Programming Language Landscape

Programming Language Landscape

Syntax, Semantics, and Implementation
Second Edition

Michael Marcotty
General Motors Research Laboratories

Henry Ledgard
Independent Consultant

SCIENCE RESEARCH ASSOCIATES, INC.
Chicago, Henley-on-Thames, Sydney, Toronto

An IBM Company

The SRA Computer Science Series

William A. Barrett, et al., *Compiler Construction: Theory and Practice, Second Edition*
Alan W. Doerr and Kenneth M. Levasseur, *Applied Discrete Structures for Computer Science*
Mark Elson, *Data Structures*
Peter Freeman, *Software Systems Principles: A Survey*
Philip Gilbert, *Software Design and Development*
A. N. Habermann, *Introduction to Operating System Design*
Michael Marcotty and Henry Ledgard, *The Programming Language Landscape: Second Edition*
Harold S. Stone, *Introduction to Computer Architecture, Second Edition*
Gregory F. Wetzel and William G. Bulgren, *The Algorithmic Process: An Introduction to Problem Solving*

Acquisition Editor	John Levstik
Project Editor	Geof Garvey
Copy Editor	Arlan Bushman
Text and Cover Design	Harry Voigt
Production Director	Steve Leonardo
Composition	The Clarinda Co.
Illustrations	Drake Maher
Cover Illustration	Franz Altschuler

Library of Congress Cataloging in Publication Data

Ledgard, Henry F., 1943–
    Programming language landscape.

    Authors' names reversed on previous ed.
    Includes bibliographies and index.
    1. Programming languages (Electronic computers)
I. Marcotty, Michael, 1931– .   II. Title.
QA76.7.L44   1985   001.64′24   85-11778
ISBN 0-574-21945-5

Printed in the United States of America.

10 9 8 7 6 5 4 3

Contents

7 Control Structures   179

8 Data Types   229

Preface

The earth, viewed through the window of an airplane, shows a regularity and repetition of features, for example, hills, valleys, rivers, lakes, and forests. Nevertheless, there is great local variation; Vermont does not look like Utah. Similarly, if we rise above the details of a few programming languages, we can discern features that are common to many languages. This is the programming language landscape; the main features include variables, types, control structures, and input-output. Again, there is local variation; Ada[1] does not look like Lisp.

This book is a broad and comprehensive discussion of the principal features of the major programming languages.

Emphasis on Teaching and Depth

There are several approaches to the study of programming languages. One is to examine several existing languages in detail, compare and contrast their salient features, and attempt to draw conclusions about underlying design principles. Another path starts with the language concepts, studies them in relative isolation, and then seeks examples of the implementation of these principles in real languages. This text follows the second approach. We believe that it is only by understanding the basic concepts first that meaningful comparisons may be drawn among various languages.

This book opens with several introductory chapters. These survey the landscape and how its features can be described. In particular, they treat syntax issues, the definition of semantics, and general implementation

---

[1] Ada is a Registered Trademark of the Ada Joint Program Office—U.S. Government.

techniques. Each of the following chapters concentrates on a single language concept. It presents a simple model of the feature, expressed in a small but complete language distilled from contemporary languages. This allows us to study an issue in depth and relative isolation. Each chapter concludes with a discussion of the way in which the concept is incorporated into some well-known languages. This permits a reasonably complete coverage of language issues.

Consideration of Human Aspects

Throughout the book, we view a programming language as a notation. The user of a notation must make a mental investment in learning before gaining any advantage. If the investment is greater than the return in mental leverage for the production of correct programs, the language fails. The mental leverage results from an increased ability by the programmer to master the details of a computation. For the investment to be low, there must be an inherent simplicity in the language, uniformly applied rules, and few special cases.

For good mental leverage, the language must provide powerful abstraction tools that allow the user to subdue the clamor of complexity and master a large program. It is essential to remember that the most important function of a programming language is to communicate the algorithm to other programmers. The language is constructed for the convenience of humans, not of machines.

A Basis on Contemporary Languages

The reader is expected to have experience with one (perhaps more) high-level language. The concepts discussed here are drawn mainly from Ada, Algol 60, Algol 68, APL, Basic, Bliss, Cobol, Fortran, Lisp, Modula-2, Pascal, PL/I, Simula 67, and Smalltalk. Among these languages, almost any programming language principle, good or bad, can be found. Obviously, there can be no attempt to present a description of all these languages.

However, the reader, even if unfamiliar with these languages, should have no difficulty in understanding this text. The chapters that describe particular language features each contain a section—"Where to Look"—that describes the realization of the feature in one or two real languages. It is expected that the reader will wish to refer to detailed manuals to obtain a deeper understanding of some of the languages mentioned. Reference material for all languages mentioned is cited in the bibliography under the name of the language. Suggestions for further reading are contained at the end of each chapter.

There is no firmly established convention for the style of writing the names of programming languages. Usage varies, with no obvious criterion, between use of upper case only and just capitalizing the initial letters—

for example, between FORTRAN and Fortran. In this text, we have adopted the rule that, if the name is pronounced as a sequence of letters, all the letters will be written in upper case, otherwise the name is treated as a normal proper noun. Examples of the application of this rule are: AED, Ada, Algol 60, APL, BCPL, Fortran, and PL/I.

For teaching, this book follows the guidelines of course CS 8, "Organization of Programming Languages," given in Curriculum '78, Communications of the ACM, March 1979. As such, it may be useful for undergraduate and early graduate courses, as well as for anyone seeking a perspective of the programming language area.

A *Study of Underlying Concepts*

Although each chapter in this book is self-contained, we treat programming languages in four successively deeper levels. The first level, Chapters 1 through 5, introduces the area of programming language, discusses a number of broad issues, such as the formal description of languages and compilers, and generally sets the landscape for the remainder of the book. The second level, Chapters 6 through 11, discusses six dominant features of most contemporary languages: assignment, control structures, data types, input/output, procedures, and nesting.

The third level, Chapters 12 through 17, treats more advanced topics, such as data definition, dynamically varying data structures, applicative languages, exception handling, concurrent processing, and modularization. The last chapter, Chapter 18, presents some views on the complexity of programming languages. Some suggested term projects are given at the end of this chapter.

Beyond a chapter that summarizes various aspects of translator design, parsing, optimization, code generation, preprocessors, and interpreters, the implementation of languages is not discussed specifically. However, where appropriate, the method of implementation is described. For example, in the chapter on block structure, the dynamic allocation of variables is discussed. The reader is thus able to see how language design, translation processes, and execution environment interact.

Acknowledgments

One of the first uses of mini-languages as a vehicle for describing language principles was in Ledgard's paper "Ten Mini-languages: A Study of Topical Issues in Programming Languages" [Ledgard 1971]. This book has gained much of its breadth from the work done by Ledgard on the design of Ada. The syntax of many of the mini-languages has also benefited from this work.

Andrew Singer provided thoughtful comments during the development of the first edition of this work. We are also grateful to J.A.N. Lee, who for many years has promoted the use of mini-languages in teaching. This book owes its inception to a mixed graduate, undergraduate course that Marcotty has been teaching at Wayne State and Oakland Universities.

The authors and publisher would like to thank the following reviewers for their valuable feedback: Dr. Richard Detmer (East Texas State University), Dr. David Rosenthal (Ithaca College), Dr. Dennis Conrady (North Texas State University), and Dr. Carl Steidly (Central Washington University).

Michael Marcotty
Henry Ledgard

ACKNOWLEDGMENTS

Cover illustration "Mesa Sunset" by Franz Altschuler. Reproduced by permission of the artist. All rights reserved.

Chapter 1 "Freiburger Alpen." Aerial photograph of the Alps near Freiburg, Switzerland. Photo by Swissair A.G.

Page 11, quotation From Alfred North Whitehead, *An Introduction to Mathematics,* Copyright © 1958, Oxford University Press. Reprinted by permission of the publisher.

Chapter 2 Portion of a painting, "Land Forms of the Earth," by Kenneth Fagg.*

Chapter 3 Enlarged portion of a U.S. Geological Survey topographic map of the Grand Canyon, Arizona.

Chapter 4 "Grand Canyon." Photograph taken in the Grand Canyon showing Sumner Butte. Photo by Don Hart. Reproduced by permission of the photographer.

Chapter 5 Kuluene River, Brazil. Photo by Emil Schulthess.

Chapter 6 Photograph taken at Guam by United Press International. The Bettmann Archive.

Chapter 7 Highway crisscross near Frankfurt, Germany. From "The World from Above," by Hanns Reich. Photo by Aero Exploration. Reproduced by permission of Hanns Reich.

Chapter 8 Yebechai rock formations, Monument Valley, Arizona. Photo by David Muench. Reproduced by permission of the photographer.

Chapter 9 Battersea Power Station, London, England. Photo by Robert Estall. Reproduced by permission of the photographer.

Chapter 10 Factory chimneys in England. From "The World from Above," by Hanns Reich. Photo by Aerofilms. Reproduced by permission of Hanns Reich.

Chapter 11 The Souf Oasis. Photo by Georg Gerster. Reproduced by permission of Photo Researchers, Inc.

Chapter 12 Balancing rock in Chiricahua National Monument, Arizona. Photo by Ed Cooper. Reproduced by permission of the photographer.

Chapter 13 "Volcano." Photo by Eliot Elisofon, Life Magazine. © 1951, Time, Inc. Reproduced by permission of the publisher.

Chapter 14 Zagros Mountains, Western Iran. From "The World from Above," by Hanns Reich. Photo by Aerofilms. Reproduced by permission of Hanns Reich.

Chapter 15 "Landslide." Photo by Nat Farbman, Life Magazine, © 1959, Time, Inc. Reproduced by permission of the publisher.

Chapter 16 Flock of sheep on highway. From "The World from Above," by Hanns Reich. Photo by Bayer Flugdienst. Reproduced by permission of Hanns Reich.

Chapter 17 Rice fields in Asia. Photo by Horace Bristol, Life Magazine, © Time, Inc. Reproduced by permission of the publisher.

Chapter 18 Mangrove Swamp, Everglades. Photo by Dan McCoy. Reproduced by permission of the photographer.

---

*SRA has made every attempt to contact the artist for permission to reproduce this work. The owner may make arrangements by contacting Rights and Permissions, Science Research Associates, Inc., 155 N. Wacker Dr., Chicago, Ill. 60606–1780.

1

Introduction

1.1 The Building of the Tower of Babel

Before 1954 almost all programming was done in machine language. Solving a problem on a computer required the detailed encoding of long sequences of instructions into numbers in binary or octal form. For the Manchester University Mark I computer in England, possibly the world's first stored program computer, instructions had to be written in binary, split into groups of five bits, and then translated into teleprinter code so that they could be entered into the machine. The resulting instructions looked like this:

```
E  @  H  O
X  E  /  :
V  E  /  :
@  @  H  B
I  @  T  /
I  @  /  C
@  @  /  N
T  C  T  A
```

Nevertheless, it was possible to write programs in this way to perform serious computations, such as those required for the St. Lawrence Seaway project.

Later, some mnemonic help was provided through the use of letter codes for operations, for example, MPY in place of 021 for multiply. This help was later augmented by the use of symbolic names instead of numeric addresses to refer to values. Programs written in this form were converted

1

into machine language through the use of a program called an *assembler.*
This form of expressing programs is referred to as an *assembler language.*
The following example of an assembler language program fragment is
somewhat more comprehensible than the previous example:

```
        LDY  #0
        LDA  $60
CHBIT   BPL  CHKZ
        INY
CHKZ    ASL  A
        BNE  CHBIT
        BRK
```

The kind of work involved in writing programs in both these forms is
illustrated by the fact that the actual writing of the instructions was called
coding rather than *programming.* Programming implies the more difficult
task of designing algorithms.

The problems with expressing algorithms in these forms were:

- The language in which the program was written contained little textual redundancy that could be used to detect errors. Almost any
  combination of characters could be executed. To tie the execution
  errors back to the faulty code was difficult and time-consuming.

- The programs had to be tailored to the particular characteristics of
  the available computer. Much effort was devoted to overcoming deficiencies of the computer's architecture, for example, no index registers, lack of built-in floating point operations, and restricted instruction sets.

- The close association between a program and a particular machine
  design not only permitted but encouraged the invention of all kinds
  of tricks to wring maximum performance from the computer. The
  correctness of programs constructed in this way was very difficult to
  verify, and it was practically impossible to discover the algorithm
  behind a program coded by a colleague.

- When a new computer replaced the old one, all this inventiveness
  was wasted; the old programs had to be thrown away and the process of building a new library started again.

Automatic Programming Systems

These shortcomings led to the development of so-called *automatic programming systems.* These systems generally provided operations such as
floating point addition and trigonometric functions, together with either
fixed or variable operands. Usually, the programmer had to write state-

ments in a rigid format that did not allow mathematical expressions to be written in anything resembling mathematical notation.

Automatic programming systems gave the programmer a synthetic "computer" with an instruction set that was different from that of a real machine. In particular, the synthetic machine generally had floating point operations, index registers, and improved input and output commands. It was much easier to program than its real counterpart. The programmer was able to think of a floating point addition as just that, and able to ignore the details of carrying it out in the hardware. The synthetic machine was thus an *abstract machine,* that is to say, a simulation of a computer that did not exist in hardware. The abstraction simplified the programming of complex operations by reducing the number of details that had to be directly controlled by the programmer.

The early automatic programming systems were costly to use since they slowed the actual machine down by a factor of five or more. Much of this time was spent in floating point subroutines. Experience with these systems, coupled with their familiarity with programming tricks, convinced programmers that any mechanical coding method would fail to apply the ingenuity that programmers believed they used constantly in their work.

The advent of computers with built-in floating point and indexing further increased the skepticism. By speeding up the floating point computations by a factor of ten, a common source of inefficiency in handwritten programs was removed. Consequently, the automatic generation of programs that were efficient, by comparison with handwritten ones, became more difficult. Those who wanted to simplify programming could only gain acceptance for their system if they could demonstrate that it could produce programs that were almost as efficient as handcoded ones in practically every case.

Development of Fortran

In this atmosphere John Backus formed a group in 1954 to develop the Fortran (FORmula TRANslator) compiler. This project was aimed at the automatic translation of mathematical formulas into machine instructions. The group hoped to bring about a radical change in the economics of scientific computing by making programming much cheaper through a drastic reduction in the time it took for a working program to be prepared. Because of the atmosphere of skepticism, the group's emphasis was on the efficiency of the translated program rather than on language design. This view is expressed by [Backus and Heising 1964]:

> [Our development group] had one primary fear. After working long and
> hard to produce a good translator program, an important application
> might promptly turn up which would confirm the views of the sceptics:
> . . . its [translated] program would run at half the speed of the hand-

coded version. It was felt that such an occurrence, or several of them, would almost completely block acceptance of the system.

It was thought that, once the ideas of an assignment statement, subscripted variables, and the DO statement had been adopted, the remaining problems of language design would be trivial! Their solution would be dictated either by the need to provide some new machine facility or by some programming task that could not be done with existing structures.

At that time, nothing was known of many issues that were later thought to be important: block and control structures, nested subprograms, and type declarations—issues that are addressed in detail in this book. The Fortran programming system was viewed as applying to just one machine, and very little thought was given to the implications of making a machine-independent programming language. As a result, certain characteristics of the machine on which Fortran was first implemented became part of the language; for example, the naming of output channels was determined by the numbering of the tape units on the IBM 704 computer.

An example of a program in the original version of Fortran, taken from [Knuth and Pardo 1976] is:

```
       DIMENSION A(11)
       READ A
   2   DO 3,8,11 J=1,11
   3   I=1-J
       Y=SQRT(ABS(A(I+1)))+5*A(I+1)**3
       IF (400.>=Y) 8,4
   4   PRINT I,999
       GO TO 2
   8   PRINT I,Y
  11   STOP
```

Programming Revolution

Fortran was just one of several programming languages that appeared in 1956 and 1957. This period was the beginning of a programming revolution. It almost seemed that each new computer, and even each programming group, was spawning its own algebraic language or favorite dialect of an existing one. Most of these languages were aimed at helping the scientific programmer and were restricted to a particular machine. Their designers were generally a small group of implementors, rather than users, drawn from a single company. A primary design objective was to produce efficient machine code, even if it meant sacrificing some clarity of expression in the language.

The objectives of the designers of Cobol (Common Business Oriented Language) were different. In 1959, a committee of representatives from several organizations was established to design a machine-independent programming language suitable for use by the business community. The committee decided that the language should make the maximum use of simple English so that managers who had no programming experience would be able to understand the programs. Many committee members felt that arithmetic operations should be specified by words like ADD and MULTIPLY rather than by the symbols + and * because these words would be more readily understood. The important thing is not whether the committee was right, but that a serious effort was being made to design a language for communication between people and computers. Because the members of the committee represented competing computer companies, considerable effort was expended to make the language independent of the hardware. The hope was to avoid any manufacturer having an unfair advantage over the competition.

Fortran and Cobol are only two examples of the many languages that have been developed for programming computers. Languages of this sort are referred to as *high-level languages* since they achieve a higher level of abstraction than machine or assembler languages by suppressing many of the complicating details.

In many cases, however, little thought has been put into the design of high-level languages. This is demonstrated in two major ways:

- The external form of the language has often been designed according to what was thought to be the easiest form for computer analysis rather than what was most natural as a means of expression.

- Economy of design and simplicity of structure are rarely seen.

The profusion of programming languages and their design weaknesses severely hinder valuable communication between programmers. We are still in the state described in Genesis as leading to the failure of the Tower of Babel project. This is despite the efforts of many very talented people working individually, in groups, in small and large committees, and even in international committees. Some have attempted to design a "universal" language. There have been several candidates for this position, but none has achieved widespread acceptance and use.

If programming languages are examined carefully, they are found to resemble each other more than their external forms would lead us to suppose. They are built on a number of basic concepts; it is the object of this book to study these concepts so that we can have a better understanding of these languages.

1.2 What Is a Programming Language?

The computer was conceived as a device that would speed up complicated and time-consuming computations. Despite this, it is not its ability
to perform arithmetic that is important in the majority of applications, but
the fact that it can store and access large amounts of data. These data form
an *abstraction* of some part of the real world.

Consider the master file used in a payroll application. Each employee is
represented by the data needed for the accounting procedures involved
in preparing the payroll. These will probably include such items as the
employee's name, social security number, and salary. Other data, such as
hair color, shoe size, and name of a favorite breakfast cereal, will probably
not be included. These, while very much part of a full description of the
employee, are irrelevant to the paycheck computation and do not form
part of the abstraction that represents the employee in the master payroll
file.

The data stored in the computer are thus a representation of real-world
objects. We speak of the data items as *abstract objects.* Associated with an
object is a set of operations that transforms it into other objects. The computation consists of applying these operations to an initial set of objects,
the input data, so as to transform them into new abstract objects that
represent the result of the computation.

We define an *algorithm* as a specification of the sequence of operations
to be performed on the initial set of objects to produce the resulting set
of objects. This algorithm must be represented in a form that can be communicated both to the computer and to other programmers. A *programming language* is a set of conventions for communicating algorithms. An
algorithm expressed in a programming language is a *program.*

Language Classifications

Although all programming languages share a number of common principles that we shall study later, the languages are of different varieties. These
may be very loosely classified according to the area of application or mode
of use.

> A *commercial language* is one that is particularly concerned with
> the manipulation of files of alphanumeric data and with the production
> of reports. Cobol is the best-known commercial language.

> A *scientific language* is one that is used mainly for the manipulation
> of numeric data. Fortran is the best-known scientific language.

> A *systems programming language* is one that is used particularly
> for writing operating systems. Such a language is typically less ma-
> chine-independent than usual high-level programming languages. For
> example, it may have facilities for addressing registers directly. Exam-
> ples of this kind of language are C, Bliss, and BCPL.

*A **command language*** is a language that is the interface between the computer user and the operating system. The statements define the programs to be executed, the conditions under which execution is to take place, and the data files to be manipulated. At present there are no machine-independent or standard forms for languages of this class. Examples include DCL for Digital Equipment's VMS and JCL for IBM's MVS. We will not discuss command languages further in this text.

*An **interactive language*** is one that is designed to allow a programmer to make changes and corrections from a terminal during execution. For example, both Lisp and APL are designed to be used interactively.

*A **procedural language*** is one that allows the user to specify a set of imperative statements that are to be performed in a particular sequence. Most contemporary programming languages are procedural.

*A **nonprocedural language*** is one in which the user does not specify the sequence of operations that are to be performed to obtain a problem's solution. Only the problem is defined; the emphasis is on what is to be done rather than how it is to be done. Well-known examples of nonprocedural languages (although some may dispute that they are, in fact, programming languages) are sort and report generators, in which the user specifies the forms of the input and the output without any description of the detailed steps required to transform the former into the latter.

*An **applicative language*** is one in which the program consists of the evaluation of a function that uses the input data as arguments and whose value is the result of the computation. "Pure" Lisp is an example of an applicative language.

*A **data-flow language*** is one that permits the flow of data between the statements of a program to be examined so that inherent parallelism is exposed. This allows the program to be executed on a special machine that takes advantage of this parallelism to achieve increased speed. Val is an example of a data-flow language.

*An **object-oriented language*** is one in which data elements are active and have some of the characteristics normally associated with programs. This is in contrast to more conventional languages where data elements are strictly passive and are acted on by programs. Active data elements respond to messages that cause them to act on themselves, possibly returning other data elements. Smalltalk is an example of an object-oriented language.

*A **real-time language*** is one that allows the programming of procedures that can be executed concurrently and can be activated in response to external signals as required. Concurrent Pascal and Ada are examples of real-time programming languages.

A special-purpose language is one that is designed with a limited objective, such as ease of use in a particular application area. For example, the language Apt is used to write programs to control machine tools.

You should recognize of course that these classifications are very informal, and that certain languages will fall into more than one category.

Implementation Schemes

The realization of a programming language in a computer system is called the *implementation.* Programming languages may be implemented in one of two ways: *compilation* or *interpretation.*

Compilation: The program written in the programming language, the *source program,* is translated into an equivalent program, the *object program,* in the machine language of the computer on which it is to be executed, the *target machine.* The object program is then executed by the target machine.

The translation from source program to object program is performed by a program generally referred to as a *translator* or *compiler,* the terms being used synonymously. The translator is executed on the *host machine,* which is generally the same as the target machine. However, if this is not feasible, for example, if the target machine is too small for the compiler to run, then the translator is executed on a larger machine, possibly of an entirely different architecture. In this case, the translator is known as a *cross compiler.* Much of the programming for minicomputers and some work for microcomputers are done through cross compilers.

The use of a compiler thus makes the execution of a program written in a programming language a two-stage process. Below are these two stages represented diagramatically:

Interpretation: The source program is not translated but is executed directly through an *interpreter.* This is a program that executes on the target machine. As each statement of the source program is executed, the interpreter examines the statement and performs the operations specified by it, generally through the use of subroutines.

Thus, in contrast to compilation, pure interpretation is a one-step process as shown in the following diagram:

The use of an interpreter allows for greater flexibility than can be achieved by direct execution. However, the penalty is that interpretation is generally much slower than direct execution. The implementation of Basic on most home and personal computers is through interpretation. Generally, the interpreter is built into the electronics of the computer, which can allow it to be executed more rapidly. Other languages that are often interpreted are APL and Lisp.

Mix of Compilation and Interpretation

There is no hard line of differentiation between compilation and interpretation. Generally, a mixture of the two techniques is used in an implementation. Although the compiler produces machine code for a real machine, an extensive support library of subroutines is usually required for execution of the object program. As the system design moves more in the direction of interpretation, the library becomes bigger and less is done by execution of compiled codes.

Interpretation and compilation merge at the point where the object program consists of a sequence of machine code subroutine invocations and where the interpreter consists of the subroutines that are invoked during execution. The amount of processing performed by the translator ranges from doing nothing, in which case the character string representation of the source program is interpreted directly, through complete translation into target machine code. An implementation of a programming language includes the translator, interpreter, and supporting subroutines.

Another alternative is for the machine code generated by the compiler not to correspond to any real machine but to an abstract machine. Generally, the abstract machine is designed so that it is easy to write an interpreter for its machine code. This simplifies the problem of program portability, that is, the movement of a program from one machine to another. While the machine independence of a language means that, in principle, a program is portable, the reality is that this requires a suitable compiler to generate code for the target machine. Generally, it is simpler to write an interpreter for an abstract machine than it is to write a compiler for a new machine. The penalty is the loss of execution speed that is inherent in the interpretation.

There is, of course, a relationship between a language and its implementation. While there may be several different ways of realizing the facilities of a language, some are inherently more difficult and expensive than others. The ability to manipulate strings that do not have a predetermined upper bound for their length, for example, offers great flexibility to the programmer; at the same time, such a facility requires expensive storage management techniques. Awareness of the associated implementation complexities allows a choice to be made between utility and cost.

1.3 Why Study Programming Languages?

Facility with English does not automatically confer the ability to understand French and German, although they are all natural languages. Nevertheless, the three languages are based on very similar principles because of their common Indo-European origin. English is blessed (or cursed) with a very tolerant grammar. Many students whose mother tongue is English have problems with languages with more rigid grammars. This is because grammatical concepts that are only slightly used in English are important in other languages and need to be understood. Although the subjunctive exists in English, its use is vanishing fast and most English-speaking people are unaware of it. In French, however, it has a very important place and must be understood before the language can be mastered. An understanding of the common grammatical basis of English and French clearly helps the student. Both languages, however, allow the same basic ideas to be communicated.

The situation is very much the same with programming languages; they differ widely in their external forms and range of facilities, yet they are based on a relatively small group of basic concepts. Programming languages are the programmer's major software tool. A tool needs to be fully understood before it can be used properly.

Of all the aspects of programming, the design of a language requires the greatest skill and judgment. The linguist [Benjamin Whorf 1956] has hypothesized that one's language has a considerable effect on the way that one thinks; indeed on *what* one *can* think. The language designer's task goes beyond programming itself and concerns itself with the symbolism that is used to express computations. Thus, if Whorf's hypothesis is correct, the skill of the designer will have a considerable effect on the range of problems that can be solved in a language. The designer must survey the many attractive features that are available for inclusion in a language and choose the most powerful set of facilities that will constitute a harmonious assembly. The objective is sufficient power with *minimal* complexity. A full understanding of the principles is required in order to evaluate an unfamiliar language.

Of course, most programmers and computer scientists do not become language designers, which is a good thing since there are already too many languages. In a sense, every programming interface, whether it be between human and program, program and program, or program and hardware, is a kind of programming language. A proper understanding of the concepts of programming languages will help make the design of these interfaces, and hence of programs, considerably easier. Success will be indicated by a program that is a pleasure to use.

1.4 What Should We Look For in a Language?

A programming language is the programmer's most important tool. A good language can lead the programmer to the correct solution of a problem in a natural and easy manner. Conversely, a poor language may add so much complexity to finding the solution that the programmer will abandon the attempt at solving the problem in favor of an easier one. A programming language thus serves a programmer in the same way that a notation serves a mathematician. As said in [Whitehead 1911]:

> By relieving the brain of all unnecessary work, a good notation sets it free to concentrate on more advanced problems, and in effect increases the mental power of the race. Before the introduction of the Arabic notation, multiplication was difficult, and the division even of integers called into play the highest mathematical faculties. Probably nothing in the modern world would have more astonished a Greek mathematician than to learn that . . . a large proportion of the population of Western Europe could perform the operation of division for the largest numbers. This fact would have seemed to him a sheer impossibility. . . . Our modern power of

easy reckoning with decimal fractions is the almost miraculous result of the gradual discovery of a perfect notation.

The primary purpose of a programming language is to help in the task of programming. Thus, it must aid in those areas that are the most difficult:

Program design: deciding and specifying what must be done and how the data are to be represented.

Understanding: explaining the working of the program to a human reader.

Verification: establishing the correctness of the program.

We turn then to some of the characteristics of a programming language that will make it useful in these areas. It will become evident that the areas are not independent and that some desirable characteristics are helpful in all three.

Program Design

In program design, the language must assist the programmer in specifying the process and the data clearly and naturally. It must be possible to construct abstractions that match the characteristics of the problem. This means that it must be possible to avoid extraneous detail that will clutter a solution.

A common deficiency in this area is the inability of a language to manipulate abstract data objects other than the few primitive types supplied by the language. For example, in Basic, Fortran, Cobol, and to a large extent PL/I, all data must be mapped into a few basic elements. The details of this representation are likely to appear in the algorithm, making it more difficult to understand.

For example, a date, if it is to be manipulated in these languages, must be represented as a number. A programmer may use operations, such as division, that are valid for numbers but that have no meaning when applied to dates. Thus, it is most important for the ease and clarity of programming that the language be able to treat abstract objects that match the problem data.

Understanding

All too often documentation is added to a program as a chore after the program has been made to work. As a result, either too little or too much detail is supplied. If there is not enough, the programmer who wishes to modify the program later will not be able to do the job reliably. If there is too much detail, it usually repeats what is written in the code and serves to obscure rather than enlighten.

A well-designed language will encourage the programmer to write so clearly that the program will be *self-documenting,* with only modest need for additional comments. Making the documentation an integral part of the program avoids the well-known trap of misleading documentation that occurs when a program is modified without corresponding changes in the separate documentation. For self-documentation to be possible, the language must allow the specification of operations and data to be made clearly and naturally.

A frequently applied criterion in the design of languages is the minimization of keystrokes on the grounds that this will help the programmer. Shopping lists are usually constructed this way, with terse phrases based on a great deal of contextual information in the writer's mind. Six months later, a shopping list is often too cryptic to be understood because the contextual information has been forgotten.

Readability is thus a much more important criterion than writability; after all, the program will probably only be written once, but read many times. It must be recognized, however, that, even though a language may be designed with the goal of program clarity, it does not follow that all programs written in that language will be clear. It is impossible to design a language in which an obscure program cannot be written.

Verification

To help with verification, the programming language must give the programmer confidence that the program is correct. Thus, it must aid the programmer to obtain either formal or informal verification. Again, one of the best ways of achieving this is for the program to have been written with such crystal clarity that it is obviously correct. Since it is probable that careless errors will always be made, the notation of the programming language should be designed so that the scope of such errors will be reduced and the bulk of them detected by the compiler.

1.5 Language Design Issues

The major areas in the design of programming languages can be categorized under three major headings:

1. The representation and treatment of data.
2. The sequence in which the statements of the program are to be executed.
3. The segmentation of the program into separate parts that can be considered individually yet combined to solve a problem.

In this book, we will be treating these areas in considerable detail. Linking these topics are a number of important issues that must be resolved during the design of a language. In each case, the problem lies in the choice of a compromise between two opposing extremes.

Redundancy

The compiler can detect many of the simple errors made by programmers through consistency checks. For this to be possible, the programmer must provide redundant information. The design issue to be resolved is the balance between the utility of checking and the extra work of providing the redundant information.

PL/I allows the implicit declaration of variables. That is, variables do not have to be declared explicitly. The designers argued that this would save the programmer trouble in cases where the attributes assumed by the translator matched those required by the programmer. The penalty for this convenience is that the compiler can no longer detect simple spelling errors in the names of variables. The occurrence of a misspelled name constitutes an implicit declaration of that name as a new identifier.

More importantly, the explicit declaration of variables does a great deal to establish the intent of the program in the reader's mind. The declarations may then be viewed as "definitions" of program objects, and the executable statements as steps in the process of computing the result.

Abstraction

As we have seen, programming languages obtain much of their advantage by reducing the complexity of programming through the suppression of details. The tension lies between omitting details and giving the programmer the depth of control needed to solve hard problems.

Often, an attempt to provide a language that can solve all problems results in a multiplicity of forms, each of them simple, that constitutes a large language. Complete understanding of the language then becomes a problem. For proper use, the programmer must be able to understand the tool completely. How many Fortran, Ada, or PL/I programmers can claim that they know the language completely? Understanding a new language often represents such a large investment in time that programmers find it impossible to change to a new language despite the acknowledged weaknesses of an old one.

The provision of more than one form to denote a concept always increases the size of a language. The additional complexity introduced by such features must be carefully weighed against their usefulness.

Cobol provides an example of questionable duplicate forms. The sequence of arithmetic statements

```
COMPUTE TOTAL-HOURS    = OVERTIME-HOURS + REGULAR-HOURS.
COMPUTE NUM-ON-PAYROLL = NUM-EMPLOYEES  - NUM-ON-VACATION
                                        - NUM-ON-LEAVE.
```

performs the same computation as the sequence of statements

```
ADD      OVERTIME-HOURS TO REGULAR-HOURS GIVING TOTAL-HOURS.
SUBTRACT NUM-ON-VACATION, NUM-ON-LEAVE FROM NUM-EMPLOYEES
                                       GIVING NUM-ON-PAYROLL.
```

and both sequences are homogeneous to the eye. However, when both notations are combined as in

```
COMPUTE  TOTAL-HOURS = OVERTIME-HOURS + REGULAR-HOURS.
SUBTRACT NUM-ON-VACATION, NUM-ON-LEAVE FROM NUM-EMPLOYEES
                                       GIVING NUM-ON-PAYROLL.
```

the symmetry of like operations becomes less visible. A designer may prefer the concise mathematical form of the first sequence or the English-like notation of the second. In any case, it would be simpler to retain a single notation in the language. We prefer the arithmetic version in this case.

In some languages that attempt to provide everything for everybody, the problem of maintaining simplicity is attacked by so-called *modularity* of design. The idea is that an individual user will only be concerned with a particular part of the language and will not need to know anything about the other parts. Thus, the language is designed so that there are a number of generally overlapping subsets. In principle, this appears acceptable.

There are many problems with this approach however. The user will still be intimidated by the whole language, and separate texts may need to be written for the individual users. The compiler, which is written for the union of all the subsets, does not take account of the fact that the user only knows part of the language. There is even the danger that a user may write something that is meaningless in the particular subset being used but valid in another subset that is not known to the programmer. When the program is executed, an unintended action will take place, one that cannot be explained in terms of the original subset.

One aspect of the suppression of details is the abstract machine represented by the language; it is a much simpler machine than the one on which the language is implemented. However, not all programming errors can be detected by the compiler. Some errors will be detected by the actual hardware. The language must be designed so that the effects of these errors can all be explained through the language without recourse to details of the implementation or the underlying real machine. To require knowledge of the real machine is to shatter the illusion of the abstract machine. The Fortran error message

```
STATE--ABEND CODE IS: SYSTEM 0200, USER 0000
IO-NONE, SCB=0F10C0, PSW IS 078D2000000A98B7E
```

has no meaning in the language; the Fortran machine does not have an SCB or PSW.

Orthogonality

An important part of a simple design is that there should not be more than one way of expressing any action in the language, that is, each component of the language should be independent of the other components. The design is then said to be *orthogonal*. In a truly orthogonal design, there are a small number of separate, basic constructions, and these are combined according to regular and systematic rules without arbitrary restrictions.

Many programming languages include composite data types, such as structures and arrays. They also allow functions, processes that map arguments into a result. A proper combination of these two orthogonal concepts, data types and functions, would permit functions to return results of any data type that is allowed as an argument.

One restriction, for example, would allow arguments to be of composite data type but permit only scalar results. This type of restriction is seen in Fortran, Algol 60, and some versions of PL/I. However, there is a danger in removing all restrictions; the complexity of the language might be increased without a corresponding gain in facility.

Implementation

The properties that we have discussed so far have been characteristics of the *design* of a language. There are also some general questions of *implementation* that must be considered. Among these are:

Availability: Are there compilers available for the language on a wide range of machines?

External support: Are the standard processes, such as sorting, solution of differential equations, and graphic display, available for use or must they be written specially?

Implementation: Is the compiler easy to use and does it produce clear diagnostics?

Efficiency: Is the compiler efficient both in the compilation process and in the object code that it produces?

Documentation: Are the language and its compiler well documented? Are the supporting documents written clearly and unambiguously?

1.6 The Study of Programming Languages

Generally, the study of programming languages is divided into two distinct parts, the *syntax* and the *semantics.* Broadly speaking, the syntax of a language is concerned with the way that a program is written and the semantics with what happens when the program is executed, that is, with its *meaning.*

A program in a language is represented outside the computer as a string composed of symbols. Commonly, the symbols comprise the character set of a keypunch or terminal, but other sets of symbols are possible. Most of the strings of symbols are not programs in the language, they are meaningless gibberish. The syntax of the language consists of rules that define strings of symbols constructed in a particular way. These strings are called *syntactically legal programs.* The syntax rules of Fortran, for example, specify that the sequence of characters

```
2 + 3 = I + 1
```

is not a valid Fortran statement.

Only a small fraction of the legal programs will execute correctly. The rules of syntax govern only the construction of programs from the symbols and have no concern with what happens when the programs are executed. The semantic rules of the language define a subset of legal programs that have a meaning. In a similar way, there are many grammatical sentences in English, such as:

```
THE SPHERICAL WALL GARGLED THE BUS
```

The semantics of English tells us that this sentence is nonsense. In Fortran, the sequence of statements

```
J = 0
K = 3 / J
```

results in division by zero. A program that contains such a sequence of symbols is said to contain a *semantic* error and to be meaningless.

The boundary between syntax and semantics is not well defined; different authors may define it differently. For example, the association of an identifier with a declaration is regarded by some as being syntactic and by others as semantic. There is a temptation to become over-involved with syntactic questions, and many textbooks succumb to this. The reason for this is primarily because there is some well-developed mathematics connected with the syntax of languages. Consequently, a much tidier presentation is possible in this area. In most programming languages, the syntax is the only part defined with any degree of formalism. Usually, the semantic rules are only expressed informally. However, the semantic questions are much more difficult.

All too often, an intuitive understanding of the semantics turns out to be woefully superficial. When an attempt at implementation is made, ramifications and discrepancies appear. What was thought to have been fully understood is discovered to have been differently perceived by various readers of the same informal description. By then, it is frequently too late to change, and incompatibilities have been cast in code. There is thus a great need for formalism that would remove the ambiguities and vagueness from semantic definitions. However, despite a great deal of work in this area, there is still little known about how to define semantics clearly. We return to this question in Chapter 4.

In Chapter 2, we discuss the elements of programming languages and the general issues of syntax and semantics and their effect on the programming process. Chapters 3 and 4 describe techniques for the formal description of syntax and semantics, and Chapter 5 gives an overview of the workings of a compiler. Chapter 6 and the following chapters treat particularly important language issues common to several currently used languages.

We introduce mini-languages at appropriate points to provide vehicles for the discussion. The idea of a mini-language is that it contains only those features that are being currently discussed. Thus, it is small enough to be easily described and understood, and the particular area of interest can be studied without worrying about interactions with other features in the language. Although heavy use of mini-languages provides a focus for discussion, examples of well-known programming languages are also cited frequently. In particular, each of the chapters 6 through 17, which discuss specific language principles, contains a section "Where to Look" that describes real programming languages where the chapter's topic is implemented.

Further Reading

There are a number of books in the general area of programming languages, and most of them are textbooks. However, there are also a number of shorter works. One of the more cleverly written of these is [Wirth 1976]. This paper discusses a number of language issues and then presents an amusing script describing the design of a hypothetical computer language. Other short papers in the general area of language design are [Hoare 1973], [Richard and Ledgard 1977], and [Wirth 1974].

A detailed description of programming the Manchester University Mark I is given in [Campbell-Kelly 1980] and an account of the early history of compilers is in [Knuth and Pardo 1976]. In 1978, a conference was held on the history of programming languages. This conference discussed the early development of a number of languages, including Fortran, Cobol, PL/I, and Basic. The proceedings of this conference appear in [Wexelblat 1981]. This book is certainly relevant to this text. An earlier and comprehensive work in this area is [Sammet 1969].

There are other texts similar in intent to this one, such as [Barron 1977], [Elson 1973], [Ghezzi and Jazayeri 1982], [Higman 1977], [Horowitz 1984], [MacLennan 1983], [Nicholls 1975], [Organick et al. 1978], [Pratt 1984], and [Tennent 1981].

Exercises

Exercise 1.1 Language Complexity

It has been the fate of languages to get larger and larger as time passes. For instance, the original version of Fortran developed in the 1950s was quite small, although admittedly with some severe limitations. Then came Fortran II, Fortran IV, and Fortran 77, each larger and more complex than its predecessor. *No* language that we know of has become smaller over time.

Choose one of the languages, Ada, Basic, Fortran, Pascal, or PL/I, and two features that you would remove from the language. Give a rationale for each deletion. This rationale should include consideration of the effects of the deletion on the remainder of the language.

Note: Do not be misled by this exercise. The design of language features is often so interconnected that removal is extremely difficult. The key to smaller and less complex languages is not simply a matter of deletion. The key is the initial underlying design.

Exercise 1.2 Areas of Application

In Section 1.2 we give a loose classification of languages according to their area of application or mode of use. Choose three such areas and an appropriate language for each area, and then describe why the language is suited to the area. For example, what is it that makes Cobol such a popular language for data processing? Illustrate the points you make with examples.

Exercise 1.3 *Machine Independence*

What does it mean to say that a programming language is machine-independent? Why is machine independence thought to be an important language design consideration? Describe some of the points that must be kept in mind when designing a machine-independent language. Illustrate your answers with examples showing both machine independence and dependence in existing languages.

Exercise 1.4 *Language Description*

What are the important concepts used in describing a programming language? Illustrate your answer with examples from an existing language description showing the application of your concepts.

Exercise 1.5 *Language Design*

What are the criteria that should be used in judging the design of the language? Illustrate your answer with examples from existing languages showing how your design criteria are both satisfied and violated by different languages.

Exercise 1.6 *Abstract Machines*

A programming language defines an abstract machine that differs from the actual host hardware. Choose a language with which you are familiar and determine the structure of the abstract machine that it defines. In what way does the abstract machine differ from the actual hardware? Give examples of restrictions (for example, features of the hardware that are not available to programmers in assembler language) and of extensions (that is, facilities that are directly available in the abstract machine but that can only be obtained by software simulation on the actual hardware).

Exercise 1.7 *Language Design for Human Use*

Based on your experience and drawing on examples taken from existing programming languages, list four principles the language designers might adopt to make the programming process as difficult as possible. (This exercise is from Richard L. Wexelblat.) You might wish to have a look at [Ledgard et al. 1981].

Exercise 1.8 Programming in Two Languages

On most interactive systems you must enter a "password" in order to start programming. This helps ensure that someone else does not have access to your files of information or does not charge you for their use of the computer facilities.

Write a program in *two* different computer languages (your choice) to prompt a user for a password. If the password is not given correctly within three tries, the program should inform the user that the passwords given are incorrect and then terminate; otherwise, the user should be informed of a successful entry, and then, at least for this exercise, terminate. Your program will define the correct password.

a. *Successful entry*

Computer	:	PLEASE ENTER YOUR PASSWORD
User	:	SHERLOCK
Computer	:	OF COURSE, GO RIGHT AHEAD

b. *Unsuccessful entry*

Computer	:	PLEASE ENTER YOUR PASSWORD
User	:	MYCROFT
Computer	:	WHO?
User	:	WATSON
Computer	:	WHO?
User	:	HOLMES
Computer	:	FORGET IT.

When you are done, comment on the most significant differences between the two languages, as expressed by your two programs.

Note: From the user's side, the two programs should have identical behavior in all respects.

Exercise 1.9 *Aim of Language Design*

Consider the following rather broad statements about what is most important in language design.

Statement 1: A programming language is essentially a mathematical notation. The keypoint is its terseness and power. (For instance, APL and Lisp might be considered in the category.)

Statement 2: A programming language must be easy to learn and to implement, as is exemplified by Basic.

Statement 3: A programming language must be able to produce readable programs. (Pascal could be considered as such.)

Statement 4: A programming language must offer power for a wide class of problems, for example, PL/I or Ada.

Pick one of these statements and write a three page report justifying your basic position.

2
Elements of a
Programming Language

A programming language is the programmer's most important tool. By simplifying the way in which algorithms are expressed, it allows the programmer to concentrate on the design of the algorithm. Through the use of redundant information, the compiler checks the consistency of the programmer's work. However, before we can use a language, there are certain things that we must know about it. This information should be in any proper description of the language.

First of all, we must know what type of objects can be manipulated in the language. Historically, programming languages have been designed to deal principally, though not exclusively, with some specific type of object. For example, Fortran and Algol programs manipulate *numbers* while Snobol programs manipulate *strings* and Lisp programs manipulate *lists*.

The next thing we need to know about a language is what kind of algorithms it can be used to specify. In principle, almost any programming language, even the simplest, can be used to specify any algorithm. It can be shown that a very simple machine consisting only of a store and the single instruction

> Change the contents of location A by subtracting the contents of location B from it; branch to location C if the result is negative, and otherwise proceed sequentially to the next instruction

can evaluate any computable function. However, such a machine will not be easy to program, and its programs will not be easy to understand. Thus, while any programming language can be used for anything (Fortran has been used for payrolls and Cobol for solving differential equations), it is important to know whether a particular kind of algorithm can be reasonably written in a language. Fortran and Cobol, for example, are not suitable for writing recursively defined functions (ones that can invoke themselves), but Algol and Pascal are.

We must know how a program in the language is to be written; that is, we must know what must be entered through the terminal or punched on the card. This is the syntactic aspect of the language. Finally, we must understand the semantics of the language, that is, what a program does when it is executed. In this chapter, we investigate the relationship between the syntax and semantics of a language and the programming process.

We will start by describing informally the syntax of a simple programming language. Despite its small size, the language displays many of the features of the larger languages that are actually used. This simple language is the first of the mini-languages that we will describe in this book. Since it provides the pattern on which all except one of the other mini-languages are based, we have called it Mini-language Core. This mini-language will provide a focus for discussion of the syntactic aspects of language design. We will then use the same approach for the semantics side of the language; that is, we will describe the semantics of the mini-language and use that as the example on which to base our discussion.

Finally, we will consider the difficulty of defining programming languages and the need for completeness and clarity in their description. This discussion will lead to the need for greater formality in the definition of languages using techniques that are introduced in Chapters 3 and 4.

2.1 Informal Description of Mini-language Core

A Mini-language Core program is introduced by the symbol `program`. Despite the fact that `program` is written with several letters, it is considered to be a unique symbol of the language. The language has several such symbols, and these will be shown in lowercase letters. The program consists of two sections: a declaration section, which follows immediately after the `program` symbol, and a statement section. The statement section follows the declaration section; it is introduced by the `begin` symbol and terminated by the `end` symbol and a semicolon. The declaration section is formed of declarations; each consists of a list of identifiers separated by commas and terminated by a colon, the symbol `integer`, and a semicolon. For example:

```
A, B: integer;
X, Y, Z: integer;
```

Statements

The statement section consists of a sequence of statements. There are five kinds of statements: assignment, if, loop, input, and output statements. Each is terminated by a semicolon.

The assignment statement consists of an identifier, the symbol :=, and an expression, in that order. The following are examples of assignment statements:

```
X := B;
X := X + 1;
```

The if statement has two forms,

```
if comparison then
    statement. . .
end if;
```

and

```
if comparison then
    statement. . .
else
    statement. . .
end if;
```

where "statement . . ." represents a sequence of statements, and if, then, else, and end are symbols. Two examples of the if statement are

```
if (X = 2) then
    A := B;
    X := X + 1;
end if;
```

and

```
if (A ≠ B) then
    X := X - 1;
else
    X := X + 1;
end if;
```

A loop statement has the form

```
while comparison loop
    statement. . .
end loop;
```

where while, loop, and end are symbols. An example of a loop statement is:

```
while (Z < X) loop
    Z := Z + 1;
    Y := Y + Z;
end loop;
```

The input and output statements are similar to each other. The input statement consists of the symbol input followed by a list of identifiers separated by commas. The output statement consists of the symbol output followed by a list of identifiers. Examples of these statements are:

```
input A;
output X, Y, Z;
```

Expressions

Expressions are built from operands (consisting of identifiers, integers, and parenthesized expressions) separated by operators. The operators are the symbols +, -, and *. The following are examples of Core expressions:

```
A + B * 3
(A + B) * 3
```

If several operators occur in an expression, the parenthesized expressions are considered as a single operand. Operands separated by the * operator are grouped together to form operands before those separated by the + and - operators. The operator * is said to have a higher *precedence* than the + and - operators. The + and - operators have equal precedence. Sequences of operands separated by operators of equal precedence are grouped in order from left to right. Thus

```
A + B * 3
```

is equivalent to

```
A + (B * 3)
```

and

```
A - B - C
```

is equivalent to

```
(A - B) - C
```

Comparisons

Comparisons consist of parentheses enclosing a pair of operands, each an identifier or integer, separated by one of the comparison operators = , ≠ , ‹ , and › . For example,

```
(A = 3)
(X ≠ Y)
(5 > Y)
```

are comparisons.

An identifier consists of a sequence of letters A through Z. Any two adjacent letters can be separated by an underscore. Thus

```
A
ALPHA
SUM_OF_SQUARES
```

are all examples of identifiers.

An integer consists of a sequence of the digits 0 through 9. Particular implementations of Mini-language Core may impose limitations on the lengths of identifiers and integers.

Constraints

In addition to the rules given for the construction of a program in Core, there are two constraints:

1. *All identifiers used in the statements of the program must be declared.*

Thus, for example, the program

```
program
    A: integer;
begin
    input    A, B;
    output   A, B;
end;
```

is illegal because the identifier B has not been declared.

2. *No identifier may be declared more than once.*

That is, no identifier may appear more than once in the declaration section of the program. For example, the declaration section

```
A, B: integer;
B, C, C: integer;
```

is illegal since both the identifiers B and C are declared more than once.

Comments

Since the purpose of a programming language is to *communicate algorithms to programmers* as well as computers, the programmer will sometimes need to annotate the program. Annotations, generally called *comments,* can provide the human reader with explanations at a higher level of abstraction than is possible in the actual programming language. From the point of view of the translator, comments do not change the program in any way; it is as if the comments were not there. The compiler's only action is to copy the comment into the listing of the source code. Nothing of the comment appears in the object program.

In Mini-language Core, as with the other mini-languages in this book, we shall use the following convention:

A comment is introduced by two contiguous hyphen symbols (that is, --). These two symbols and the remaining characters on the same line are treated as the text of the comment and have no effect on program execution. A comment can occur in the program at any point where a blank may appear.

For example, we may have

```
INCHES := FEET * 12;  -- make conversion to inches
```

Since this convention is uniform throughout the mini-languages in this book, it will not be mentioned when describing them. Comments will, however, be used frequently in examples.

A comment on comments. You may notice that the above comment is quite superfluous in describing the program's meaning. Generally, we believe that such in-line (as distinct from header) program comments should be rare. Good mnemonic names and other programming conventions can make the use of in-line comments virtually nonexistent. In this text our major use of in-line comments will be to make points about the language (not the program).

2.2 Informal Semantics of Mini-language Core

We now discuss the semantics of the mini-language whose written form was described in the previous section.

A declaration in Mini-language Core specifies one or more identifiers that can be used as variables in a program. Each declared variable can take on only integer values. An integer is a nonnegative whole number, for example:

0   16   1776   12345

The maximum value of an integer is defined by a particular implementation and may vary from one implementation to another according to the characteristics of the host machine. However, the maximum value will never be less than 99999.

The execution of a statement causes the actions defined below to take place. The statements in a statement sequence are executed in the order in which they appear. However, some statements are compound in that they enclose other statement sequences. The execution of a compound statement and its enclosed statements is defined below. A program terminates *normally* after the execution of its last statement.

It is possible for the action specified by a statement to be meaningless. An attempt to execute such a statement causes the program to terminate *abnormally.* In addition, the execution of a loop statement, defined below, can result in its contained statements being executed endlessly. Hence, some programs may never terminate.

Thus, there are only three possible outcomes to the execution of a program:

■ Normal termination

■ Abnormal termination

■ Nontermination

The exact meaning of a program is defined only for programs that terminate normally.

Assignment Statements

An assignment statement causes the value of the expression at the time of execution to be associated with a variable. For example, we may have:

```
A := 0;     -- value of A is set to 0
B := B + 1; -- value of B is incremented by 1
```

Execution of an assignment statement takes place as follows:

1. The expression given on the right of the assignment statement is evaluated according to the rules given below. If the expression contains any variables, their current value is used in the equation.
2. The value obtained from the evaluation of the expression becomes the current value of the variable on the left of the assignment.

Provided that the evaluation of the expression does not terminate abnormally, the assignment statement will execute normally.

Input Statements

An input statement causes one or more integer values to be read from an external source, one value for each identifier given in the list of identifiers. Subsequent execution of the same or other input statements causes further values to be read. Each input value in the external source must be separated by one or more blank characters. An end-of-line boundary is treated as a single blank character. If the external data source contained

```
   0           5
  16
```

then the input statement

```
input A, B, C;
```

would read these values into the variables A, B, and C respectively. For this set of data values, the input statement is thus equivalent to the assignments:

```
A := 0;
B := 5;
C := 16;
```

There are three kinds of error that can occur during the execution of an input statement:

1. The external data source contains fewer values than there are identifiers in the input statement. This is an *insufficient data* error.
2. The integer value read from the external data source is greater than the maximum allowed by the implementation. This is a *size* error.
3. One of the characters read from the external data source is an illegal character, i.e., other than a digit or blank. This is an *illegal character* error.

If any of these errors occur, the program is abnormally terminated.

Output Statements

Execution of an output statement causes the value of each of the variables in the list to be printed. Each value is preceded by the name of the variable and an = symbol. For example, the output statement

```
output A, B, C;
```

assuming that the values of A, B, and C are as given above, would result in the output:

```
A = 0    B = 5    C = 16
```

The output from an output statement starts on a new line and consists of the name of a variable, the = symbol, and the value, each separated by a single blank. The length of an output field is thus:

```
length(identifier)  +  length(integer-value)  +  3
```

Fields are separated by three blanks. The length of an output line is defined to be 72 characters. If there is insufficient room left on a line to accommodate the next output field, a new line is started. An output field is not split between lines unless its length is greater than 72 characters.

There is one error that can occur during the execution of an output statement:

- One of the variables in the list has not had a value assigned to it. This is the *undefined value* error.

If Statements

An if statement is a compound statement headed by a comparison. The comparison allows the programmer to make a choice of which statements are to be executed. The simplest form of an if statement contains only a comparison and one enclosed sequence of statements, for example:

```
if (A = 0) then
    INDEX   := INDEX - 1;
    PRODUCT := PRODUCT * INDEX;
    output INDEX, PRODUCT;
end if;
```

Here, the two assignment statements and the output statement are executed only if the variable A has the value zero. If the value of A is not equal to zero, then none of the contained statements is executed.

If statements may have an else part, which contains an alternative sequence of statements to be executed if the comparison is false. For example, we may have:

```
if (A = 0) then
   INDEX   := INDEX - 1;
   PRODUCT := PRODUCT * INDEX;
   output INDEX, PRODUCT;
else
   INDEX   PRODUCT := INDEX + 1;
   SUM     := SUM + INDEX;
   output INDEX, SUM;
end if;
```

Here, depending on the value of A, either the first three enclosed statements are executed or the second three enclosed statements are executed. An if statement terminates abnormally if the evaluation of the operands in the comparison leads to an error, as defined below.

Loop Statements

A loop statement is a compound statement that specifies that the statements within the loop are to be executed repeatedly as long as the comparison at the head of the loop is true. For example, we may have:

```
while (CHANGE > 99) loop
   DOLLARS := DOLLARS + 1;
   CHANGE  := CHANGE - 100;
end loop;
```

Here the value of CHANGE is compared with 99. If it is greater than 99, the two enclosed assignments are executed and the process is repeated. If, for example, the value of CHANGE were initially 265, then the two assignments in the loop would be executed. The value of CHANGE would then be 165 and the loop would be executed a second time. At this point, the value of CHANGE would be 65 and the execution of the loop statement would be complete. If the initial value of CHANGE were 65, the enclosed assignment statements would not be executed at all.

As in the if statement, the loop statement terminates abnormally if evaluation of the operands in the comparison leads to an error.

Expressions

An expression defines the computation of a value. The operators +, -, and * denote addition, subtraction, and multiplication. The operators are evaluated in order of decreasing precedence, defined by the syntax of the language. Table 2.1 shows a number of example expressions and the order in which their components are evaluated. The lowercase letters denote temporary storage that is used to retain values for later use as they are computed.

There are three errors that can arise during the evaluation of an expression:

1. A variable in the expression has not previously had a value assigned to it. This is an *undefined value* error.

2. One of the operations leads to a value greater than the maximum permitted value defined by the implementation. This is an *overflow* error.

3. One of the operations leads to a value less than zero. This is the *negative value* error.

The occurrence of any of these errors causes abnormal termination of the program.

Table 2.1 **Evaluation of Expressions**

Expressions	Sequence of Values Computed	Equivalent Expressions
A + B + C	x ← A + B y ← x + C	(A + B) + C
A - B - C	x ← A - B y ← x - C	(A - B) - C
A + B * C	x ← B * C y ← A + x	A + (B * C)
A * B + C	x ← A * B y ← x + C	(A * B) + C
A * B + C * D	x ← A * B y ← 10 C * D z ← x + y	(A * B) + (C * D)
A * (B + C) * D	x ← B + C y ← 10 A * x z ← D * y	(A * (B + C)) * D

Comparisons

A comparison consists of two operands separated by one of the comparison operators, ⟨, =, ≠, ⟩, meaning less than, equal to, not equal to, and greater than, respectively. If v1 is the value of the operand x1 and v2 is the value of the operand x2, then the result of the comparison:

```
(x1 < x2) will be true if v1 is less than v2
(x1 = x2) will be true if v1 is equal to v2
(x1 ≠ x2) will be true if v1 is not equal to v2
(x1 > x2) will be true if v1 is greater than v2
```

Otherwise, the result of the comparison will be false.

Should the evaluation of one of the operands lead to an error, the program will be terminated abnormally.

Examples

```
program
   COUNT, LIMIT: integer;
    LAST_TERM, THIS_TERM, NEXT_TERM: integer;
begin
   COUNT     := 0;
   LAST_TERM := 1;
   THIS_TERM := 1;
   input LIMIT;
   while (COUNT < LIMIT) loop
      output LAST_TERM;
      NEXT_TERM := LAST_TERM + THIS_TERM;
      LAST_TERM := THIS_TERM;
      THIS_TERM := NEXT_TERM;
      COUNT     :=COUNT + 1;
   end loop;
end;
```

Example 2.1 **Program to Print the Fibonacci Series**

As a complete example of a program in Mini-language Core, the program shown in Example 2.1 generates the Fibonacci series where, after the first two terms, each term is the sum of the previous two. If the value read by the input statement were 10, the output would be:

```
LAST_TERM = 1
LAST_TERM = 1
LAST_TERM = 2
LAST_TERM = 3
LAST_TERM = 5
LAST_TERM = 8
LAST_TERM = 13
LAST_TERM = 21
LAST_TERM = 34
LAST_TERM = 55
```

Should the value read from the external data source be sufficiently large, the program will terminate with an overflow error during the execution of the statement:

```
NEXT_TERM := LAST_TERM + THIS_TERM;
```

The following is a very simple program with one assignment statement.

```
program
    A: integer;
begin
    A := A + 1; -- A has not been initialized
    output A;
end;
```

When the expression in this assignment statement is evaluated, the variable A has had no value assigned. Thus, this program terminates abnormally and no output is generated.

2.3 Language Design and the Programming Process

A programming language is a very complex tool whose design requires many compromises. It must provide a notation that carries a mental load for the programmer and therefore must be natural to use. Yet, it must be adequate for describing a wide variety of real-world problems, many of them beyond the imagination of the language designer. However, if the language becomes too broad in its scope, it will become too complex for the programmer to master. The design of the language will have great effect on the ease with which the programmer can use it. In this section we will discuss some aspects of the relationship between language design and ease of programming.

In a large measure, the syntax of a language controls the clarity of programs. This does not mean that programs written in a language with a perfectly designed syntax, assuming that such a thing were possible, would necessarily be easy to read. It is always possible to write obscure programs, whatever the language.

A second effect of the design of the syntax is the number of errors that are made during the writing of the program. These errors may not be due to incorrect thinking, but occur because the syntax does not conform to the programmer's intuition. For example, from their experience with both natural language and mathematics, people are used to certain ways of using spaces and punctuation. Programming languages that vary from these normal uses are likely to cause needless errors.

If frequency counts of the types of syntax errors that occur were available, they would provide an interesting way of comparing languages. Each language would have its own set of characteristic errors, which would generally reflect the weak spots in its design. There have been several experimental studies of the relationship between programming language design and programming errors see for example, [Gannon and Horning 1975].

We now discuss particular aspects of syntax and some considerations that should be borne in mind. It must be emphasized that this is only representative of the questions that need to be weighed during the design process.

Free Form versus Fixed Form

Some programming languages have rigid requirements on the form in which statements in the program are to be written. Originally, all statements in Fortran had to start in column 7, and the programmer was unable to indicate the structure of the program through indentation of the statements. Such rigid requirements remain current in some Fortran and Basic implementations. If we consider the way in which we normally use blanks, indentation, and other layout techniques when we write prose, it is remarkable that this convention has survived so long. It is very important that the programmer be allowed to use white space to enhance the overall readability of the program.

One of the design considerations of Fortran was that blanks could be ignored at all points in a program; the compiler would rely on other delimiters to analyze the program. For example, the two statements

```
DO 13 K = 1,3
```

and

```
DO 13 K = 1.3
```

are both valid statements. The first is the start of an iterative statement that loops with the variable K having the successive values 1, 2, and 3. The second is an assignment statement that assigns 1.3 to the variable DO13K. One of the arguments for the philosophy of ignoring blanks is that, when Fortran first came out, there were no Fortran coding sheets and programmers wrote their programs on blank paper; as a consequence, it was feared that keypunchers would find it too difficult to count blanks accurately. A result of this convention is that we still see Fortran programs written without any blank characters at all.

By itself, the rule that blanks play no part in the syntax of Fortran is not dangerous. It is only when it occurs in conjunction with a rule that variables do not have to be declared that danger occurs. If the language required that all variables be declared, then the second statement would not be valid unless the programmer had declared a variable DO13K, an unlikely event. It has been said that just such a mistyping of a comma as a period caused the loss of a Venus probe, a heavy price to pay for the slip of a finger.

Just as free form encourages the use of horizontal white space, it should also encourage the use of vertical white space. The language and the compiler should allow empty lines to appear in the source program. In addition, there should be some way of controlling the layout of the listing of the source program produced by the compiler. This would allow separate sections of a program to be started on separate pages.

Comments

There are various conventions for comments:

- Start the comment in a specific column and continue to the end of the line. This is sometimes used in low-level languages like assemblers. The use of free format in higher-level languages prevents the use of this convention.

- Use a symbol to make a complete line into a comment. Fortran uses a letter C in column 1 for this purpose. The main disadvantage is that it does not permit a comment to be put on the same line as the statement it annotates.

■ Start the comment with a special symbol and terminate it with a special symbol. This is a common convention. Algol 60 uses the symbol **comment** to mark the start and continues to a semicolon. Pascal uses { to mark the beginning and } as a terminator. With this method, it is possible to put a comment into the middle of a statement and continue the statement on the same line, as in

```
if BASE_PTR = nil {the list is absent} then
```

which is not possible with the other two conventions. This advantage is, however, offset by a danger that, since the end of line plays no part in marking comments, the omission of the terminator can cause part of the program to be treated as a comment by the compiler—generally with bad consequences. The convention might be improved by making the end-of-line an alternative terminator.

■ Start the comment with a special symbol and continue to the end of the line. This is the convention used in Ada and is the one we have adopted for the mini-languages used in this book. This method seems to have advantages in readability, convenience of use, and reliability.

Semicolons

It has become common practice to use semicolons as punctuation in programs. There are, however, two views on their usage. They can be used either to terminate or to separate statements. In the Mini-language Core fragment

```
while (LIMIT > COUNT) loop
   NEXT_TERM  := LAST_TERM + THIS_TERM;
   LAST_TERM  := THIS_TERM;
   THIS_TERM  := NEXT_TERM;
   COUNT      := COUNT + 1;
end loop;
```

the semicolon is used to terminate the four assignments and the one loop statement.

If the semicolon had been used as a separator, there would be no semicolon after the fourth assignment since that statement does not need separating from the next statement in the sequence. Instead, the end of the sequence would be marked by the symbols end loop. PL/I has adopted the convention of using the semicolon as a terminator, while Algol 60, Pascal, Bliss, and several others use it as a statement separator. Pascal makes things more difficult by also using the semicolon as a terminator in the declarative part, thus making the placement of the semicolons very confusing.

In an experiment reported in [Gannon and Horning 1975], errors with separators were ten times more likely than errors with terminators. It seems that the rule where a statement is always terminated by a punctuation mark is easier to understand and remember than the rule that a punctuation mark is required whenever one statement is being separated from another. Such a rule reflects usage in normal prose.

Reserved Words

Mini-language Core uses symbols like while, loop, and if in the construction of the statements. These serve the dual purpose of differentiating one kind of statement from another and of making the programs easy to read. We have used lowercase letters to distinguish these symbols from the identifiers that can be constructed by the programmer. In some languages, the luxury of upper and lower case is not possible because of the implementation hardware. In such cases, the fixed symbols of a language are called *keywords* and have the same representation as identifiers.

There are three main techniques used to distinguish keywords from identifiers:

- Precede them by a special symbol, for example, $. A loop statement in the Mini-language Core might then become:

```
$WHILE (A < B) $LOOP
    A := A + X;
$END $LOOP;
```

  The special symbol here is obtrusive and seriously affects the readability of a program.

The other two techniques are really opposed to each other and will be discussed together.

- Define the keywords to be *reserved words,* that is, forbid the programmer from using these keywords as identifiers.
- Rely on context to make the distinction. That is, to say

```
WHILE := LOOP;
```

  is an assignment statement because of the symbol :=.

These last two conventions are debated. Ada, Pascal, and Cobol have chosen reserved words, while PL/I has no reserved words. The arguments may be summarized as follows:

- If keywords are reserved then there is no danger of a loss of readability due to the programmer choosing identifiers that clash with keywords. While it is true that a perverse PL/I programmer could write

```
IF IF = THEN THEN
THEN = ELSE;
```

  it is likely that the programmer would soon tire of this.

- If a reserved word language is extended, it is quite likely that new keywords will be required. This will extend the list of reserved words and render illegal existing programs that have used these new keywords as identifiers before they were made keywords. A proposed revision to the Cobol standard received many objections because the addition of more than 50 reserved words would, as reported by [Dubnow 1981], "be at the cost of changing millions of lines of source code."

- In a reserved word language, the keywords provide fixed markers in the syntax that allow the compiler to make better recovery in the face of syntax errors and give more meaningful error messages.

This matter is not fully resolved.

2.4 The Definition of Programming Languages

Programming languages are usually defined informally. Typically, such descriptions employ normal prose, mixed with the use of tables, equations, and examples. The descriptions of our mini-languages in this book use this method. There are many questions related to the definition of programming languages:

- How can we present a precise definition of a language so that it is comprehensible to the average user?

- How can we use proper terminology and, at the same time, avoid the use of computer jargon typically associated with the definition of a language?

- How can we find abstractions for issues that are noted for their excessive detail, for example, input and output or arithmetic with real numbers?

- How can we describe the precise conditions under which a program is erroneous?

■ How can we isolate those portions of a language that are dependent on the implementation?

■ Last, is there a real need for formal definitions of semantics?

We treat these issues next.

Presentation of a Language

One of the key decisions in describing a language is the order in which the concepts are presented. Typically, language descriptions take a bottom-up approach; that is, low-level ideas, for example, numbers, identifiers, and character sets, are described first. The description slowly expands to include higher-level parts of the language, for example, procedures, nesting of declarations, and, finally, programs.

This method presumes that the lower-level concepts are easier to understand, and that a slow building of the user's knowledge will eventually lead to a comprehension of a complete program. Unfortunately, this method of description forces the reader to learn many features of a language whose utility may not be apparent until much more of the language is understood. As a result, there is some reason to believe that languages should be defined the other way around. This is the top-down order.

In a top-down presentation, the higher-level concepts are given first, defined in terms of constructions that are to be specified later. All of the mini-language descriptions and all of the tables describing the syntax are arranged in this way. The category program is defined by the first production in terms of categories defined in subsequent productions.

We argue that a top-down description of a language leads to a more rapid comprehension. Often, the lower-level items, such as numbers and expressions, are common to most languages, and the reader need not waste time rehearsing concepts that are already well known. More importantly, the general structure is outlined at the beginning and the details filled in subsequently according to the needs of the reader.

A definition intended for beginning programmers is likely to be organized differently from one for use by an experienced programmer as a reference. A description intended for beginners can appeal to little in the way of background knowledge, whereas a programmer might use a language definition to answer detailed questions about the language. Typical of such questions are: Is a semicolon needed here? Under what conditions will a particular construct lead to abnormal termination? What happens if I write this statement? Obviously, the choice of a good organization for a reference manual is a difficult issue and may be neither top-down nor bottom-up. Certainly, a comprehensive index to any language description is essential.

People learn by examples, and with programming languages this is particularly true. Unfortunately, most language descriptions do not give realistic examples. The use of program fragments without a context or without a concern for style and clarity is all too frequent. For example, constructs like

```
while (I < J) loop
    J := J - 1;
end loop;
```

or even worse,

```
while (I < J) loop J := J - 1; end loop;
```

are hardly illuminating. Their identifiers give no inkling of the parts played by the variables I and J in the computation.

It may be argued that the development of good examples is difficult, and indeed it is. In this text, we too have occasionally used somewhat less than meaningful examples. On this point, we can only say, the better the examples, the better the language description.

Terminology

We now speak more about the words with which a language is described. A reference manual for a programming language is a compromise between a legal document describing the exact meaning of every feature in the language and a prose description suitable for the human reader. Typically, such descriptions introduce terminology and notations that have a special meaning with respect to the computer language.

One of the keys to the precision and clarity with which a language is described is the terminology used. Consider the simple and familiar term *value*. A value presumably denotes some object that can be constructed in a program. Thus, it makes sense to speak of the value of an expression, the value existing on some input or output device, or the value returned by a function. This term is, however, used in other contexts.

For example, we often speak of the *value* associated with a parameter of a procedure, or the *value* of a variable given on the left side of an assignment statement. In these contexts, the meaning of the term *value* is not quite so obvious. For example, the value associated with a parameter to a procedure may, in fact, mean the location of the corresponding argument. Similarly, the value of the variable on the left side of an assignment statement may also denote a location, rather than some object computed by the programmer. We consider this question in much greater detail in Chapter 6.

Similar problems arise with the two familiar terms *operator* and *operation*. We often speak of the addition operator and sometimes speak of the addition operation. Similarly, we speak of the assignment operator and sometimes of the assignment operation. Frequently, a clear definition of these two terms is not given.

In our description of the mini-languages, we have made the following rather narrow distinction between these two terms. An operator can be applied to values to produce another value. Thus, we speak of the addition operator or the equality operator. An operation is an action causing an effect on the internal state of the program. Thus, we speak of an assignment operation and an input or output operation. This difference between an operation and an operator is one we also draw between a procedure and a function in Chapter 10.

There are many such related questions. What is scope? What is an "attribute"? What does it mean for an object to have a location? We discuss these specific points in later chapters.

Style of writing presents another problem. We are taught in writing classes to use synonyms to avoid tedious repetition. In a precise definition, this will leave the reader wondering about the difference in meaning between the synonyms.

These are typical of the kinds of issues that make the description of a programming language difficult. It is certainly true that the description of a programming language requires a great deal of care.

Specifying Details

Many features of a programming language involve numerous details. In Fortran, for example, the form and meaning of FORMAT statements is quite complicated because of the many options specifying the type and field width of items. A careful specification of all of the format options in Fortran typically takes pages and pages of text.

Another area of particular difficulty is the detailed behavior of arithmetic for floating point numbers. Specifying the resolution to which each arithmetic computation is evaluated, maximum and minimum values, the number of significant digits, and rounding or truncation conventions can be quite elaborate.

Errors

Programmers do not intend their programs to terminate abnormally. Nevertheless, errors occur, often to the great surprise of the programmer.

The specification of the conditions under which a program will terminate abnormally is an important part of any programming language description. All too often error conditions are not clearly defined.

In Mini-language Core there are several conditions that can lead to abnormal termination of a program. These are:

1. *Undefined value* error.
2. *Overflow* error.
3. *Negative value* error.

4. *Insufficient data* error.

5. *Size* error.

6. *Illegal character* error.

In addition, a program may be erroneous if it contains a loop that does not terminate.

Because Mini-language Core is such a small language, it has been possible to keep the number of semantic errors to a very small number. In real programming languages defining all the possible execution time errors is much more difficult, yet a complete definition must do so.

Implementation Dependencies

It is a fond wish for high-level programming languages to be independent of the host machine and operating system on which they run. The program that runs on machine X should also run on machine Y without modification. To some degree, this is achieved. It is usually possible to move a program in one of the standard languages from one implementation to another without too much difficulty. This is because most programs make use of those parts of the language that are well understood and avoid the fringe areas.

Nevertheless, there are some areas that commonly give problems, for example:

- *Maximum length of identifiers:* Because of different machine characteristics, different implementations of the same language may find it convenient to set different bounds on the lengths of identifiers or discriminate between identifiers on different numbers of characters.

- *Arithmetic precision:* The different word lengths of various machine architectures encourage arithmetic of different precision. This variance is compounded by a variety of number representations that bring computed results that may not be equal. For example, rounding on a two's complement machine may not give the same answer as rounding on a machine that uses a base ten representation.

- *Character sets:* The character sets can be different from one implementation to another. While it is true that the sequence of letters in the alphabet is likely to be consistent, other important details are not. The two most popular character encodings are the ASCII set, which is a standard in the United States, and the EBCDIC scheme of IBM. In the ASCII code, the digits precede the letters; in EBCDIC, the letters come first.

  The choice of character set is generally made by the manufacturer of the hardware and is "built into" the hardware. It would therefore be difficult to implement a language that called for the ASCII character set on a machine that was designed for EBCDIC. Every time that two character strings were compared, special measures would have to be used, rather than making direct use of the hardware instructions.

Even beyond these kinds of issues, there is a tacit assumption that the implementation has adhered to the "standard" definition of the language. All too often this is not the case.

The definition of a language must therefore take care to separate those parts of the language that are to be consistent across all implementations from those that are left to the implementor's discretion. Some typical situations include:

1. *Minimum requirement.* The definition may specify some minimum requirements, for example, the minimum number of digits precision to represent an integer. An implementation may make extensions beyond this minimum, but a program that makes use of integers that have greater precision than the specified minimum might not be transportable from one implementation to another.

2. *Implementation defined.* Here, the language specification requires that the documentation supplied by the implementor should augment the language definition by supplying certain details, such as the maximum number of characters used in discriminating identifiers.

3. *Deliberately undefined.* Certain details of a language can be left explicitly undefined, for example, the order in which subscript expressions in an array reference are evaluated. By leaving them deliberately undefined, the programmer would know that programs that depend on these details are likely not to be movable from machine to machine; indeed, different versions of the same compiler may treat them differently.

In any case, a complete definition of a language must adopt a position on all details of the language.

Need for Formal Definitions

Computer science has already made considerable progress without having a generally accepted formal technique for defining programming languages, just as the English language was well developed before the advent of Johnson's *Dictionary of the English Language* in 1755. However, the lack of general use of formal definitions has not been without some hard consequences. For example:

- Language designers do not have good tools for careful analysis of their decisions.

- Standardization efforts have been impeded by the lack of an adequate formal notation.

- It is impossible to make a contract with a vendor for a compiler and be assured that the product will be an exact implementation of the language.

- It is difficult to write reference manuals and tutorial texts without glossing over critical details.

- The answers to detailed questions about a programming language frequently have to be obtained by trying an implementation or hoping for a consensus from several implementations.

Most of these problems would be avoided if there were good formal definitions for the languages. There would then be a single source for the precise details of each language, and no question would be left unanswered. Importantly, there would be a tendency to improve the design of a language by bringing its complexities out into the open. It is easy to say, "Language X is block structured and jumps out of blocks are permitted." But without a formal description of language X, the consequences are not so obvious.

Among the characteristics that are important to the successful use of any method are:

1. *Completeness:* There must be no gaps in the definition. In particular, there must be no questions about the syntax or semantics of the language that cannot be answered by means of the definition.

2. *Clarity:* Users of the definition must be able to understand the definition and to find answers to their questions easily. While it is obvious that some facility with the language is essential before being able to understand the definition fully, the amount of effort required should be small.

3. *Naturalness:* The naturalness of a notation has a very large effect on the ability of a user to understand a definition. The naturalness of a notation is more important than its conciseness, although there is a relation between the two.

4. *Realism:* Although the designer of a language may wish to be free from such mundane restrictions as finite numeric ranges and bounded storage, these restrictions are realities of an implementation. The definition provided by the designer, which is the implementor's manufacturing specifications, must specify exactly where

restrictions or choices can be made and where the designer's unobstructed landscape must be modeled exactly.

In the next two chapters, we will describe techniques for the formal definition of syntax and semantics.

Further Reading

There are really not many works on the syntax of programming languages, aside from work on formal grammars and methods of implementation. The larger issues of readability and presentation of programs are seldom discussed.

One thoughtful work on the subject of syntax is Chapter 2 of the Rationale for the Design of the Ada Programming Language; *see [Ichbiah et al. 1979]. This discusses numerous issues concerning the presentation of the syntax of a programming language. An entirely different but relevant work is [Gannon and Horning 1975], which describes an experiment intended to compare the utility of various forms for expressing programming language constructs.*

There are several reviews of the effects of language design on the reliability of programming. [Horning 1979] considers many of the aspects of language design and includes a very complete bibliography. [Shaw et al. 1981] compares four languages—Fortran, Cobol, Jovial, and Ada—from the point of view of their meeting the requirements of software engineering methods. [Feuer and Gehani 1982] compare the designs of C and Pascal from the point of view of their utility in programming a variety of applications.

An interesting view of the role of language definition is presented in [Ashcraft and Wadge 1982]. The authors' thesis is that formal definitions should be used prescriptively rather than descriptively. That is to say, a formal language definition should be developed concurrently with the design of the language. The definition will make plain the complexities of the language and alert designers to areas that need attention.

Exercises

Exercise 2.1 *Learning the P's and Q's of Syntax*

There are many little and often annoying details that must be learned in a language. Some of these are covered in the following true-false quiz. Try it on Mini-language Core.

   a. The first nonblank character in a program must be the p in program.
   b. The last nonblank character in a program must be a semicolon.
   c. The identifier end may be used as the name of an integer variable.
   d. Only one statement may appear on a line.
   e. The following sequence of characters is a well-formed comment:

   ```
   -- The symbols -- may be used in comments.
   ```

   f. The statement

   ```
   SOCIAL_SECURITY_NUMBER := 022325795;
   ```

   is a well-formed assignment statement.
   g. The sequence 2 22 43 is an integer.

Exercise 2.2 *Comments*

Investigate the comment conventions in the languages Fortran, PL/I, Pascal, Algol 60, Ada, APL, and Lisp. Compare them from the point of view of ease of use and possibility of causing programming errors.

Exercise 2.3 *Unreserved Keywords*

One consequence of avoiding the use of reserved words in PL/I is that the expression following the keyword WHILE in a do statement with the while option must be in parentheses, for example,

```
DO WHILE(A = B);
```

whereas parentheses are not required round the expression between the IF and THEN keywords in an if statement, for example,

```
IF A = B THEN
```

Develop an explanation for this rule.

Exercise 2.4 *Writing a Reference Manual*

Consider the following strange-looking language.

A program is a sequence of string replacement rules of the form

```
L    ->   R
```

where L and R are strings of characters. Some of the rules may have a period after the arrow, as in

```
L    ->. R
```

In both cases, the replacement R may be an empty string. The input to each program is itself a character string.

A program is executed as follows. The sequence of rules is scanned for the first rule, such that the string L given on the left side occurs within the input string S. Then the leftmost occurrence of L within S is replaced by R, giving a new input string S'. This process is reiterated until a rule with a period is executed, or until no substitution is possible, at which point the program terminates.

The final value of the input string is the output of the program.

This language, described in [Markov 1954], is known as a Markov Normal Algorithm and can, in fact, express any computable operation. For example, the program

```
B    ->   D
C    ->   F
D    ->   I
```

transforms the string COBBLER into the string FIDDLER, and the program

```
B    ->   D
C    ->.  T
D    ->   I
```

transforms the string COBBLER into the string TODDLER.

Consider, as another example, the following program for taking a parenthesized string of letters from the alphabet {O, P, T, S} and producing a string where the initial letters are reversed:

```
OO*    ->    O*O
OP*    ->    P*O
OT*    ->    T*O
OS*    ->    S*O

PO*    ->    O*P
PP*    ->    P*P
PT*    ->    T*P
PS*    ->    S*P

TO*    ->    O*T
TP*    ->    P*T
TT*    ->    T*T
TS*    ->    S*T

SO*    ->    O*S
SP*    ->    P*S
ST*    ->    T*S
SS*    ->    S*S
(O*    ->    O(
(P*    ->    P(
(T*    ->    T(
(S*    ->    S(

()     ->.
)      ->    *)
```

For example, the input

```
(STOP)
```

gives the output

```
POTS
```

Now for the exercise. Write a reference manual for this "programming language." In the course of writing your reference manual, you will discover that you will have to specify some details not covered in our informal description. You should draw on your experience and inventiveness to supply these details.

Exercise 2.5 *Negative Values*

Mini-language Core, as it is defined in this chapter, does not permit negative values. Specify changes to the description to allow negative values. This will require changes to both the syntax and the semantics of the language.

Exercise 2.6 *Language and the Programming Process*

Section 2.3 discusses some aspects of the effects of language design on the programming process. Sections 1.4 and 1.5 describe other language design issues. Discuss how these, too, might affect the programming process.

3

Syntax

In this chapter we describe how the outward appearance of a programming language, that is, its syntax, can be defined. In Chapter 2 we described the syntax of Mini-language Core in an informal way. Starting from this informal view of the syntax, we identify the syntactic components of the language that are fitted together to form the fabric of the complete language.

Although we have taken great care in writing the prose description of Mini-language Core, there are still likely to be things that are not clear. Few real languages are so carefully defined. They are, of course, much larger and their descriptions are subject to the vagaries of English prose. In this chapter we will discuss more formal techniques for the description of syntax and show how these techniques can be applied to the description of Mini-language Core. This will lead us to the choice of a particular method that we will use throughout the rest of this book.

3.1 The Syntactic Components of Programming Languages

A program consists of a hierarchy of *syntactic units.* At the highest level we have the complete program. In Mini-language Core, the complete program consists of the three symbols `program`, `begin`, and `end`, together with everything contained within the framework they provide. In other programming languages there may be other large structural units. For example, in PL/I a program may consist of several separate external procedures that have been individually translated and subsequently linked together for execution.

At the next level of syntactic structure there are declarations and statements. Each of these units is one of a number of specific forms. Some statements contain expressions: these are syntactic units of arbitrary size built according to certain rules, with subunits separated from each other by operators.

At the bottom of the syntactic scale are the *lexical* elements, the symbols from which programs in the language are constructed. In the case of Core, the lexical elements are

```
begin  else  end  if  integer  input  loop  output  program

then   while

0 1 2 3 4 5 6 7 8 9

A B C D E F G H I J K L M N O P Q R S T U V W X Y Z

/   ,   :   ;   +   -   *   <   >   =   ≠   (   )   :=
```

and the blank character, which, when we need to represent it explicitly, will be denoted by the symbol ⍁.

The set of symbols from which a language is constructed is its *vocabulary*. Some of these symbols are always used by themselves, for example, begin, end, +, and *. Others are used to construct larger syntactic units such as identifiers and integers. Identifiers and integers are always terminated by one of the special symbols, shown in the last row of the lexical elements above, or by blanks. The symbols used to terminate identifiers and integers are known as *delimiters*. In all the mini-languages used in this book, at any point where a delimiter can occur in a program, an arbitrary number of blanks may be inserted or a new line started.

3.2 The Description of Syntax

In our informal description of Mini-language Core in Section 2.1, we gave a long-winded description of the rules for writing a program in Core. Such a description also suffers from the imprecision of English and its possible ambiguities. It is even difficult to know whether the description is complete. For example, is it legal to have a program without a declaration or without any statements? Of course, once such questions have been thought of, it is possible to amplify the informal description to include their answers. However, what about all the other possible questions?

There is thus a need for a more formal way of describing the syntax of programming languages. In this section we will describe the most common approaches to this problem.

Some Basic Notions

- A *grammar* is a set of rules that defines the set, generally infinite, of all sentences that can be written in a language.
- A *sentence* of a language is a finite sequence of symbols from a vocabulary constructed according to the rules of the language's grammar.
- A *vocabulary* or *alphabet* is a finite set of symbols.
- A *symbol* is an atomic entity, which is represented by a graphic, for example, +, (, a letter, or a digit.

In some languages like Mini-language Core, complete words, for example, begin, may be treated as symbols. Such symbols can be distinguished from identifiers, which are also constructed from letters, by using a different typeface, making them reserved words, or some other device, such as introducing them with a special symbol, as discussed in Chapter 2.

The following are examples of languages:

L1. The set of strings of length greater than zero composed of the symbols 0 and 1. These two symbols constitute the vocabulary of L1.

L2. The set of strings consisting of *n* occurrences of the symbol A followed by *n* occurrences of the symbol B. The vocabulary of this language consists of the symbols A and B. The grammar states that there are equal numbers of occurrences of the symbol A and of the symbol B. The strings

```
AAAABBBB
AB
```

are examples of sentences in L2.

L3. The set of grammatical sentences in English. The vocabulary here consists of the words of the English language; the grammar is the grammar of English, which requires, for example, that the form of a verb match the subject of the verb. Thus HE IS A MAN is legal, while HE ARE A MAN is not.

In describing these languages, the sentences were defined by giving rules for constructing them from a vocabulary. These rules form the grammar or the *rules of syntax* (often referred to as simply the *syntax* of the language). In the languages L1 and L2, the rules are quite specific; L1 and L2 are very simple languages. In the case of L3, use was made of the vague term "grammatical sentences." The rules of English grammar are very complex and ill-defined in many places. Luckily, programming languages are not nearly as complex as English, and we are able to produce reasonably simple and precise grammars for them.

3.3 Grammars for Describing Syntax

In the analysis or parsing of English sentences, the words in a sentence are placed in different categories according to their functions in the sentence. In the simple sentence THE MAN EATS THE APPLE, THE MAN is the subject and EATS THE APPLE is the predicate. The subject consists of an article followed by the noun MAN. The predicate consists of the verb EATS followed by the direct object THE APPLE, which is an article and a noun.

We can represent this analysis by a tree-like structure known as a *parse tree:*

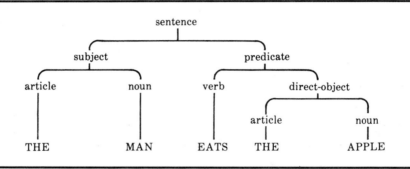

In this parse tree there are two kinds of named points, generally called *nodes.* One type of node represents the words of the original sentence. These appear at the ends of the branches of the tree and are called *terminals.* They appear in uppercase letters, as they do in the original sentence. The terminals taken in left-to-right order form the original sentence. The other type of node, written here in lowercase letters, are *nonterminals* and bear the names of the grammatical categories they represent. These are often called *syntactic categories.*

Each nonterminal of the parse tree has one or more *subnodes* connected by a line drawn from the bottom of the node. Each subnode is either a terminal or a nonterminal. Except for one nonterminal (the *root* of the tree), each symbol has exactly one *parent* node. The grammar of a language consists of a set of rules that specify for each nonterminal precisely what subnodes it may have and in what order they may appear.

For our example sentence, we can write a grammar as:

sentence	∷= subject	predicate
subject	∷= article	noun
predicate	∷= verb	direct-object
direct-object	∷= article	noun
article	∷= THE	
noun	∷= MAN	
noun	∷= APPLE	
verb	∷= EATS	

The ∷= symbol indicates that the item to the left has the items on the right as subnodes. This symbol is not part of the language being defined by the grammar but is part of yet another language, one used to describe languages. Such a language is called a *syntax meta-language.* In this grammar there is precisely one syntactic category that does not appear on the right of a rule, this is the *goal* of the grammar and will be the root of the parse tree.

The rules of a grammar can be used to generate all the sentences of a language. If we use our simple grammar, starting with the syntactic category sentence, we can see that the only possible subnodes are subject and predicate. Indeed, there is no choice possible until we come to noun, at which point we can choose between MAN and APPLE. There are thus only four possible trees that we can draw with this grammar. They correspond to the sentences:

```
THE MAN EATS THE APPLE
THE MAN EATS THE MAN
THE APPLE EATS THE APPLE
THE APPLE EATS THE MAN
```

These are the four sentences that constitute the language defined by this grammar. Because of this use of a grammar to produce sentences, the rules are often known as *productions.*

An alternative way of using a grammar is to analyze a given sentence to see if it is a syntactically correct sentence of the language. This is done by using the rules of the grammar to attempt to construct a tree whose terminals, taken in left-to-right order, form the given sentence. If it is possible to construct such a tree, then the sentence is in the language. The analysis of a sentence in this way is called *parsing.*

Grammars are thus used in two ways:

1. *Generatively* to construct all possible sentences in the language. A grammar for Mini-langue Core used generatively would potentially produce all possible Core programs. We use "potentially" because there are an infinite number of Core programs possible.

2. *Analytically* to determine whether a given string is a sentence in the language. The analytical use of a grammer for Mini-language Core would be to check whether a given Core program was syntactically correct.

Context-free Grammars

In our use of the grammar to construct the four sentences, when it came to choosing a subnode for noun the second time, no account was taken of our first choice. That is, whenever we make a choice, we are not able to allow our choice to be affected by any of the categories and terminal symbols that already exist in the partial derivation tree. Our choice is made without *context*.

A rule of a grammar where context is considered would have the form

```
w  x  y  ::=  w  z  y
```

where w, y, and z are sequences of terminals and nonterminals and x is a nonterminal. The sequences w and y provide the context that defines where the nonterminal x can be replaced by the sequence z.

As an example of this, consider the Mini-language Core program

```
program
    declare A;
begin
    input A;
end;
```

If w represented the sequence of terminals `program declare A; begin` and y the sequence `end ;`, we might have the context-sensitive rule

```
w  input-statement  y  ::=  w  input A;  y
```

This denotes that `input A;` can be replaced by the nonterminal input-statement in the context of a declaration of A as an identifier.

A grammar where no account of context is taken when making a substitution is a *context-free language.* Context-sensitive grammars are more complex than context-free grammars because of the need to express the fact that a substitution in one part of the derivation tree can influence the structure in another part. Almost all languages, both natural and artificial, have context sensitivities. Programming languages generally have some context-sensitive rules. As we shall explain later, the rule in Mini-language Core that an identifier may not be declared more than once in a program is an example of a context-sensitive rule.

To avoid the added complexity of context, the syntax of programming languages is generally defined in a context-free form with additional, usually informal, rules describing the context sensitivities.

A context-free grammar requires the specification of four items:

1. A vocabulary of nonterminal symbols.

2. A vocabulary of terminal symbols.

3. A set of productions of the form

x ::= y

where x is a nonterminal drawn from the nonterminal vocabulary and y is a combination of symbols drawn from the combined terminal and nonterminal vocabularies.

4. A goal symbol that is to be the root node of all parse trees. Sometimes, the term *distinguished symbol* is used for the goal symbol.

Derivations

In general, the repeated application of the productions gives sequences of symbols, both terminal and nonterminal, that can be *derived* from the goal symbol. These sequences are the *sentential forms* of the language defined by the grammar G. Any string that contains only terminal symbols and that can be derived from the goal symbol is a *sentence* of the language defined by G.

We would show the derivation of the sentence

THE MAN EATS THE APPLE

as a sequence of pictures that show the parse tree growing:

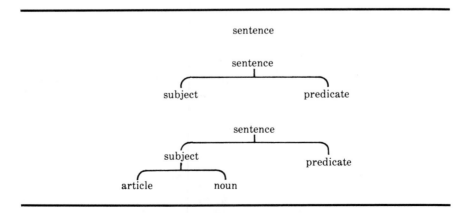

and so on. An alternative method is to show the entire derivation as

```
sentence
    →    subject    predicate
      →    article    noun    predicate
        →    THE    noun    predicate
          →    THE    MAN    predicate
            →    THE    MAN    verb  direct-object
              →    THE    MAN    EATS    direct-object
                →    THE    MAN    EATS    article    noun
                  →    THE    MAN    EATS    THE    noun
                    →    THE    MAN    EATS    THE    APPLE
```

where each line represents the terminal nodes of the parse tree in its
current state of development. The arrow at the beginning of the lines
means "is derived from the previous line by the application of a single
rule." At each application of a rule, a single nonterminal is replaced by one
or more symbols. Thus, this representation shows the order in which the
substitutions are made. The last line of the derivation contains only terminal symbols of the grammar and no further substitutions can be made.

3.4 The Backus-Naur Form

Probably the most common meta-language for specifying the context-free
syntax of programming languages is the Backus-Naur Form, sometimes
called Backus Normal Form, generally abbreviated to BNF. This was introduced in 1959 by John Backus as a method for the definition of the syntax
of Algol 60. The first version of the meta-language was improved shortly
thereafter by Peter Naur.

The meta-symbols of BNF are:

::=	meaning "is defined as"
|	meaning "or"
< >	angle brackets used to surround category names

The angle brackets distinguish category names from terminal symbols,
which are written exactly as they are to be represented.

A BNF rule defining a nonterminal has the form:

The nonterminal being defined

The meta-symbol :: =

Then a sequence of alternatives consisting of strings of terminals and nonterminals, where the alternatives are separated by the meta-symbol | .

For example, the BNF production for a Mini-language Core program is:

```
<program>     ::=    program
                         <declaration-sequence>
                     begin
                         <statement-sequence>
                     end ;
```

This shows that a Mini-language Core program consists of the keyword program followed by the declaration sequence, then the keyword begin and the statement sequence, finally the keyword end and a semicolon. The nonterminal symbol <program> is the goal symbol.

The statements of the Mini-language Core can be specified in BNF as a set of productions:

```
<statement>  ::=  <assignment-statement>
<statement>  ::=  <if-statement>
<statement>  ::=  <loop-statement>
<statement>  ::=  <input-statement>
<statement>  ::=  <output-statement>
```

This may be abbreviated

```
<statement>  ::=  <assignment-statement>
     |   <if-statement>
     |   <loop-statement>
     |   <input-statement>
     |   <output-statement>
```

In the BNF definition of Mini-language Core, there is a clash between the greater-than and less-than symbols used in the comparison and the printed brackets of the BNF notation. In order to avoid the clash, the symbols that are part of the Mini-language are underlined in the definition. Thus:

```
<comparison-operator>  ::=  ≤  |  =  |  ≠  |  ≥
```

Recursive Productions

The informal definition of Mini-language Core specifies an integer to be an arbitrary sequence of digits. Thus, we might think that this would be represented in BNF as

```
<integer>  ::=  <digit>
            |  <digit>  <digit>
            |  <digit>  <digit>  <digit>
```

and so on, with an arbitrary number of alternatives corresponding to all possible lengths of integers.

However, each of the alternatives, after the first, really consists of an <integer> followed by a single <digit>. Thus, to avoid the need for an arbitrary number of alternatives, we write:

```
<integer>  ::=  <digit>
            |  <integer>  <digit>
```

This type of definition, where the defined nonterminal is part of the definition itself, is called a *recursive definition*.

A recursive definition can only be used provided that there is some way of terminating it. The single production

```
<a>  ::=  <a>  A
```

is useless since it is impossible to produce a line containing only terminal symbols. In our definition of <integer>, the alternative

```
<integer>  ::=  <digit>
```

provides the means for terminating the recursion.

Canonical Derivations

The definition for <integer> given in the last section requires a rule for <digit>. By adding this, we can define integers in Mini-language Core by the small grammar:

```
<goal>     ::=  <integer>

<integer>  ::=  <digit>
            |  <integer>  <digit>

<digit>    ::=  0 | 1 | 2 | 3 | 4 | 5 | 6 | 7 | 8 | 9
```

This small grammar allows us to derive all legal integers. For example, abbreviating <integer> by i and <digit> by d, we have two possible derivations of the integer 193:

```
        <goal>                <goal>
   →      i              →      i
     →      i  d            →      i  d
       →      i  d  d          →      i  3
         →      d  d  d          →      i  d  3
           →      1  d  d          →      9  3
             →      1  9  d          →      d  9  3
               →      1  9  3          →      1  9  3
```

There are many possible derivations, depending on the order in which the nonterminals are chosen for replacement. It is convenient to be able to single out a particular derivation as being *the* derivation. This is generally called the *canonical derivation*. The choice of canonical derivation is essentially arbitrary; the usual choice is the one where, at each stage in the derivation, the left-most nonterminal is the one that is replaced. This corresponds to the derivation of 193 on the left. Although the definition of canonical derivation is arbitrary, once the choice has been made, it must be used consistently.

Ambiguous Grammars

One possible grammar for simple expressions involving only multiplication and addition is:

```
<goal>          ::=  <expression

<expression>  ::=  <expression>  +  <expression>
                |  <expression>  *  <expression>
                |  <identifier>

<identifier>    ::=  X  |  Y  |  Z
```

In this grammar, the sentence

```
X + Y * Z
```

has two distinct canonical derivations.

The first is:

```
        <goal>
  →     <expression>
    →     <expression> + <expression>
      →     <identifier> + <expression>
        →     X + <expression>
          →     X + <expression> * <expression>
            →     X + <identifier> * <expression>
              →     X + Y * <expression>
                →     X + Y * <identifier>
                  →     X + Y * Z
```

Its corresponding parse tree is:

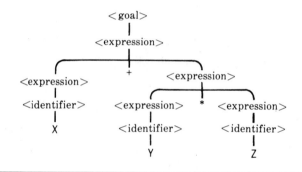

The second derivation is:

```
        <goal>
  →     <expression>
    →     <expression> * <expression>
      →     <expression> + <expression> * <expression>
        →     <identifier> + <expression> * <expression>
          →     X + <expression> * <expression>
            →     X + <identifier> * <expression>
              →     X + Y * <expression>
                →     X + Y * <identifier>
                  →     X + Y * Z
```

Its corresponding parse tree is:

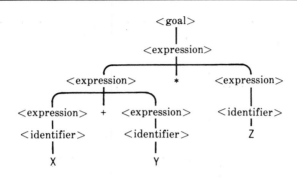

If, as in this case, the rules of a grammar permit more than one canonical derivation of a sentence of the language, the grammar is said to be *ambiguous*.

If the only use for grammars were to determine whether a string belongs to the language, this ambiguity would be of little importance. The number of ways of generating a string would not be relevant. However, for programming languages, part of the meaning of a program is sometimes specified in terms of the corresponding syntactic structure. The existence of more than one structure could imply more than one meaning for the program.

In the example that we have just shown, the two trees correspond to two different evaluation sequences for the operators * and +. In the first tree, the Y and the Z are bound together by the * operator, and it is the result of this operation that is added to X. If we take * to mean multiplication, this derivation corresponds to the precedence specified in the informal definition of Mini-language Core. Note that the ambiguity is syntactic and has severe consequences when meaning is ascribed to the symbols.

The second derivation shows that X and Y are added together and the result is multiplied by Z. It is as if the expression had been written:

(X + Y) * Z

If we are to avoid this ambiguity, we must restructure our grammar and ensure that it defines a single correct meaning for the sentences representing expressions. The following grammar does this:

```
<expression>  ::=  <factor>
              |    <expression>  +  <factor>

<factor>      ::=  <identifier>
              |    <factor>  *  <identifier>

<identifier>  ::=  X  |  Y  |  Z
```

The corresponding parse tree is:

Although it is possible to determine whether certain grammars are ambiguous, it is not possible to do this in general. Similarly, although there are arbitrarily many context-free grammars for any context-free language, it is not always possible to determine whether two grammars define the same language.

Programming languages, including the higher-level ones, differ fundamentally from natural languages. Programming languages have a smaller vocabulary and a simpler fixed grammar. More importantly, they are formal languages; that is, every grammatical statement has one and only one meaning and that meaning can be abstracted by a simple procedure from the structure of the statement. In a natural language, on the other hand, ambiguity is common, and the parsing of statements that are grammatically correct can often be done only from the meaning of the words.

Compare, for example, the two sentences:

```
TIME FLIES LIKE AN ARROW
FRUIT FLIES LIKE A BANANA
```

They both have the same structure, yet they are parsed differently. In one, FLIES is a verb and in the other a noun.

The if statement in PL/I has an optional else part just as it does in Mini-language Core. Consider the form of a nested if statement in PL/I.

```
IF  boolean-expression-1  THEN
IF  boolean-expression-2  THEN
statement-1;
ELSE
statement-2;
```

To which if statement does the else clause belong? PL/I has solved this potential ambiguity by defining the syntax so that the else clause is associated with the last uncompleted if statement, that is, with the second one. Mini-language Core avoids the problem through the use of the end if symbols.

Some problems cannot be resolved so easily. Consider, for example, the Ada assignment statement:

```
I  := F(J);
```

Is the reference to F an invocation of a function procedure or to an element of an array F? In Pascal this problem is solved by writing the two kinds of reference as F(J) and F[J] respectively. In Ada, information from the declaration of F must be used to make the differentiation. This is called *contextual information.*

Context Sensitivity Again

It must be recognized that there are certain things that cannot be represented in BNF. Consider, for example, the Mini-language Core rule that an identifier may not be declared more than once in a program. This rule cannot be defined in BNF.

Suppose there were only three possible identifiers allowed in Core and only one declaration were allowed in a program. The declaration statement could then be defined in BNF as:

```
declaration ::= A: integer;        | B: integer;
             | C: integer;         | A, B: integer;
             | A, C: integer;      | B, C: integer;
             | B, A: integer;      | C, A: integer;
             | C, B: integer;      | A, B, C: integer;
             | B, A, C: integer;   | B, C, A: integer;
             | A, C, B: integer;   | C, A, B: integer;
             | C, B, A: integer;
```

that is, all legal possibilities are specified. In the actual Mini-language Core, there is an infinite number of possible identifiers. Thus, there would have to be an infinite number of alternatives to show the set of legal declarations.

The problem is one of context. In Mini-language Core, the declaration

```
A: integer;
```

is legal if it does not occur in the same program with another declaration of A, that is, in the context of another declaration of A. BNF is a context-free grammar and can only show a *context-sensitive* rule with an infinite number of productions. Thus, in any BNF description of the syntax of a programming language, the context-sensitive rules must be given separately.

Context-free Syntax of Mini-language Core in BNF

Table 3.1 shows a BNF definition of the context-free syntax of the Mini-language Core. In the form shown there, some of the structure of programs and statements has been indicated by the use of indentation on the right side of a production. This indentation is not part of the definition and has been added for clarity.

Even with the indentation, the BNF definition presents some readability problems. These are mainly concerned with the specification of optional parts and sequences. Consider, for example, the production for the <if-statement> shown in Table 3.1.

```
<if-statement>  ::=  if  <comparison>  then
                          <statement-sequence>
                     end if ;
               |     if  <comparison>  then
                          <statement-sequence>
                     else
                          <statement-sequence>
                     end if ;
```

This requires two productions to specify that the else part is optional. To see exactly which parts are optional, the two alternatives must be examined closely.

The production for <statement-sequence> in Table 3.1 is:

<statement-sequence> ::= <statement>
            | <statement> <statement-sequence>

To represent the sequence as being of arbitrary length, a recursive production must be used. Finally, the use of the $^<$ and $^>$ symbols to enclose the names of syntactic categories makes the definition less readable.

The three problems can be solved with the following extensions to BNF:

- **Optional Items:** These are enclosed in brackets, thus introducing the additional meta-symbols [and].
- **Sequences:** The . . . symbol (the ellipsis) is introduced as another meta-symbol to indicate the repetition of the preceding category, or group of categories contained in brackets, an arbitrary number of times.
- **Typefaces:** The names of BNF categories will be written without < and > but in a typeface different from that of the language being defined.

Using these extensions, the production for the if statement becomes:

if-statement ::= if comparison then
              statement. . .
      [else
           statement. . .]
      end if ;

Table 3.2 shows the definition of the context-free syntax of Mini-language Core using these extensions to BNF. We will use this extended form of BNF to define the mini-languages used in the later chapters.

As with BNF, where there is a clash between a meta-symbol and a symbol of the Mini-language, the symbol that is part of the Mini-language will be underlined. For example,

variable ::= identifier
      | identifier [expression]

The definitions of identifier and integer are the same in all of the mini-languages and, for simplicity, their productions will be omitted from future syntax definitions.

Table 3.1 **Context-free Syntax of Mini-language Core in BNF**

\<program\>	::=	program
		   \<declaration-sequence\>
		begin
		   \<statement-sequence\>
		end ;

\<declaration-sequence\>	::=	\<declaration\> | \<declaration\> \<declaration-sequence\>
\<statement-sequence\>	::=	\<statement\> | \<statement\> \<statement-sequence\>
\<declaration\>	::=	\<identifier-list\> : integer ;
\<identifier-list\>	::=	\<identifier\> | \<identifier\> , \<identifier-list\>
\<statement\>	::=	\<assignment-statement\> | \<if-statement\> | \<loop-statement\> | \<input-statement\> | \<output-statement\>
\<assignment-statement\>	::=	\<identifier\> := \<expression\> ;

\<if-statement\>	::=	if \<comparison\> then
		   \<statement-sequence\>
		end if ;
		| if \<comparison\> then
		   \<statement-sequence\>
		else
		   \<statement-sequence\>
		end if ;

Table 3.1 **continued**

<loop-statement>	::=	while <comparison> loop <statement-sequence> end loop ;
<input-statement>	::=	input <identifier-list> ;
<output-statement>	::=	output <identifier-list> ;
<comparison>	::=	(<operand> <comparison-operator> <operand>)

<expression>	::=	<factor>
		  | <expression> + <factor>
		  | <expression> - <factor>

<factor>	::=	<operand> | <factor> * <operand>

<operand>	::=	<integer>
		  | <identifier>
		  | (<expression>)

<comparison-operator>	::=	$\leq$ | = | $\neq$ | $\geq$

<identifier>	::=	<letter>
		  | <identifier> <letter>
		  | <identifier> _ <letter>

<integer>	::=	<digit> | <integer> <digit>

<letter>	::=	A | B | C | D | E | F | G | H | I
		  | J | K | L | M | N | O | P | Q | R
		  | S | T | U | V | W | X | Y | Z

<digit>	::=	0 | 1 | 2 | 3 | 4 | 5 | 6 | 7 | 8 | 9

Table 3.2 **Mini-language Core**

---

program	::=	`program`
		    declaration. . .
		`begin`
		    statement. . .
		`end ;`

declaration	::=	identifier [, identifier]. . . : `integer ;`
statement	::=	assignment-statement | if-statement | loop-statement | input-statement | output-statement
assignment-statement	::=	identifier := expression ;

if-statement	::=	`if` comparison `then`
		    statement. . .
		    [`else`
		        statement. . .]
		`end if ;`

loop-statement	::=	`while` comparison `loop`
		    statement. . .
		`end loop ;`

input-statement	::=	`input` identifier [, identifier]. . . ;
output-statement	::=	`output` identifier [, identifier]. . . ;
comparison	::=	(operand comparison-operator operand)
expression	::=	[expression +] factor | [expression -] factor
factor	::=	[factor *] operand
operand	::=	integer | identifier | (expression)
comparison-operator	::=	‹ | = | ≠ | ›
identifier	::=	letter [[_] letter] . . .
integer	::=	digit. . .
letter	::=	A | B | C | D | E | F | G | H | I | J | K | L | M | N | O | P | Q | R | S | T | U | V | W | X | Y | Z
digit	::=	0 | 1 | 2 | 3 | 4 | 5 | 6 | 7 | 8 | 9

3.5 Other Context-free Syntax Definitions

Although BNF is the best-known method for defining the context-free syntax of a programming language, several other techniques are in use.

The Cobol Notation

The Cobol syntax notation was developed by the Short-Range Subcommittee commissioned by CODASYL (the Committee on Data Systems Languages) to develop a business-oriented programming language. As described in [Sammet 1978], although there are many similarities between BNF and the Cobol notation, the development of these two meta-languages was parallel and independent. This notation has been used, in addition to defining standard Cobol, for the description of PL/I.

Unlike BNF, which is used to define complete programs, the Cobol meta-language is used to define only small parts of the language, particularly statements. Some basic elements of the notation are

- **Vertical bar** separates alternatives. Alternatives may also be listed vertically within brackets or braces.

- **Brackets** enclose an optional syntactical unit.

- **Braces** group elements of a syntactical unit or a vertically listed choice.

- **Ellipsis** indicates repetition of the immediately preceding syntactical unit one or more times.

As an example of this notation, Table 3.3 shows the definition of the Mini-language Core if statement.

Table 3.3 Syntax of Mini-language Core If Statement: using the Cobol Notation

---

```
if comparison then
    statement. . .
[ else
    statement. . . ]
  end if;
```

where "comparison" is

	integer		integer	
(	identifier	⟨ | = | ≠ | ⟩	identifier	)
	(expression)		(expression)	

Syntax Diagrams

An entirely different method of syntax definition is the graphic representation known as *syntax diagrams* or charts. This method has been used to define the syntax of Pascal in [Wirth 1973] and Fortran in [ANSI 1978].

The rules take the form of flow diagrams. The possible paths represent the possible sequences of symbols. Starting at the beginning of a diagram, a path is followed either by transferring to another diagram if a rectangle is reached or by reading a basic symbol contained in a circle or box with rounded ends. For example, an identifier in Mini-language Core is defined by the diagram shown below.

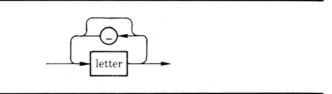

Table 3.4 shows the definition of the context-free syntax of Mini-language Core by syntax charts.

Table 3.4 **Syntax of Mini-language Core
Defined by Syntax Charts**

PROGRAM

DECLARATION

STATEMENT

EXPRESSION

Table 3.4 **continued**

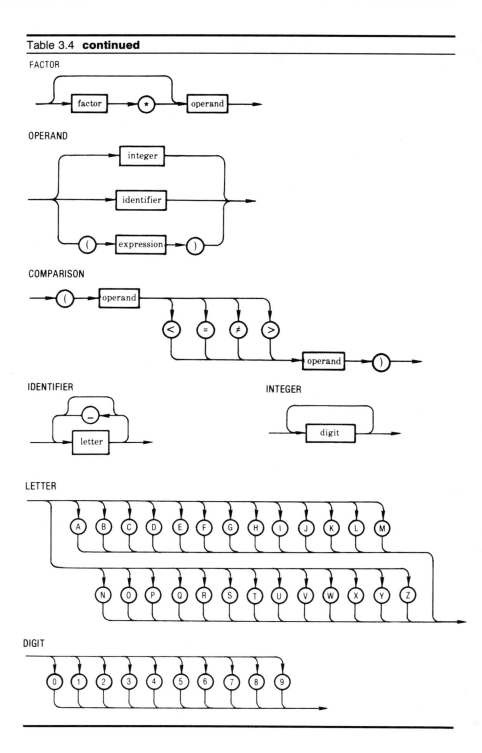

3.6 Specification of Context-Sensitive Rules

Mini-language Core has two context-sensitive rules. These require that all identifiers referenced in statements must be declared and that no identifier may be declared more than once. As we have seen, the BNF meta-language can only define the context-free syntax of a language. In this section, we introduce an extension of BNF called an *attribute grammar* that permits the formal specification of context-sensitive rules.

BNF defines a derivation tree for each syntactically correct program of the language. An attribute grammar extends this by associating atributes with the nodes of a derivation tree. Attributes can be of two kinds: *inherited* attributes, whose values are obtained from the immediate parent node in the derivation tree, and *synthesized* atributes, whose values are obtained from the immediate descendants in the tree.

Attribute values are obtained from nodes by the application of evaluation rules associated with the context-free productions of the grammar. An evaluation rule associated with a production is applied to all instances of the production in the derivation tree. Intuitively, a synthesized attribute of a node represents information about the internal constituents of the construct represented by the node, and an inherited attribute represents information about the context in which the node occurs.

The context-sensitive constraints of a language are expressed by conditions attached to productions in the grammar. These conditions specify relations between attribute values that must be satisifed to meet the context-sensitive requirements of the language.

There is no generally adopted convention for specifying the attribute evaluation rules. Different authors use different techniques. As an example of this method of specifying context-sensitive rules, we will show the additions required to the BNF syntax of Mini-language Core for an attribute grammar that expresses its two context-sensitive rules.

In this grammar, shown in Table 3.5, attributes are represented by names in normal type that are not enclosed in the angle brackets that surround syntactic categories. Attributes are shown following the syntactic category to which they apply. Synthesized attributes are prefixed by an upward-pointing arrow; inherited ones by a downward-pointing arrow. The attributes of a given category are always written in the same order.

Table 3.5 **Context-Sensitive Attribute Grammar
for Mini-language Core**

\<program\>	::=	program
		    \<declaration-sequence\> $\downarrow$ <u>empty-env</u> $\uparrow$ env
		begin
		    \<statement-sequence\> $\downarrow$ env
		end ;

\<declaration-sequence\> $\downarrow$ env$_1$ $\uparrow$ env$_2$	::= |	\<declaration\> $\downarrow$ env$_1$ $\uparrow$ env$_2$ \<declaration\> $\downarrow$ env$_1$ $\uparrow$ env$_3$ \<declaration-sequence\> $\downarrow$ env$_3$ $\uparrow$ env$_2$
\<statement-sequence\> $\downarrow$ env	::= |	\<statement\> $\downarrow$ env \<statement\> $\downarrow$ env \<statement-sequence\> $\downarrow$ env
\<declaration\> $\downarrow$ env$_1$ $\uparrow$ env$_2$	::=	\<identifier-list\> $\downarrow$ env$_1$ $\uparrow$ env$_2$: integer ;
\<identifier-list\> $\downarrow$ env$_1$ $\uparrow$ env$_2$	::= |	\<declared-id\> $\downarrow$ env$_1$ $\uparrow$ env$_2$ \<declared-id\> $\downarrow$ env$_1$ $\uparrow$ env$_3$, \<identifier-list\> $\downarrow$ env$_3$ $\uparrow$ env$_2$
\<declared-id\> $\downarrow$ env$_1$ $\uparrow$ env$_2$	::=	\<identifier\> $\uparrow$ name <u>insert declaration</u> $\downarrow$ env$_1$ $\downarrow$ name $\uparrow$ env$_2$ condition: name does not exist in env$_1$
\<statement\> $\downarrow$ env	::= | | | |	\<assignment-statement\> $\downarrow$ env \<if-statement\> $\downarrow$ env \<loop-statement\> $\downarrow$ env \<input-statement\> $\downarrow$ env \<output-statement\> $\downarrow$ env
\<assignment-statement\> $\downarrow$ env	::=	\<reference\> $\downarrow$ env := \<expression\> $\downarrow$ env ;

\<if-statement\>
$\downarrow$ env
	::=
	
	|
		if \<comparison\> $\downarrow$ env then
		    \<statement-sequence\> $\downarrow$ env
		end if ;
		if \<comparison\> $\downarrow$ env then
		    \<statement-sequence\> $\downarrow$ env
		else
		    \<statement-sequence\> $\downarrow$ env
		end if ;

\<loop-statement\>	::=	while \<comparison\> $\downarrow$ env loop \<statement-sequence\> $\downarrow$ env end loop ;

Table 3.5 continued

<input-statement>	::=	input <reference-list> ↓ env ;
<output-statement>	::=	output <reference-list> ↓ env ;
<reference-list> ↓ env	::= |	<reference> ↓ env <reference> ↓ env , <reference-list> ↓ env
<comparison> ↓ env	::=	(<operand> ↓ env <comparison-operator> <operand> ↓ env)
<expression> ↓ env	::= | |	<factor> ↓ env <expression> ↓ env + <factor> ↓ env <expression> ↓ env - <factor> ↓ env
<factor> ↓ env	::= |	<operand> ↓ env <factor> ↓ env * <operand> ↓ env
<operand> ↓ env	::= | |	<integer> <reference> ↓ env (<expression> ↓ env)
<comparison-operator>	::=	≤ | = | ≠ | ≥
<reference> ↓ env	::=	<identifier> ↑ name condition: name must be in env
<identifier> ↑ name$_1$	::= | |	<letter> ↑ name$_1$ <identifier> ↑ name$_2$ <letter> ↑ name$_3$ underline{concatenate} ↓ name$_2$ ↓ name$_3$ ↑ name$_1$ <identifier> ↑ name$_2$ _ <letter> ↑ name$_3$ underline{concatenate} ↓ name$_2$ ↓ name$_3$ ↑ name$_1$
<integer>	::=	<digit> | <integer> <digit>
<letter> ↑ name	::= | |	A underline{give value to attribute} ↓ A̲ ↑ name B underline{give value to attribute} ↓ B̲ ↑ name . . . Z underline{give value to attribute} ↓ Z̲ ↑ name
<digit>	::=	0 | 1 | 2 | 3 | 4 | 5 | 6 | 7 | 8 | 9

Table 3.6 **Attributes and Evaluation Rules**

Attribute: name	{name of a variable}
Values:	character strings of arbitrary length
Constants:	A, B, . . . Z
Evaluation Rules:	<u>give value to name</u> ↓ <letter> ↑ name
	{takes a letter and returns a name with that value}
	<u>concatenate</u> ↓ $name_1$ ↓ $name_2$ ↑ $name_3$
	{$name_3$ is the concatenation of $name_1$ and $name_2$}
Attribute: env	{environment, i.e., "symbol table"}
Values:	lists of names
Constants:	<u>empty-env</u> = φ
Evaluation Rules:	<u>insert declaration</u> ↓ env_1 ↓ name ↑ env_2
	{name is added to env_1 to produce env_2}

The highest-level rule is:

```
<program>  ::= program
                    <declaration-sequence>   ↓ empty-env   ↑ env
               begin
                    <statement-sequence>   ↓ env
               end ;
```

The value of the attribute env represents the environment of the program and contains a list of all the declared identifiers. The term *environment* is generally used to denote the set of identifiers in a program together with the values associated with them during execution, that is, the variable storage. Here, since we are not concerned with execution, *environment* is used more restrictively to mean just the set of identifiers in the program. We shall use the term in the more general sense later in the book. The value of env is synthesized in the subtree of the <declaration-sequence> node and is transferred to the inherited attribute of the <statement-sequence> node. In general, attribute evaluation rules that are simple value transfers are shown by the use of identical attribute names.

The name <u>empty-env</u> denotes a constant attribute value that represents an empty environment with no identifiers in it. In general, constant attribute values are denoted by double underlining. Table 3.6 lists the set of possible values for each attribute type, the names of the constant values used in the attribute grammar, and the operations associated with the attribute type.

The attribute evaluation rule of this production can be summarized as: the constant value <u>empty-env</u> is passed down to <declaration-sequence> as an inherited attribute where it is modified and returned as a synthesized attribute ↑ env. If we look at the left side of the production for <declaration-sequence>:

<declaration-sequence> ::= <declaration> ↓ env₁ ↑ env₂
↓ env₁ ↑ env₂ | <declaration> ↓ env₁ ↑ env₃
 <declaration-sequence> ↓ env₃ ↑ env₂

we see that the first of these is received as ↓ env₁ and the second is returned as ↑ env₂. Finally, the production for <program> shows that the synthesized attribute ↑ env received from <declaration-sequence> is transferred and passed down to <statement-sequence> as the inherited attribute ↓ env.

Any order of evaluation of the attributes that leads to well-defined values in the derivation tree is allowed. If we take the second alternative in the production for <declaration-sequence>, the evaluation of the env attribute will be as follows:

1. The value env₁ is inherited from <declaration-sequence> on the left of the production;
2. This value is passed down to <declaration> and the synthesized attribute value of env₃ is obtained from the subtree of <declaration>;
3. The value of env₃ is then passed down to <declaration-sequence> on the right side and the value env₂ is obtained as a synthesized attribute from <declaration-sequence> on the right side;
4. The value env₂ is then passed up as a synthesized attribute to <declaration-sequence> on the left of the production.

This process is illustrated in the following diagram:

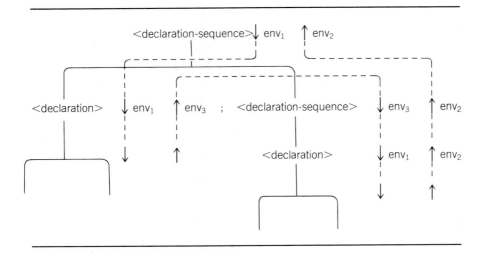

This shows part of the derivation tree for a <declaration-sequence> with more than one <declaration>. The solid lines indicate the structure of the syntactic derivation tree, and the broken lines show the transfer of values of the env attribute between the nodes as specified by the productions.

From the production for <declaration-sequence>, we can follow the value of the inherited ↓ env attribute down through the productions for <declaration> and <identifier-list> to the production for <declared-id>:

<declared-id>   ::=   <identifier>   ↑ name
↓ env$_1$ ↑ env$_2$ <u>insert declaration</u>   ↓ env$_1$ ↓ name   ↑ env$_2$
                    condition: name does not exist in env$_1$

In this production, the evaluation of the attribute value requires more than a simple transfer of value between nodes. The evaluation here is carried out by adding the synthesized attribute name to env$_1$ to produce env$_2$. This is shown by the operation <u>insert declaration</u>, which is informally defined in Table 3.5. This production also has a condition associated with it; this requires that the attribute name must not already exist in the attribute env before it is inserted. This condition corresponds to the context-sensitive rule that an identifier may not be declared more than once.

Attribute grammars are therefore able, through the use of attribute values, evaluation rules, and conditions, to express context-sensitive rules that cannot be expressed in standard BNF.

Further Reading

On the subject of formal grammars, perhaps the most comprehensive treatment is given in [Cleaveland and Uzgalis 1976], which discusses the notion of context-free grammars as well as development of BNF that allows context-sensitive rules to be defined. This is done through the use of macro productions that will generate the infinite number of productions needed. Chapter 2 of [Pagan 1981] contains another description of BNF and a discussion of two techniques for the context-sensitive specification of syntax.

The idea of adding inherited and synthesized attributes to context-free grammars to specify context-sensitive rules was orignally described in [Knuth 1968a].

Exercises

Exercise 3.1 *Writing Context-free Grammars*

A simple grammar for expressions is:

```
expression  ::=  term
                 |  expression  +  term
term        ::=  operand
                 |  term  *  operand
operand     ::=  X  |  Y  |  Z
```

Extend this grammar to include the subtraction and division operators, the use of parentheses to change precedence, and a prefix minus operator.

Exercise 3.2 *Operator Precedence*

Each of the two grammars G1 and G2 below defines the syntax of expressions involving identifier operands and the operations

+	infix plus
-	prefix and infix minus
*	multiplication
/	division
**	exponentiation

These two grammars differ slightly in the order in which operations are evaluated.

Explain the effects of this difference, illustrating your answer by showing the differences in the two parse trees for at least three sentences defined by the grammars. Describe the practical significance of this difference and give arguments in favor of choosing one of the grammars for describing the expressions.

Grammar G1

expression	::=	expression-1
		| expression + expression-1
		| expression - expression-1
expression-1	::=	expression-2
		| expression-1 * expression-2
		| expression-1 / expression-2
expression-2	::=	identifier
		| - expression-2
		| expression-3
expression-3	::=	identifier ** expression-2

Grammar G2

expression	::=	expression-1
		| expression-1 + expression
		| expression-1 - expression
expression-1	::=	expression-2
		| expression-2 * expression-1
		| expression-2 / expression-1
expression-2	::=	expression-2 ** expression-3
		| expression-3
expression-3	::=	identifier
		| - identifier

Exercise 3.3 *Writing a Grammar to Describe Trees*

Consider the following trees:

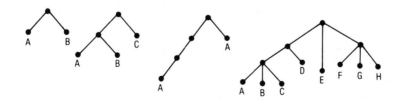

These trees can be represented by the lists:

(A B)
((A B) C)
(((A)) A)
(((A B C) D) E (F G H))

Write a grammar using the BNF variant of Table 3.2 to describe lists with one letter nodes.

Exercise 3.4 *Extensions to Context-free Grammars*

A context-free grammar is sometimes either inadequate or clumsy for expressing some restrictions in the language it defines. As such, many forms of *extension* have been proposed.

One form of extension allows a grouping of n counters designated c_1, c_2, and so on, which may take on integer values. In the extended grammar, a rule is written

[p] left-side   ::= right-side [a]

where [p] is a *predicate,* a condition that must be satisfied before the rule is applied and [a] is an *action* to be performed after the rule is applied. The predicates and actions are expressions involving only counters and integer constants. For example, we may have:

$[c_2 < c_1 + 3]$ left-side ::= right-side $[c_2 := c_2 + 1]$

A rule may be without a predicate or action. A rule with no predicate may be applied just as the rules of a conventional context-free grammar are applied.

Suppose the following context-free rules are used to define the syntax of identifiers and integers:

identifier	::=	letter
identifier	::=	identifier letter-or-digit
letter-or-digit	::=	digit
integer	::=	digit
integer	::=	integer digit

Assume the grammar has 26 rules for the nonterminal letter, each rule having a distinct letter as its right side. Similarly, there are 10 rules for the nonterminal digit to define the decimal digits.

Extend the rules to enforce the restriction that identifiers have no more than 10 characters and integers have no more than five digits.

Could a context-free grammar *without* extensions be used to effect this sort of a length restriction? If not, explain why. If so, write a new set of rules for limiting integers to five digits.

Exercise 3.5 *Describing BNF with BNF*

Write a grammar to describe the BNF variant used in Table 3.2. Since the symbols you will be using in the meta-language will be the same as those of the language being described, you will have to use the technique of underlining such symbols in the language being described. This technique was introduced in Section 3.4. Your grammar will begin something like:

```
grammar    ::= production. . .
production ::= variable ::= right-side
```

Exercise 3.6 *Proper Terminology*

Imagine for the moment that you are writing a glossary of terms for Mini-language Core. Give precise definitions for each of the following terms, using at most two sentences for each definition:

program	integer
declaration	value
statement	operator
identifier	operand
expression	location
comparison	

Exercise 3.7 *Attribute Grammars*

As defined in Table 3.2, Mini-language has no limit to the depth to which statement-sequences can be nested through if statements and loop statements. Suppose that there were an implementation defined limit to this depth. Define the modifications to the attribute grammar for Mini-language Core shown in Tables 3.5 and 3.6 to define this limit.

Exercise 3.8 *Context-Sensitive Rules*

Choose a language with which you are familiar, for example, Fortran, Pascal, or Ada, and list ten of its context-sensitive rules.

4
Semantics

The semantics of a language provide a meaning to its expressions, statements, and programs. In Section 2.2 we gave an informal but complete description of the meaning of all constructs in Mini-language Core. The problem of defining the semantics is very difficult. The goal, of course, is to specify the meaning of every syntactically valid construct so that its behavior can be understood unambiguously.

There are two important concerns. First, the definition of the language must be *complete*—there must be no room for ambiguity as to the meaning of any construct. Second, the language should be defined in such a way that a programmer can *easily* refer to the language definition to answer questions about the language. These two goals, completeness and clarity, are not easy to satisfy separately and are very difficult to achieve together.

The semantics of most programming languages are, as we have done for Mini-language Core, defined informally. Generally, only the context- free syntax is defined formally; the semantics are defined informally in terms of concepts that are presumably well understood by the reader. Examples of these are:

Mathematical Properties: The semantics are described by reference to common mathematical properties. The evaluation of expressions in Mini-language Core, for example, was defined using the principles of integer arithmetic.

Mechanical Models of Computation: The semantice are defined through the mechanical properties of the machine. We did this in explaining the sequence of statement execution. We assumed the model of statements being processed one by one, based on the way in which computer instructions are executed. Concepts like if statements and loop statements can be explained in terms of these properties. For example, the statements within the loop are executed repeatedly for as long as the comparison at the head of the loop is true.

Abstraction: Use is made of higher-level concepts for the phenomena being explained. For example, data that are received from an input device, such as a typewriter terminal, consist of a sequence of character codes. Some of these character codes represent the data, while others control the device, representing a new line, tabbing, or backspace. We can define the semantics of the input statement by the abstraction of fields in lines separated by blank characters. Such a field is a group of characters representing the conceptual unit of an integer. Thus, the execution of the input statement can be viewed as an abstracted operation that reads a succession of numbers from some external source of data.

None of these techniques, however, provides the precision and completeness that is required of a full definition of the semantics of a programming language. In this chapter, we provide an introduction to three techniques for the formal definition of semantics. They are very different in approach, notation, and level of abstraction. They may be summarized, in increasing order of abstraction, as:

The Operational Approach. The meaning of each language construct is defined by describing the effect of its execution on a hypothetical machine. This machine is intended to be so simple that there can be no possible misunderstanding of the way in which it works.

The Denotational Approach. Here, each language construct is defined in terms of mathematical entities (numbers, truth values, functions, etc.) that model their meaning.

The Axiomatic Approach. Meaning is specified entirely in terms of the formal statements that can be made about the effect of executing a language construct.

Since a complete study of these approaches lies far beyond the scope of this book, we limit our description in this chapter to the minimum that is required to define Mini-language Core. Even here, we have further limited ourselves in the interests of providing a clear overview of the techniques. For the purposes of the definitions given here, we have modified the semantics of the output statement so that its output is limited to the integer value of the variable rather than the name of the variable, an equals symbol, and the value (as described in Section 2.2). We have also omitted detection of some error conditions such as overflow and negative-value.

4.1 The Abstract Program

The boundary between the syntax of a language and its semantics is essentially arbitrary. Different authors take different positions; for example, some would place the context-sensitive rules in the semantic part while others would do as we do and consider it to be part of the syntax. Our position is roughly based on the action of a compiler. We classify those aspects of the language apart from code generation and optimization as being syntactic and all matters that are normally handled at runtime as being semantic.

The written form of a program contains many items that are purely syntactic in purpose and have no semantic content. This is because a program is nonlinear in structure and, due to hardware limitations, the written form is a linear encoding of this structure. For this encoding to be unambiguous, delimiter symbols such as `program`, `declare`, `;`, and parentheses are inserted into the program. These delimiters are sometimes referred to as "syntactic sugar" and serve to make the written program more palatable to the eye.

Abstract Syntax

If we remove the purely syntactic content from the syntax of Mini-language Core, we obtain its *abstact syntax*. Table 4.1 shows an extended BNF description of the abstract syntax. This syntax really defines a program in Mini-language Core as being a tree. It generally follows the form of the definition of Mini-language Core shown in Table 3.2 with all language symbols deleted. Another major change is that the abstract program no longer contains any declarations or identifiers. A variable is defined as an integer, which represents the address of the storage location that contains the variable's value. This is in keeping with the idea that an abstract program represents only the semantic content of the program; the actual identifier used does not matter. For example, the two programs

```
program                     program
   A, B: integer;              X, Y: integer
begin                       begin
   input A, B;                 input X, Y;
   A := A - B + 3;             X := X - Y + 3;
   output A;                   output X;
end;                        end;
```

are precisely equivalent and would correspond to exactly the same abstract program.

The function of a semantic definition of a language is to define the meaning of an abstract program. Although we have used extended BNF as a method of defining the abstract syntax of Mini-language Core, each of the techniques of semantic definition has its own representation and notation for abstract programs. Table 4.1 introduces the concept of an abstract syntax through a familiar notation. Other notations will be introduced as required.

Table 4.1 **Mini-language Core**

program	::=	statement. . .
statement	::=	assignment-statement
		if-statement
		loop-statement
		input-statement
		output-statement
assignment-statement	::=	variable expression
if-statement	::=	comparison then-clause [else-clause]
then-clause	::=	statement. . .
else-clause	::=	statement. . .
loop-statement	::=	comparison statement. . .
input-statement	::=	variable. . .
output-statement	::=	variable. . .
comparison	::=	operand comparison-operator operand
expression	::=	operand arithmetic-operator operand
operand	::=	integer
		variable
		expression
comparison-operator	::=	⟨ | = | ≠ | ⟩
arithmetic-operator	::=	+ | - | *
variable	::=	integer

4.2 Operational Definitions

Even in informal definitions of programming languages, operational definitions are used; that is, a construct is defined in terms of its execution on
a hypothetical machine. For example, in the [IBM 1976] definition of PL/I,
one of the forms of the do-statement is defined in the following style:
The do-statement with the form:

```
LABEL:    DO variable = expression1 TO expression2
                              BY expression3
                              WHILE(expression4)
                              UNTIL(expression5);

              statement-1;
              . . .
              statement-m;
LABEL1:   END;
NEXT:     statement;
```

is exactly equivalent to the following expansion:

```
LABEL:    P  = ADDR(variable);
          E1 = expression1;
          E2 = expression2;
          E3 = expression3;
          V  = E1;
LABEL2:   IF ((E3 >= 0) & (V > E2)) or ((E3 < 0) & (V < E2))
                THEN
              GO TO NEXT;
          IF (expression4) THEN
                ;
          ELSE
              GO TO NEXT;
          statement-1;
          . . .
          statement-m;
LABEL1:   IF (expression5) THEN
              GO TO NEXT;
LABEL3:   V = V + E3;
          GO TO LABEL2;
NEXT:     statement;
```

where P is a compiler created pointer; V is a compiler-created based variable based on P and with the same attributes as variable. . . .
    In this example, a complex statement in the language is described algorithmically through simpler statements in the language.

VDL Definition

One of the earliest proposals for the rigorous definition of a programming language was the suggestion in [Garwick 1963] that an actual implementation be used. The major objections to this technique are the inevitable encroachment of the host hardware into the language being defined and the highly restricted availability of the definition. To escape these objections the IBM Vienna Laboratories developed the idea of a hypothetical machine as proposed in [McCarthy 1962], [Elgot and Robinson 1964], and [Landin 1965] on which to make an implementation. This work led to the Vienna Definition Language (VDL) and was used originally for a formal definition of PL/I [Lucas and Walk 1969].

In a VDL definition, the semantics of a programming language are defined in terms of what happens when a program in the language is executed on a hypothetical computer that is not based on any real hardware. This is the *abstract machine.* It has a state with general components and some primitive instructions. The meaning of a program is defined by the sequence of changes in the state of the abstract machine as the program is executed. The rules of execution are defined by an algorithm, the Interpreter.

The state of the abstract machine used as the base of a VDL definition of Mini-language Core would have five components:

1. *The program:* the abstract program
2. *The control:* defining the part of the abstract program currently being interpreted
3. *The store:* the storage part of the abstract machine
4. *The input file*
5. *The output file*

The idea underlying this type of formal definition is that, although the abstract machine is divorced from reality, it is simple enough that it is impossible to misunderstand its operation. Once the abstract program has been understood, one merely has to trace through it, step by step, to determine its precise meaning.

VDL Notation for Objects and Abstract Syntax

In VDL, both the abstract machine and program are *objects* that are represented as trees. There are two classes of objects: *elementary objects,* which have no components, and *composite objects,* which have a finite number of immediate components that are also objects. These correspond to terminal and nonterminal nodes of the tree representation.

A major difference between the representation of VDL objects and the conventional representation of trees is that with VDL objects the links

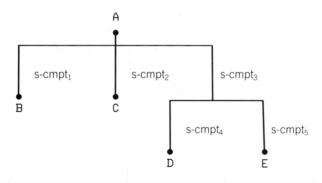

Figure 4.1 **A Composite VDL Object**

between nodes are named, whereas with trees it is the nodes that are named. The names on the links are *selectors.* Selector names are arbitrary with the convention that they begin with "s-". Figure 4.1 shows a composite object A that has three components distinguished by the selectors s-cmpt$_1$, s-cmpt$_2$, and s-cmpt$_3$. The immediate component s-cmpt$_1$ of A is denoted by s-cmpt$_1$(A). This is the elementary object B. We can apply selectors to objects that have been selected. For example, since D is the s-cmpt$_4$ component of s-cmpt$_3$(A), we can denote D by s-cmpt$_4 \circ$s-cmpt$_3$(A). One special elementary object, the *null object,* denoted by Ω, serves to indicate the absence of some component, for example, s-cmpt$_4$(A) = Ω since A does not have an immediate component that can be selected by s-cmpt$_4$.

The composite object s-cmpt$_3$(A) has two components, s-cmpt$_4$ and s-cmpt$_5$. These components are the elementary objects D and E. The construction of s-cmpt$_3$(A) can be described as two selector-object pairs:

$$\text{s-cmpt}_3(A) \equiv (<\text{s-cmpt}_4 : D>, <\text{s-cmpt}_5 : E>)$$

and the complete construction of the composite object A can be shown by three selector-object pairs:

$$A \equiv \{<\text{s-cmpt}_1:B>, <\text{s-cmpt}_2:C>, <\text{s-cmpt}_3:\{<\text{s-cmpt}_4:D>, <\text{s-cmpt}_5:E>\}>\}$$

To specify subclasses of objects, predicates that are true for members of the subclass and false for all other objects are used. By convention, names used for predicates begin with "is-", for example, is-Ω(Z) will be true if and only if Z is a null object.

There is a need for objects that represent *lists* of other objects of the same kind. By convention, all objects that satisfy the predicate is-x-list are lists of objects that satisfy the predicate is-x. The *i*-th element of the list is selected by the selector elem(i). The empty list is denoted by $<>$ and the usual list functions of length, head, tail, and cat (denoting concatenation) are defined.

Objects can be modified by using the μ operator. The result of the application $\mu(\mathsf{A} :<\text{s-cmpt}_1:\mathsf{F}>)$ is constructed from a copy of A by first deleting the component s-cmpt$_1(\mathsf{A})$, if it exists, and then adding a component $<\text{s-cmpt}_1:\mathsf{F}>$.

The Abstract Machine

The abstract machine used to define Mini-language Core is specified by its machine state ξ, which is defined by the two predicate definitions:

$$
\begin{array}{lll}
\text{is-}\xi & = & (<\text{s-program} & : & \text{is-abstract-program}>, \\
& & <\text{s-control} & : & \text{is-control}>, \\
& & <\text{s-storage} & : & \text{is-value-list}>, \\
& & <\text{s-input} & : & \text{is-integer-list}>, \\
& & <\text{s-output} & : & \text{is-integer-list}>)
\end{array}
$$

$$
\text{is-value} \quad = \quad \text{is-integer} \quad | \quad \text{is-UNDEFINED}
$$

The component of the state selected by s-program is the abstract program and will be defined in the next subsection. The component selected by s-control is a special object that represents the control state of the abstract machine. We will describe this object when we discuss the interpretation of the abstract program. The storage component of the machine holds the integer values of variables. In the state ξ, the current value of the i-th variable will be elem(i)∘s-storage(ξ). The predicate is-integer not defined any further with the understanding that it is satisfied only by an integer. The input and output components model the input and output files of the program.

The Abstract Program

Table 4.2 defines the predicate is-abstract-program. This is really a translation into VDL notation of the BNF abstract syntax for Core shown in Table 4.1.

Table 4.2 **is-abstract-program for Core**		
is-abstract-program	=	is-statement-list
is-statement	=	is-assignment-statement | is-if-statement | is-loop-statement | is-input-statement | is-output-statement
is-assignment-statement	=	(<s-variable : is-variable>, <s-expression : is-expression>)
is-if-statement	=	(<s-compare : is-comparison>, <s-then-clause : is-statement-list>,
is-loop-statement	=	(<s-compare : is-comparison>, <s-body : is-statement-list>)
is-input-statement	=	(<s-read : is-variable-list>)
is-output-statement	=	(<s-write : is-variable-list>)
is-comparison	=	(<s-left-operand : is-operand>, <s-right-operand : is-operand>, <s-operator: is-comparison-operator>)
is-expression	=	is-integer | is-variable | is-infix-expression
is-infix-expression	=	(<s-left-operand : is-operand>, <s-right-operand : is-operand>, <s-operator: is-arithmetic-operator>)
is-operand	=	is-integer | is-variable | is-expression
is-comparison-operator	=	is-LT | is-EQ | is-NE | is-GT
is-arithmetic-operator	=	is-plus | is-minus | is-multiply
is-variable	=	(<s-address : is-integer>)

The Interpreter

The remaining part of the VDL definition of Mini-language Core consists of a specification of the way in which the abstract program is interpreted by the machine. This is defined as a set of operations which are specified as a set of algorithms. These algorithms constitute the *interpreter* and may be thought of as the machine's "microcode."

Table 4.3 **The Core Machine Interpreter**

execute–statement–sequence(*sequence*) =
   is-<>(*sequence*)→ Ω
   T   → **execute–statement–sequence**(tail(*sequence*))
                         execute–statement(head(*sequence*))

execute–statement(*statement*) =
   is-assignment-statement(*statement*)→ **execute–assignment–statement**(*statement*)
   is-if-statement(*statement*)   → **execute–if–statement**(*statement*)
   is-loop-statement(*statement*)   → **execute–loop–statement**(*statement*)
   is-input-statement(*statement*)   → **execute–input–statement**(*statement*)
   is-output-statement(*statement*)   → **execute–output–statement**(*statement*)

execute–assignment–statement(*statement*) =
   store(s-address∘s-variable(*statement*), *value*)
      value: **evaluate–expression**(s-expression(*statement*))

execute–if–statement(*statement*) =
   evaluate–comparison(s-compare(*statement*)) = T →
                    execute–statement–sequence(s-then-clause(*statement*))
   T → **execute–statement–sequence**(s-else-clause(*statement*))

execute–loop–statement(*statement*) =
   evaluate–comparison(s-compare(*statement*)) = T →
                      execute–loop–statement(*statement*)
                      execute–statement–sequence(s-body(*statement*))

execute–input–statement(*statement*) = **input**(s-read(*statement*))

execute–output–statement(*statement*) = **output**(s-write(*statement*))

evaluate–expression(*expression*) =
   is-integer(*expression*) → PASS: *expression*
   is-variable(*expression*) → **evaluate–variable**(*expression*)
   T   → **calculate**(*left-value, right-value,* s-operator(*statement*))
        left-value: **evaluate–expression**(s-left-operand(*statement*))
        right-value: **evaluate–expression**(s-right-operand(*statement*))

evaluate–comparison(*comparison*) =
      compare(*left-value, right-value,* s-operator(*statement*))
      left-value: **evaluate–expression**(s-left-operand(*statement*))
      right-value: **evaluate–expression**(s-right-operand(*statement*))

calculate(*value-1, value-2, operator*) =
   is-PLUS(*operator*)   → PASS: *value-1 + value-2*
   is-MINUS(*operator*)   → PASS: *value-1 − value-2*
   is-MULTIPLY(*operator*) → PASS: *value-1 × value-2*

Table 4.3 **continued**

compare(*value-1, value-2, operator*) =
    is-LT(*operator*) & (*value-1* < *value-2*) → PASS: T
    is-EQ(*operator*) & (*value-1* = *value-2*) → PASS: T
    is-NE(*operator*) & (*value-1* ≠ *value-2*) → PASS: T
    is-GT(*operator*) & (*value-1* > *value-2*) → PASS: T
    T → F

evaluate–variable(*variable*) =
    is-UNDEFINED(elem(s-address(*variable*))(s-storage(ξ))) → ERROR
    T → PASS:elem(s-address(*variable*))(s-storage(ξ))

store(*location, value*) =
    s-storage: μ(s-storage(ξ); <elem(*location*): *value*>)

input(*variables*) =
    is-<>(*variables*) → Ω
    T   → **input**(tail(*variables*))
                               store(s-address∘head(*variables*), *value*)
                               value: **input–file**

input–file =
    is-<>∘s-input(ξ) → ERROR
    T   → μ(ξ: <s-input: tail∘s- input(ξ)>)
                          PASS: head∘s-input(ξ)

output(*variables*) =
    is-<>(*variables*) → Ω
    T   → **output**(tail(*variables*))
                              output–file(*value*)
                          value: **evaluate–variable**(head(*variables*))

output–file(*value*) = μ(ξ: <s-output : s-output(ξ) cat *value*>)

The initial state of the Core machine consists of:

- the abstract program to be interpreted,
- an empty store,
- an input component consisting of a list of integers that constitute the program's input file,
- an output component that is an empty list, and
- a control component that contains the first instruction to be executed, **execute–statement–sequence**(t) where t is the statement-sequence component of the abstract program.

The meaning of the program is then defined as the contents of the output component when execution completes.

The control part of ξ is a composite object with machine operations at the nodes. Since Core has no side effects, this can be treated as if it were a stack of machine operations, some with arguments. The operation most recently added to the stack is the next one to be executed. The execution of an operation may:

— add new operations to the stack

— insert a value into the argument list of an operation already on the stack

— change some other components of ξ

An operation is removed from the stack when its operation is complete. The operations of the Core machine are defined in Table 4.3.

The initial operation in the stack, **execute–statement–sequence**, is defined as:

execute–statement–sequence(*sequence*)   =
   is-<>(*sequence*) → Ω
   T   → **execute–statement–sequence**(tail(*sequence*))
                                    execute–statement(head(*sequence*))

This definition takes the form of a conditional expressed in the form:

$$p_1 \rightarrow e_1, \ p_2 \rightarrow e_2, \ \ldots \ p_n \rightarrow e_n$$

where each predicate p is an expression whose value is either true (T) or false (F) and each of the e's is an expression. The value of the conditional is the value of the first expression e_i for which p_i is true, there is always at least one p_i that is true.

The definition of the operation **execute–statement–sequence** specifies that:

1. if the statement list *sequence* is empty, then nothing (signified by Ω), is added to the control stack. In this way, the stack will become empty and the Core machine will halt at the end of the interpretation.

2. if the statement list *sequence* is not empty, then the pair of operations:

   > **execute–statement–sequence**(tail(*sequence*))
   > **execute–statement**(head(*sequence*))

   replaces the current operation on the stack.

Thus, the next operation to be executed is **execute–statement**. The argument of this operation is the first statement from the statement list *sequence,* making this statement the next statement in the program to be interpreted. When this is completed, **execute–statement–sequence** will become the next operation on the stack to be executed. Its argument is the statement list *sequence* with its first element deleted.

The way in which statements are interpreted is shown by the operation **execute–assignment–statement**:

> **execute–assignment–statement**(*statement*) =
>   **store**(s-address∘s-target(*statement*), *value*)
>   *value*: **evaluate–expression**(s-source(*statement*))

Its execution causes it to be replaced on the stack by the operation pair:

> **store**(s-address∘s-target(*statement*), *value*)
>   *value*: **evaluate–expression**(s-source(*statement*))

Here, "*value*:" specifies that the execution of **evaluate–expression** will return a value, denoted locally as *value,* which will be substituted into the argument list of the as yet unexecuted **store** operation on the stack. In this way, the value of the expression on the right of the assignment is passed to the operation that inserts into storage.

The notation PASS: in, for example,

> **evaluate–variable**(*variable*) =
>   is-UNDEFINED(elem(s-address(*variable*))(s-storage(ξ))) $\rightarrow$ ERROR
>   T $\rightarrow$ PASS:elem(s-address(*variable*))(s-storage(ξ))

denotes that, when the value of *variable* is not UNDEFINED, its actual value will be returned by the operation. Here, its value is obtained by using its address component as a subscript to elem. This value is itself a function that extracts the value from the storage component of ξ.

In addition to returning a value, an operation can also change other parts of ξ through the μ operator. For example, in the **read–file** operation

$$
\begin{aligned}
\textbf{read–file} &= \\
\text{is-}{<}{>}\text{∘s-input}(\xi) &\rightarrow \text{ERROR} \\
\text{T} &\rightarrow \mu(\xi: <\text{s-input: tail∘s-input}(\xi){>}) \\
&\quad \text{PASS: head∘s-input}(\xi)
\end{aligned}
$$

if the input file is empty, the program is in error. Otherwise, the operation returns the first element of the input file as its value and modifies the input file by deleting its first element.

4.3 Denotational Definitions

The denotational approach to defining semantics was developed by Strachey and Scott, for example, see [Scott and Strachey 1971]. Over the years this method of defining semantics has gained considerable popularity. It can be argued that this method is the only one that addresses fundamental semantic issues. Unfortunately, it has been often associated with a great deal of specialized and often complex notation. This has hampered the understanding of its underlying ideas.

This approach to the definition of semantics is based on the idea that each construct in a programming language can be defined in terms of mathematical entities that model its meaning. These entities are the *denotations.* As a very simple example of this, we can say that the numerals:

$$\text{VI} \quad 110_2 \quad 12_4 \quad 陆 \quad 여섯$$

are all denotations of the same number, the number also denoted by 6. Note the difference between *numeral,* the written form, and *number,* the meaning of the numeral. To define the meaning of a numeral, we must specify how it can be mapped into a number. The numerals are said to be in the *syntactic domain,* the numbers are in the *semantic domain,* and the mapping is specified by a *semantic function.*

As an introductory example, we will consider the binary numerals. The syntactic domain of all binary numerals will be denoted by **Bin**. We will use uppercase bold letters as symbols to represent typical elements of the domain, for example,

B: **Bin**

specifies that **B** represents an element of **Bin**. If we need to represent more than one element of the domain, subscripts will be used. Thus, $\mathbf{B}_1$ and $\mathbf{B}_2$ would represent any two elements of **Bin**.

The construction of the syntactic domain is defined by BNF-like rules for the abstract syntax. In the case of binary numerals, these would be:

B ::= 0 | 1 | **B**0 | **B**1

The semantic domain is the set of natural numbers plus zero. The convention is to use a lowercase Greek letter to represent an element of a semantic domain:

μ: **N** = {0, 1, 2, . . .}

Semantic functions, conventionally represented by uppercase script letters, map elements of the syntactic domain into elements of the semantic domain. For binary numerals, we show this by:

$\mathcal{N}$: **Bin** → **N**

and $\mathcal{N}$ is defined by a set of *semantic equations,* one for each part of the syntactic domain. The left side of a semantic equation shows the application of the semantic to an argument consisting of a representative element of the syntactic domain. As a notational convenience, special brackets, [[and]], are used round the syntactic arguments. The equations for $\mathcal{N}$ are:

$$\mathcal{N}[\![0]\!] = 0$$
$$\mathcal{N}[\![1]\!] = 1$$
$$\mathcal{N}[\![\mathbf{B}0]\!] = 2 \times \mathcal{N}[\![\mathbf{B}]\!]$$
$$\mathcal{N}[\![\mathbf{B}1]\!] = 2 \times \mathcal{N}[\![\mathbf{B}]\!] + 1$$

As can be seen, this defines $\mathcal{N}$ as mapping binary numerals into numbers.

Mini-language Core

The denotational definition of binary numerals serves as an introduction to the notation. In our definition of Mini-language Core, we will extend this notation as required. The complete definition is shown in Table 4.4.

The syntactic domains are quite straightforward. The list of them together with their symbols is:

P:	**Prog**	programs
S:	**Stmt**	statements
V:	**Var**	variables
W:	**Vars**	lists . of one or more variables
E:	**Exp**	expressions
C:	**Comp**	comparisons
R:	**Rel**	relations
O:	**Opr**	operations
I:	**Num**	integer constants
D:	**Dig**	decimal digits

Table 4.4 **Denotational Definition of Mini-langauge Core**

Syntactic Domains

P:	**Prog**	programs
S:	**Stmt**	statements
V:	**Var**	variables
W:	**Vars**	lists of one or more variables
E:	**Exp**	expressions
C:	**Comp**	comparisons
R:	**Rel**	relations
O:	**Opr**	operations
I:	**Num**	integer constants
D:	**Dig**	decimal digits

Abstract Syntax Rules

$$
\begin{aligned}
\textbf{P} &::= \quad \textbf{S} \\
\textbf{S} &::= \quad \textbf{S}_1 \; ; \; \textbf{S}_2 \mid \textbf{V} := \text{E} \mid \texttt{if } \textbf{C} \texttt{ then } \textbf{S} \texttt{ end if} \\
&\quad \mid \texttt{if } \textbf{C} \texttt{ then } \textbf{S}_1 \texttt{ else } \textbf{S}_2 \texttt{ end if} \mid \texttt{while } \textbf{C} \texttt{ loop } \textbf{S} \texttt{ end loop} \\
&\quad \mid \texttt{input } \textbf{W} \mid \texttt{output } \textbf{W} \\
\textbf{W} &::= \quad \textbf{V} \mid \textbf{W}_1 , \textbf{W}_2 \\
\textbf{C} &::= \quad \textbf{E}_1 \; \textbf{R} \; \textbf{E}_2 \\
\textbf{E} &::= \quad \textbf{V} \mid \textbf{I} \mid \textbf{E}_1 \; \textbf{O} \; \textbf{E}_2 \\
\textbf{I} &::= \quad \textbf{D} \mid \textbf{I} \, \textbf{D} \\
\textbf{O} &::= \quad + \mid - \mid * \\
\textbf{R} &::= \quad < \mid = \mid \neq \mid > \\
\textbf{D} &::= \quad 0 \mid 1 \mid 2 \mid 3 \mid 4 \mid 5 \mid 6 \mid 7 \mid 8 \mid 9
\end{aligned}
$$

Semantic Domains

γ:	**St**	$= \textbf{En} \times \textbf{Fi} \times \textbf{Fi}$
ϕ:	**Fi**	$= \textbf{N}^*$
σ:	**En**	$\doteq \textbf{Var} \to \textbf{N}$
υ:	**N**	$= \{. \; . \; ., -2, -1, 0, 1, 2, . \; . \;\}$
τ:	**T**	$= \{\textit{true, false}\}$

Semantic Functions

$\mathcal{M}$:	**Prog**	$\to \textbf{Fi} \to \textbf{Fi}$
$\mathcal{S}$:	**Stmt**	$\to \textbf{St} \to \textbf{St}$
$\mathcal{C}$:	**Comp**	$\to \textbf{En} \to \textbf{T}$
$\mathcal{E}$:	**Exp**	$\to \textbf{En} \to \textbf{N}$

Table 4.4 **continued**

	Semantic Equations

$\mathcal{M}[\![P]\!]\phi_0$ $= (\mathcal{S}[\![P]\!](<\perp, \phi_0, nil>)) \downarrow 3$

$\mathcal{S}[\![S_1 ; S_2]\!]$ $= \mathcal{S}[\![S_2]\!]\circ\mathcal{S}[\![S_1]\!]$

$\mathcal{S}[\![V := E]\!]$ $= <\sigma[\mathcal{E}[\![E]\!]\gamma/V], \phi_1, \phi_2>$
      where $\sigma = \gamma \downarrow 1, \phi_1 = \gamma \downarrow 2,$
      $\phi_2 = \gamma \downarrow 3$

$\mathcal{S}[\![input\ W_1 , W_2]\!]$ $= \mathcal{S}[\![input\ W_1 ; input\ W_2]\!]$

$\mathcal{S}[\![output\ W_1 , W_2]\!]$ $= \mathcal{S}[\![output\ W_1 ; output\ W_2]\!]$

$\mathcal{S}[\![input\ V]\!]\gamma$ $= (\phi_1 = nil \rightarrow \perp, <\sigma[head(\phi_1)/V],$
      $tail(\phi_1), \phi_2>)$ where $\sigma = \gamma \downarrow 1,$
      $\phi_1 = \gamma \downarrow 2, \phi_2 = \gamma \downarrow 3$

$\mathcal{S}[\![output\ V]\!]\gamma$ $= <\sigma, \phi_1, append(\phi_2, \sigma[\![V]\!])>$
      where $\sigma = \gamma \downarrow 1, \phi_1 = \gamma \downarrow 2,$
      $\phi_2 = \gamma \downarrow 3$

$\mathcal{S}[\![if\ C\ then\ S\ end\ if]\!]\gamma$ $= (\mathcal{C}[\![C]\!](\gamma \downarrow 1) \rightarrow \mathcal{S}[\![S]\!]\gamma, \gamma)$

$\mathcal{S}[\![if\ C\ then\ S_1\ else\ S_2\ end\ if]\!]\gamma$ $= (\mathcal{C}[\![C]\!](\gamma \downarrow 1) \rightarrow \mathcal{S}[\![S_1]\!]\gamma, \mathcal{S}[\![S_2]\!]\gamma)$

$\mathcal{S}[\![while\ C\ loop\ S\ end\ loop]\!]\gamma$ $= (\mathcal{C}[\![C]\!](\gamma \downarrow 1) \rightarrow$
      $\mathcal{S}[\![while\ C\ loop\ S\ end\ loop]\!]\circ\mathcal{S}[\![S]\!]\gamma, \gamma)$

$\mathcal{C}[\![E_1 < E_2]\!]\sigma$ $= (\mathcal{E}[\![E_1]\!]\sigma < \mathcal{E}[\![E_2]\!]\sigma \rightarrow true, false)$

$\mathcal{C}[\![E_1 = E_2]\!]\sigma$ $= (\mathcal{E}[\![E_1]\!]\sigma + \mathcal{E}[\![E_2]\!]\sigma \rightarrow true, false)$

$\mathcal{C}[\![E_1 \neq E_2]\!]\sigma$ $= (\mathcal{E}[\![E_1]\!]\sigma \neq \mathcal{E}[\![E_2]\!]\sigma \rightarrow true, false)$

$\mathcal{C}[\![E_1 > E_2]\!]\sigma$ $= (\mathcal{E}[\![E_1]\!]\sigma > \mathcal{E}[\![E_2]\!]\sigma \rightarrow true, false)$

$\mathcal{E}[\![E_1 + E_2]\!]\sigma$ $= \mathcal{E}[\![E_1]\!]\sigma + \mathcal{E}[\![E_2]\!]\sigma$

$\mathcal{E}[\![E_1 - E_2]\!]\sigma$ $= \mathcal{E}[\![E_1]\!]\sigma - \mathcal{E}[\![E_2]\!]\sigma$

$\mathcal{E}[\![E_1 * E_2]\!]\sigma$ $= \mathcal{E}[\![E_1]\!]\sigma \times \mathcal{E}[\![E_2]\!]\sigma$

$\mathcal{E}[\![E]\!]\sigma$ $= \sigma[\![V]\!]$

$\mathcal{E}[\![ID]\!]\sigma$ $= 10 \times \mathcal{E}[\![I]\!]\sigma + \mathcal{E}[\![D]\!]\sigma$

$\mathcal{E}[\![0]\!]\sigma$ $= 0, \mathcal{E}[\![1]\!]\sigma = 1, . . ., \mathcal{E}[\![9]\!]\sigma = 9$

The abstract syntax follows closely to that given earlier in this chapter.

```
P    ::=   S
S    ::=   S1 ; S2  |  V := E  |  if C then S end if
           |  if C then S1 else S2 end if  |  while C loop S end loop
           |  input W  |  output W
W    ::=   V  |  W1 , W2
C    ::=   E1 R E2
E    ::=   V  |  I  |  E1 O E2
I    ::=   D  |  I D
O    ::=   +  |  -  |  *
R    ::=   <  |  =  |  ≠  |  >
D    ::=   0  |  1  |  2  |  3  |  4  |  5  |  6  |  7  |  8  |  9
```

The need for a syntactic domain for a sequence of statements was avoided through the abstract syntax rule

$$\textbf{S} ::= \textbf{S}_1 \; ; \; \textbf{S}_2$$

The fact that this grammar is ambiguous is of no consequence since this definition starts with an abstract program; we are not concerned with parsing here.

The next part of the definition is the semantic domains, these are the sets of mathematical objects into which the constructs of the abstract program will be mapped by the semantic functions. Here, we have used the terms "domain" and "set" synonymously. From a strictly mathematical point of view, this is not correct; however, for the purposes of this introduction, we will not have any problems. The two basic domains are those of truth values and integers. These can be defined by enumeration. To each of these, we add a special object, $\perp$ ("bottom"), which represents an undefined value. The two domains are thus:

$$\upsilon\colon \textbf{N} = \{. \; . \; ., \; -2, \; -1, \; 0, \; 1, \; 2,. \; . \; ., \; \perp\}$$
$$\tau\colon \textbf{T} = \{\textit{true}, \; \textit{false}, \quad \} \qquad\qquad \perp$$

Generally, the appearance of $\perp$ will indicate that an error has occurred.

The domain of files is defined by

$$\phi\colon \textbf{Fi} = \textbf{N}^*$$

that is, the domain of all finite lists of elements drawn from the domain of numbers including $\perp$.

The domain of environments represents the storage part of a computation and is defined as

$$\sigma\colon \textbf{En} = \textbf{Var} \rightarrow \textbf{N}$$

An environment is a function that maps variables from the syntactic domain **Var** into numbers from the semantic domain **N**.

Finally, the domain **St** of states:

$$\gamma\colon \textbf{St} = \textbf{En} \times \textbf{Fi} \times \textbf{Fi}$$

defines the state domain **St** to be a *product* of three domains, the store or environment domain **En** and two file domains **Fi**. That is, an element γ of **St** is an ordered triple of elements from these three domains. Given γ, the three components can be extracted by the expressions $\gamma \downarrow 1$, $\gamma \downarrow 2$, and $\gamma \downarrow 3$. Thus, $\gamma \downarrow 1$ is the environment component, $\gamma \downarrow 2$ is the input file, and $\gamma \downarrow 3$ is the output file.

The top semantic function $\mathcal{M}$ is defined to be a function of the form **Prog** $\rightarrow$ **Fi** $\rightarrow$ **Fi**. This means that if we apply $\mathcal{M}$ to a particular program **P**, in $\mathcal{M}[\![P]\!]$, we will obtain some function that maps an input file into an output file. The specification of the function is given by the semantic equation

$$\mathcal{M}[\![P]\!]\phi_0 \;=\; (\mathcal{S}[\![P]\!](<\perp,\ \phi_0,\ \text{nil}>))\!\downarrow 3$$

where $\mathcal{S}$: **Stmt** $\rightarrow$ **St** $\rightarrow$ **St** is the semantic function for statements. This equation states that the meaning of **P** with initial input file ϕ_0 is the output file that is the third component of the state produced by $\mathcal{S}$ when it is applied to **P** with the initial state $<\perp,\ \phi_0,\ \text{nil}>$. The first component of this initial state specifies that the entire environment contains only undefined values, the second component is the input file ϕ_0, and the output file is empty.

$\mathcal{S}$ is defined by a set of semantic equations, covering each statement type. Sequences of statements are covered by the equation

$$\mathcal{S}[\![S_1\ ;\ S_2]\!] \;=\; \mathcal{S}[\![S_2]\!]\circ\mathcal{S}[\![S_1]\!]$$

This specifies that the state transformation function obtained by applying $\mathcal{S}$ to the sequence $S_1\ ;\ S_2$ is the equivalent of the function obtained by applying $\mathcal{S}$ to S_2 composed with the function obtained by applying $\mathcal{S}$ to S_1. For example,

$$\mathcal{S}[\![X := 5;\ \text{output } X]\!] \;=\; \mathcal{S}[\![\text{output } X]\!]\circ\mathcal{S}[\![X := 5]\!]$$

thus

$$\mathcal{M}[\![X := 5;\ \text{output } X]\!]\phi_0 \;=$$
$$((\mathcal{S}[\![\text{output } X]\!]\circ\mathcal{S}[\![X := 5]\!])(<\perp,\ \phi_0,\ \text{nil}>))\!\downarrow 3$$
$$(\mathcal{S}[\![\text{output } X]\!](\mathcal{S}[\![X := 5]\!](<\perp,\ \phi_0,\ \text{nil}>)))$$

The semantic equation for assignment statements is

$$\mathcal{S}[\![V := E]\!] \;=\; <\sigma[\mathcal{E}[\![E]\!]\sigma/V],\ \phi_1,\ \phi_2>$$
$$\text{where } \sigma = \gamma\!\downarrow 1,\ \phi_1 = \gamma\!\downarrow 2,\ \phi_2 = \gamma\!\downarrow 3$$

The semantic function $\mathcal{E}$ is the function for expression evaluation. When $\mathcal{E}$ is applied to an expression, it yields a function that maps an environment into a number. In other words, it makes use of the environment, which provides the correspondence between variables and values, to calculate the value of the expression. The notation $\sigma[\mathcal{E}[\![E]\!]\sigma/V]$ shows that in the environment the value of the variable **V** is updated with the value of the expression **E**. The two file components in the state are unchanged.

As an example of how an undefined value might occur, consider the semantic equation for the read statement,

$$\mathscr{S}[\![\text{input } \mathbf{V}]\!]\gamma = (\phi_1 = \text{nil} \rightarrow \bot, <\sigma[\text{head}(\phi_1)/\mathbf{V}], \text{ tail}(\phi_1), \phi_2>)$$
$$\text{where } \sigma = \gamma\!\downarrow 1, \ \phi_1 = \gamma\!\downarrow 2, \ \phi_2 = \gamma\!\downarrow 3$$

This is a conditional expression, which has the form

$$t \rightarrow e_1, \ e_2$$

This has the value e_1 if the boolean expression t is true, otherwise it has the value e_2. Thus, if the input file ϕ_1 is empty, the value is $\bot$, otherwise it is the first element in the file and the file is modified by deleting the first element. This is the end-of-file error in Core. Undefined values are propagated through the functions and, if the program is in error, may appear in the output file. The meaning of an erroneous program is thus undefined.

4.4 Axiomatic Definitions

The axiomatic definition differs significantly from the operational approach described in Section 4.2. Instead of relying on a model of execution, the definition of the constructs of the language is designed so that it is possible to prove properties about programs built from the constructs. The meaning of a construct is given in terms of *assertions* about the computation state before and after execution of the construct. The definition associates an axiom with each kind of construct in the language. The axiom states what can be asserted after execution of the construct, based on what was true before. Thus, the definition of a statement is expressed as:

$$\{ \ P \ \} \quad \text{statement} \quad \{ \ Q \ \}$$

Here, P is the set of assertions that are true before execution of the statement, and Q the set of assertions that can be derived from P after execution of the statement.

For the assignment statement, we have the axiom

$$\{P[\text{expression/identifier}]\} \quad \text{identifier} := \text{expression} \quad \{P\}$$

The notation P[expression/identifier] denotes the set of assertions obtained from P by replacing all occurrences of the identifier by the *value* of the expression. In a sense, the axiom for assignment appears to be the wrong way around, since we are deriving the assertion that must be true before assignment from the assertion that is true afterward. This initially counter-intuitive definition reflects the fact that any assertion derived after execution of the statement must be true when the identifier is replaced by the expression before execution of the statement. Thus, for example, we have

```
{(A + B + C) > 0}  D := A + B;  {(D + C) > 0}
```

As another example, consider the loop statement of Mini-language Core

```
while comparison loop
    loop-body
end loop;
```

We know that when the loop terminates (provided that it does) the comparison will be false. In addition to asserting that the comparison is false, it will be possible to make other assertions after execution of the loop. These will depend on what was true before the loop was executed and on the effect of executing the sequence of statements that comprise the loop body. In particular, it is possible to state that those assertions that were true before execution of the loop and that are not made false by execution of the loop body will still be true after the loop has terminated. These assertions are known as the *loop invariant* and are denoted by P[inv]. Thus, the axiom for the loop statement is

$$\{P[inv]\} \quad \text{loop-statement} \quad \{P[inv] \ \& \ not(comparison)\}$$

Rule of Proof

Generally, an axiom is expressed as a *rule of proof* (also called rules of inference or deduction). A rule of proof allows the truth of certain assertions to be deduced from the truth of other assertions. The general form of the rule is:

$$\frac{A_1, A_2, \ldots, A_n}{A}$$

where $A_1, A_2, \ldots, A_n$, and A all represent assertions. This rule means that, given the truth of $A_1, A_2, \ldots, A_n$, the truth of A may be inferred.

The axiom for loop statements can then be expressed as:

$$\frac{\{P \ \& \ comparison\} \ \text{loop-body} \ \{P\}}{\{P\} \ \text{while comparison loop loop-body end loop} \ \{P \ \& \ not(comparison)\}}$$

In addition to rules for the constructs of the language, the definition will include some generally useful rules of proof that are independent of the language being defined. Two examples of this are the "rules of consequence":

$$\frac{\{P\}\ S\ \{Q\},\ Q \Rightarrow R}{\{P\}\ S\ \{R\}}$$

$$\frac{P \Rightarrow Q,\ \{Q\}\ S\ \{R\}}{\{P\}\ S\ \{R\}}$$

The first of these states that, if P is true before S is executed then Q will be true afterwards, and that from Q we can derive R. This in turn says that the truth of P before S is executed implies the truth of R after its execution.

Finally, the semantics of the operators are defined by the axioms for integer arithmetic on the values used for the language. For example,

$$\forall\ x,\ y \quad x + y = y + x$$

expresses the commutativity of addition for all integer values. This axiom should be read as "For all integers x and y, the value of $x + y$ is equal to the value of $y + x$." These axioms describe conventional integer arithmetic, which does not entirely correspond to the computer representation of integer arithmetic. Exercise 4.5 addresses this issue.

Axiomatic Definition of Mini-language Core

The axiomatic definition of Mini-language Core is given in Table 4.5. Axiomatic definitions of the statements show nothing about *how* the statements are executed. They describe only assertions about *value*s before and after execution. Our attention is turned away from the mechanics of execution toward more static assertions. The assertions that are true *after* executing one statement are those that are true *before* executing the next statement. By using the first-order predicate calculus to link assertions, it is possible to derive assertions about results at the termination of a program.

The technique of axiomatic definition grew out of work described in [Floyd 1967], where assertions were attached to links of flowcharts. The application to the definition of programming languages has been mainly developed in [Hoare 1969]. It was used to define some of the semantics of Pascal in [Hoare and Wirth 1973].

Table 4.5 **Axiomatic Definition of Mini-language Core**

$$\frac{\{P\}\ S\ \{Q\},\ Q \Rightarrow R}{\{P\}\ S\ \{R\}}$$ 　　　　　　　　　　　　　　　　Consequence-1

$$\frac{P \Rightarrow Q,\ \{Q\}\ S\ \{R\}}{\{P\}\ S\ \{R\}}$$ 　　　　　　　　　　　　　　　　Consequence-2

$$\frac{\{P\}\ S\ \{Q\},\ \{P'\}\ S\ \{Q'\}}{\{P\ \&\ P'\}\ S\ \{Q\ \&\ Q'\}}$$ 　　　　　　　　　　　　　Conjunction

$$\frac{\{P\}\ S\ \{Q\},\ \{P'\}\ S\ \{Q'\}}{\{P\ |\ P'\}\ S\ \{Q\ |\ Q'\}}$$ 　　　　　　　　　　　　　Disjunction

$$\frac{\{P\}\ S_1\ \{Q\},\ \{Q\}\ S_2\ \{R\}}{\{P\}\ S_1\ ;\ S_2\ \{R\}}$$ 　　　　　　　　　　　　Composition

$$\frac{\{P\}\ \mathtt{input}\ W_1\ ;\ \mathtt{input}\ W_2\ \{Q\}}{\{P\}\ \mathtt{input}\ W_1\ ,\ W_2\ \{Q\}}$$ 　　　　　　　Input list

$$\frac{\{P\}\ \mathtt{output}\ W_1\ ;\ \mathtt{output}\ W_2\ \{Q\}}{\{P\}\ \mathtt{output}\ W_1\ ,\ W_2\ \{Q\}}$$ 　　　　Output list

$\{IN\ =\ <K>L\ \&\ P[K/V]\}\ \mathtt{input}\ V\ \{IN\ =\ L\ \&\ P\}$ 　　　Input

$OUT\ =\ L\ \&\ P\ \&\ V\ =\ K\}\ \mathtt{output}\ V\ \{OUT\ =\ L<K>\ \&\ P\ \&\ V\ =\ K\}$
　　　　　　　　　　　　　　　　　　　　　　　　Output

$\{P[E/V]\}\ V\ :\ =\ E\ \{P\}$ 　　　　　　　　　　　　　Assignment

$$\frac{\{P\ \&\ B\}\ S\ \{Q\},\ P\ \&\ \neg B \Rightarrow Q}{\{P\}\ \mathtt{if}\ B\ \mathtt{then}\ S\ \mathtt{end\ if}\ \{Q\}}$$ 　　　　　If-then

$$\frac{\{P\ \&\ B\}\ S_1\ \{Q\},\ \{P\ \&\ \neg B\}\ S_2\ \{Q\}}{\{P\}\ \mathtt{if}\ B\ \mathtt{then}\ S_1\ \mathtt{else}\ S_2\ \mathtt{end\ if}\ \{Q\}}$$ 　　　If-then-else

$$\frac{\{P\ \&\ B\}\ S\ \{P\}}{\{P\}\ \mathtt{while}\ B\ \mathtt{loop}\ S\ \mathtt{end\ loop}\ \{P\ \&\ \neg B\}}$$ 　　Loop

Table 4.5 **continued**

∀ x, y x + y = y + x	Commutativity
∀ x, y x * y = y * x	
∀ x, y, z (x + y) + z = x + (y + z)	Associativity
∀ x, y, z (x * y) * z = x * (y * z)	
∀ x, y, z x * (y + z) = x * y + x * z	Distributivity
∀ x x + 0 = x	Identity
∀ x x * 1 = x	
∀ x x + (-x) = 0	Additive inverse
∀ x, y x - y = x + (-y)	Subtraction
∀ x, ¬(x < x)	Irreflexivity
∀ x, y (x < y) | (x > y) | (x = y)	Trichotomy
∀ x, y, z (x < y) & (y < z) ⇒ (x < z)	Transitivity
∀ x, y ¬(x < y < (x + 1))	Discreteness
∀ x, y (x > y) ⇒ (y < x)	Define >
∀ x, y (x ≠ y) ⇒ (x = y)	Define ≠
∀ x, y, z, w (x ≥ y) & (z ≥ w) ⇒ (x + z) ≥ (y + w)	
∀ x, y, z, w (x ≥ y) & (z ≥ w) ⇒ (x - z) ≥ (y - w)	
∀ x, y, z (x ≥ 0) & (z ≥ y) ⇒ (x * z) ≥ (x * y)	
∀ x, y, z (x ≥ 0) & (x * y) ≥ (x * z) ⇒ (y ≥ z)	

4.5 The Differing Roles of Definition Methods

The purpose of a programming language definition is to specify the meaning of all programs in that language. Each of the three definitions of Mini-language Core given in this chapter does that; however, they use very different models and notation. Following the topics suggested by [Pagan 1981], we may summarize some of the applications of language definitions under the headings of language standardization, user reference, program proofs, and language design.

Language Standardization: Programming languages need to be standardized for reasons of communication and portability. If there is a standard, it will help communication between organization and organization so that programs can be shared, between programmer and programmer so that understanding of algorithms can be shared, and between program and program so that data can be shared. Language standardization helps us to realize the goal of being able to move a program from one computer to another. The success of a definition technique in specifying a language standard depends largely on its completeness and level of detail. The operational method has been used to define PL/I in [ANSI 1976] and the denotational method for

Ada in [Department of Defense 1980b]. In both cases, the notation used was substantially different from that presented in this chapter.

User Reference: Programmers need to resolve detailed questions about facets of the language that are often omitted from informal language definitions. The only formal notation that has received widespread acceptance among users is BNF and its variants for context-free syntax. The operational definition of PL/I in [ANSI 1976], even though its notation was much less formal than the VDL shown in this chapter, was criticized by [Weiss 1975] as:

. . . [having moved] so far toward abstract and algorithmic statement and so far from the common English language as to make it virtually incomprehensible unless one first learns the special metalanguage created just for this standard and then studies the entire document in detail, almost without reference to any prior knowledge of PL/I. That is, in their effort to achieve precision the authors of this standard have chosen to make great sacrifices of comprehensibility.

The question of what formalisms could be of use to programmers is a matter of opinion; however, one could argue that the operational method stands the best chance since its algorithmic style is most familiar to programmers.

Program Proofs: Since program testing can never prove its correctness, more formal methods of verification are required. If proofs are to have any pretense at mathematical rigor, the properties of the programming language must be formalized. For this purpose, the axiomatic technique goes a long way in providing the necessary tools; however, so far, no realistic language has been completely formalized using this method. One of the closest has been the definition of Pascal in [Hoare and Wirth 1973], which is incomplete since it does not provide a definition for functions with side effects and goto statements among other details. It is possible that the denotational technique could serve as a tool for proving programs. The operational method does very little in this regard since it is equivalent to executing the program on a computer.

Language Design: Normally, formal descriptions are used as specifications of languages that have already been designed. [Tennent 1977] and [Ashcroft and Wadge 1982] make a good case for the formalisms to be used as tools in the design of new languages. This is the *prescriptive,* as opposed to the *descriptive,* approach. In the preceding paragraph, we noted that the axiomatic definition of Pascal in [Hoare and Wirth 1973] was incomplete because it did not handle functions with side effects and goto statements. These were omitted because they were very difficult to formalize. As we shall see in subsequent chapters, these are precisely the features of a language that tend to make programs difficult to understand and unreliable. Since the complexity of a language's design is reflected to some extent in its definition, whichever of the methods is used, they can all serve to improve language design. However, the generally held opinion by language theorists is that the denotational approach has the greatest potential in this area because its mathematical underpinnings can provide better insights into the structure of the language.

We can see from this discussion that the different approaches have individual strengths and are better suited for particular applications. It is not helpful to regard the three approaches as *competing* or that one method is *better* than the others. They are really different aspects of the same problem presented with differing levels of detail. It has been suggested by [Donahue 1976] that the best way to give a complete, useful semantic description is by defining the language at more than one level of abstraction. He has proposed the term *complementary definitions,* where complementary is used in terms of the utility of the separate definitions for specific purposes.

4.6 The Correctness of a Program

It is a common view that a program is either correct or incorrect. Correctness is thus viewed as some kind of absolute property of a program. Strictly speaking, this view may be valid, but in practice it is not always helpful.

The language definition, the programmer, and the user of a program each have different views of correctness. The following is a list of various interpretations of correctness in order of increasing difficulty of attainment.

1. The program contains no context-free syntax errors.
2. The program contains no context-free or context-sensitive syntax errors.
3. The program contains no syntax errors and executes to a normal termination.
4. The program contains no syntax errors and there exists some set of input data for which the program executes to normal termination to yield the correct results.
5. The program contains no syntax errors and, for a typical set of input data, executes to normal termination to yield the correct results.

6. The program contains no syntax errors and, for deliberately difficult sets of test data, executes to normal termination to yield the correct results.

7. The program contains no syntax errors and, for all possible sets of input data that are valid according to the problem specification, executes to normal termination to yield the correct results.

8. The program contains no syntax errors and, for all possible sets of input data, executes to normal termination to yield the correct or reasonable results.

The beginning programmer will, for a short while, be happy with level 1 or 2. Eventually the programmer will generally be satisfied with level 6. The user, of course, would like to see all programs at level 8 but must come to realize that this may be prohibitively expensive.

From the point of view of the definition of most programming languages, any program that has no syntax errors and executes to normal termination is a correct program and has a meaning. That the program does not produce correct results from the programmer's point of view does not destroy its validity. It is still a correct program written to a specification other than the one that the programmer intended.

Example

As a simple example of what is involved in proving the correctness of a program, consider the following sequence of Mini-language Core statements intended to perform division of a nonnegative integer X by a positive integer Y to produce a quotient Q and a remainder R.

```
Q := 0;
R := X;
while(R ≥ Y) loop
    R := R - Y;
    Q := Q + 1;
end loop;
```

If these statements produce the required result, then the assertion

$$\{(X = Q \times Y + R) \ \& \ (0 \leq R) \ \& \ (R < Y)\} \qquad \text{(A–1)}$$

must be true when they complete execution.

If we take the axiom for the loop statement

$$\frac{\{P \ \& \ B\} \ S \ \{P\}}{\{P\} \ \text{while } B \text{ loop } S \text{ end loop } \{P \ \& \ \neg B\}}$$

we note that the assertion at the end of the loop (provided that it terminates) consists of two parts, the loop invariant P and the condition for loop termination, B. One of the components of the assertion A–1, $(R < Y)$, is the condition for the termination of the while loop. If we can show that the remaining two components were true before execution of the loop and that executing the body of the loop does not change their truth then, by the loop statement axiom, we shall have proved our statement sequence.

Before executing the statement sequence, the assertion

$$\{(X \geq 0) \;\&\; (Y > 0)\}$$

follows from the initial conditions for the algorithm. After executing the two assignment statements, the assertion

$$\{(X \geq 0) \;\&\; (Y > 0) \;\&\; (R = X) \;\&\; (Q = 0)\}$$

will be true. From this assertion, we can derive the assertion

$$\{(X = Q \times Y + R) \;\&\; (R \geq 0)\} \tag{A–2}$$

which is to be shown to be the loop invariant.

It now remains to show that A–2 is, in fact, unchanged when executing the body of the loop. We have just demonstrated that A-2 is true before entering the loop, combining this with the condition that $(R \geq Y)$, which must be true for the body of the loop to be executed, we have

$$\{(X = Q \times Y + R) \;\&\; (R \geq 0) \;\&\; (R \geq Y)\} \tag{A–3}$$

After executing the assignment statement

```
R := R - Y;
```

will still leave $(R \geq 0)$ true since $(R \geq Y)$ was true before executing it. Hence the assertion

$$\{(X = Q \times Y + (R - Y)) \;\&\; (R \geq 0)\} \tag{A–4}$$

derived from A–3, will hold just before executing the assignment

```
Q := Q + 1;
```

Following execution of this assignment, the assertion

$$\{(X = (Q + 1) \times Y + (R - Y)) \;\&\; (R \geq 0)\} \tag{A–5}$$

will hold. We can derive A–2 from A–5 by elementary algebra. Thus, A–2 is an invariant of the loop and the sequence of statements achieves its desired result.

Some languages allow the programmer to include assertions as part of the program. These can then be checked against the statements in the program either during compilation with the help of a theorem prover, or during execution with extra machine instructions. For such languages, the programmer's view of correctness of results has some meaning. However, it should be remembered that the statements and the assertions are really two different ways of saying the same thing. There is nothing magic about a mathematical proof nor is there any guarantee of its correctness. A mathematical proof is no more reliable than the mathematician who makes it and the mathematicians who are convinced by it. Even if the proof of a program is correct, all that can be said is that the assertions match the statements in the program. There can be no guarantee that what was written down matched what the programmer or user had in mind.

Further Reading

On a subject as broad as semantics the possible readings are numerous. We list but a few.

The general subject of language design, and semantic issues in particular, is treated in [Hoare 1973] and [Richard and Ledgard 1977]. Both of these papers are quite readable and tend to emphasize directions in design rather than specific proposals for improvement. A much more rigorous but somewhat less readable exposition of the language design area is given in [Ichbiah et al. 1979]. This document, Rationale for the design of the Ada programming language, *examines almost every area of language design.*

[Strachey 1972] gives another view of programming languages. This short report presents a thoughtful analysis of programming languages by simply discussing the kinds of objects denoted by programming constructs.

In the area of formal definition, a rather elaborate survey is given in [Marcotty et al. 1976]. This paper not only surveys the area of formal definition techniques but presents a small language similar to Mini-language Core whose syntax and semantics are defined using four different formal techniques.

Another comparative view of formal definition techniques is given in [Donahue 1976]. Papers on the origins of definition techniques include in [Strachey 1966] and [Landin 1963].

The Vienna Definition Language approach to defining semantics has received considerable attention in the literature. A fundamental paper on this topic is [Lucas and Walk 1969]; [Lee 1972] also describes this technique.

The functional or denotational approach to defining semantics has evolved over the years. Surveys of this approach are given in [Stoy 1977] and [Gordon 1979]. Of these, the text by Stoy is more comprehensive, and the paper by Gordon is more readable by the uninitiated. The origins of this approach are discussed in [Scott and Strachey 1972] and [Scott 1970]. [Donahue 1976] offers a fairly comprehensive bibliography on this approach. A survey of the denotational approach is also given in [Tennent 1976].

There are a large number of works on axiomatic definition of languages and proofs of program correctness. The early work by [Floyd 1967] gives one of the first attempts at work in this area. Also of importance are the work [Hoare 1969] and the classic axiomatic definition of Pascal given in [Hoare and Wirth 1973]. Again, a good bibliography in this area as well as a comparison of axiomatic approaches with the denotational approach are given in [Donahue 1976]. An interesting view of the role of program proving in language design is contained in [DeMillo et al. 1979].

Exercises

Exercise 4.1 Defining a Language

The description of Mini-language Core was quite carefully written. Nevertheless, a thorough reading of the description reveals a number of points in which the exact meaning of a program is not explicitly stated. Enumerate four such points.

Note: Problems like those found above are commonplace in language descriptions. In commonly used (and thus much larger) languages, the possibilities for imprecision are much greater.

Exercise 4.2 Programming in Mini-language Core

The numbers on the pages of a book go in ascending order; the first page is 1, the second, 2, and so forth.

If you are a typesetter in a printing shop, you need to have sufficient digits to print the page number for each page. For example, in a book with only 51 pages, you need:

5 Zeros	7 Fives
16 Ones	5 Sixes
15 Twos	5 Sevens
15 Threes	5 Eights
15 Fours	5 Nines

Assuming you never have to print a book with more than 1,000 pages, write a program in Mini-language Core to input the number of pages in a book and to output the number of each digit required.

Exercise 4.3 Proofs of Correctness

The following program computes the greatest common divisor of X and Y.

```
program
    X, Y, GCD: integer;

begin
    input X, Y;
    while (X = Y) loop
        if (X > Y) then
            X := X - Y;
        else
            Y := Y - X;
        end if;
    end loop;
    GCD := X;
    output GCD;
end;
```

Using the mathematical properties of greatest common divisors, for example,

```
gcd(X, Y)  =  gcd(Y, X)
gcd(X, Y)  =  gcd(X+Y, Y)
```

give a formal proof of correctness for this program.

Exercise 4.4 The Go Stones Problem

The following problem is adapted from a book by Gries:

The Japanese game of Go is played with black stones and white stones. A box contains some of these black and white stones. The following process is to be repeated as long as possible:

Randomly select two stones from the box. If they are the same color, throw them out, but put another black stone in. (Enough extra black stones are available to do this.) If they are different colors, place the white one back into the box and throw the black one away.

Performing this process reduces the number of stones in the box by one. Repetition of the process must terminate with exactly one stone in the box. The question is: what, if anything, can be said about the color of the final stone based on the number of white stones and the number of black stones initially in the box. It will help you to solve the problem if you look for a loop invariant.

Exercise 4.5 *Loop Invariants*

In Section 4.4 we alluded briefly to invariant relations of loops. Suppose Mini-language Core included arrays. Then in the loop

```
I := 1;
X := A[1];
while (I ≠ N) loop
    I := I + 1;
    if (A[I] > X) then
        X := A[I];
    end if;
end loop;
```

the invariant relation is that X contains the maximum value of the first I elements of the array A. Verify that executing the body of the loop does not change the invariant relation.

Consider next the following program fragment to reverse the order of the first N values in the array A:

```
LOWER := 1;
UPPER := N;
while (LOWER < UPPER) loop
    TEMP      :=  A[LOWER];
    A[LOWER]  :=  A[UPPER];
    A[UPPER]  :=  TEMP;
    LOWER     :=  LOWER + 1;
    UPPER     :=  UPPER - 1;
end loop;
```

Determine the invariant relation of the loop and then show that this relation, together with the condition for loop termination (LOWER ≥ UPPER), demonstrates that the program has executed correctly.

Exercise 4.6 *Computer Arithmetic*

None of the sample definitions given in this chapter reflects the fact that computer arithmetic is different from normal integer arithmetic as is used in mathematics. Computer arithmetic is subject to the bounds imposed by the hardware on the size of the maximum value that can be stored. Each implementation must define maximum and minimum values to be applied. When a program attempts to compute a value outside this range, the implementation must either declare the program to be in error, or substitute some standard value within the permitted range for the result. Choose one of these alternatives and modify the three definitions of Mini-language Core accordingly.

Exercise 4.7 *Error Conditions*

The semantic definitions given in this chapter all omit any detection of an overflow error condition during expression evaluation. For each definition, show which lines must be changed and how they should be changed to define the overflow condition.

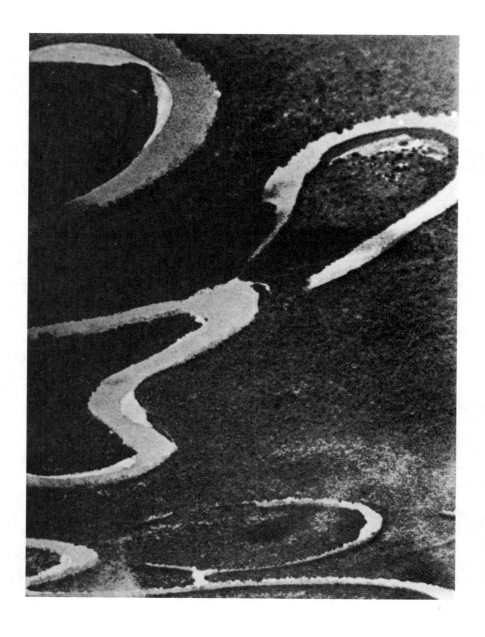

5

The Translation Process

The compiler is the programmer's most important software tool. It provides an automatic link between the abstraction of a high-level language and the minute detail of an actual machine language. This chapter describes the general working of a compiler. It does not deal with its theoretical aspects; its object is to give the reader an appreciation of the working of the various parts of a compiler. An understanding of this mechanism is of considerable assistance in appreciating the way in which languages are designed.

A compiler is a program that is used to transform a program, the *source program,* from the source language into an equivalent *object program* in the target language. Frequently, but by no means universally, the source language is a high-level language and the target language is some form of machine language.

An implementation can be viewed as a sequence of two processes:

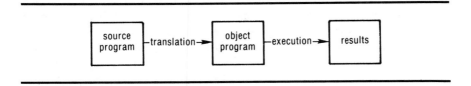

Usually, these two processes are separate, but the dividing line can vary considerably. The translation phase may merely transform the source program into some internal form that does not correspond to the architecture

125

of any real machine. As described in Section 1.2, the execution may be an interpretation of this by another part of the translator. Some languages, such as APL and Lisp, are implemented in this way so as to achieve extra flexibility.

5.1 Overview of the Translation Process

The translation process may be divided into two subprocesses: *analysis* and *generation.*

Analysis

During the analysis phase, the source program is parsed and an abstract representation of the program, the *abstract program,* is built. The abstract representation of the program can take a number of forms depending on the design of the translator. It can be in the form of a tree having a construction similar to the parse tree. Another alternative is for it to consist of a sequence of instructions for a hypothetical machine, typically one where each instruction has an operator, two operands, and a result.

In the original source form, the program is represented as a character string with only a single dimension, although a program really has two dimensions. Programmers will frequently show this fact by indenting their program in a way that makes the nesting of the structures obvious. To achieve this mapping of two dimensions on to one, the source program contains a number of syntactic symbols whose sole function is to indicate the two-dimensional structure of the program—for example, semicolons to separate the statements and symbols or keywords such as begin to show the major structure of the program. In the abstract form, the program does not contain these syntactic symbols because it is represented as a two-dimensional structure and has no need for them. While the abstract representation of the program is being built during analysis, some equivalent of the derivation tree is constructed. Generally, only a part of the derivation tree is present in the translator at any one time, since it is too big to exist in its entirety.

Generation

During the generation phase of the compiler, the abstract program is converted into the equivalent object program. This part is sometimes known as the *code generation* phase. Although we have shown the code generation to be a separate phase from the analysis, this is not always the case, and the part of the object program corresponding to the beginning of the source program may be generated before the end of the source program has been parsed.

If the parsing and code generation are combined, the translator is frequently known as a *single-pass compiler.* Most translators for large languages require several passes over the program being translated. Often the actual number of passes depends on the parts of the language that are used in a particular source program. The decision that a single-pass compiler will be used imposes certain constraints on the source language. These constraints are required to ensure that sufficient information is available to generate code before the source program has been completely parsed. This means that, for example, variables must be declared before they are referenced so that their type is known at the time the code is to be generated.

Scanning, Parsing, and Completion

The analysis phase may itself be divided into three subprocesses: scanning, parsing, and completion.

During the scanning process, the source program is divided into *tokens,* the basic syntactic units from which a program can be constructed. It is the function of the parsing part to take the tokens and build the derivation tree whose root is the goal symbol of the grammar and whose terminals are the tokens. The completion process takes the derivation tree and constructs the abstract program from it. This process involves abstracting those parts concerned with the meaning of the program from those that have only syntactic functions. In addition, the completion will add some things, making details explicit that were only implicit in the source program.

Optimization and Code Generation

The generation phase converts the abstract program to the object program. This phase of the compiler often involves two parts, *optimization* and *code generation.*

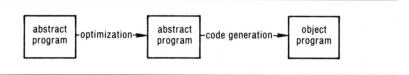

The goal of optimization is to make the object program as small and as fast as possible. To do this, transformations are applied to the abstract program that make it more efficient but do not change its meaning. The term *optimization* is somewhat of a misnomer, since to produce a truly optimal version of a program would generally involve discarding the original program and substituting the best possible algorithm for performing the desired task. All that can generally be achieved is a better program than can be produced without optimization.

The transformations during optimization are generally independent of the target machine for the compilation. The characteristics of this machine become of great importance during the final stage of the compilation, code generation. At that point, the abstract program is translated into the machine instructions and data representation of the target machine. The object program is output in a form suitable for the target machine's operating system. Some functions called for in the program may require the use of library subroutines. The code generation stage must construct the necessary calls for these subroutines so that they can be incorporated in the final object program.

Even during the code generation phase, some transformations akin to those that are done during optimization can take place. The difference between these and the previous ones is that the characteristics of the target machine are taken into account. Typical of these transformations is the movement of constant address calculations to the outside of loops.

5.2 The Lexical Scan

The scanner reads the sequence of characters (letters, digits, and special symbols) that constitute the program and produces a sequence of meaningful tokens. Each token represents a sequence of characters that can be treated as a single logical entity. Identifiers, numbers, operators, language symbols like begin, and semicolons are typical tokens of the Mini-language Core. There are two kinds of tokens: those that represent fixed sequences of characters such as := , begin , or a comma, and those that represent classes of character strings such as identifiers or numbers.

In extracting the tokens from the sequence of characters, the scanner discards semantically irrelevant portions of the input text, for example, comments and blanks. In the course of building the tokens, a low-level check is made on the correctness of the program's syntax. Thus, illegal characters, improper keywords, illegal numbers, etc., will be rejected.

All tokens have a type, and those that represent classes have a value as well. For example, an identifier token might have the value COUNT. As an example of the sequence of tokens, consider the Core program:

```
program
    -- program to read in a number,
    -- add 7 to it, and output the result.
    A, B: integer;
begin

    input A;
    B := A + 7; -- compute the result.
    output B;

end;
```

The sequence of tokens corresponding to this program that would be used as input to the parsing process is:

Token Type	Token Value
program-symbol	
identifier	A
comma-symbol	
identifier	B
colon-symbol	
integer-symbol	
semicolon-symbol	
begin-symbol	
input-symbol	
identifier	A
semicolon-symbol	
identifer	B
colon-equals-symbol	
identifier	A
plus-symbol	
integer	7
semicolon-symbol	
output-symbol	
identifier	B
semicolon-symbol	
end-symbol	
semicolon-symbol	

Notice that the tokens show nothing of the comments, blank lines, or indentation that were in the program. The sequence of tokens would have been just the same if the program had been written as:

```
program A, B: integer; begin input A;
B := A + 7; output B; end;
```

A program like this is no more difficult for the lexical analyzer; it is just more difficult for the human reader. All the syntactic symbols required to reflect the two-dimensional structure of the program are contained in the sequence of tokens. These will be used during the parsing process.

In languages, such as PL/I, where there is no distinction between keywords and identifiers, they will all be treated as identifier tokens, and the parsing process will distinguish between the two from context.

5.3 Parsing

The basic function of the parsing phase is to build a unique parse tree from the sequence of tokens produced by the scanner. This parse tree is then traversed in an appropriate order by the code generation phase to produce the translation of the program in the target language. Note that the parse tree need never be built explicitly. The dynamic structure of the parsing algorithm may model the structure of the tree and be its only representation. The walk-through of the tree to generate the target program may well take place at the same time as it is being built.

There are two classes of parsing techniques: *top-down* and *bottom-up*. Each class is characterized by the order in which the productions of the derivation tree are recognized. The top-down parser builds the tree by starting with the root, the goal symbol, and by working down to produce a tree whose terminal nodes match the sequence of tokens in the source program. The bottom-up technique replaces right sides of productions by the corresponding left-side symbol until only the goal symbol remains. These two strategies for parsing have been extensively studied.

Top-down Parsing

In the top-down method, we start with the goal symbol and then scan the input to find the syntax elements that are on the right side of its syntax rule. In the case of the Mini-language Core, the rule is:

```
program ::= program
               declaration. . .
            begin
               statement. . .
            end ;
```

Thus, the highest level of top-down parser for Core will perform the following steps:

1. Check that the first token is a `program`-symbol.
2. Call a subroutine to parse one or more declarations, parse-declaration-sequence.
3. Check that the next token is a `begin`-symbol.
4. Call a subroutine to parse one or more statements, parse-statement-sequence.
5. Check that the next two tokens are `end`-symbol and semicolon-symbol and that there is nothing following them in the input stream.

The subroutine parse-declaration-sequence repeatedly calls the parse-declaration subroutine until it returns an indication that there are no more declarations. The parse-declaration routine:

1. Checks that the next token is an identifier.
2. Tests whether the next token is a comma-symbol or colon-symbol. If it is a comma-symbol, step 1 is repeated.
3. Checks that the next two tokens are an `integer`-symbol followed by a semicolon-symbol.

The parse-statement-sequence subroutine examines the next token, which indicates the kind of statement, and calls the appropriate statement parsing subroutine. As an example of these, consider the parse-loop-statement subroutine; its action is based on the grammar rule for the loop statement:

```
loop-statement ::= while comparison loop
                        statement. . .
                   end loop ;
```

Thus, it performs the following steps:

1. Checks that the next token is a `while`-symbol.
2. Calls the parse-comparison subroutine.
3. Checks that the next token is a `loop`-symbol.
4. Calls the parse-statement-sequence subroutine.
5. Checks that the next three tokens are `end`-symbol, `loop`-symbol, and semicolon-symbol in that order.

Note that, in the course of parsing the loop statement, the parse-statement-sequence subroutine was called. This is the subroutine that invoked the parse-loop-statement subroutine. We have a case of indirect recursion. It is for this reason that this parsing technique is called *recursive descent*.

Backtracking

In this very superficial account of top-down parsing, we have not explained what is to happen if any of the checks fail. If at any point a mismatch between the expected token and the actual token occurs, this means that the parsing process has made an incorrect decision at some previous stage or that there is an error in the input program. We will discuss the case of errors in the source program later. To get a better idea of how a mismatch can occur even when the source program is syntactically correct and what must be done, we will consider the parsing of an expression using the simple grammar that was introduced in Chapter 3:

1	\<expression\>	: : =	\<factor\>
2		|	\<expression\> + \<factor\>
3	\<factor\>	: : =	\<identifier\>
4		|	\<factor\> * \<identifier\>
5	\<identifier\>	: : =	X
6		|	Y
7		|	Z

Suppose that the input token stream corresponded to the expression

X + Y * Z

We can follow the action of the parser by representing it in two columns: the one on the left representing the syntactic category to be matched and the one on the right showing the successive states of the input. The process starts as:

\<expression\>   X + Y * Z

The process consists of applying productions in the grammar to the element in the left column until the left-most syntactic category matches the head of the right column. At this point, they can both be eliminated. Thus, we might go through the following steps:

\<factor\>
                            X + Y * Z
\<identifier\>   X + Y * Z
                            + Y / Z

But now, we have a problem: the left column is empty but the right one is not. This means that an incorrect choice of production was made earlier. The algorithm must *backtrack* to that point and make a different choice. The problems of making the proper choice of production and avoiding being caught in a recursive loop are well beyond the scope of this summary. For details of how it can be done, the reader is referred to [Davie and Morrison 1981].

Bottom-up Parsing

In bottom-up parsing techniques, the derivation tree is built from the terminal nodes up to the root node. As the parsing progresses, the input is scanned from left to right, and the input is converted into a list of subtrees from which the complete tree will be constructed. At any stage, there are two alternatives from which the parsing algorithm must choose. It could *shift* a symbol from the head of the input over to the list of subtrees on a stack and form a new primitive subtree on the top of the stack. Alternatively, it could *reduce* one or more of the subtrees at the right end of the list of subtrees to a single subtree, using one of the production rules. A set of subtrees that can be reduced is known as a *handle* since they are grasped together to make the reduction.

In general, a parser will shift until the right end of the list of trees contains a handle and then reduce it. This technique, known as the shift-reduce principle, was introduced in [Floyd 1961]. The parsing algorithm will usually make use of tables, which are constructed from the grammar by a special program, to base its decisions on shifting or reduction. These tables determine, given the subtrees at the top of the stack and the leading token on the input, whether to shift or reduce. If reduction is performed, the tables also determine the production to be applied. As an example of bottom-up parsing, we show the parsing of the same expression that we considered earlier. In the action column, S stands for Shift and R for Reduce. With each reduction the number of the production to be applied is shown:

Action	Stack	Input
S		X + Y * Z
R 5	X	+ Y * Z
R 3	\<identifier\>	+ Y * Z
R 1	\<factor\>	+ Y * Z
S	\<expression\>	+ Y * Z
S	\<expression\> +	Y * Z
R 6	\<expression\> + Y	* Z
R 3	\<expression\> + \<identifier\>	* Z
S	\<expression\> + \<factor\>	* Z
S	\<expression\> + \<factor\> *	Z
R 7	\<expression\> + \<factor\> * Z	
R 3	\<expression\> + \<factor\> * \<identifier\>	
R 4	\<expression\> + \<factor\>	
R 2	\<expression\>	

There are two occasions in the above parsing where the stack consists of

<expression> + <factor>

At the first, the decision to shift was based on the fact that the leading input token was *. Had it been a +, the action would have been to reduce, using production 4.

There are many other more complicated bottom-up parsing techniques. For more descriptions of these, the reader is referred to the literature cited in the section on Further Reading.

Somewhat greater attention has been given to bottom-up techniques since they are more efficient and the development work was conducted at a time when parsing efficiency was thought to be very important. It turns out that parsing is a relatively small part of the whole translation process; the generation of the object program takes the larger part of the time. Another often cited attraction of the bottom-up technique is that it is possible to take a grammar specified in BNF and generate tables automatically for a parser. This means that changes to the syntax of a language can be accommodated quickly. It also ensures that the language being parsed matches the language specified in the written syntax. More recently, techniques have been developed for the automatic generation of tables for top-down parsers so that this is no longer a particular advantage for bottom-up techniques.

Error Recovery

Parsing would be much simpler if all programs supplied were syntactically correct. Unfortunately, some users submit programs with syntax errors. The parsing algorithm must be able to cope with this problem and provide helpful information to the programmer. Detecting the first error, providing a report on it, and then quitting is generally not an acceptable solution since the user may have to wait a long time to get a response from the system.

The underlying philosophy of error recovery is to change an incorrect program to the "nearest" syntactically correct one and to attempt to continue with the parsing. The "correction" is not intended to make a correct program out of an erroneous one but to provide a firm base from which parsing can continue. It is important to avoid as much as possible the situation where a single error causes a cascade of error messages because no firm base for restarting parsing can be found.

Careful design of a language can also help in error recovery. This involves building redundancy into the syntax so that the compiler may use the extra symbols as landmarks for recovery. In the case of Mini-language Core, the different markers at the end of statement sequences—end loop;, end if;, and end;—would be of assistance in error recovery.

While both top-down and bottom-up parsing techniques have their own problems with error recovery, in general, top-down methods have the advantage since more contextual information is available. This contextual information can be of great help in providing meaningful messages to the user.

5.4 Completion of the Abstract Program

The result of the parse process is the derivation tree that corresponds to the source program. The process of completing the abstract program takes the derivation tree and converts it into an intermediate form from which the object program will be generated. In general, this process consists both of deleting items from the tree and of adding links or nodes. Since the abstract program is concerned purely with the meaning of the program, those parts of the derivation tree that serve only to reflect the syntactic structure of the original program are often deleted at this point. They serve no purpose in the generation of code.

The adding of nodes serves to make explicit some parts of the source program that were only implicit. For example, in a language like PL/I where certain things are determined by default, those attributes that are not explicitly declared are manufactured through the application of some contextual rules. If there is no declaration for an identifier, then one is constructed, possibly with some attributes obtained from the context in which references to the identifier occur. An identifier, MASTER, that appears in the context

```
OPEN FILE(MASTER);
```

will be given the attribute FILE in its constructed declaration. At the end of the synthesis process, all the contextual implications of the source program will have been made plain, and the abstract form of the program will be complete.

Symbol Tables

Another important part of the completion process is the association of references to identifiers with the appropriate declaration. In a language like Ada where the rules for making this association are rather complex, this can involve a considerable amount of processing. The central data structure of the compiler through which this association is established is the *symbol table*.

Conceptually, a symbol table is a dictionary providing a correspondence between identifiers and their properties. These properties include names, their attributes, and machine addresses. It is referenced constantly during compilation: during syntax analysis for its construction and during code generation for its information.

Generally, the symbol table is constructed during the parsing of the declarations. As the identifiers are declared, they are entered into the table together with their type attributes. These attributes specify the kind of values that are to be associated with the identifiers during the program's execution and thus determine the kind of operations that can be performed on these values. This, in turn, controls the details of the code that is to be generated. In addition, the symbol table contains the machine addresses at which the variables are to be stored during execution. This information also is required for code generation.

Internal Representations

The internal form of the abstract program can vary from one compiler to another. Apart from trees, internal representations in common use include postfix notation, quadruples, and triples.

In postfix notation, the operators follow their operands. The expression

```
A + B * C
```

appears in postfix notation as

```
A B C * +
```

This form is especially useful for producing code for stack machines.

A quadruple consists of an operator, its two operands, and the location of the result of the operation, which may be a temporary location under the control of the compiler. The above expression can be represented by a pair of quadruples

```
* B C temp1
+ A temp1 temp2
```

One of the disadvantages of quadruples is the number of temporary variables that must be described. The use of triples eliminates this problem. A triple consists of an operator and its two operands. There is no field for the result. Instead, the triples are numbered and a later triple that uses the result of the operation refers to it through the use of the triple's number. Thus, for the above expression we would have the triples

```
1: * B C
2: + A 1:
```

The choice of which kind of internal representation to be used in a compiler often depends upon what kind, if any, of manipulations are to be performed on the program before the actual generation of the object code. These manipulations are the subject of the next section.

5.5 Optimization

Optimization refers to the process of rearranging and changing the program being compiled to produce a more efficient object program. There are two different kinds of optimization:

1. Modification of the original source program. This class of program transformation is independent of the target machine on which the program will be executed. Generally, these modifications could have been performed by the programmer on the source program.

2. Modification of the generated code. Here, the transformations are aimed at improving the efficiency of the program when it is run on a particular processor. This is beyond the power of the programmer to perform.

Typical Transformations

Typical transformations that can be done during source program optimization are:

■ *Folding:* performing operations whose operands have values that are known during compilation.

For example,

```
I := 4 + J - 5;
```

can be transformed to

```
I := J - 1;
```

A less obvious example is that the pair of assignments

```
I := 3;
J := I + 2;
```

can be transformed to

```
I := 3;
J := 5;
```

- *Elimination of redundant operations:* This generally involves factoring out common subexpressions.

  For example, the three assignments

  ```
  A := 6 * (B + C);
  D := 3 + 7 * (B + C);
  E := A * (B + C);
  ```

  can be transformed to

  ```
  TEMP := B + C;
  A    := 6 * TEMP;
  D    := 3 + 7 * TEMP;
  E    := A * TEMP;
  ```

  where TEMP is a new variable created by the compiler to hold the value B + C.

- *Loop optimization:* Usually this means moving expressions whose values do not change within a loop out of the loop.

  Consider, for example, the Mini-language Core loop statement:

  ```
  while (COUNT < LIMIT) loop
     input SALES;
     VALUE := SALES * (MARK_UP + TAX);
     output VALUE;
     COUNT := COUNT + 1;
  end loop;
  ```

  The computation of the value MARK_UP + TAX is performed each time the loop is executed, yet its value does not change. The loop is transformed to

  ```
  TEMP := MARK_UP + TAX;
  while (COUNT < LIMIT) loop
     input SALES;
     VALUE := SALES * TEMP;
     output VALUE;
     COUNT := COUNT + 1;
  end loop;
  ```

Program Analysis

Although the examples of optimization transformations just given are shown as transformations of the source program, in most compilers it is the abstract program that is transformed. To make these transformations, the program must be analyzed.

The first step in doing this is to determine the flow of control in the program. The program is divided into *basic blocks* consisting of sequences of consecutive instructions that are always executed from start to finish. That is, a basic block can only be entered at the first instruction and left at the last. The basic blocks are then linked according to the flow of control specified by the statements in the program. This structure is the flow graph of the program.

Many of the transformations require knowing the places in a program at which a value is assigned to a variable and where that value is subsequently used. This definition-reference relationship is determined from the flow graph, and the analysis of the flow of data from its point of definition to its point of reference is known as *data flow analysis.* The algorithms that perform this kind of analysis are complex and, where the program has a large number of variables, very time-consuming. It is important to realize that optimization costs computation time and is only economical if the gains in object program efficiency will recover the machine time expended on achieving it. Generally, this is only possible if the program will be executed many times or intrinsically requires a great deal of computer resources to execute.

In all cases, the transformation must preserve the meaning of the program. The compiler must make a very careful analysis of the program to make sure of this and, if there is the slightest doubt, the form of the program must be left unchanged. We shall see in later chapters that the design of a language can have a profound effect on what transformations can be performed. Depending on the skill with which the source program was written, factors of about two in improvement may be obtained by using optimization techniques.

However, it should not be thought that optimization is intended to compensate for poor programming. For example, consider the checking of subscript ranges during execution. It is desirable to detect all attempts to reference outside the limits of an array since these are sources of very subtle programming errors. Unfortuantely, range checks are expensive and can result in considerable loss of execution speed. For this reason, they are generally omitted although it is freely admitted that this is a dangerous sacrifice of safety. Optimization offers a reasonable alternative to omitting subscript range checking altogether. Data flow analysis can show that many range checks are superfluous. If the index has satisfied the check at one point in the program, then there is no need to check it again unless its value has been changed in the interval. Other checks can be safely moved to a section of code that is less frequently executed. The result will be a more efficient program that has not sacrificed an important reliability check.

5.6 Code Generation

During this process, the abstract internal form of the source program is converted into the object program in the target language. The details of addressing, use of registers, and operation codes all depend on the particular target machine, real or abstract. The precise form of the object program, whether its addresses are absolute or relocatable, will depend on the operating system used on the target machine. The code generation process depends heavily on the target machine and operating system.

Code Templates

Although it is possible to produce the object code during the program completion process or even during the parsing process, for large languages it is more usual to use a separate set of code generation routines. Typically, each such routine will have a skeletal structure or *code template* corresponding to a particular structure in the source language. The code template is parameterized so that the actual sequence of machine instructions can be varied according to the context in which it is to be applied.

In simple cases, the parameters are only used to accommodate differing addressing modes for the data. In more complicated cases, there may be considerable variation in the sequences of machine instructions generated under differing circumstances. Consider, for example, the assignment statement

```
A := B cat C;
```

where the values of two character string variables, B and C, are to be concatenated and the result assigned to a third string variable A. The following considerations will materially change the details of the generated code:

1. The operands may be of fixed or varying length. Much of the complexity of the code generator will depend on this fact alone. If both operands are of fixed length, it will be possible to calculate the length of the result during code generation. In this case, the generated code will be much simpler than if the length of the result must be determined during execution.

2. Depending on the characteristics of the variable A, the resulting character string may have to be truncated or padded with blanks before assignment to A.

3. If the variable A is the same as one or both of the operands, temporary storage will be required.

4. Depending on the length of the result, differing instructions sequences may be required. Some machines have a limit on the number of characters that can be copied in a single instruction.

In machines with several address, arithmetic, or index registers, the code generators must interact with an algorithm that allocates the registers. The design of this algorithm is crucial to the generation of efficient code since the careful use of registers can avoid the use of temporary storage and the recalculation of addresses.

Difficulty of Code Generation

A study of textbooks on compilers might lead one to believe by the number of pages devoted to parsing that it is more difficult than code generation. This is not the case. The design of code generators for the production of efficient programs is extremely difficult. It is less well understood than the design of parsing algorithms and hence is more difficult to describe.

Essentially, the success of code generation depends on the number of special cases that can be identified and optimized. However, the detection of special cases requires compiler execution time and is not always economical. For example, the typical code that might be generated for the prefix minus operator in the expression -A might be

```
LOAD A
COMPLEMENT
```

and for the expression --A

```
LOAD A
COMPLEMENT
COMPLEMENT
```

It might be argued that it would be more efficient in this situation to omit the two complement operations since they cancel each other out. However, to detect this special case, every time a prefix minus occurred the expression code generator would have to check whether there was a second one. Since an expression with two prefix minus operators is extremely rare, it is not economical to make this test in the hope of saving these two instructions.

Certain local optimizations can be achieved during code generation. One technique is to analyze a small range of instructions. This is known as *peephole optimization*. A characteristic of this process is that one optimization may spawn others, and thus the improvement obtained is iterative. Examples of the kind of improvements that can be obtained by this technique are the deletion of redundant load and store instructions, the deletion of unreachable code, and algebraic simplification.

The design of code generators calls for great skill and good judgment. Although there have been many generalized code generation schemes proposed, they have not received the same level of adoption as have the standard parsing algorithms.

5.7 Preprocessors

A preprocessor is a simple translator that is applied to the source program before it is submitted to the compiler. Typically, a programmer finds that certain constants are required in the text of the program. The programmer defines identifiers that are to represent the constants and, whenever the one of the constants is required, simply writes the identifier. Before the program is compiled it is passed through the preprocessor, which replaces all occurrences of the identifiers with the defined sequence of instructions. This both simplifies the task of the programmer in writing the program and also makes the program easier to read.

A very simple example of this, using the notation of the programming language C, is

```
#define TABLESTART      0
#define TABLEEND      250
#define TABLESTEP       5
```

This is an instruction to the preprocessor to replace every occurrence of the identifiers TABLESTART, TABLEEND, and TABLESTEP by 0, 250, and 5, respectively. The head of a loop statement to step through a table can then be written

```
for (tabindex = TABLESTART; tabindex <= TABLEEND;
                       tabindex = tabindex + TABLESTEP)
```

instead of

```
for (tabindex = 0; tabindex <= 250; tabindex = tabindex + 5)
```

which is what will result after the substitutions have been made by the preprocessor. This technique also makes the program more easily modifiable since changes to the constant values can be made by simple changes to the definitions rather than searching for and modifying all occurrences of the constants, a tedious and error-prone operation.

It is also possible to define substitutions of this sort with parameters so that the replacement text depends on the way in which the identifier is used. For example

```
#define AUGMENT(A)    A = A + 1
```

will cause the statements

```
AUGMENT(LINE_COUNT);
AUGMENT(INDEX);
```

to be replaced by

```
LINE_COUNT = LINE_COUNT + 1;
INDEX = INDEX + 1;
```

before being analyzed by the compiler.

The #define serves as a command to the preprocessor. This command is executed immediately and causes the preprocessor to store the replacement specification that follows. More sophisticated preprocessors can have a range of commands that are executed as they are found by the preprocessor. These commands can specify conditional replacement so that a given identifier is only replaced when certain conditions are satisfied. They can also define the string to replace the identifier to be computed by arithmetic and string operations.

Context-Sensitive Replacements

The preprocessor replacement of an identifier is performed in a context-free manner. Generally, a string of characters enclosed in quotation marks is treated as a single character-string token and no identifiers inside it are replaced. That is, except for the conditional replacement mentioned in the previous paragraph, an occurrence of the given identifier in the source program is always replaced by the specified string, irrespective of the context in which the identifier is used. It is generally impossible to restrict the replacement to certain statement types. For example, it would be impossible to specify that every occurrence of an assignment statement with the identifier on its left side is to be followed by an output statement to print its new value.

To specify such context-sensitive replacements, the preprocessor must have the ability to recognize patterns of syntactic categories in the source language. To continue with the example, a pattern of the form:

```
"COUNTER" := <expression> ;
```

would have to be specified. The replacement string would then have to contain a reference to the <expression> token:

```
COUNTER := <expression> ;
output COUNTER;
```

Since the syntactic definition of an expression is particular to a language, there has to be a very close relationship between the preprocessor and the compiler to achieve such context-sensitive definitions. The preprocessors for the languages C and PL\I are examples of this close relationship although neither of them has taken advantage of it to permit context-sensitive replacements.

Language Extension

In some ways, a preprocessor can be regarded as a means of extending the source language. Although a great deal of extension can be achieved in this way, the base language can only be extended in terms of itself. Thus, it is difficult to make a preprocessor that would extend Fortran with pointer variables because there is no way to describe them in Fortran. For such extensions to be possible, the base language would have to include a method for defining the machine language to be emitted for such extensions.

5.8 Interpretation

Compilers analyze the statements of a program in a high-level language and produce machine instructions that can be executed in a second step. Pure interpreters also analyze the statements but then execute subroutines to simulate the execution of the source program. Other interpreters may in fact produce an internal form of the source program in the form of instructions for a hypothetical machine before proceeding to simulate the execution of the program.

The general form of a pure interpreter is:

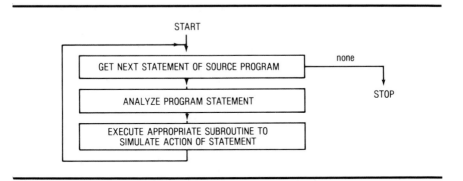

A consequence of this way of working can be illustrated during the execution of a loop. For example, consider the sequence of Basic statements

```
10 CT = 0
20 PRINT "XXXXX"
30 CT = CT + 1
40 IF CT < 5 THEN 20
```

Here, the statements inside the loop (lines 20, 30, and 40) will be analyzed each time the loop is traversed. This increases the execution time during interpretation. It also accounts for the fact that many Basic programming manuals for home computers advise users to remove blanks and comments from their programs to improve their execution speed. During interpretation, blanks and comments have to be analyzed before it can be determined that no action is required. It also accounts for the fact that a syntax error in a Basic program may only be discovered long after it has been thought to be working. This happens when a program has been insufficiently tested and not all paths through the code have been executed. Statements in the program are not checked for syntax errors until they are executed.

To reduce the time penalty, many interpretation schemes mix both compilation and interpretation methods. That is, they analyze the complete program and translate it into machine code for a hypothetical machine. This is then interpreted in the way that we have just described. Examples of this are the UCSD Pascal implementation described in [Overgaard 1980] and the Intcode interpreter for BCPL described in [Richards and Whitby-Stevens 1979].

A somewhat different technique is that of a *threaded list* interpreter. This was first described by [Bell 1973]. The underlying principle is that code to be interpreted consists of addresses of subroutines to be executed to perform the action of the program. The actual interpreter then becomes very simple since all that is required is to load the address and branch to it. On return from the subroutine, the next address is loaded and so on. The lists are said to be threaded because subroutines can themselves be written in interpreted code.

Further Reading

There are many books that describe the construction of compilers, and the following is only a partial list. The theory of compilers is described in detail in [Aho and Ullman 1972] and [Lewis et al. 1976]. A survey of parsing techniques is contained in [Aho and Johnson 1974]. At a more practical level there are [Gries 1971], [Lee 1974], [Aho and Ullman 1977]. The discussion of recursive descent parsing in [Davie and Morrison 1981] is also of a practical nature. [McKeeman et al. 1970] provides a description, including a complete listing, of a simple compiler. Another good general textbook on compilers is [Hunter 1981], while an excellent description of the process of designing and constructing a commercial compiler for a large subset of PL/I is in [Anklam et al. 1982].

The subject of program optimization is a topic of its own with a large literature. In addition to material covered in the references mentioned in the previous paragraph, much of the work has been described by Frances Allen, particularly in [Allen 1969], [Allen 1970], and [Allen and Cocke 1972]. The subject is also discussed by a number of different authors in [Muchnick and Jones 1981], which also contains a large bibliography. The use of data flow analysis to remove redundant subscript range checks is described in [Markstein et al. 1982].

[Brown 1974] provides a good discussion of preprocessors. Two examples of the way in which languages can be extended through the use of simple string replacement preprocessors are contained in [Beckermeyer et al. 1974] and [Kernighan and Plauger 1974]. The first introduces the ability to handle asynchronous interrupts into a block-structured language. The second implements a structured version of Fortran, called Ratfor for Rational Fortran.

General information on interpreters can be found in section 1.4.3 of [Knuth 1968b] and [Glass 1969]. A very detailed practical discussion of the building of an extensible compiler interpreter using the idea of threaded interpretive code is in [Loeliger 1981]. The interpreter described there is very similar to that used to implement the Forth language described in [Brodie 1981].

Exercises

Exercise 5.1 *Compiler Messages*

Give three examples of messages that might be generated by each of the following compiler processes:

1. Preprocessor
2. Scanner
3. Parser
4. Completion
5. Optimizer
6. Code generation
7. Execution time library

Not all the messages need be caused by errors in the source program.

Exercise 5.2 *Error Diagnostics*

Write a complete list of possible error diagnostics for Mini-language Core. For example, the list might include

```
SEMICOLON EXPECTED
UNDECLARED IDENTIFIER
KEYWORD program IS NOT THE FIRST SYMBOL
```

It has been argued that error messages should be defined before implementation. Do you agree with this view?

Exercise 5.3 *Error Messages*

Choose a compiler for one of the languages, Fortran, Pascal, or Basic. Identify and list five error messages. Rewrite the messages to make them more helpful in finding the actual problem.

Exercise 5.4 *Optimization*

The following program in Core does not do anything sensible. However, apply the optimization techniques of folding, elimination of redundant operations, and loop optimization to transform it into a more efficient program.

```
program
    A, B, C, D, E: integer;
begin
    input A;
    B := 1;
    C := 2;
    if (A < 5) then
        D := B * C + 3;
        while (C ≠ 10) loop
            E := B + C;
            C := C + 1;
            if (A > 3) then
                D := A * B + D;
            else
                while (E < 10) loop
                    D := A * B * C + E;
                    E := E + 1;
                end loop;
            end if;
            E := A * B + D;
            A := A + 1;
        end loop;
    else
        D := B * C + A;
    end if;
    B := C * D;
    C := B - D;
    output A, B, C, D;
end;
```

Explain and justify each transformation that you make.

Exercise 5.4 *Execution Efficiency*

Ultimately, any claim to the efficiency of a program must be borne out by actually running the program. Write a program to read a number N and output the sum of integers 1 through N. Get actual runtime figures for N = 2, 200, and 2,000.

6

Names, Locations, and Values

A programming language is designed for the manipulation of objects, for example, numbers, strings, people's names, colors, and so forth. An object that is to be operated on by a program has two attributes:

1. The place where it is stored; this is its location.

2. Its value; this value may change during the course of the program's execution.

We use the term *location* rather than *address,* since address is a hardware concept that may have no meaning in a programming language. An object can occupy only one location, yet it may occupy several hardware addresses. For example, on a byte-addressed machine, a number may occupy more than one byte. The value of a pointer variable in PL\I may often be thought of as an address, and the built-in function ADDR encourages this thought; in fact, the pointer value might not be a physical address but an index into a vector of actual addresses. In general, for a given location, we can always obtain the value that is stored there.

The objects manipulated by a program are identified by names. However, sometimes a name is used to mean the location of an object; at other points in the same program, the name can be used to mean the value stored at that location. For example, in the Pascal statement

```
J := J + 1;
```

the J on the left is used to refer to a location, while the one on the right means the value stored at that location. We can separate these two uses by saying that the J on the left gives a *reference* and the J on the right gives a *value*. Thus, a reference identifies a location at which a value is stored. Some writers use the terms *l-value* (left value) for location and *r-value* (right value) for the value stored in the location.

Mini-language Ref, defined next, will help clarify some of the issues involved in names.

6.1 Mini-language Ref

Mini-language Ref derives its reference mechanism from Algol 68. Its context-free syntax is defined in Table 6.1.

A program consists of a sequence of declarations followed by a sequence of statements. Each identifier used in these statements must appear exactly once in the declarations.

Constant Values

If we declare the value associated with an identifier to be constant, for example

```
PAGE_LENGTH: integer = 63;
```

then the identifier becomes a name for the constant value 63. Following this declaration, the identifier PAGE_LENGTH cannot appear on the left side of an assignment nor in an input statement.

The two assignments

```
X := PAGE_LENGTH;
```

and

```
X := 63;
```

are equivalent. A declaration of this sort has two advantages. First, the meaning of the constant value in the program is more easily understood from the name than its value. And second, should the value have to be altered, only one declaration in the program need be changed to produce a new version of the program.

Variables

If the value associated with the identifier is to be variable, then different kinds of values can be associated with the identifier, depending on the type specification. If the type specification contains no occurrences of the symbol ref, the associated identifiers refer to integer values. If the type specification contains a single ref symbol, the values themselves are ref-

Table 6.1 **Mini-language Ref**

program	::=	`program`
		    declaration. . .
		`begin`
		    statement. . .
		`end` ;

declaration	::=	identifier [, identifier]. . . : type ;
type	::=	`integer` = integer | [`ref`. . .] `integer`
statement	::=	assignment-statement | input-statement | output-statement
assignment-statement	::=	identifier := expression ;
input-statement	::=	`input` identifier [, identifier]. . . ;
output-statement	::=	`output` identifier [, identifier]. . . ;
expression	::=	[operand +] operand
operand	::=	integer | identifier

erences to integer values; that is, the values identify locations in which integer objects are stored. If the type specification contains two `ref` symbols, the values to which the associated identifiers refer are references to locations that contain references to integer values, and so on. This is the technique of indirect addressing, well known to assembler language programmers.

In each case, starting with an identifier and following the chain of references, one eventually finishes at a location that contains an integer value. The number of links is defined by the number of `ref` symbols in the specification of the type. Since the language does not impose an upper bound on the number of `ref` symbols in a declaration, there are arbitrarily many different types in any program.

Example of a Program

The executable statements are assignment statements, input statements, and output statements, all of which have familiar syntax.

Consider the very simple program:

```
program
   OFFSET: integer = 32;
   X:       integer;
begin
   input X;
   X := X + OFFSET;
   output X;
end;
```

This program reads in a positive integer value, adds 32 to the value, and prints the result.

This simple program uses the identifier X to refer directly to an integer value. This variable, like all variables, must be given a value, either by assignment or input, before it can be used in an expression.

When we declare a variable, like OFFSET, as having a constant value, we are saying that the identifier is identically equal to a fixed integer value. At any point in the program where it would be correct to use the numeral 32, it would also be correct to use the identifier OFFSET. In fact, OFFSET and 32 are two different names for the same integer value. The *mode* of the identifier OFFSET is integer. That is, OFFSET is the name of an integer value.

The identifier X, declared to be of type integer, has associated with it an integer value that can be changed during program execution. The identifier X is identically equal to a location that can contain an integer value. We say that the mode of X is reference-to-integer.

Executing the assignment

```
X := OFFSET;
```

associates a new value with X. The identifier OFFSET is identically equal to the integer value 32. This is the value copied into the location referred to by X.

Dereferencing

In the declaration

```
Y: ref integer;
```

we have a variable whose value is a reference-to-integer. Thus, the mode of Y is a reference-to-reference-to-integer.

Executing the assignment

```
Y := X;
```

sets the value of Y to be a reference to the integer value to which X refers. Executing the assignment

```
X := 7;
```

does not change the value of Y, still a reference to the integer value to which X refers, but it does change that integer value. Thus, the integer value that is at the end of the chain of references that starts with the identifier Y is changed.

To obtain the integer value at the end of this chain of references, the value of Y must be *dereferenced* twice, corresponding to the two occurrences of *references-to* in the mode of Y. The dereference operation performs one step in following a chain of references. This mechanism is extended for variables declared with more than one ref symbol.

The operator + represents addition. To evaluate an expression that consists of the + operator and operands that are identifiers, the value of each identifier is dereferenced as many times as needed to obtain an integer value.

Legal Assignments

For an assignment statement to be legal, the identifier on the left must not be declared as a constant, and one of the following cases must be true:

1. The expression consists of either:
   —more than one operand, or
   —an integer, or
   —a single identifier that has been declared to be a constant
   and the identifier on the left is declared without any ref symbols.

2. Or, if 1 above is not true, there can only be one identifier on the right side. In this case the number of ref symbols in the declaration of the identifier on the left side can be at most one greater than the number of ref symbols in the declaration of the identifier on the right side.

For example, given the declarations

```
A: integer = 5;
B: integer;
C: ref integer;
D: ref ref integer;
```

both the assignments

```
B := A;
C := D;
```

satisfy the requirements above. On the other hand, the assignments

```
C := A;
D := B;
```

both violate the conditions and are thus illegal.

Execution of a legal assignment is as follows:

1. In the first case above, the value of the expression (which by definition is an integer value) is copied into the location associated with the identifier on the left.

2. *Case 2.1:* The number of ref symbols in the declaration of the identifier on the right is one less than the number of ref symbols in the declaration of the identifier on the left.

   In this case, a reference to the location associated with the identifier on the right is copied into the location associated with the identifier on the left.

   Case 2.2: The number of ref symbols in the declaration of the identifier on the right is greater than or equal to the number of ref symbols in the declaration of the identifier on the left.

   In this case, the value contained in the location associated with the identifier on the right is obtained. This value refers to a location. The dereferencing operation is performed a number of times equal to the excess number of ref symbols in the declaration of the identifier on the right. The resulting value is copied into the location associated with the identifier on the left.

For the assignment to be executed without error, it must be possible to perform the required number of dereference operations. Notice that in case 2.2, each time a value is obtained from a location, that location must contain a defined value; that is, the location must have had a value assigned to it either by an assignment statement or by an input statement.

```
program
   INT_A, INT_B: integer;
   REF_INT_C, REF_INT_D: ref integer;
   REF_REF_INT_E, REF_REF_INT_F: ref ref integer;

begin
   INT_A := 1;
   INT_B := 2;

   REF_INT_C := INT_A;
   REF_INT_D := INT_B;

   REF_REF_INT_E := REF_INT_C;  -- state shown in Figure 6.1

   REF_INT_C := INT_B;  -- state shown in Figure 6.2

   INT_A := REF_REF_INT_E;
   input    REF_REF_INT_E;
   output   REF_INT_D;  -- state shown in Figure 6.3
end;
```

Example 6.1 **Dereferencing in Mini-language Ref**

Example of Dereferencing

Input and output statements specify the reading and writing of integer values. On input it must be possible to dereference each identifier by the number of ref symbols given in its declaration. On output it must be possible to dereference each identifier in the output statement fully to obtain an integer value. Otherwise, the input or output action is in error.

As an illustration of the dereferencing mechanism, consider the program of Example 6.1. After the fifth assignment has been executed, two chains of references will have been set up, and the state will be as shown schematically in Figure 6.1. The symbols used in Figure 6.1 are:

rectangle	▭	name
circle	○	location containing integer value shown in circle
single-pointed shape	⬡	location containing reference-to-integer value whose name appears in shape
double-pointed shape	⬡	location containing reference-to-reference-to-integer value whose name appears in shape

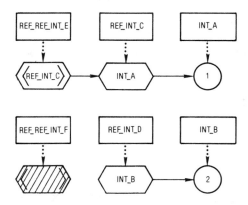

Figure 6.1 **State After Execution of Fifth Assignment in Example 6.1**

Any of the shapes except the rectangle may be shaded to indicate that the location contains an undefined value. In Figure 6.1, it should be noted that REF_REF_INT_F has not been assigned a value.

The next assignment

```
REF_INT_C := INT_B;
```

causes the value of REF_INT_C to refer to the location associated with INT_B. No other value is changed. The situation after executing this statement is as shown in Figure 6.2.

The final assignment causes the value of REF_REF_INT_E to be dereferenced twice to obtain the integer 2, which is copied into the location associated with INT_A. The input statement causes a value, say 3, to be read from the input file and assigned to the variable found by following the chain starting at REF_REF_INT_E. The semantics of Mini-language Ref require that this chain be set up by a sequence of assignment statements before an input statement is executed. The result is depicted in Figure 6.3. The final statement thus prints the value 3.

Notice that an attempt to execute

```
output REF_REF_INT_F;
```

in place of the given output statement is in error, since the value of REF_REF_INT_F is undefined and cannot be dereferenced to produce an integer.

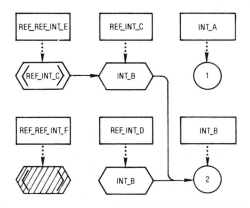

Figure 6.2 **State After Executing** `REF_INT_C := INT_B;`

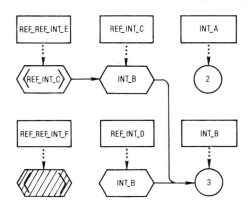

Figure 6.3 **Final State of Example 6.1**

6.2 Declarations

Consider a declaration of a variable, such as:

```
A: integer;
```

This states that A is the name of a variable that can take integer values. A is a reference to a location that can contain an integer value. Building on the symbols of the previous section, we can represent the relation as

where the double line linking the name rectangle to the single-pointed reference-to-integer shape indicates that the two are identically equal.

A declaration of a variable creates this structure with an undefined value in the location. Once the location associated with the identifier A has been created, it cannot be changed although the value stored in the location can be. Since A always refers to a location that can only contain an integer object, it always refers to an integer.

In general, a location can only contain a value of a particular type, an integer, or a reference-to-integer, for example. For this reason, we use different shapes in the diagrams.

When we say that a location can only take a particular kind of value, we are referring to an abstract model of storage. When this model is implemented on an actual machine, our abstract storage is mapped into a physical store that is made of bits grouped into bytes or words. There, all values are stored in the same basic units of physical storage, irrespective of their type. The programming language performs the mapping between the abstract concept of a location and the actual storage address. At a particular time, the language also ensures that only one type of value can be stored at the address corresponding to a specific location. At some other time, the first location will no longer exist and some other location, which can take a different type of value, will be mapped into the same address. The same address thus serves to model two different locations; however, the two locations do not coexist in time, and our rule that a location can only take one type of value stands.

Role of Locations

The role of locations is made clear in Algol 68, where the declaration

```
real X
```

is an abbreviation for the declaration:

```
ref real X = loc real
```

Here X is a constant whose value is a reference to a real value; `loc real` is a generator that acquires the location that is to be defined as the value of X; that is, X is identically equal to a reference-to-real value that is given by `loc real`. In this case we have

Thus,

```
real X
```

actually declares X to be the name of a constant value, the location where a real value may be stored. Thus, the location associated with X cannot change, but the real value that is stored in the location can.

The effect of a declaration is therefore to create a "new" location, that is, one that is currently unused, and to associate that location with the identifier being declared. The correspondence between identifiers and locations, *bindings*, defines the environment. Hence, a declaration changes the environment.

Pointer Variables

The Mini-language Ref declaration

```
REF_A: ref integer;
```

specifies that REF_A is a variable that refers to a location that can contain reference-to-integer objects. That is to say, the only values that can be assigned to REF_A are references to locations that contain integer values.

Variables of this kind are termed *reference variables* or *pointer variables.* This can be represented by the diagram

The Pascal declaration

```
REF_A:  ↑integer;
```

is exactly equivalent to the Mini-language Ref declaration. If we wish to obtain the integer value referred to by REF_A in Pascal, we write REF_ A ↑ ; the upward-pointing arrow signifies the dereferencing operation.

In contrast to the pointer variables of Pascal and Ada, which are restricted to referencing a particular kind of value, the pointer variables in PL/I can reference values of any kind. The declaration of a pointer variable in PL/I is written as:

```
DECLARE P POINTER;
```

If we have an integer variable declared by

```
DECLARE I FIXED;
```

we may assign to P the location of I by the assignment

```
P = ADDR(I);
```

To be able to refer to this integer value through P, we must declare what is called a based variable:

```
DECLARE B_INT FIXED BASED;
```

The based attribute specifies that the location of this variable will be supplied by the value of a pointer variable. The actual reference is expressed as P -> B_INT.

In a similar way, we could also use P to reference a floating point value. We could do this with the declarations

```
DECLARE F        FLOAT;
DECLARE BASED_F FLOAT BASED;
```

and the assignment of a location to P by

```
P = ADDR(F);
```

The actual reference to the floating point value is then written as P -> BASED_F.

In each of the pointer references, the P provides the location of the value, and the reference to the based variable specifies whether it is an integer or floating point value that is being referenced. The PL/I language requires that the kind of object to which the value of P refers must match the declaration of the based variable used in the reference. Thus, it would be an error if, immediately after the assignment P = ADDR(I); was made, the reference P -> BASED_F were made since there is no match between the object referred to by P and the declaration of BASED_F.

This restriction on the way in which pointer variables can be used in PL/I is the equivalent of the restriction placed on pointer variables in Pascal and Ada. The difference is that in PL/I the restriction can only be enforced during execution, whereas in Pascal and Ada the compiler can check it. The trade-off is that PL/I pointers offer greater flexibility at the cost of execution checking for equal reliability.

6.3 Assignments

A new variable does not have a value until one has been explicitly assigned to it. A program that attempts to obtain the value of a variable before it has been assigned is in error. Returning to our mini-language, suppose we have the declaration

```
A, B: integer;
```

and the two assignments:

```
A := 5;
B := A;
```

The digit 5 is the name of a constant whose value is the integer 5, and so execution of the first assignment puts a copy of the integer object 5 into the location associated with the identifier A. This gives:

The meaning of the second assignment is: obtain the value associated with A and copy it into the location associated with B. Thus, the execution of this second assignment may be represented as:

In a language like PL/I, for example, it is possible to have two names that refer directly to the same value. The PL/I declaration

```
DECLARE X FIXED,
        Y FIXED DEFINED X;
```

gives rise to the naming structure:

Value versus Location

As we have seen, when a name is used in a program, sometimes it refers to its location and sometimes to the object contained in that location. Consider, for example, the Pascal program

```
program EXAMPLE (INPUT, OUTPUT);
    var
        A: INTEGER;

    procedure P (var B: INTEGER);
    begin
       B := B + 2
    end;

begin
    A := 1;
    A := A + 1;
    P(A)
end.
```

Here A is used with two distinct meanings. In the expression

```
A + 1
```

A denotes some *value*. Once we are given the value of A, we can perform the required addition without concern about the name of A or the location of the value of A.

On the left side of the assignment, A denotes some *location*. Once we are given this location, we can proceed with the assignment without concern about the name A or its value.

In the procedure invocation P(A), A means its location; on invocation, the parameter B of procedure P is associated with the *location* of A. Hence the occurrence of B on the left side of

```
B := B + 2
```

refers to the location of A (whose value is to be changed), whereas the occurrence of B on the right side denotes the value stored in the location of A.

An Alternative

In Mini-language Ref, assignment is always performed by copying values. An alternative to this scheme is used in what are often called object-oriented languages. Objects are actually the values that are manipulated by the language, and the location associated with a variable contains a pointer to an object. That is, there is an extra level of indirection, and the value of a variable is always the location of its data object value. When an assignment is made, the target variable is set to point to the object that is being assigned.

Thus, instead of the assignment

```
A := B;
```

taking place according to the diagram

the assignment proceeds as

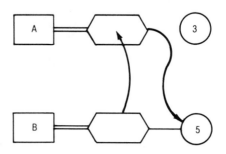

In the first case, the object 3 is replaced by the object 5. In the second, A is set to refer to the same object to which B refers. At the same time, the object 3 becomes inaccessible to the program. Its space can be reclaimed by an automatic process known as *garbage collection*. This is performed by a run-time language support system that acquires those portions of storage that have been previously allocated but are no longer accessible to the program. Usually, the garbage collector is automatically invoked when the storage that is available for allocation is nearly exhausted. A survey of garbage collection techniques is contained in [Pratt 1975].

When the assignment involves an expression, for example:

```
A := A + 3;
```

a new object is created and the target variable is set to refer to it. This implementation of the assignment is sometimes known as *pointer semantics.*

Targets

A frequent form of assignment statement involves a target that also appears in the expression, for example, the one just shown, or in its more general form:

```
A := A + e;
```

where e is an expression. Certain languages provide abbreviations of this common form, for example:

Cobol	`ADD e TO A.`
Algol 68	`A +:= e;`
C	`A += e;`

These forms allow the compiler to optimize address computation. The language C has generalized this principle to include all operations including modulus, right and left shifts, and the logical operations. Thus, for example

```
X *= Y + 1;
```

is the equivalent of

```
X = X * (Y + 1);
```

It is also possible to have assignment statements with *multiple targets.* In PL/I, we can have a statement of the form

```
ref₁, ref₂, . . . ,refₙ = exp;
```

where ref_1, ref_2, . . . ,ref_n are target references and exp is an expression. The expression is evaluated and its value is assigned to all the targets. In certain cases, where side effects can occur, the order of assignment can be important to the result. Exercise 6.4 investigates this situation.

Multiple Assignments

Another variant of the assignment statement is the *multiple assignment* of the form:

```
ref₁, ref₂,. . .,refₙ := exp₁, exp₂,. . .,expₙ;
```

where, in addition to having several targets on the left, we have the same number of source expressions on the right. This assignment really corresponds to the *simultaneous execution of the set of assignments*

```
ref₁ := exp₁;
ref₂ :⁼ exp₂;
       .   .   .
refₙ := expₙ:
```

Thus, this form allows the interchange of the values of the variables X and Y to be expressed as

```
X, Y := Y, X;
```

instead of the more cumbersome form

```
T := X;
X := Y;
Y := T;
```

where T is the name of a temporary location chosen by the programmer. Of course, the assignments do not actually take place simultaneously. The compiler generates machine code that will produce the same effect as if they were executed simultaneously. This may involve the use of temporary locations; however, this complexity is handled by the compiler, and the programmer does not have to be concerned.

6.4 Statements as Expressions

An example of an Algol 68 form of the assignment with multiple targets is

```
A := B := C := 5;
```

Its working is slightly different from that discussed in the previous section. In both Algol 68 and C, an assignment has a value, the value that is assigned to the target. Thus, the above assignment could be considered as an abbreviation for

```
A := (B := (C := 5)));
```

and execution proceeds by assigning the value 5 to C. This assignment statement is treated as an expression that has the value and the side effect of performing the assignment. The value of the assignment statement can then be assigned to B, and so on.

This view of assignments allows them to be written in more general expressions, for example, in Algol 68

```
while (N := N + 1) < A do
```

where the result of incrementing the variable N is compared with the value of A to determine if the body of the loop should be executed. A typical example from C is

```
while ((C = getchar()) != EOF)
```

The function getchar is a standard function that obtains the next character from input. Thus, this statement obtains the next character, assigns it to C, and (if it is not the end-of-file marker) executes the body of the loop.

Expressions with side effects also have other uses in C. The operation ++ is used in the following way:

++A increments A, and has the value of A after being incremented.

A++ increments A, and has the value of A before being incremented.

Two examples taken from [Kernighan and Ritchie 1978] illustrate the way in which these forms are used.

The first is a program that copies one array of characters, s1, onto another, s2, under assumption that s2 will be big enough. It relies on the fact that the s1 is terminated by the null character denoted by 0 and copies this character onto s2.

```
copy (s1, s2)
char s1[], s2[];
{   int i;
    i = 0;
    while ((s2[i] = s1[i]) != ' 0')
++i;
```

In the second example, we have a fragment from a program that deletes all occurrences of the character X from an array of characters s. We need to copy the character and increment the target index j only when the character is not an X. This is done by

```
if (s[i] != 'X')
    s[j++] = s[i];
```

inside the loop that increments i every iteration.

It is not clear whether these abbreviations really make a program easier to understand.

Algol 68 generally treats all statements as expressions; the general term "unit" is used and units always have values. An if statement has a value, the value of its then part or its else part, depending on the value of the condition. Thus, the expression

```
if P then 3 else 7 fi;
```

will have the value 3 if P has the value true, and otherwise it will have the value 7. This expression can be used as the source expression in an assignment

```
X := if P then 3 else 7 fi;
```

Although, to make it look more like an expression, the language allows an alternative notation

```
X := (P | 3 | 7);
```

Extensions of this idea allow expressions of this form that have locations as their value to be used as assignment targets:

```
(P | X | Y) := 5;
```

Algol 68 has applied this idea with great consistency so that left and right parentheses mark the boundaries of a unit, and a unit can be used in any context where a value is required. Within a unit, there may be declarations of local values; in fact, a procedure is a unit.

6.5 Where to Look: Algol 68, Smalltalk

In Mini-language Ref, since there is no limit to the number of ref symbols that can be used in a declaration, there are potentially an infinite number of different types. This system has been modeled on Algol 68, which has a rich and elaborate type structure.

It should be noted that Algol 68 uses the term "mode" where other languages, and this book, use the term "type." In our description of Mini-language Ref, we have distinguished between the two terms. We have used "type" to describe the value associated with an identifier and "mode" to describe the identifier itself. Thus, the relationship between mode and type is that mode has one more level of indirection than type. In what follows, we will continue with this usage; however, the reader must be aware that this does not follow the usual Algol 68 practice.

Algol 68

Algol 68's powerful type structure has been achieved by building orthogonally on a small number of independent primitive concepts. The general form of a declaration in Algol 68 is

type identifer

in contrast to the Mini-language Ref form

identifier : type ;

There are five primitive Algol 68 types. In addition to the four common int, real, bool, and char, there is a fifth that is used for completeness. Since all statements, including the call statement, have a value, they also have a type. Procedures that do not return a value must have a type to pass back to the call statement that invokes them. The additional type void is used to cover this case.

As with Mini-language Ref, the concept of a reference is used as a mechanism for defining new types. Thus, there are declarations such as

ref int RI;

which correspond to

RI: ref integer;

in Mini-language Ref.

The general rule of assignment follows that of Mini-language Ref. The mode of the target determines whether dereferencing (or any other conversion) is required on the source value. If the mode of the right side is not the type to which the left side refers, dereferencing is applied automatically as often as required.

Algol 68 also matches Ref in the naming of constants. Again the general form is

type identifier = expression

where the expression can be evaluated during compilation. This idea is extended to include procedure constants, for example:

```
proc MAX = (int A, B) int:
              if (A > B) then
                 A
              else
                 B
              fi;
```

It is this uniformity of notation and consistent application of forms that makes the language particularly expressive; however, the concepts that are included in this are not simple, and the consequences are difficult to grasp.

Smalltalk

Smalltalk is an object-oriented language. An object is a dynamically allocated location to which a name can be bound. For example,

```
A ← 7.
B ← A + 2.
```

binds A to the object 7 and B to the object 9. Variables like A and B designate objects rather than contain them as with Algol 68. The mechanism is one of pointer semantics. An object can contain named cells that refer to other objects, and since these references are all the same size, variables can refer to any kind of object, irrespective of their type. When we return to a description of Smalltalk in Chapter 17, we will see that objects are in fact more complicated than just pointers to other objects and contain the mechanism for manipulating objects. In a sense, they are not passive entities as in languages like Pascal or Ada, but active ones.

Further Reading

More than any other, the concept of assignment separates programming languages from conventional mathematical systems. Without assignment, the world of programming languages would be quite different.

Perhaps the most thoughtful work on the topic of assignment is a very early one, [Strachey 1967]. This paper may be difficult to obtain, but it presents a number of early fundamental ideas about programming languages.

A good introduction to Algol 68 with many examples can be found in [Lindsey and van der Meulen 1975]. The definitive description of Smalltalk is in [Goldberg and Robson 1983].

Exercises

Exercise 6.1 *Names, Locations, and Values*

The occurrence of an identifier can imply the use of either the location associated with the identifier, or the value associated with the identifier. Which of these uses of the identifier A is made in the following PL/I or Pascal statements? Not all are from the same program.

	PL/I	Pascal
a.	A = 3;	A := 3
b.	B = A;	B := A
c.	CALL A;	A
d.	A(1) = 2;	A[1] := 2
e.	ALLOCATE A;	NEW(A)
f.	X = A -> Y;	X := A
g.	GOTO A;	
h.	OPEN FILE(A);	RESET(A)

Exercise 6.2 *Explicit Dereferencing*

We have already remarked that in many languages the two instances of the identifier I in the assignment statement

```
I = I + 1;
```

denote either the location associated with I or the value contained in that location. In the systems programming language Bliss [Wulf et al. 1971], an identifier always denotes a location and not the object stored at that location. To access the object stored in the location, the programmer must explicitly dereference the identifier with the . prefix operator. Thus, the assignment would have to be written:

```
I := .I + 1;
```

Consider a variant of Mini-language Core in which the same rule obtains. Using this variant, write a program that builds an equivalent structure and produces the same output as the program shown in Example 6.1.

Exercise 6.3 *Mini-language Ref*

Consider the fragment of Ref program:

```
program
      ONE        :   integer constant = 1;
      TWO        :   integer constant = 2;
      A, B       :   integer;
      RC, RD     :   ref integer;
      RRE, RRF   :   ref ref integer;
      RRRG, RRRH:    ref ref ref integer;

begin
      A    :=   ONE;
      B    :=   A + ONE;
      RC   :=   A;
      RD   :=   B;
      RRE  :=   RC;
      RRF  :=   RD;
      RRRG :=   RRE;
      RRRH :=   RRF;
end;
```

Given the state after executing this fragment, for each of the following statements state whether it is legal (and describe its effect) or illegal (and give reasons).

a. A   := RRRG + B;

b. RRRH := RC;

c. RC   := RRRH;

d. RC   := RRRH + RD;

e. RRRH := RRE;

f. RRF   := RRRG;

g. RRF   := RRRG + TWO;

h. input RC;

i. RD   := RC;

j. B   := RRRG;

Exercise 6.4 *Multiple Assignment*

PL/I has the multiple assignment statement of the form

```
ref₁, ref₂, . . ., refₙ = exp;
```

where ref_1, ref_2, through ref_n are references and `exp` is an expression. There are a number of possible rules for executing this kind of statement, for example:

1. Evaluate `exp` to obtain a value `val`
    For i = 1 to n step 1
        evaluate ref_i to obtain a location loc_i
        assign `val` to location loc_i

2. Evaluate `exp` to obtain a value `val`
    For i = n to 1 step -1
        evaluate ref_i to obtain location loc_i
        assign `val` to location loc_i

3. Evaluate ref_1 to obtain a location loc_1
    Evaluate `exp` to obtain a value `val`
    Assign `val` to loc_1
    For i = 2 to n step 1
        evaluate ref_i to obtain location loc_i
        assign `val` to location loc_i

4. Evaluate ref_n to obtain a location loc_n
    Evaluate `exp` to obtain a value `val`
    Assign `val` to loc_n
    For i = n - 1 to 1 step -1
        evaluate ref_i to obtain location loc_i
        assign `val` to location loc_i

5. For i = 1 to n step 1
        evaluate ref_i to obtain a location loc_i
    Evaluate `exp` to obtain a value `val`
    For i = 1 to n step 1
        assign `val` to location loc_i

6. Evaluate `exp` to obtain a value `val`
    For each value of i, 1 <= i <= n, taken in undefined order
        evaluate ref_i to obtain location loc_i
        assign `val` to location loc_i

There are, of course, other possible sets of rules. Discuss the possible advantages and disadvantages of each of the six given rules, with examples. Choose one of these methods or another that you feel would be the best and explain why.

Note: You may start by considering the assignment

```
A(J - 1), J, A(J + 1) = J + 1;
```

where A is an array. Also, the possible semantics of the statements have been described in an algorithmic manner. These algorithms are for definitional purposes only and are not intended as implementation models.

Exercise 6.5 *Reference Variables*

There are two different views of reference variables. In Mini-language Ref, like Algol 68, Pascal, and Ada, a reference (or pointer) variable may only designate an object of a specific type which is specified before the program is compiled. The other view, exemplified by PL/I, is that a pointer variable can designate any kind of object. Discuss the relative advantages and disadvantages of these two views of reference variables.

Exercise 6.6 *Declarations*

All the mini-languages and many real languages, such as Pascal and Ada, require that the declaration of a variable occur before it is used. For example, in Pascal you can say

```
const
    NUMITEMS = 10;
var
    A: array [1 .. NUMITEMS] of INTEGER;
```

but not

```
var
    A:    array [1 .. NUMITEMS] of INTEGER;
const
    NUMITEMS = 10;
```

Discuss the advantages and disadvantages of this requirement, both from the point of view of the user and of the implementor.

Exercise 6.7 *Uninitialized Data Objects*

Discuss the advantages and disadvantages of the following different approaches to handling data objects created by declarations:

1. Compel the programmer to define in the declaration the value that the data object is to be given when it is created.

2. Analyze programs during compilation, using data flow analysis, to detect possible uses of undefined values and signal them as errors.

3. Automatically initialize new data objects to values that are likely to cause problems if they are used during execution, such as the largest possible integer.

4. Automatically initialize new data objects to values that might be of use to the programmer during execution, for example, zero for integer variables.

5. Automatically initialize the data object to some special value such that, if it is referenced, there will be an error detected during execution.

7

Control Structures

The power of computers comes in large part through the programmer's ability to specify the sequence in which the statements of the program are to be executed. The execution sequence is defined by such techniques as loop and if statements. Statements of this sort are called *control structures.*

The choice of control structures in a language has long been a subject of controversy, and for good reason. One of the keys to clarity is the set of control structures used.

Although a great deal has been written on the subject of control structures, the debates and polarized opinions remain. On one side, we have the view that only conditional and simple loop structures should be used. On the other side, there is the view that high-order structures, such as exits, are essential to good programming. In this chapter we treat both the simple conditional and looping structures as well as the goto statement and high-order structures.

7.1 Mini-language Control

To provide a focus for our discussion, we define a mini-language whose essential ingredient is, of course, a set of control structures. The syntax of this language, Mini-language Control, is specified in Table 7.1. As in most of our mini-languages, a program consists of a declaration section followed by a sequence of executable statements. Each of the variables used in a program must be declared exactly once.

Table 7.1 **Mini-language Control**

---

program	::=	`program`
		    declaration. . .
		`begin`
		    statement. . .
		`end` ;

declaration	::=	identifier [, identifier]. . . : `integer` ;
statement	::=	[identifier :] simple-statement
simple-statement	::=	assignment-statement | if-statement | loop-statement | exit-statement | goto-statement | input-statement | output-statement
assignment-statement	::=	identifier : = expression ;

if-statement	::=	`if` condition `then`
		    statement. . .
		[`else`
		    statement. . .]
		`end if` ;

loop-statement	::=	[`while` condition] `loop` statement. . . `end loop` ;
exit-statement	::=	`exit` (integer) ;
goto-statement	::=	`goto` identifier ;
input-statement	::=	`input` identifier [, identifier]. . . ;
output-statement	::=	`output` identifier [, identifier]. . . ;
condition	::=	[condition `and`] comparison | [condition `or`] comparison
comparison	::=	(operand comparison-operator operand)
expression	::=	[expression +] operand | [expression -] operand
operand	::=	integer | identifier | (expression)
comparison-operator	::=	‹ | = | ≠ | ›

Control Structures

In Mini-language Control, there are five ways in which the next statement to be executed may be specified:

1. Sequentially
2. Conditionally
3. Repetitively
4. Exit from a loop
5. Unconditional transfer

In sequential execution the statements are executed in the order in which they are written, for example:

```
input X, Y;
X := X + 1;
Y := Y + 1;
output Y, X;
```

Conditional execution in Mini-language Control is expressed by the if statement. In its full form this statement is:

```
if condition then
    statement . . .
else
    statement . . .
end if;
```

Execution of an if statement begins by the evaluation of the condition. If its value is true, then the sequence of statements between the then and else symbols is executed. If its value is false, the sequence of statements between the else and end if symbols is executed. In both cases, after execution of the appropriate statement sequence, execution continues after the if statement.

In an alternative form of the if statement, the else part is omitted:

```
if condition then
    statement . . .
end if;
```

In this case, if the condition evaluates to true, the statement sequence between the then and end if symbols is executed. Otherwise, execution continues after the if statement.

The iterative control structure in Mini-language Control is the loop statement, which specifies that a sequence of statements, the *body of the loop,* is to be executed repeatedly. There are two forms of loop statement, of which the while loop is the more conventional. In the while loop, the loop body is prefixed by a condition. This structure has the form:

```
while condition loop
    -- statements forming the body of the loop
end loop;
```

Each time control arrives at the top of the loop, the condition is evaluated. If the condition evaluates to false, no action is taken and execution continues after the loop. If its evaluation gives the value true, the body of the loop between the loop and end loop symbols is executed. When execution of the loop body is complete, the condition is reevaluated for another possible execution of the loop body.

Thus, *before* any execution of the body of the loop, the condition at the head of the loop is evaluated; it is the result of this evaluation that determines whether the body is to be executed or the loop is to be terminated. Note that the value of the condition, were it to be evaluated *during* the execution of the loop body, has no effect on the termination of the loop. If the condition has the value false initially, the body of the loop is never executed; in this case, the loop statement has no net effect.

A condition is either a comparison, or a condition and a comparison separated by one of the logical operators and and or. A comparison consists of two integer operands separated by a comparison operator, all enclosed in parentheses. A condition consisting of a condition separated from a comparison by the and operator evaluates to true only if both the condition and the comparison evaluate to true. A condition consisting of a condition separated from a comparison by the or operator evaluates to true if either or both the condition and the comparison evaluate to true.

The forms of execution control described thus far are common to many languages. In addition to these, Mini-language Control has some less common methods of specifying execution sequence. There is an alternative form of the loop statement that is a simple loop without a while clause:

```
loop
    -- statements forming the body of the loop
end loop;
```

The statements within the loop are executed repeatedly until an exit or goto statement transfers control out of the loop as described below. Thus, this form of the loop statement must include at least one of these statements to have a program that will terminate normally.

An exit statement has the form

```
exit (i);
```

where i is an integer greater than zero. Execution of an exit command causes termination of the *i* enclosing loops. For example, consider the loop:

```
loop
    -- statements to obtain data values
    if (INPUT_VALUE = 0) then
        exit(1);
    end if;
    -- statements to process data values
end loop;
-- statements following loop
```

This loop continues to obtain and process data until `INPUT_VALUE` is 0, at which point the exit statement is executed and the loop is terminated by transferring control to the statement following the loop. The value of *i* must be less than or equal to the number of enclosing loops.

Consider next the sketch:

```
begin
    . . .
    loop
        . . .
        loop
            . . .
            exit (2);       -- inner and outer loops terminated
        end loop;
    end loop;
    -- continuation point (a)
    . . .
    exit (1);       -- illegal, no enclosing loop
    . . .
end;
```

Here execution of

```
exit (2);
```

terminates execution of both enclosing loops with execution continuing at point (a). The statement

```
exit (1);
```

is illegally placed since there are no loops bracketing it.

Statements within a program may be prefixed by a label consisting of an identifier, for example:

```
HERE:   A := A + 1;
```

A label prefix is a declaration of an identifier (in this case, HERE) as a label constant referencing the statement that follows the colon. The label prefix marks the statement to be one to which control can be transferred by a goto statement. Since the label prefix acts as a declaration, a label identifier cannot be the same as an identifier declared as a variable or as any other label.

The form of a goto statement is

```
goto label-constant  ;
```

For example, we may have:

```
HERE:     A := A + 1;
          .  .  .
THERE:    A := A + 2;
          .  .  .
          if (X > 10) then
             goto HERE;
          else
             goto THERE;
          end if;
```

Any statement within the program may be labeled, and execution of a goto statement causes execution to continue at the referenced statement. If no label exists, the goto statement is illegal. However, a goto statement can transfer control into and out of loops and to a statement within the then or else parts of an if statement. For example, in the following sequence:

```
goto INNER_LOOP;
.  .  .
loop
   .  .  .
   loop
      INNER_LOOP: A := A + 1;
      .  .  .
      goto THEN_PART;
   end loop;
   .  .  .
end loop;
if (A = 3) then
   THEN_PART: output B;
end if;
```

both kinds of transfers of control are legal.

Flow of Control Rules

Generally speaking, we can state the flow of control rules of Mini-language Control as follows:

- Statements in a sequence are executed in the order in which they appear unless a loop, if, goto, or exit statement is encountered.

- Execution of a loop statement prefixed by a while clause causes the condition in the while clause to be evaluated. If the value is true, the enclosed statement sequence is executed and then, provided that executing the statement sequence does not transfer control out of the loop, the loop statement is reexecuted. If the value of the condition is false, execution of the program continues after the loop statement.

- Execution of a loop statement without a while clause causes the enclosed statement sequence to be executed repeatedly. An exit, or goto statement, that transfers control out of the loop is required to terminate the loop.

- Execution of an if statement causes the execution of the statement sequence following the `then` symbol if the condition is true; otherwise the statement sequence following the `else` symbol, if it exists, is executed.

- Execution of `exit(`*i*`)` causes control to be passed to the statement immediately following the *i*th loop enclosing the exit statement.

- Execution of a goto statement causes control to be passed to the statement labeled by the identifier in the goto statement.

Other Features

Programs in Mini-language Control, of course, have variables. All variables in a program must be declared. A variable can only have integer values.
The remaining statements in the language are the familiar:

- Assignment statements
- Input statements
- Output statements

Examples

We next turn to some example programs. Example 7.1 shows a simple program for converting nautical or 24-hour clock time into the 12-hour notation. A flag AM_OR_PM specifies morning (0) or afternoon (1). For example, if 1830 is given as input, the program outputs:

```
HOURS = 6   MINUTES = 30   AM_OR_PM = 1
```

The basic structure of this program is quite simple. The integer value of the nautical TIME is input, and the number of HOURS and the number of MINUTES are calculated. If the number of HOURS or MINUTES is out of range for a valid time, the value input for TIME is printed. Otherwise, the appropriate 12-hour values are printed.

Examples 7.2, 7.3, and 7.4 all treat the same problem, calculating the sum of a number of items. Example 7.2 performs this using a while loop that terminates when all the items have been summed, that is, when the value of COUNT equals the number of items.

Example 7.3 shows the use of a simple one-level exit from a loop. When the value of COUNT is equal to the number of items, the loop is terminated.

Example 7.4 performs the calculation in the same way as Example 7.3 except that, in this example, the loop is terminated by a goto statement. When the goto statement is executed, control continues at the output statement prefixed by the label DONE.

```
program
    -- This program reads in an integer value representing the time
    -- on a 24-hour clock and prints out the corresponding 12-hour
    -- clock time.  If the input value does not represent a correct
    -- time, the input value is printed.

    TIME, HOURS_AND_MINUTES, HOURS, MINUTES, AM_OR_PM: integer;
begin
    input TIME;
    HOURS_AND_MINUTES := TIME;
    HOURS             := 0;
    while (HOURS_AND_MINUTES > 99) loop
        HOURS_AND_MINUTES := HOURS_AND_MINUTES - 100;
        HOURS             := HOURS + 1;
    end loop;
    MINUTES := HOURS_AND_MINUTES;

    if (HOURS > 23) then
        if (HOURS = 24) and (MINUTES = 0) then
            AM_OR_PM := 0;
            HOURS    := 12;
            output HOURS, MINUTES, AM_OR_PM;
        else
            output TIME;
        end if;
    else
        if (MINUTES > 59) then
            output TIME;
        else
            AM_OR_PM := 0;
            if (HOURS = 0) then
                HOURS := 12;
            else
                if (HOURS > 11) then
                    AM_OR_PM := 1;
                    if (HOURS > 12) then
                        HOURS := HOURS - 12;
                    end if;
                end if;
            end if;
            output HOURS, MINUTES, AM_OR_PM;
        end if;
    end if;
end;
```

Example 7.1 **A Mini-language Control Program**

```
program
    -- This program reads in an integer specifying the number
    -- of integer items and then reads in the items.
    -- It outputs the sum of the integers.

    COUNT, NUM_ITEMS, NEXT_ITEM, SUM: integer;

begin
    input NUM_ITEMS;
    COUNT := 0;
    SUM   := 0;
    while (COUNT < NUM ITEMS) loop
        input NEXT_ITEM;
        SUM   := SUM + NEXT_ITEM;
        COUNT := COUNT + 1;
        end loop;

    output SUM;
end;
```

Example 7.2 **Use of a While Loop**

```
program
    -- This program reads in an integer specifying the number
    -- of integer items and then reads in the items.
    -- It outputs the sum of the integers.

    COUNT, NUM_ITEMS, NEXT_ITEM, SUM: integer;

begin
    input NUM_ITEMS;
    COUNT := 0;
    SUM   := 0;
    if (NUM_ITEMS > 0) then
        loop
            input NEXT_ITEM;
            SUM   := SUM + NEXT_ITEM;
            COUNT := COUNT + 1;
            if (COUNT = NUM_ITEMS) then
                exit (1);
            end if;
        end loop;
    end if;

    output SUM;
end;
```

Example 7.3 **Use of a Simple Exit**

```
program
    -- This program reads in an integer specifying the number
    -- of integer items and then reads in the items.
    -- It outputs the sum of the integers.

    COUNT, NUM_ITEMS, NEXT_ITEM, SUM: integer;

begin
    input NUM_ITEMS;
    COUNT := 0;
    SUM   := 0;
    if (NUM_ITEMS > 0) then
        loop
            input NEXT_ITEM;
            SUM   := SUM + NEXT_ITEM;
            COUNT := COUNT + 1;
            if (COUNT = NUM_ITEMS) then
                goto DONE;
            end if;
        end loop;
    end if;

    DONE: output SUM;
end;
```

Example 7.4 **Use of a Simple Goto Statement**

7.2 Basic Control Structures and Flowgraphs

In the study of flow of control, it is useful to represent a program as a *flowgraph.* This is a set of nodes, denoting actions in the program, connected by directed lines that show the flow of control. The flowgraph represents the sequence in which the actions occur during program execution. There are three kinds of nodes:

- *Basic actions:* These are represented by rectangles and denote actions that can change the values of variables but cannot alter the flow of control. Thus, a basic action node has only one flow line leaving it.

- *Conditions:* These are represented by diamond shapes and denote actions that can change the flow of control but cannot alter the values of variables. A condition node has two flow lines leaving it, implying that a binary choice of flow sequence is being made.

- *Joins:* These are represented by a simple junction of flow lines. Joins do not denote any action and thus cannot change the values of variables and have only a single flow line leaving them.

D-structures

We now discuss a class of simple control structures called D-structures (D for Dijkstra; see [Bruno and Steiglitz 1972].) A D-structure is either a

- **Basic action:** For example, an assignment statement, procedure call, or input-output statement;

or one of the following forms, themselves composed of D-structures:

- **Sequence**

s_1 s_2 . . . s_n

where s_1 through s_n are D-structures.

- **Conditional structure**

```
if c then
    s₁
else
    s₂
end if;
```

where c is a condition and s_1 and s_2 are D-structures.

- **Iterative structure**

```
while c loop
    s
end loop;
```

where c is a condition and s is a D-structure.

D-structures may be represented in the form of flowgraphs as shown in Figure 7.1. We use the convention in all flowgraphs that the true branch is always shown on the left of the condition node.

Since the basic actions are such that no transfers of control can occur during their execution, we can say that they are *one-in, one-out* structures; that is, control enters by only one path and leaves by only one path. The assumption we have made is that there is no mechanism by which control can return from a procedure to a statement other than the one immediately following the call statement. D-structures built from one-in, one-out actions are themselves one-in, one-out structures.

A program that is constructed entirely from D-structures is itself a D-structure. Consequently, it will have only one entry and one exit. Mini-language Control programs that use only the assignment, if (with the else clause), while loop, input, and output statements correspond exactly to the construction rules for D-structures.

A program that is a D-structure can be readily diagrammed as a planar flowgraph. Figure 7.2 shows a Mini-language Control program and the corresponding flowgraph.

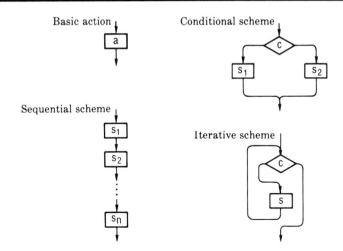

Figure 7.1 **Flowgraph Representation of D-Structures**

```
program
    -- This program reads a number of integer
    -- values and prints their maximum value.

    NUM_VALUES, CURRENT_MAX,
    NEW_VALUE,  VALUE_COUNT: integer;

begin
    input NUM_VALUES;
    VALUE_COUNT := 0;
    CURRENT_MAX := 0;
    while (VALUE_COUNT < NUM_VALUES) loop
        input NEW_VALUE;
        if (NEW_VALUE > CURRENT_MAX) then
            CURRENT_MAX := NEW_VALUE;
        end if;
        VALUE_COUNT := VALUE_COUNT + 1;
    end loop;

    output CURRENT_MAX;
end;
```

Figure 7.2 **A Mini-language Control Program and its Flowgraph**

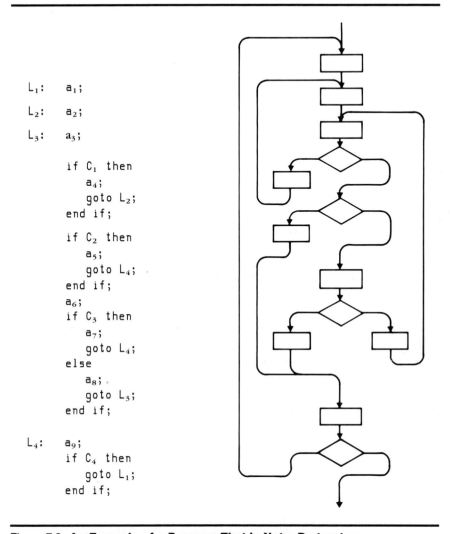

```
L₁:    a₁;

L₂:    a₂;

L₃:    a₃;

       if C₁ then
          a₄;
          goto L₂;
       end if;

       if C₂ then
          a₅;
          goto L₄;
       end if;
       a₆;
       if C₃ then
          a₇;
          goto L₄;
       else
          a₈;
          goto L₃;
       end if;

L₄:    a₉;
       if C₄ then
          goto L₁;
       end if;
```

Figure 7.3 **An Example of a Program That is Not a D-structure**

More generally, the flow of control of any program, whether D-structure or not, can be depicted as a flowgraph. Figure 7.3 shows the flowgraph of a program that is not a D-structure. The program corresponding to the flowgraph, also shown in Figure 7.3, is written with explicit transfers of control. Here, execution of a statement

    goto label;

results in program execution continuing at the statement prefixed by the label.

Beyond D-structures, we can identify other classes of control structure.

D'-structures

D'-structures consist of D-structures plus some extensions built from them; among these are:

1. If statements with only a single branch

2. Multi-way branching case statements

3. Until loops

4. For loops

The first of these is in Mini-language Control and the remaining three will be described in Section 7.4. This set of D'-structures contains the set of Pascal control structures apart from the goto. As defined here, all D'-structures are one-in, one-out structures in the sense that any well-defined loop has one entry and one exit.

RE_1-structures

An RE_1-structure is composed of basic actions, sequences, if-then-else structures, loop structures, and exit statements that leave a single enclosing loop, that is, exit (1) statements. For example, we may have:

```
loop
    . . .
    if c₁ then
        exit (1);
    end if;
    . . .
    if c₂ then
        exit (1);
    end if;
end loop;
```

Note that a while loop of the form

```
while (A = B) loop
    -- statements
end loop;
```

is equivalent to the RE_1-structure:

```
loop
   if (A ≠ B) then
      exit (1);
   end if;
   -- statements to be repeated
end loop;
```

RE_n-structures

An RE_n-structure is composed of basic actions, sequences, if-then-else, and loop structures, together with exit statements of the form $exit(i)$;, where i is a positive integer between 1 and n. On execution, the statements within a loop are to be repeated indefinitely until an exit statement is encountered. The execution of the exit statement causes termination of the i enclosing loops.

L-structures

An L-structure is defined as any structure without restrictions on the transfers of control. An L-structure corresponds to a program with free use of labels and goto statements.

This set of control structures embraces most of the control structures found in conventional languages.

7.3 Theorems on Control Structures

The best known theorem on control structures is that stated in [Boehm and Jacopini 1966], which shows that D-structures are sufficient for the construction of any program. This result, virtually unnoticed at first, has had a far-reaching effect on programming and has spawned much controversy about the proper use of control structures. A proof that is less formal than the original one is contained in [Mills 1972].

The basic conclusion can be stated simply as:

For any proper program there exists an equivalent program that is a D-structure.

"Any proper program" means any computer program, no matter what control structures it contains, provided:

1. There is precisely one entry and one exit to the entire program.

2. For every node in the flowgraph representation of the program, there is at least one path from the entry point, through that node, to the exit point.

This latter restriction rules out programs containing infinite loops and statements that are not reached by the flow of control from the program's entry point.

An *equivalent program* is a program that will always give the same result as the original one for the same input data. Two equivalent programs may have very different flowgraphs. For example, we can compare two programs that calculate the square root of their input. One obtains the result by successive approximation, while the other uses a table look-up method. These two programs will be equivalent if their results are exactly equal for all possible input values.

The proof of the existence of an equivalent D-structure program consists of a step-by-step method of deriving a D-structured flowgraph that is equivalent to the flowgraph for the original program. This derived flowgraph corresponds to a D-structure program equivalent to the original one. The derived D-structure program may contain actions, conditions, or variables that were not in the original program.

The importance of this theorem is that it *guarantees* that any problem can be programmed using only D-structures. If you keep to using only D-structures from the very start, you are sure to have enough ammunition to write your program. In particular, if your programming language includes only the following control statements

1. Sequences of one or more statements

2. Conditional statements of the form

```
if condition then
    statement. . .
else
    statement. . .
end if;
```

3. Loops of the form

```
while condition loop
    statement. . .
end loop;
```

or their equivalent, then this is all you need, at least theoretically.

Of lesser importance is the method by which the theorem is proved. It is a proof by construction consisting of an algorithm that takes an arbitrary flowgraph and keeps on transforming it according to the rules until an equivalent D-structure is reached. In many instances the converted program will be less efficient and far less clear. There are methods of mechanical restructuring that are more effective, (for example, [Arsac 1979]), but this topic is far beyond the scope of this text. The important point is that restructuring a poorly designed algorithm in a mechanical way will probably not improve it. A clear structure should be there from the outset.

Conversion to Equivalent Form

We now consider the relative power of control structures by examining the conversion of a control structure to an equivalent form. The minimum requirement that we place on the conversion of a control structure S into a control structure T is that it preserve the function of the structure; that is,

For every input, T computes the same result as S.

If this condition holds, we say that the two structures are *functionally equivalent*. We also say that a control structure S is *more powerful* than a structure T if the conversion of S to T requires the introduction of new actions, conditions, or variables. Finally, we say that a structure S is *semantically equivalent* to T if the conversion of S to T does not require any new actions, conditions, or variables.

We might now ask: under which conditions is a control structure convertible to a D-structure without introducing new boolean variables or changing the particular actions and conditions of a program? The answer to this question, given by [Kosaraju 1974], lies in the detection of a loop with two or more distinct exits. In general, an L-structure is convertible to a semantically equivalent D-structure if and only if the structure does not contain a loop with more than one distinct exit. If a structure contains only loops with one exit, conversion can be made by rearrangement and possible duplication of the existing actions and predicates.

For example, consider the program schema of Figure 7.4. This is a typical structure that cannot be converted to a D-structure without new variables or actions. Here we have a loop through a_3, a_5, a_7 with two exits, one through a_6 and the other through a_8. Note that the branch to a_4 is not an exit from this loop, since the flow of control must return to a_3, via a_2.

[McCabe 1976] shows that any program that is not written with just D-structures will contain at least two of the following control situations:

Branching out of a loop

Branching into a loop

Branching into a decision

Branching out of a decision

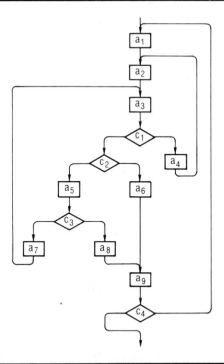

Figure 7.4 **An L-Structure Not Convertible to a D-Structure**

For example, the path from c_3 to a_8 in Figure 7.4 branches both out of a loop and out of a decision. This result gives a basis for understanding why departures from the pure use of D-structures apparently increase the complexity of programs.

A Hierarchy of Control Structures

There have been numerous attempts to discover the limitations of D-structures as well as to explore the expressive power of other control structures. These results show that there are programs that cannot be converted to D-structure form without changing the length, execution time, or basic actions of a given program. One of the more important results, due to [Kosaraju 1974], answers the question: how do the different types of structures relate to each other?

The basic results are outlined in Figure 7.5. A downward line connecting one class of structures to another class means that the upper class is

Figure 7.5 **A Hierarchy of Control Structures**

in general only convertible to the lower one with the introduction of new actions and variables. The main results shown in Figure 7.5 may be summarized as:

- D and D'-structures are semantically equivalent; that is, the basic D-structures can provide a simple means of expressing the extensions embraced by D'-structures.

- D and D'-structures are less powerful than RE_1-structures. Thus, to write a program using only D or D'-structures, we may have to introduce new boolean variables and actions to achieve the desired effect.

- If no prior bound is placed on the index n, *any* structure is convertible to an RE_n-structure. This is the meaning of $RE_\infty \equiv L$ in Figure 7.5.

- For any finite value of n, there exist L-structures that cannot be converted to RE_n-structures without the introduction of new actions and conditions.

Implications of the Results

From the programmer's viewpoint, the results suggest that there may be control situations where more powerful control structures (e.g., RE_1 or L-structures) are preferable to D or D'-structures because, for example, they do not require new control variables, conditions, or actions. Aside from questions of efficiency, the results also suggest that the use of stronger control structures like RE_n-structures and their variants may obviate the need for goto's and control variables. In a later section, we show an example that, in fact, presents evidence *counter* to these suggestions.

7.4 Other One-in, One-out Control Structures

There are other one-in, one-out control structures that allow the clear expression of some algorithms. These structures are available in some programming languages, particularly those designed more recently. In this section we will discuss several of these structures. All have the important property that they are one-in, one-out.

By a one-in, one-out control structure, we mean a control structure that always has one entry and one exit, and for which any substructure also has precisely one entry and one exit. For example, in a structure of the form

```
if  condition  then
      statement-1
      statement-2
      statement-3
end  if;
```

our definition excludes the use of any statement, say statement-2, to cause an explicit branch out of the if-then statement.

An If Statement Extension

As you may have noticed in Example 7.1, the simple form of the if statement in Mini-language Control is not very satisfactory when there are many possible conditions. The statement becomes deeply indented and difficult to understand. A simple language design approach to this problem would be to extend the definition of the if statement to:

```
if-statement  ::=  if  condition  then
                         statement. . .
                   [  elsif  condition  then
                      statement. . .  ]. . .
                   [  else
                      statement. . .  ]
                      end  if ;
```

This is similar to that found in the programming language Ada. Execution of this form of the statement consists of evaluating each of the conditions in the order in which they appear until the first one with the value true is encountered. At this point, the corresponding sequence of statements is executed. After execution of the statement sequence, control passes to the statement following the if statement. If none of the conditions evaluates to true, the statement sequence that follows the else symbol is executed if it exists; otherwise control passes directly to the statement following the if statement.

This form of the if statement is useful in problems where a choice of actions is determined by the first of several conditions that is true. For example, it allows statements like:

```
if (DISCRIMINANT > 0) then
    PRINT ('TWO REAL ROOTS');
elsif (DISCRIMINANT = 0) then
    PRINT ('ONE ROOT');
else
PRINT ('TWO IMAGINARY ROOTS');
end if;
```

This is clearer than using the nested if-then-else statement:

```
if (DISCRIMINANT > 0) then
    PRINT ('TWO REAL ROOTS');
else
    if (DISCRIMINANT = 0) then
        PRINT ('ONE ROOT');
    else
        PRINT ('TWO IMAGINARY ROOTS');
    end if;
end if;
```

With many conditions, the point becomes even more evident.

Case Statement

An important one-in, one-out structure found in many languages is the case statement. It is a form of conditional statement where the actions to be carried out depend on the value of an expression given at the head of the case statement. In a simple form, it has a structure like that found in Ada:

```
case expression of
    when value-1 => statement . . .
    when value-2 => statement . . .
        . . .
    when value-n => statement . . .
end case;
```

Here the expression following the `case` symbol is evaluated, and its value is compared in turn with each of the values that follow the `when` symbols. As soon as a match is found, the corresponding sequence of statements is executed.

There are many variants of this kind of statement. One of the most useful contains an *otherwise* option to cover any values not explicitly given. For example, we may have:

```
case I of
    when 0     =>    -- what to do if the value of I is 0
    when 1     =>    -- what to do if the value of I is 1
        . . .
    otherwise =>    -- what to do for all other values of I
end case;
```

There are a number of questions that must be resolved by the language designer when specifying such a statement. For example:

- Must all the conditions be mutually exclusive?
- Are the conditions evaluated strictly in the order in which they appear?
- Suppose that none of the conditions evaluate to true. Is it an error if there is no otherwise option?

Guarded Command

A particularly elegant form for specifying selection is that of *guarded commands* proposed in [Dijkstra 1975]. The general form of the construct is:

```
if condition-1 → statement. . .
☐  condition-2 → statement. . .
    . . .
☐  condition-n → statement. . .
fi
```

Each of the conditions condition-1, condition-2,. . ., condition-n is called a *guard*. The semantics of this statement are that the statement sequence that follows the first of the guards that evaluates to true is executed and then control passes to the statement following the if statement. At least one of the guards must evaluate to true, otherwise the statement is in error.

The elegance of this construct becomes particularly apparent when it is seen in conjunction with the iterative form:

```
do condition-1  →  statement. . .
   ☐ condition-2  →  statement. . .
   . . .
   ☐ condition-n  →  statement. . .
od
```

In this form, looping continues until none of the guards evaluates to true. Thus, we have both the conditional and iterative constructs with essentially the same form. In Chapter 16 we shall examine a version of these constructs that are used to control the interaction of concurrent processes.

While Loop Variant

For iteration structures, there are numerous useful forms. One of them is a variant of the while loop where, instead of testing the termination condition before each iteration, it is tested after the body of the loop has been executed. Thus, at least one iteration of the loop is guaranteed. This can be expressed in the form:

```
loop
    statement. . .
end loop when condition;
```

In most existing languages this structure is written with a syntax using the keywords *repeat* and *until,* for example:

```
repeat
    statement. . .
until condition;
```

This form of loop is especially useful when the condition depends on a value that is initialized within the loop, for example:

```
repeat
    -- some statements
    input X;
    -- other statements
until (X = 0);
```

For Loop Structure

Another useful form is the *for loop,* where the number of iterations of a loop is specified beforehand; at each iteration a variable, called the *control variable,* is assigned one of a sequence of values. A simple example can be shown by a loop that computes the sum of 100 input values:

```
SUM := 0;
for I := 1 to 100 loop
    input X;
    SUM := SUM + X;
end loop;
```

This structure also has many alternative forms. For example, we may have a loop that terminates when either the control variable completes its assigned values or when a condition is satisfied:

```
SUM := 0;
for I := 1 to 100 while (not END_OF_INPUT_FILE) loop
    input X;
    SUM := SUM + X;
end loop;
```

Here, too, there are a number of points that must be resolved by the language designer, for example:

- Can the value of the control variable be changed inside the body of the loop?
- What is the value of the control variable immediately after terminating the loop?

All of these structures illustrate a general point. Even within the basic framework of one-in, one-out structures, of which D-structures are a part, it is possible to provide considerable expressive power.

7.5 The Goto Statement and Label Values

In recent years there has been a great deal of discussion of the goto statement. Although not the first to speak against its use, [Dijkstra 1968a] provided the first argument against it that was really noticed. He said:

> For a number of years I have been familiar with the observation that the quality of programmers is a decreasing function of the density of goto statements in the programs they produce.

Reaction was strong. Many people appeared to have misunderstood what Dijkstra was saying. He was not arguing against all transfers of control, which would be ridiculous since the power of a computer stems from conditionals and loops, but rather against the use of undisciplined transfers of control. In this section we examine the properties of the goto statement and label values.

"Come From" Statement

Among the contributions to the debate on the goto statement, there was a tongue-in-cheek suggestion in [Clark 1973] that the goto statement could be eliminated in favor of a *come from* statement. For example, in Fortran:

```
10      J = 1
11      COME FROM 20
12      WRITE (6,40) J
        STOP
13      COME FROM 10
20      J = J + 2
40      FORMAT(I4)
```

Here, after executing statement 10, control is transferred to statement 13. Although Clark's suggestion was intended as a spoof, there was a large grain of truth contained in it, and it highlights the difficulty with the goto statement.

In a program with many goto statements, we are likely to have this kind of situation:

```
...
goto LA;
...
goto LA;
...
LA:   ...
...
goto LA;
...
```

At any point in a computation, there is a particular value associated with each of the program's variables. The set of these values constitutes the *computation state* at that point in the program. Thus, when control is transferred to the statement labeled LA, the computation state will depend on the point from which control came. To understand the program, the programmer must be aware of all the possible states and therefore must be able to keep in mind the state at each goto statement. Thus, it is not so much a goto problem as a come from problem.

Static and Dynamic Forms of Programs

There are really two forms of a program:

- the *static form* in which the program was written and which can be read from top to bottom in the normal way
- the *dynamic form,* which represents the actual sequence in which the statements are executed.

The problem of understanding a program is one of reading the static form and understanding the dynamic form from it. To do this, requires a mental leap. The greater the difference between the two forms, the harder it is to make this mental leap. Programs that contain goto statements are likely to have dynamic forms that are very different from their static forms. This is the real problem associated with goto statements.

Problem of Label Variables

The problem of goto's is made worse when the language permits the use of label variables. These variables can be given label values; that is, they can reference statements in the program for purposes of control flow. A goto statement that references a label variable causes transfer of control to a point in the program defined by the value of the label variable when the goto is executed. To understand the execution of the program, the reader must know the value of the label variable. The use of label variables makes the understanding of a program much more difficult. Exercise 7.10 illustrates this point.

7.6 Conclusions

When all is said and done, the practicing programmer is primarily interested in solving *problems* using the set of control structures provided by a particular language. Although theorems on the *conversion* of one form of structure to another may be of some practical interest in that they show the situations where the introduction of new variables may be required, conversion is not the basic issue.

Of much greater importance is the question of naturalness of expression. That is, can the control structures of the language under consideration form a natural expression of the algorithm needed to solve the current problem? In particular, are there problems for which D- or D'-structures do not provide solutions that are as clear as the more powerful control structures? We now present an example aimed at resolving this issue.

An Example Problem

We have chosen a problem that is apparently difficult for D'-structures; its solution seems to require the ability to leave nested loops both to restart and to terminate the loops. For this problem, we must write a program segment that sets the value of a variable LEGAL_NAME_FLAG to 1 or 0, depending on whether a given PL/I qualified name is a legal or illegal reference.

Data structures in PL/I may be declared with nested components, for example:

```
DECLARE 1 A,
          2 B,
            3 C CHARACTER (5),
            3 D FIXED;
DECLARE 1 X,
          2 B,
            3 C FLOAT,
            3 E FLOAT;
```

A reference to a structure element is legal if, and only if, it designates a unique component of a structure. Using the declarations of A and X above, the references A, A.B, A.B.C, A.C, and B.E are all legal. However, both references B and B.C are ambiguous and hence illegal. The reference B.C could refer to either A.B.C or to X.B.C.

Assumed Primitives

To solve this problem, a number of primitives are assumed:

1. A linked list of entries, called QUALIFIED_NAME, that contains a separate entry for each identifier component of the qualified name to be tested.

2. A linked list of entries called SYMBOL_TABLE, which contains a separate entry for each identifier declared in a program. An identifier declared in more than one structure has an entry corresponding to each occurrence.

3. A function BASE_ID, which, when applied to QUALIFIED_NAME, yields the rightmost or lowest-level entry in the name. For example, the BASE_ID of the qualified name A.B.C is the entry for C.

4. A function NEXT, which, when first applied to SYMBOL_TABLE, gives the first entry, and on subsequent applications to a symbol table gives succeeding entries in the symbol table. Repeated applications thus provide each entry of the symbol table in some unspecified order, terminated by a null entry.

5. A function FATHER, which can be applied to either a qualified name entry or symbol table entry. In either case, it yields the next higher-order entry in the corresponding linked list, or the null entry if there is no father entry. For example, in the linked list for A.B.C, the father of the entry for C is the entry for B, and the father of the entry for A is the null entry.

Each of these primitives is illustrated in Figure 7.6. Finally, we assume that FALSE and TRUE are constants with the respective values 0 and 1.

Example 7.5 shows a solution to this problem using RE_2-structures. This solution makes use of exit statements for escapes from one and two levels of loops. A *mechanical conversion* of this program to a D or D'-structure is impossible without the introduction of new boolean-valued variables. While not intrinsically bad and often making for clearer programs, in this case the additional boolean variables increase the complexity of the program.

However, by starting again from the original problem statement, it is possible to devise a new functionally equivalent solution using D-structures. This solution, shown in Example 7.6, requires neither new variables nor excessive copying of code; its clarity compares very favorably with the solution using RE_2-structures. Thus, the expected superiority of RE_2-structures over D-structures is not supported by the example.

Entry for the Qualified Name A.B.C.

Symbol table for the declarations:

```
DECLARE 1 A,
        2 B,
          3 C,
          3 D;
DECLARE 1 X,
        2 B,
          3 C,
          3 E;
```

Figure 7.6 **Primitives for the Qualified Name Problem**

```
NAME_BASE         := BASE_ID(QUALIFIED_NAME);
DIRECT_HIT        := FALSE;
NUM_PARTIAL_HITS := 0;

loop
   TABLE_ENTRY := NEXT(SYMBOL_TABLE);
   if (TABLE_ENTRY = NULL) then
      exit(1);
   end if;
   if (TABLE_ENTRY = NAME_BASE) then
      LOCAL_TABLE_ENTRY := FATHER(TABLE_ENTRY);
      LOCAL_NAME_ENTRY  := FATHER(NAME_BASE);
      SKIP              := FALSE;
      loop
         if (LOCAL_NAME_ENTRY = NULL) then
            if (LOCAL_TABLE_ENTRY = NULL) then
               if (SKIP = TRUE) then
                  NUM_PARTIAL_HITS := NUM_PARTIAL_HITS + 1;
               else
                  DIRECT_HIT := TRUE;
                  exit(2);
               end if;
            else
               NUM_PARTIAL_HITS := NUM_PARTIAL_HITS + 1;
            end if;
            exit(1);
         else
            if (LOCAL_TABLE_ENTRY ≠ NULL) then
               if (LOCAL_TABLE_ENTRY = LOCAL_NAME_ENTRY) then
                  LOCAL_NAME_ENTRY := FATHER(LOCAL_NAME_ENTRY);
               else
                  SKIP := TRUE;
               end if;
               LOCAL_TABLE_ENTRY := FATHER(LOCAL_TABLE_ENTRY);
            end if;
         end if;
      end loop;
   end if;
end loop;

if (DIRECT_HIT = TRUE) or (NUM_PARTIAL_HITS = 1) then
   LEGAL_NAME := TRUE;
else
   LEGAL_NAME := FALSE;
end if;
```

Example 7.5 **A Solution Using RE$_2$-Structures**

```
TABLE ENTRY       := NEXT(SYMBOL TABLE);
NAME_BASE         := BASE_ID(QUALIFIED_NAME);
DIRECT_HIT        := FALSE;
NUM_PARTIAL_HITS := 0;

while (TABLE ENTRY ≠ NULL) and (DIRECT HIT = FALSE) loop
   if (TABLE_ENTRY = NAME_BASE) then
      LOCAL_TABLE_ENTRY := FATHER(TABLE_ENTRY);
      LOCAL_NAME_ENTRY  := FATHER(NAME_BASE);
      SKIP              := FALSE;

      while (LOCAL_NAME_ENTRY ≠ NULL) and
                             (LOCAL_TABLE_ENTRY ≠ NULL) loop
         if (LOCAL TABLE_ENTRY = LOCAL_NAME_ENTRY) then
            LOCAL_NAME_ENTRY := FATHER(LOCAL_NAME_ENTRY);
         else
            SKIP := TRUE;
         end if;
         LOCAL_TABLE_ENTRY := FATHER(LOCAL_TABLE_ENTRY);
      end loop;

      if (LOCAL_NAME_ENTRY = NULL) then
         if (LOCAL_TABLE_ENTRY = NULL) then
            if (SKIP = TRUE) then
               NUM_PARTIAL_HITS := NUM_PARTIAL_HITS + 1;
            else
               DIRECT_HIT := TRUE;
            end if;
         else
            NUM_PARTIAL_HITS := NUM_PARTIAL_HITS + 1;
         end if;
      end if;
   end if;
   TABLE_ENTRY := NEXT(SYMBOL_TABLE);
end loop;

if (DIRECT_HIT = TRUE) or (NUM_PARTIAL_HITS = 1) then
   LEGAL_NAME := TRUE;
else
   LEGAL_NAME := FALSE;
end if;
```

Example 7.6 **A Solution Using D-Structures**

Three Basic Conclusions

We draw three basic conclusions from our discussion of Mini-language Control.

■ From the programmer's viewpoint, theoretical results based on the conversion of one program form to another need not be of practical significance.

The formal results discussed earlier in this chapter suggest the limitations of one-in, one-out structures. The supporting evidence rests mainly on the impossibility of converting (under particular restrictions) control schema into equivalent forms limited to one-in, one-out structures. However, the practicing programmer is rarely concerned with converting programs from one form to another. Concern is centered on the naturalness with which a particular set of control structures can express the algorithmic solution to the problem at hand.

For the programmer then, the acid test of the "power" of control structures must involve their use in the solution of specific problems typical of those met in programming. Of course, the potential strengths and weaknesses indicated by the theoretical results will guide the choice of particular test problems. For example, the Qualified Name problem was originally chosen to illustrate the weakness of D and D′-structures in dealing with exit problems. To make the comparison, separate solutions to the same problem were *independently* programmed using the control structures under investigation.

Inevitably, the conventions of a programming language dictate the way that the solution to a problem is expressed. Developing each solution from the original problem statement will ensure that the peculiarities of one set of control structures do not become obstacles to the clear expression of another solution using a different set. Each Qualified Name solution was shaped by the particular characteristics of the control structure being used. Had the solution based on the RE_2-structure been *converted* into one using D′-structures, we would have had to introduce additional complexity as well as several new variables. The result of this comparison shows that it is easy to gain the wrong impression by considering theoretical results that are based only on conversion under restricted conditions.

■ The need for higher-level (above D or D′) control structures remains unproven.

There have been many, many works suggesting new control structures, higher than D and D′. These higher control structures are generally techniques for implementing exits from containing structures. In our opinion, such exits reduce clarity. The basic function of a control structure is to provide clarity by operational abstraction. Thus, the reader of a program should be able to take a level at a time, without having to bother with the inner details to find the exit conditions. For this reason, one-in, one-out structures like D and D' provide very effective abstractions.

We believe that there is no good evidence for the need of these higher forms. For these higher forms to be advantageous, the gain in naturalness, clarity of expression, and efficiency in solving problems must be sufficient to offset the additional complications introduced to both the language and its compiler.

■ The utility of the goto is seriously questioned.

In some ways it is strange that the discussion of the goto statement has been included with that of the higher-level control structures. On the one hand, the goto statement is the most powerful control structure from the point of view of the Kosaraju hierarchy presented earlier. On the other hand, as [Dijkstra 1968] said, "The goto statement as it stands is just too primitive; it is too much an invitation to make a mess of one's program."

Generally the arguments advanced in favor of the use of the goto statement are for clarity and efficiency. [Knuth 1974] said that "Sometimes it is necessary to exit from several levels . . . and the most graceful way to do this is a direct approach via the goto or its equivalent." Here, its equivalent would appear to be a more disciplined form such as an exit statement. While one example does not make a theorem any more than one swallow makes a summer, our Qualified Name example does not seem to support this contention. The use of a disciplined form of exit statement is preferable to the use of the goto statement for the same purpose.

The argument for efficiency, that the goto statement allows for more efficient programs, is frequently made. That is, by clever use of the goto statement a more efficient algorithm can be constructed. However, in almost every large program, efficiency obtained by clever use of control structures is a tiny fraction of the overall cost. While no optimizing compiler can be expected to perform *macro-efficient* optimizations, such as converting a linear search into a binary one, redundant tests and repeated actions are typical of the *micro-efficient* conditions that can be eliminated by good optimizing compilers, rare though they may be at the present time. It is this type of optimization that is the province of the compiler and not that of the programmer, who should be primarily interested in developing *clear* macro-efficient programs. Indeed, it is becoming clear that general optimization can be done automatically with greater effect when the program is built from D-structures.

Finally, we admit that any recommendation for a good set of control structures is subjective. However, we must conclude from this examination that D-structures and their variants, with all their simplicity, lead the practicing programmer toward clear and effective solutions.

7.7 **Where to Look:** Pascal, Ada

The languages Pascal and Ada provide examples of most of the control constructs that we have considered in this chapter.

Pascal

The control structures of Pascal are:

1. Compound statements of the form:

```
begin
    statement;
    statement;
    statement
end
```

2. If statement of the form:

```
if  condition  then
    statement
[   else
    statement  ]
```

Only a single statement is allowed in each part; however, this could be a compound statement that contains a statement sequence.

3. Case statement of the form:

```
case expression of
    constant  :  statement;
    constant  :  statement;
    constant  :  statement
end
```

Only a single statement is allowed in each case; however, this could be a compound statement. The case labels can also consist of lists of constants separated by commas.

4. While loop of the form:

```
while condition do
    statement
```

The single statement can be a compound statement.

5. Repeat until loop of the form:

```
repeat
    statement. . .
until  condition
```

6. For loop of the form:

```
for variable := expression [down]to expression do
    statement
```

where the control variable can either increase or decrease. The single statement can be a compound statement.

7. Goto a label constant. Transfers of control are limited to a single procedure. Label constants have the form of an unsigned integer so that they can be of little mnemonic assistance to the reader.

Ada

The control structures of Ada are similar to those of Pascal with some modifications to add expressive power and clearer syntax:

1. Sequence of statements.

2. If statement with the form

```
if condition then
    statement. . .
[   elsif condition then
        statement. . .   ] . . .
[   else
        statement. . .   ]
end if ;
```

3. Case statement of the form:

```
case expression is
    when values => statement. . . ;
    when values => statement. . . ;
    . . .
    when others => statement. . . ;
end case;
```

where "values" denotes a set of possible values or ranges of values for the expression at the head of the statement.

4. Loop statement with the basic form:

```
loop
    statement. . .
end loop;
```

As in the loop of the same form in Mini-language Control, this loop is only terminated by an exit or goto statement. The basic form of the loop can have header clauses of the form:

```
while condition loop
```

or

```
for variable in [ reverse ] value-range loop
```

to provide loops where the terminating condition is stated.

5. Exit statement of the form:

```
exit [ identifier ] [ when condition ] ;
```

Without any of the optional parts, this statement transfers control to the end of the innermost enclosing loop, as does exit(1) in Mini-language Control. The identifier, if present, gives the label of the enclosing loop to be exited. If the when clause is attached, the exit only takes place if the condition evaluates to true.

6. Goto statement which transfers control to another statement in the same procedure and at the same or an outer level of statement nesting.

Further Reading

The practice of using only one-in, one-out control structures is generally attributed to Dijkstra. His famous Letter to the Editor [Dijkstra 1968a] hurled the challenge to the goto statement. A later work [Dijkstra 1972a] presents a thoughtful treatise on programming, in which only one-in, one-out control structures were used. These two works are classics in the area.

[Mills 1972] provides easy to understand proof of the Boehm and Jacopini theorem. Another form of this theorem that gives the stronger result that for every proper program there exists an equivalent program that is a D-structure with one occurrence of the iterative structure is in [Cooper 1967]. An interesting account of the history of these two forms of the theorem is in [Harel 1980].

Two readings relevant to this chapter stand out. The first is [Kosaraju 1974], where the results on control structures are carefully explained. Beware though, this paper is surely for those with a mathematical mind. The second reading [Knuth 1974] presents arguments that we have criticized here. Though Knuth summarizes well the arguments given by those supporting the use of higher-order control structures, a counterview is expressed in [Ledgard and Marcotty 1975].

Exercises

Exercise 7.1 *Programming Mini-language Control*

Write a program in Mini-language Control to check the relationship between the height and weight of men. The input consists of pairs of integers representing a man's height and weight respectively. The input is terminated by a height of zero.

If the height is less than 62, then the man is in category 1. If the height is greater than 75, then the man is in category 2. Otherwise, if the man's weight is less than 124 plus 4 times the amount by which the man's height exceeds 62, the man is in category 3. If the man's weight is greater than 143 plus 4 times the amount by which the man's height exceeds 62, the man is in category 4. Otherwise, the man is in category 5.

For each pair of numbers input, output the corresponding category number.

Make a second version of your program using a variant of Mini-language Control that also contains the alternative forms described in Section 7.4.

Exercise 7.2 *Elimination of Goto's*

Restructure the following program to eliminate as many goto's as possible by using the other control structures of Mini-language Control.

```
program
    X, MAX_VALUE: integer;
begin
    input MAX_VALUE;
    goto C;
1: if (X = 0) then
       goto I;
    else
       goto E;
    end if;
5: if (X > MAX_VALUE) then
       goto F;
    else
       goto D;
    end if;
9: output X;
    goto G;
3: input X;
    goto A;
6: X := X + 1;
8: X := X + X;
    goto I;
4: X := X + 2;
    goto H;
7: output MAX_VALUE;
end;
```

Exercise 7.3 *Conversion of a Flowgraph*

Convert the flowgraph shown below into a functionally equivalent one
built from sequence, if-then-else, and do-while structures only. You
can introduce boolean variables if needed. The aim is to produce the
clearest possible flowgraph for the algorithm. Compare the clarity of
your new structured flowgraph with the original unstructured one.

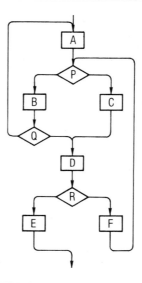

Exercise 7.4 *Designing an If Statement*

In the design of any language feature, a choice must be made among alternative designs. Consider the following alternative syntax equations for if statements:

1. *Extended Mini-language Control:*

```
if-statement      ::=   if  condition  then
                            statement. . .
                        [ elsif  condition  then
                            statement. . .    ] . . .
                        [ else
                            statement. . .    ]
                        end if ;
```

2. *Pascal-like:*

```
if-statement      ::=   if  comparison  then
                            unit-statement
                        [ else
                            unit-statement  ]

unit-statement    ::=   statement
                    |   begin
                            statement. . .
                        end;
```

3. *Choice-like:*

```
if-statement      ::=   select
                            when  comparison  => statement. . .
                        [   when  comparison  => statement. . . ] . . .
                        end select;
```

In alternative 3, the first true comparison determines which statements are executed. Faced with the above choices, choose one alternative and justify your choice.

Exercise 7.5 *Conversion of a Program*

Consider the following program:

```
program
    X: integer;
begin

        input X;
    L1: if (X > 10) then
        goto L2;
        end if;
        X := X + 1;
        if (X < 5) then
        goto L2;
        end if;
        X := X + 1;
        goto L1;
    L2: output X;
end;
```

Convert the program to a D-structure *without* introducing new variables or show that it cannot be done.

Exercise 7.6 *Prettyprinting of Control Structures*

One design requirement for features in a programming language is that they be able to be displayed in a readable fashion. Consider the following alternatives for Mini-language Control:

a.
```
    if (X > Y) then X := Y;
                    else Y := X;
    end if;
```

b.
```
    if (X > Y) then
        X := Y;
    else
        Y := X;
    end if;
```

c.
```
    if (X > Y)
        then
            X := Y;
        else
            Y := X;
    end if;
```

Each of these versions is debatable. In the general use where there may be several contained statements, nested structures leading to wide lines of text, or no else part, the issue is even more debatable.

Your problem is to choose one of the following positions and support it with a three- or four-page position paper. Even if you disagree with them all, you must choose one.

1. Any prettyprinting conventions should be chosen by the programmer. In particular cases, options (a), (b), or (c) may be individually desirable, and each should be allowed.

2. All conditional statements should be displayed as in option (b) above. No exceptions should be allowed.

3. All conditional statements should be displayed as in option (c) above. No exceptions should be allowed.

4. Prettyprinting is an overrated issue. It tends to emphasize small concerns at the expense of more important issues.

Don't be bashful.

Exercise 7.7 *Use of Various Control Structures*

[Knuth 1974] contains a text processing example. Suppose that we are processing a stream of text character by character and that we want to read and print the next character. However, if the character is a slash (/), we want to *tabulate* instead (that is, to advance the output to the next tab-stop position on the current line); moreover, two consecutive slashes mean a *carriage return* (that is, to advance the output to the beginning of the next line). After printing a period (.), we also want to insert an additional space in the output.

The following code adapted from Knuth clearly does the trick.

```
input X;
if (X = SLASH) then
    input X;
    if (X = SLASH) then
        return the carriage;
        goto DONE;
    else
        tabulate;
    end if;
end if;
output X;
if (X = PERIOD) then
    output SPACE;
end if;
DONE: ...
```

Write two other solutions to this program, one using only D- or D'-structures and the other using exit statements as well.

In both cases, you should strive for the clearest possible program. You will probably find it best to start from the problem statement rather than to try to convert the above program. Finally, compare your solution with the one shown above.

Exercise 7.8 *Use of Various Control Structures*

The meaning of the informally expressed program shown below should be quite clear even though it is unstructured.

```
                 Set MAX to N
                 If N <= 1 go to DONE
                 Set I to 1

LOOP:            Set J to 1
                 Set FLAG to false

COMPARE:         If TABLE[J] < TABLE[J+1] go to INC
                 Set TEMP to TABLE[J]
                 Set TABLE[J] to TABLE[J+1]
                 Set TABLE[J+1] to TEMP

INC:             Set J to J+1
                 If J < MAX go to COMPARE
                 If FLAG is false go to DONE
                 Set I to I + 1
                 Set MAX to MAX-1
                 If I < (N+1) go to LOOP

DONE:            Exit
```

a. Rewrite this program using only the D- or D'- structures of Minilanguage Control. To do this you may need additional boolean variables. Preserve the form of the algorithm as much as possible.

b. Rewrite the program using exit statements in addition to the D and D' statements of Mini-language Control, but no goto's. Again, preserve the form of the original algorithm as much as possible.

c. Write the clearest functionally equivalent program to the given program, using any control structures you wish. The form of the original algorithm may be changed provided that the new version performs the same net computation.

Exercise 7.9 *The Zahn Control Structure*

The Zahn control structure, see [Knuth 1974] is a loop to be repeated until one of a number of events occurs. When this happens, the loop is terminated. Exit from the loop invokes a specific action determined by the event that caused the exit. A possible syntax for this in Mini-language Control would be:

```
zahn-statement    ::=  loop until event [or event]. . .
                           begin
                               body-statement. . .
                           end;
                       then
                           event => statement. . .
                           [ event => statement. . .  ]. . .
                       end loop;

body-statement    ::=  event ;
                     |  statement

event             ::=  identifier
```

Write a program to solve the Qualified Name problem given in Section 7.6 using Mini-language Control extended to include the Zahn structure.

Note: You may not use while loops to solve the problem.

Exercise 7.10 *Restructuring a Difficult Program*

The algorithm shown on the facing page is a sorting program reproduced from the collected algorithms of the ACM[1]

The algorithm is written in Algol 60 and is not formed from D- and D'-structures. Write a program that uses only D- and D'-structures and that carries out the same algorithm as Stringsort, that is, it moves the data in exactly the same way as the original. You should strive to produce the clearest program that you can; this may certainly involve choosing new names for the variables. To rewrite the algorithm, you will first have to understand how Stringsort algorithm works. You will find that mechanical restructuring of the algorithm will not improve its clarity. What can you say about the efficiency of your version of the algorithm compared with the original version?

ALGORITHM 207
STRINGSORT
J. Boothroyd
English Electric-Leo Computers, Ltd,
Staffordshire, England

procedure *stringsort* (a, n);   **comment** elements $a[1] \cdots a[n]$ of
$a[1:2n]$ are sorted into ascending sequence using $a[n+1] \cdots a[2n]$
as auxiliary storage. Von Neumann extended string logic is employed to merge input strings from both ends of a sending area into
output strings which are sent alternately to either end of a receiving
area. The procedure takes advantage of naturally occurring ascending or descending order in the original data;
value n;   **integer** n;   **array** a;
begin integer d, i, j, m, u, v, z;   **integer array** $c[-1:1]$;
   switch $p := jz1$; *str i*;   **switch** $q := $ merge, $jz2$;
oddpass: $i := 1$; $j := n$; $c[-1] := n + 1$; $c[1] := 2 \times n$;
allpass: $d := 1$;   **go to** firststring.
merge: **if** $a[i] \geq a[z]$
       then begin go to p[v];
         *jz*1:   **if** $a[j] \geq a[z]$
            then *ij*:   **begin if** $a[i] \geq a[j]$
                    then *str j*: **begin** $a[m] := a[j]$;
                       $j := j - 1$ **end**
                    else *str i*: **begin** $a[m[:= a[i]$:
                       $i := i + 1$ **end**
               end
            else begin $v := 2$; **go to** *str i* **end**
         end
       else begin $u := 2$;
          *jz*2:   **if** $a[j] \geq a[z]$
            then go to *str j*
            else begin $d := -d$; $c[d] := m$;
                 firststring: $m := c[-d]$;
                   $v := u := 1$;
                go to *ij*
              end
         end;
$z := m$; $m := m + d$; **if** $j \geq i$ **then go to** $q[u]$;
if $m > n + 1$ **then begin comment** evenpass; $i := n + 1$;
             $j := 2 \times n$; $c[-1] := 1$; $c[1] := n$; **go to**
          allpass **end**
           else if $m < n + 1$ **then go to** oddpass
end stringsort;

Exercise 7.11 *Guarded Commands*

Consider a variant of Mini-language Control where the if statement and loop statement are described by the syntax:

```
if-statement      ::=  if
                           when  guard  =>  statement . . .
                       [   when  guard  =>  statement . . . ]  . . .
                       end if;


loop-statement    ::=  loop
                           when  guard  =>  statement . . .
                       [   when  guard  =>  statement . . . ]  . . .
                       end loop;


guard             ::=  condition-expression
```

During execution of the if statement, the statement sequence corresponding to an arbitrarily chosen true guard is executed. At least one of the guards must be true, otherwise the program terminates abnormally. Execution of the loop statement takes place in the same way except that, if no guard is true, no action is performed and the loop is terminated. Execution of the loop statement is repeated until none of the guards is true.

Rewrite the program in Example 7.1 using this version of Mini-language Control with guards.

8
Data Types

A program is useful because it models a real-world process. To do this, it manipulates abstract objects that represent real-world objects. The closer the properties of an abstract object mirror those of the corresponding real-world object, the more effective will be the program and the easier it will be to understand.

Early programming languages permitted only numbers as abstract objects; everything had to be represented by numbers. Since early programming was largely computational, the mapping between real and abstract was generally simple, though by no means perfect. With improvements in the design of programming languages, more varied and useful kinds of objects have been allowed.

In this chapter we discuss the kinds of objects that can be an intrinsic part of languages. We begin by describing Mini-language Type, which can operate on different kinds of objects, that is, data of various types. This mini-language serves as a basis for a discussion of the concept of *type* in programming languages. This discussion is limited to the *primitive types* of a language, that is, the types that are part of the language. In Chapter 12, we take up the issue again, with a discussion of techniques that allow the programmer to specify new data types that closely match the real objects of a given problem.

8.1 Mini-language Type

The context-free syntax of Mini-language Type is given in Table 8.1. Note here that the symbol ƀ represents the single blank character.

Table 8.1 **Mini-language Type**

program	::=	`program`
		    declaration. . .
		`begin`
		    statement. . .
		`end ;`

declaration	::=	identifier [, identifier]. . . : type ;
type	::=	simple-type | array-type | record-type
simple-type	::=	`integer` | `string` | `boolean`
array-type	::=	`array [` bounds `]` of type

record-type	::=	`record`
		    identifier : type ;
		[identifier : type ;]. . .
		`end record`

bounds	::=	integer .. integer
statement	::= |	assignment-statement | if-statement input-statement | output-statement
assignment-statement	::=	variable := expression ;

if-statement	::=	`if (` expression `) then`
		    statement. . .
		[`else`
		    statement. . .]
		`end if ;`

As usual, a program in Mini-language Type consists of a sequence of declarations followed by a sequence of statements. The declarations specify the type of value that can be associated with each identifier. The statements define the operations to be performed on values associated with declared variables.

Simple and Composite Types

A declaration specifies that a given list of identifiers can refer only to objects of the given type. The types in Mini-language Type are either simple or composite. The simple types include the integers (for example, 10 and 1776), strings of characters (for example, 'ABC' and '123'), and the bool-

Table 8.1 **continued**

input-statement	::=	input variable [, variable]. . . ;
		output variable [, variable]. . . ;
	::=	
expression	::=	[operand operator] operand
operand	::=	variable | integer | string
	|	boolean | (expression)
variable	::=	identifier | variable . identifier
	|	variable [expression]
string	::=	' character. . . '
boolean	::=	true | false
operator	::=	< | = | ≠ | > | + | - | * | div
	|	cat | and | or
character	::=	letter | digit | special- character
special-character	::=	ƀ | + | - | * | / | : | ; | _
	|	. | , | $ | % | < | = | ≠ | >

ean values true and false. Note that the integer 123, denoting the numeric value one hundred and twenty-three, is different from the string '123', denoting the three characters for the digits representing one, two, and three.

The composite types in Mini-language Type are arrays of a given simple type and record structures. For example, an array TABLE with ten integers is declared as

```
TABLE: array [1..10] of integer;
```

and a record structure COMPLEX_NUM representing a complex number is declared as

```
COMPLEX_NUM: record
                REAL_PART: integer;
                IMAG_PART: integer;
             end record;
```

All identifiers referenced in the program must be declared exactly once. A reference to a variable is either:

- An identifier whose declared type is simple.

- An identifier declared to be an array followed by a bracketed expression; in which case, it denotes some array component whose type is specified in the declaration for the identifier. This is a *subscripted reference.*

- An identifier, possibly subscripted, declared to be a record followed by a dot and an identifier, which must be the name of some component of the record associated with the first identifier. This is a *qualified reference.*

A reference to a variable must always have sufficient subscripts and qualifications so that the reference is to a simple integer, string, or boolean value.

For example, using the declaration of TABLE above, the variable TABLE[3] is of type integer and denotes the third element of the array TABLE. Similarly, using the declaration of COMPLEX_NUM above, COMPLEX_NUM.REAL_PART is of type integer and denotes a component of the record structure named COMPLEX_NUM.

Notice that if TABLE were declared to be an array of strings, then TABLE[3] would be of type string and the statement

```
TABLE[3] := 'XXXX';
```

would assign the string XXXX to the third element of TABLE.

Statements

There are four varieties of statement in Mini-language Type, each of the usual form:

1. An assignment statement. Both the variable and the expression must be of the same simple type.
2. An if statement. The conditional expression must be of boolean type.
3. An input statement.
4. An output statement.

Variables may be combined by operators in an expression to form new values. The operators +, -, *, and div are defined over integers to yield their conventional result.

The relational operators < and > are defined over integers and give a result of type boolean. The equality operators = and ≠ are defined over any two objects of the same simple type and also yield a result of type boolean.

The operators and and or are defined over two boolean values and perform the boolean "and" and "or" operations on the two values. The operator cat is defined over two string values and yields the string consisting of the concatenation of the two values.

For example, consider the declarations:

```
X, Y, I, J: integer;

ITEM_FOUND, NO_MORE_ITEMS: boolean;
TEXT: string;

TABLE: array[1..10] of integer;
ITEM:  array[1..10] of string;

COMPLEX_NUM: record
                REAL_PART: integer;
                IMAG_PART: integer;
             end record;
```

The following expressions are legal:

Expressions of type integer:

```
223
(X+2)
(X div 10)
(2 * (X - Y))
TABLE[I]
COMPLEX_NUM.REAL_PART
```

Expressions of type string:

```
'UUW'
TEXT cat 'ABC'
ITEM[I] cat ('A' cat ITEM[J])
```

Expressions of type boolean:

```
true
(ITEM[I] = 'A')
TABLE[I] = COMPLEX_NUM.REAL_PART
ITEM_FOUND
ITEM_FOUND or NO_MORE_ITEMS
```

Here we see a number of expressions whose values are integer, string, or boolean.

Note: For simplicity, no precedence rules specifying the order of operations are given for Mini-language Type, as all expressions with more than one operator must be parenthesized.

Examples

The following program is illegal:

```
program
    A: integer;
begin
    A := 'XYZ';   -- A is not of type string
end;
```

This example shows a fundamental property of most languages with several types. Once a variable is declared to have a certain type, in this case integer, the type cannot be changed during execution. It is thus illegal to assign values of another type (for example, string) to it.

The next program is also illegal:

```
program
    A, B: integer;
begin
    A := 0;
    B := (3 or A);   -- or is an illegal operation for integers
end;
```

The error here is the attempt to use an operation that is only applicable to boolean values and applying it to two integer values.

The next example can give an error during execution:

```
program
    A: integer;
begin
    input A;   -- input value might not be an integer
    A := A + 1;
    output A;
end;
```

If a variable is declared to be of a certain type and thus can take on only values within that type, an attempt to input a value of a different type will result in an error during execution. In particular, if the input statement attempts to read a string or a boolean value, an execution error occurs.

Finally, the following shows a program that adds two complex numbers:

```
program
    I, J, RESULT: record
                    REAL_PART: integer;
                    IMAG_PART: integer;
                    end record;

begin
    input I.REAL_PART, I.IMAG_PART;
    input J.REAL_PART, J.IMAG_PART;

    RESULT.REAL_PART := I.REAL_PART + J..REAL_PART;
    RESULT.IMAG_PART := I.IMAG_PART + J.IMAG_PART;

    output RESULT.REAL_PART, RESULT.IMAG_PART;
end;
```

This illustrates the use of record variables.

8.2 The Meaning of Type

A view of programming is shown in Figure 8.1. The problem to be solved by the computer is presented as a real-world algorithm that manipulates real-world objects. For example, the algorithm takes objects, such as names, hours worked, and salaries, and produces a payroll.

Programming consists of describing a computer model of the real-world algorithm through a programming language. To model the algorithm, the programmer must choose a representation of the objects in the problem from the possibilities afforded by the programming language.

The choice of representation can have a great effect on the clarity and correctness of the computer algorithm. Thus, for example, a floating point number would not be a suitable representation of a telephone number, since there are likely to be inaccuracies introduced in converting it to and from the real-world form. Since the number is used only for identification, we never perform arithmetic operations on it. It would make no sense to talk about the average telephone number of one's friends. A character string representation would be better in this case.

With each set of objects of a particular type that can be manipulated in a programming language, there is a corresponding set of operations that can be performed on objects. In Mini-language Type, addition, subtraction, multiplication, division, and the four comparison operations can be performed on integer objects. However, concatenation and tests of equality and inequality are the only valid operations for string objects.

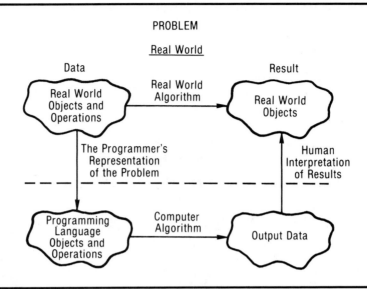

PROBLEM

Real World

Figure 8.1 **Model of a Typical Programming Task**

A consequence of a particular choice of representation of a real-world object is the set of operations that can be performed on the object in the model. Each operation permitted by the language should have a corresponding meaning in the real-world. For example, if dates were represented by integers, it would mean that all the operations that are available for integers could be performed on the modeled dates. While two dates may be subtracted to give a time interval, there is no analogue of the addition, multiplication, or division of dates in the real-world.

This view of programming leads to a definition of types:

A type is a collection of objects and a set of operations that can be validly performed on the objects.

For example, the type dollars may be viewed as a collection of quantities, $1, $2, etc., along with certain operations. For example, it is meaningful to "add" or "subtract" two dollar amounts to yield another dollar amount. It is also meaningful to "multiply" a dollar amount by an integer or a percentage to yield another dollar amount.

Generally, sophisticated types such as dollars and percentages are not included directly within a programming language. Rather, most programming languages, like Mini-language Type, provide a few basic types that the programmer must use to define meaningful computations on a class of real-world objects. Languages that allow the programmer to define data types that are a close match to the problem objects will be discussed in Chapter 12.

8.3 Primitive Types

In this section we discuss several kinds of primitive types: boolean types, integer types, and other numeric types.

Boolean Types

Perhaps the simplest of all types found in programming is the boolean type. This type contains only two values, true and false. Operations on values of this type vary from language to language, as do the operations for almost every type. Typical operators include:

not: a unary operator for negating a boolean value.

or: a binary operator for computing the logical "or" of two boolean values.

and: a binary operator for computing the logical "and" of two boolean values.

In general, the evaluation of an expression of the form

operand operator operand

involves the evaluation of both operands before the complete expression can be evaluated. The properties of the *and* and *or* operators make it sometimes possible to evaluate the complete expression without evaluating the second operand. For the *or* operation, if the value of the first operand is true, then the value of the complete expression will be true, regardless of the value of the second operand. Similarly, for the *and* operation, if the value of the first operand is false, then, whatever the value of the second operand, the value of the complete expression will be false.

We could define two new boolean operators cand and cor for Minilanguage Type that would take advantage of these properties of *and* and *or.* The cand operator would be the same as the and operator except that if the value of the first operand were false then the value of the expression would be false, irrespective of the value of the second operand. That is, the cand operator would give the value false even if evaluating the second operand would lead to an error. Consider, for example, the assignment

```
BOOLEAN_VAR := (Y ≠ 0) and ((X div Y) < 3);
```

According to the definition of and, both operands must be evaluated before the value of the complete expression can be obtained. Hence, a program containing this statement would be in error because, if the value of Y were 0, then evaluating the expression X div Y would involve division by zero. On the other hand, the assignment

```
BOOLEAN_VAR := (Y ≠ 0) cand ((X div Y) < 3);
```

would avoid this problem. A similar definition applies to the cor operator. Operators of this type are known as *short circuit* operators and are included in certain languages.

Additional operators are usually provided for mapping nonboolean values into true or false. The most common, of course, is the equality operator. This operator maps two values, for example, two integers or two arrays, into true if the values are equal, and into false otherwise.

Some languages do not have boolean values in the pure sense. For example, in PL/I the bit string '0'B is treated as false and '1'B is treated as true. Cobol allows only indirect use of boolean values. Instead, it permits conditional expressions, for example

```
IF (X = Y) THEN . . .
```

but does not permit boolean valued variables or functions that return boolean values.

Character and String Types

The manipulation of characters is fundamental to many programming problems, since communication with users is generally via sequences of characters. The real requirement is not to handle characters by themselves but to manipulate sequences of several characters. These sequences are usually known as *strings*.

There are two kinds of operations that can be performed on strings:

1. Those that treat strings in their entirety: comparison, assignment, and building longer strings through concatenation.
2. Those that require the decomposition of strings into substrings.

This differentiation is reflected by the two, essentially opposing, approaches used to provide string manipulation in languages.

String as the Primitive Type

Access to constituent substrings is provided by means of special operations and functions. Typical of these operations is the substring function of PL/I. This function has the form

```
SUBSTR(s, n, m)
```

where ᔆ is a string value (variable or constant), and ᴨ and ᴍ are integer values denoting respectively the starting position of the substring and its length. Thus, the value of

```
SUBSTR('ABCDEFG', 3, 2)
```

is the substring CD. In addition, an operation, generally concatenation, is provided for building a string out of substrings. This is the approach that we have taken in Mini-language Type. For simplicity, no substring operation has been supplied.

A Single Character as the Primitive Type

A string is treated as an array of characters. This approach has been taken in Pascal and Ada. We will return to this method in Section 8.4 when arrays are discussed.

The approach taken by Mini-language Type has been to say that all variables declared to be of type string can take string values of any length. To implement this kind of string satisfactorily requires a complex dynamic storage management capability, which may explain why such facilities are comparatively rare in languages. We discuss the storage management problems in Section 11.3. The simple alternative to the variable length method is to require that all string variables be declared with a length. When a string value is assigned to a string variable, the value will be padded on the right with blanks if it is too short or truncated if it is too long.

In addition to the fixed-length string approach, PL/I also offers a halfway position between that and the implementation problems of completely variable length. The declaration

```
DECLARE STR CHARACTER(20) VARYING;
```

specifies that STR can be assigned string values up to a maximum length of 20 characters. Above that length, the values are truncated as is done for fixed-length strings. A similar approach is taken in some implementations of Basic.

Numeric Types

Numerical calculations have always had an important role in the use of computers. All programming languages manipulate numeric data. Even in languages designed for nonnumeric work, Snobol for example, there is a need for numbers to act as counters, field widths, and control values in computation.

An important difference between the numeric values in programming languages and those in mathematics is that the computer values all have finite representations. Thus, they are frequently approximations to their real-world equivalents. There is no way that a completely accurate value of π can be represented in a computer. The need to represent objects with a wide range of number values, even if the representations were approximate, resulted in the floating point form.

Numeric types generally fall into one of three classes:

1. **Integer:** used for exact arithmetic on whole numbers within a fixed range.

2. **Fixed point:** used for noninteger values with a fixed number of digits before and after the radix point.

3. **Floating point:** used for noninteger values with a fixed number of significant digits and a widely varying magnitude.

Lexical Issues

The written form of numeric values is largely determined by conventional usage. To aid readability, some languages allow a break character to divide lengthy sequences of digits. For example, the denotations

```
1000000    --PL/I, Mini-language Type
1 000 000 -- Algol 60, Fortran
1_000_000 -- Ada
```

are different ways of writing the same integer.

The written representation of fixed point numbers is generally of the form:

digit-sequence . digit-sequence

For clarity, neither digit sequence should be null and the radix point should always be required.

The written form of floating point values has an essential difference from integer and fixed point values because of the need for an exponent. Frequently, the beginning of the exponent part is marked with the letter E, for example:

```
3.14259E0
10E+2
```

With the above syntax rules, it is possible to determine the type of all written numeric values. In languages where there are no implicit type conversions, it is possible to enforce the rule that only constants of the appropriate type can be used in assignments and expressions. This discipline has the important advantage that different types of arithmetic are distinguished; the exact computations are separated from the approximate.

Integer Types

In programming languages, the integer type has a finite set of values, the largest of which is determined either by an implementation or by the language definition. Integers are by far the most common of the numeric types. Since integers can be represented exactly on all digital computers, the usual operations of addition, subtraction, and multiplication can be provided without surprising results, even if the actual machine representation is in a base other than the conventional decimal. Should the result of these operations be outside the finite range of permitted values, an execution error will result.

In many languages, the integer type also includes the operators:

div for integer division,
mod for the remainder after integer division.

For example,

```
5 div 3   =   1
5 mod 3   =   2
```

In addition, relational operators like < and = are usually defined over integers and yield a boolean result.

Fixed Point Types

Values of a fixed point type are similar to integers in that they are uniformly spaced over a range. Two quantities are required to specify this range:

Precision: the total number of digits used for representing the value.

Scale: the number of digits in the fractional part of the value.

Thus the number 123.4567 has a precision of 7 and a scale of 4. This definition is equally applicable to numbers represented in bases other than the conventional decimal; for example, the fixed point binary number 11011.11101101 has a precision of 13 and a scale of 8.

Languages that provide a fixed point type generally allow the user to declare variables with different precisions and scales. Because these two quantities must be taken into account, the operations on fixed point values are more complex than the corresponding operations on integer values.

The concept of fixed point assignment is reasonably simple to define. The value must be copied into the target location so that its radix point is in the correct place. We align decimal quantities in this way when we write them down on paper. Fixed point variables, however, have the added problem that their precision and scale are fixed. The language must define what is to happen when the precision and scale of the assigned value do not match those of the target variable.

If the value has more fraction digits than the target, then the value must be truncated to fit, either with or without rounding. If the value has more digits before the point than the target, the situation is more serious. A radical decision is to disallow any assignments that might lead to this situation. While this restriction can be detected during compilation, it is probably too severe for most users. The alternative is to define such assignments to be execution errors. This requires special checking during execution, which may be thought to be too expensive. However, to ignore such cases is likely to lead to unreliable programs.

The operations of addition, subtraction, and multiplication present further complications. In each of these, there is the possibility that the precision of the result will exceed that of either operand. For example, if X is a fixed point variable with precision 5, scale 3, and value 12.345, then the value of the expression X*X is 152.399025. This has a precision of 9 and a scale of 6.

In an actual implementation, there will be an upper bound to the precision of a fixed point number. There is a problem similar to the one with assignment just described. Again, the radical solution of forbidding any expressions whose result might exceed this bound on the precision is too restrictive. We must expect that the result of some expressions will exceed the bound and that possible truncation may occur. It is the task of the language designer to find the most useful method for controlling this loss of information, for example, by causing the program to terminate abnormally. Other possibilities are discussed in Chapter 15.

The amount of truncation must be calculated during compilation. Otherwise we would be duplicating the effect of floating point arithmetic. There are two main approaches, truncation at the right end and truncation at the left end. Truncation at the right, while avoiding the loss of significant digits, involves a loss of accuracy in all results. This abandons the accuracy of fixed point computation without gaining the flexibility of floating point. Truncation at the left end preserves accuracy, but brings the same problem that exists in assignment of detecting loss of significant digits during execution.

The operation of division is still more complicated because of the potential requirement for infinite precision to represent the quotient. A discussion of this is beyond the scope of this book. A more complete discussion of fixed point arithmetic is to be found in [Nicholls 1975].

Floating Point Types

A floating point value has two parts, a *fraction* and an *exponent*. The fractional part is sometimes called the *mantissa*. It represents the significant digits of the value. The exponent is a scaling factor to be applied to the fraction to obtain the proper value.

From the programmer's point of view, the major characteristics of floating point values are:

- There is only a finite set of values.
- They may not contain the set of integers as a subset.
- They are not uniformly distributed.

In some languages, for example, Fortran, Pascal, and Ada, the floating point type is referred to as a *real* type. As can be seen from these properties, this is probably an unfortunate choice of name since the behavior of the floating point type is considerably different from the real numbers of mathematics. For example, because of limited precision, floating point numbers cannot represent a number such as π or the base of natural logarithms, e. Many implementations use internal representations with a non-decimal base. A consequence of this and the limited precision is that some common decimal fractions cannot be completely represented. Repeated conversions between internal floating point forms and external base-ten form may lead to considerable inaccuracies. An interesting discussion of this is to be found in [Matula 1968].

The fact that some sets of floating point values does not contain the integers as a subset leads to many anomalies in floating point arithmetic. These contribute to the complexity and inaccuracy of floating point computations. Most programmers do not care about the minute details of how their computer performs floating point arithmetic. It is only when they ensure by a test that x is not equal to y before dividing by $(x - y)$ and they still get a divide-by-zero error that they begin to wonder. Most programming languages do not define the details of floating point computation. This is because language designers are disinclined to specify machine capabilities that are not available on all machines. Thus, languages generally reflect the least common denominator of available features.

There have been proposals that aim at standardizing floating point operations. One of these, [Brown 1981], maintains that a computer's floating point arithmetic may be defined by a few environmental parameters which allow the arithmetic to be specified in a machine-independent manner. A counterproposal in [IEEE 1981] requires the special representation of the values that are obtained from invalid operations, for example, those that lead to overflow or division by zero. These special values, known as "NaN's" (Not a Number), are analogous to the undefined value $\perp$ discussed in Section 4.3. Values of this type will be further discussed in Chapter 12. A full discussion of floating point arithmetic is beyond the scope of this book; for further information, see [Knuth 1969].

Operations

One feature that is common to the three numeric types is the set of arithmetic operators. Although these operators are written with the same symbol for each type, they specify somewhat different actions. For example, fixed point addition maintains the position of the radix point, whereas floating point addition adjusts its position to accommodate a range of values.

The use of a single symbol to denote an operation whose meaning is determined by the operand types is called *overloading* or polymorphism. Probably the two most common overloaded operations are the relations = and ≠, which generally apply to all types.

As well as denoting addition of arithmetic operands, the symbol + is sometimes used to denote concatenation of string operands. The + operator is then an overloaded operator whose meaning changes considerably as its operand types change.

Conversions

In our everyday pencil and paper calculations, we treat all numeric data as being of a single type, numbers. We do not think whether they are integers, rationals, or irrationals. In programming, things are not so simple; there are different numeric types with separate representations.

In Mini-language Type, there is only one numeric type, integer, so the problem of assigning one type of numeric value to a variable of another does not arise. In most languages, this problem exists and these assignments are usually allowed. The same numeric value may have different representations in separate numeric types. The mappings between these representations are generally called *conversions*. Algol 68 and Pascal use the term *coercion*. Conversions from integer to fixed point, from fixed point to floating point, and from floating point to complex can generally be done without loss of information. A coercion of this sort is called a *widening*.

As the number of numeric data types in a language increases, so does the number of possible conversions. Some languages, for example, Pascal and Algol 68, insist that almost all conversions be done through the explicit use of a function. For example, to convert a real value to an integer in Algol 68, the function *entier* is used. At the other end of the scale, PL/I has the deliberate policy of defining all mappings between data types whenever they have a reasonable meaning. These implicit conversions can lead to programming errors that are accepted by the compiler as a reasonable conversion. The advantage of the Pascal and Algol 68 kind of approach is that the programmer is made aware of almost all conversions. We support this view.

8.4 Array Types

A fundamental property of the values belonging to the simple types is that they are indivisible without special action, for example, the use of a *substring* function. The modeling of objects, such as a deck of cards, a birth certificate, or a bank account, brings up the general issue of *composite* types. Objects of a composite type are not indivisible, but have components bearing some relation to each other.

Every programming language offers one or more built-in composite types. Among others, Fortran has arrays, Cobol has record structures, Pascal has sets, Lisp has lists, and APL has vectors.

The composite types in a language are critical to the ease with which real-world objects can be represented. For example, representing a bank account is quite easy in Cobol and representing a network is quite easy in Lisp, but not necessarily vice versa. In this section we discuss an elementary composite type, the array, where all the components are of the same type. In the next section, we discuss a different composite type, the record. The components of records can be of differing types.

The array is perhaps the most familiar composite type in programming. An array is basically a mapping from a range of contiguous integers to a set of elements. These integer values are called the *index* or *subscript* values.

In its simplest form, an array is a representation of a table. For example, consider a table that represents the number of people waiting in line at each of five counters. In Mini-language Type this array might be declared by:

```
QUEUE_LENGTH: array [1..5] of integer;
```

An important property of an array is that the value of any one of its elements can be changed without affecting the value of any of the other elements.

The range of index values of an array defines the number of elements of the array; this is the *size* of the array. In most programming languages the range of index values must be specified by the programmer.

The point at which the size of an array must be known is a subject of considerable difference in programming languages. For example, consider the following cases:

```
A: array [1..5] of integer;
```

Here the size of the array is defined at the time the declaration is written:

```
N: integer constant = 5;
A: array [1..N] of integer;
```

Here the size of the array is defined at the time the declaration of the constant N and the array declaration are written.

Next, consider

```
procedure F (N: integer):
   A: array [1..N] of integer;
```

In this procedure fragment, N is a parameter whose value is established when the procedure is invoked. Thus, the size of the array is only determined at execution time and can vary from one invocation to another. Such an array is called a *dynamic array.*

Finally, consider:

```
type VECTOR is array (INTEGER range <>) of FLOAT;
type VECTOR_REF is access VECTOR
A: VECTOR_REF;

A := new VECTOR(1..100);
```

In this fragment of Ada, the array A has an access type, which means that its value is allocated at run time. This value does not exist until the *new* operation is executed. In the declaration of A, the number of elements is specified as being determined by an initially unspecified integer range. This range is given at the time the storage for the array is obtained by executing the new operation. In this example, the array will have 100 elements.

Generally, once the size of an array has been established, it does not change during its existence. Algol 68, however, allows the size of arrays declared with flexible bounds to be changed by assignment. APL takes this generality a step further. Any variable may have an array as its value. This value may be changed just by assigning a different array to the variable, and the bounds may be changed with this assignment. Assigning to a subscript works rather differently. It means that the current array value of the variable is to be retained rather than destroyed by the assignment and that only specified elements of the array are to be modified.

Usually, languages permit arrays to have more than one index. For example, in an extension to Mini-language Type, one might write the declaration

```
B: array [1..5, 1..10] of integer;
```

Such an array can be thought of as a rectangular arrangement of elements with five rows and ten columns. Usually, each of the sets of bounds is referred to as a *dimension.* The array B has two dimensions. An array of one dimension is often called a *vector.*

An important abstraction provided by an array is that the programmer does not need to take account of the actual order in which the elements are stored. For an array with one dimension, there is only one reasonable way possible. For an array with two dimensions, there are two reasonable possibilities. Either the successive elements of a row are stored in adjacent memory locations—row major order—or the successive elements of a column are stored in adjacent memory locations; this is column major order. These orderings apply analogously to arrays with more than two dimensions. The choice between the two methods of storing is an implementation decision that does not affect the order of subscripts and only very rarely concerns the programmer.

Conceptually, the elements of an array may be of any type, including simple types and other composite types, including arrays. In practice, most languages place restrictions on the types of elements, often restricting the elements to simple types.

The basic operation on an array is element selection, that is, a reference to the value of an element in the array. This operation is usually denoted by giving a bracketed expression following the array name. For example, for the array A, a reference to an element is denoted by

```
A(3)
A(I)
A(I + 1)
```

in Ada, Fortran, and PL/I, but by

```
A[3]
A[I]
A[I + 1]
```

in Mini-language Type, Pascal, and Algol.

Sometimes it is convenient to be able to reference a subpart of an array as a single entity. In Algol 68 it is possible to treat the three elements of A with subscripts 2, 3, and 4 as an array by the reference A[2;4]. This is called a *trimmed* reference. A similar concept is found in the Ada *slice*. If B is a one-dimensional array, then the reference B(2..8) references elements 2 through 8.

Assignment to array elements is allowed in every language with array types. In some languages the assignment operation is also allowed on complete arrays. For example, if A and B are 10-element arrays of integers, then

```
A := B;
```

copies the values in B to A. This raises the issue of arrays of constant values, a feature that is present in few languages. For example, one might allow the initialization of A to be specified as

```
A := (1..10 => 0);
```

as is done in Ada. Most languages, however, allow assignment only on an element-by-element basis, as in Mini-language Type.

A Note on Strings

As mentioned in Section 8.3, an alternative to the primitive type string is the use of arrays of elements of the primitive type character. The rationale behind this view is that the basic unit is really the character, and the composite type array properly reflects the construction of the string. However, to provide the proper access to substrings and variable length strings, we need a mechanism like trimmed references and flexible bounds as in Algol 68. This poses considerable implementation problems. Conceptually, we believe that representing strings as arrays is unwieldy, and that strings deserve to be a type in their own right.

8.5 Record Types

A programmer must often deal with objects having a number of different components. For example, a driving license may be viewed as an object having a:

```
Driver: a name consisting of a
         First name:     a string of letters
         Middle initial: a single letter
         Last name:      a string of letters

License number:   eight digits

Expiration date: a calendar date consisting of a
         Month: a number from 1 to 12
         Day:   a number from 1 to 31
         Year:  a four digit number

Driving code: a character
```

The type used for collections of related objects is often called a *record*. Basically, a record type contains a collection of components, each of which may be of a different type. Each component has a name and a value.

For example, a record of type LICENSE can be declared in Mini-language Type by:

```
LICENSE: record
   DRIVER: record
      FIRST_NAME     : string;
      MIDDLE_INITIAL: string;
      LAST_NAME      : string;
   end record;
   LICENSE_NUM: string;
   EXPIRATION_DATE: record
      MONTH:  integer;
      DAY:    integer;
      YEAR:   integer;
   end record;
   DRIVING_CODE: string;
end record;
```

Notice, for example, that though the original description of the license specifies the license number as a number, it is really a sequence of digits. It does not make sense to multiply a license number by five. Similarly, the month, day, and year of expiration are not really integers, although it is convenient to perform limited numerical calculations, for example, computing when to send out the renewal notice two months before expiration.

The basic operation on record types is component selection. For example, to refer to the driving code component, we write

```
LICENSE.DRIVING_CODE
```

This is the method used in Ada, PL/I, Pascal, and Euclid. Algol 68 and Cobol take a different point of view, by writing:

```
DRIVING CODE of LICENSE    -- Algol 68
DRIVING-CODE in LICENSE    -- Cobol
```

This approach seems to focus more attention on the component, while the Ada, PL/I, Pascal, and Euclid view attaches more importance to the record as a whole.

The value of the reference LICENSE.DRIVER is also a record, so that it is possible to write:

```
LICENSE.DRIVER.LAST_NAME
```

A reference to the component of a record behaves just as a reference to the component of an array. For example, we may have:

```
LICENSE.LICENSE_NUM         := '022325795';
LICENSE.EXPIRATION_DATE.YEAR := LICENSE.EXPIRATION_DATE.YEAR + 4;
```

The basic difference between the method of selecting components in arrays and records is that, in arrays, the component can be calculated by means of a subscript expression evaluated at the time of reference. With a record, the component must be selected at the time the program is written; the choice cannot be changed during execution.

In practice, record types may have several components that are themselves records, and references to these components are common. As a result, references to records may become long and tedious. Consider the simple problem of assigning the following values to the components of the name of a DRIVER:

```
LICENSE.DRIVER.FIRST_NAME     := 'HENRY';
LICENSE.DRIVER.MIDDLE_INITIAL := 'F';
LICENSE.DRIVER.LAST_NAME      := 'LEDGARD';
```

There are several solutions to this problem. One solution, similar to PL/I and Cobol, allows omission of component names as long as the shortened reference can be uniquely identified. For example, if there were no other records in the program with the component names FIRST_NAME, MIDDLE_INITIAL, or LAST_NAME, the above sequence could be written as:

```
FIRST_NAME     := 'HENRY';
MIDDLE_INITIAL := 'F';
LAST_NAME      := 'LEDGARD';
```

This solution has one severe disadvantage in that to understand which record variable is being referenced requires knowledge of the declarations for all record variables. It also tends to produce awkward naming conventions in the attempt to keep component names distinct from each other.

Another solution, offered by Pascal, is the inclusion of a statement specifying a local context for a statement sequence. For example, the above sequence may be written as:

```
with LICENSE.DRIVER do
   begin
   FIRST_NAME     := 'HENRY';
   MIDDLE_INITIAL := 'F';
   LAST_NAME      := 'LEDGARD';
   end;
```

Here, the with clause provides the top-level qualifier over the part of the program contained between the begin and end. The Pascal solution has a disadvantage when other variables are included in the body of the with statement, in that it is not always clear to the reader which references need qualification.

Still another solution, offered by Cobol, Euclid, and Ada, allows the programmers to declare a name as a shorthand reference to record components. For example, we may declare something such as:

```
ME: renames LICENSE.DRIVER;
```

and then have:

```
ME.FIRST_NAME     := 'HENRY';
ME.MIDDLE_INITIAL := 'F';
ME.LAST_NAME      := 'LEDGARD';
```

This convention avoids the disadvantages of the other two solutions but still requires all record variables to be qualified by a prefix. However, if the prefix is chosen carefully, this will add to the clarity of the program.

Variant Records

As mentioned earlier, there are cases where the information within a record may be missing or where additional information may be required when another record component has certain values. In our license example, a driver may not have a middle initial, and the driving code may indicate a special or a restricted permit requiring other information. This kind of structure is generally handled with a record *variant.*

A record type with a variant part must have a special component called a *tag* and a selection mechanism giving the various substructures for possible values of the tag. For the selection mechanism denoting the variant, we shall use a case-like notation, similar to that for case statements. This method is borrowed from Ada.

To represent our license example in full, we can write the declaration of Example 8.1. Here, the component DRIVING_CODE is used as a tag, and the following case structure defines the record variant. When the value of the tag is S, the information for a special vehicle type is included; when its value is R, the information for a restricted permit is included; when the tag HAS_MIDDLE_INITIAL has a false value, the variant is explicitly stated as being null or empty.

Selecting a component of a variant record is just the same as for an ordinary record. Thus, provided that the value of the tag field DRIVING_CODE is 'S', we may reference LICENSE.PASSENGER_PERMIT. However, it would be an error to reference LICENSE.DAYLIGHT_ONLY. This field does not exist when the value of the tag field is 'S'. It only exists when the tag's value is 'R'. If an assignment is made to the tag field to change its value, the components of the old variant are destroyed and the components of the new variant are created.

Each variant of a record type can take a separate set of values. Thus, the complete record type with all its variants can take the union of these sets of values. It is common to refer to such record types as *unions* and to refer to those that contain a tag field to distinguish between the variants as *discriminated unions*. Those unions where the language does not insist on the tag field are known as *free unions*.

Algol 68 provides an example of unions. To take a simple case, a variable could be declared to be a union of integer and boolean values. The value of such a variable is either of type integer or type boolean, depending on which type of value was last assigned to the variable. The tag is automatically maintained by the system in a hidden field that is not directly accessible by the programmer. The language requires that, each time the value of the union variable is used, the programmer must provide explicit checks to determine if the current value is of the correct type. This underlines the fact that the checks that a reference is in accordance with the current value of the tag field must be made dynamically.

Variant records, while useful, raise some difficulties with reliability and implementation. First, there is the question of assignment to the tag field. The value of the tag is set when the record object is created. While the program must be able to assign values with an ordinary statement to components of the record, assignment of a new value to the tag is a very different question. To change the tag really implies a change in the structure of the record. From the implementation view, this could imply a change in the amount of storage required for the record. Ada specifically forbids the assignment to tags unless the complete record is being assigned to. This ensures that the fields of the record all remain consistent when the variant changes. However, dynamic checks are still required whenever a reference is made, and it seems likely that most systems will omit these checks in the name of efficiency. Pascal allows the tag field to be changed to provide an escape from type checking if the programmer wishes it for some special purpose.

Another serious problem is the design of a readable syntax. It is not obvious from the above syntax that DRIVER has potentially four components, and nested record types with variants make the problem even more acute.

Record Mapping

Once the programmer has defined a record, the layout of the fields in the computer storage must be determined. This is generally done by the compiler. It must be done according to a well-defined set of rules to ensure compatibility between separately compiled parts of a complete program.

```
LICENSE: record
   DRIVER: record
      FIRST_NAME: string;
      LAST_NAME : string;

      HAS_MIDDLE_INITIAL: boolean;   -- tag
      case HAS_MIDDLE_INITIAL of
          when true  => MIDDLE_INITIAL: string;
          when false => null;
      end case;
   end record;

   LICENSE_NUM: string;

   DRIVING_CODE: string;   -- tag
   case DRIVING_CODE of

      when 'S' => record
         VEHICLE_TYPE    : integer;
         PASSENGER_PERMIT: boolean;
         ZONE_CODE       : boolean;
      end record;

      when 'R' => record
         CORRECTIVE_LENSES: boolean;
         DAYLIGHT_ONLY    : boolean;
         AUTO_TRANSMISSION: boolean;
      end record;

      else    => null;
   end case;

   EXPIRATION_DATE: record
      MONTH: integer;
      DAY  : integer;
      YEAR : integer;
   end record;
end record;
```

Example 8.1 **A Record Variant**

Generally, the precise way in which the fields are laid out is of little consequence to the programmer. The actual addresses usually have no meaning in the language. On the other hand, where interlanguage communication is required, as for instance when data generated by a Cobol program is being processed by a PL/I program, then the mapping from declaration to addresses becomes important. Two languages may map their records differently, and appropriate programming will be required for the records produced in one language to be read in the other.

The simplest mapping would be to put each component of a record immediately adjacent to its declared neighbors. This is practical only in a computer where each bit of storage can be addressed individually. On most computers only groups of bits, for example, words or bytes, are accessed directly. Information that does not fall on these particular boundaries requires extra machine instructions, generally masking and shifting, for access. To avoid this, *padding* must be inserted between the end of one field and the beginning of the next. Thus, there is a choice between inefficient programs and inefficient use of storage. PL/I takes account of this by allowing the programmer to specify for each field whether it is to be ALIGNED on a storage boundary to permit efficient access at the cost of extra storage.

In addition to the question of storage use versus execution time, the language itself places two requirements on the storage mapping. First, the mapping of a record component must be independent of its position in the record that contains it. Second, to access a component of a record, the attributes of only those subitems that occur between the beginning of the record and the component being referenced need be known. These are both needed to allow access to parts of a record without having knowledge of the whole record, for example, when a component of a record is passed as an argument to a separately compiled procedure.

A more complete description of the problem of storage mapping, including a discussion of particular algorithms, is contained in [MacLaren 1970].

8.6 Type Checking

The partitioning of objects into types allows each assignment to be checked for a match between source value and target variable. The validity of each operation for its operands can also be verified. If these tests can be made during compilation, *before* execution, then we say that the type checking is *static*. Ada, Fortran, and Algol 68, for example, have static type checking. These three languages allow the type checking to be complete although the type checking may not be done rigorously in all implementations. Such languages are said to be *strongly typed*. Pascal, because it allows the tag field of variant records to be changed, has exceptions to strong typing.

If the type checking can only be done *during* execution, then the type checking is *dynamic.* APL and Smalltalk are examples of dynamically typed languages.

The essential difference between statically and dynamically typed languages is that in a statically typed language, the type is associated by declaration with an identifier. In a dynamically typed language, the type is associated with the value. This is implemented by storing type information with each value. Any type of value can be assigned to a variable. Before any operation is applied to a value, the type of the value is examined to see if it is compatible with the operation. In the case of overloaded operations, the type of the value will determine the precise details of how the operation is to be performed. This will generally mean that the operations will be the work of library subroutines.

Dynamic type checking is usually simple to implement. However, since the checkup is performed during execution, there is a considerable machine time penalty. Furthermore, since type errors can only be found by execution, it is generally impossible to verify that a program contains no type errors. It is often claimed that dynamic typing allows the programmer greater flexibility; however, it is not clear that this gain is sufficient to offset the loss of reliability.

Some languages avoid the idea of type altogether. These are generally the high-level *systems programming* languages. Examples of such languages are Bliss and BCPL. In Bliss, any contiguous set of bits in storage can be named and from the language's point of view, merely contains a pattern of bits. Various operations, such as integer arithmetic, comparison, or boolean operations, may be applied to these bit patterns. The interpretation placed on a particular bit pattern and the consequent transformation performed by the operator is an intrinsic property of the operator and not of its operands.

The argument for type checking is one of security. A language that regards the store as a homogeneous array of words is very error prone. It is only possible to make trivial checks on the use of data. The rationale behind strong type checking, as opposed to dynamic type checking, is that a large number of errors can be detected before the program is run when it is feasible to make extensive checks.

The counterargument is that strong typing removes a lot of the flexibility that programmers find useful, particularly in systems programming. Two examples illustrate this kind of flexibility:

- The need for arrays of heterogeneous elements. For example, in an interpreter, a stack for expression evaluation may have to consist of integer, floating point, and boolean components. Although each element in the stack assumes only one fixed type during its lifetime, the underlying static array element appears to have a varying type. This could be achieved by Algol 68 unions.

- The realization of implicit type conversions. For instance, a floating point variable might need to be treated as a bit string for printing its internal representation during error analysis of numerical computation. PL/I provides a conversion function, UNSPEC, for precisely this purpose.

The arguments between the two views continue with no resolution in sight.

8.7 Where to Look: `Fortran, PL/I`

Fortran

Fortran offers only a restricted set of data types. These are:

- integers
- floating point values—"reals"
- double precision floating point values
- complex values
- boolean data—"logical"
- character strings
- files

The only aggregate data types that are offered are arrays and strings of fixed declared length. In keeping with the language's orientation toward engineering and scientific computation, there is an extensive set of arithmetic operations and mathematical functions together with relational and boolean operations.

PL/I

In contrast, PL/I offers a wide range of data types. These are:

- fixed point numbers with a declared precision and scale factor
- floating point numbers with a declared precision
- complex numbers whose components can be either fixed or floating point numbers
- character strings of either a fixed declared length or of varying length up to a declared maximum

- hybrid character string numeric values that can be treated as either fixed point numbers or character strings
- bit strings of either a fixed declared length or of varying length up to a declared maximum
- locator values—absolute and relative pointers that can be used to reference other values as discussed in Chapter 6
- labels
- entry values that can be used to identify procedures for invocation
- files

Arrays and records provide the kind of data structuring described in this chapter. Variant records are not available. There is a large range of built-in operations and functions available in the language. Automatic conversion between data values of different types is provided in all cases where some meaning can be ascribed to the conversion. Many operations may be applied to entire arrays or records as operands.

Further Reading

In the literature, works solely on the concept of type have been overshadowed by the rather large effort in the area of type definition discussed in Chapter 12. Nevertheless, we mention here a few relevant references.

An early work [Morris 1973] discusses the now prevalent view of a type, which is characterized by a set of objects as well as operations over the objects. A later paper [Brosgol 1977] discusses a number of issues relevant to types.

A paper by [Haberman 1973] presents a critique of the view of types in the programming language Pascal. As is often the case in this text, type issues are also extensively discussed in the rationale for the preliminary version of Ada [Ichbiah et al. 1979].

Exercises

Exercise 8.1 *Programming in Mini-language Type*

On many computer systems, a calendar date is expressed in six-digit form. For example,

```
02 22 43
```

means the month 02, day 22, year 1943, or in more familiar terms we use day to day:

```
FEBRUARY 22, 1943
```

Write a program in Mini-language Type to read in three integer numbers and output the corresponding date in day-to-day notation. If the integers do not represent a valid date, an appropriate message should be printed.

For example, with

```
13 22 43
```

the output should be:

```
NOT A VALID DATE
```

Don't forget about leap year.

You must take note that, in the mini-languages, each printed value is prefixed by the variable name and an equal sign. Thus, your output may be something like:

```
MONTH = FEBRUARY
DAY = 22
YEAR = 1943
```

Exercise 8.2 *Strong Typing*

In Section 8.6 we mentioned that the strong typing in Pascal is not complete because the tag field of a variant record can be changed during execution. Explain how some type checking in Pascal can be defeated in this way. It is said that such loopholes are necessary in certain applications such as systems programming. Discuss this argument.

Exercise 8.3 *Mixed Mode*

Some languages with multiple data types (modes) allow *mixed mode* expressions. In PL/I, for example, an expression may involve operands of many different types that are converted at run time if necessary to compatible modes before the operators are applied. In other languages, operands that are not of the correct mode for an operation must be explicitly converted by using a set of functions provided in the language for that purpose.

For example, if J were an integer, in PL/I one could write the expression

```
(J + '3')
```

while in the other class of languages, one would have to write this as

```
(J + CHAR_TO_INT('3'))
```

where CHAR_TO_INT is a function which performs character string to integer conversion. What are the advantages and disadvantages of each scheme?

Exercise 8.4 *Literals for Arrays*

In some languages it is possible to write values for both composite objects and for simple objects. For example, in Ada, a ten-element array A may be set to zero with the assignment:

```
A := (1..10 => 0);    -- named notation
```

For a five-element array where elements are

```
11, 14, 10, 16, and 11
```

we may write

```
(11, 14, 10, 16, 11)    -- positional notation
```

where the array elements are listed in positioned order, or alternatively,

```
(1 => 11; 2 => 14; 3 => 10; 4 => 16; 5 => 11)    -- named notation
```

where the index values are identified. Discuss the pro's and con's of these two notations.

Exercise 8.5 *Array Access*

Consider a language in which arrays may have many dimensions. The number of dimensions and the bounds on the dimensions are fixed by the declaration and may not be changed dynamically. Suppose a particular array has n dimensions with lower bounds l_1, l_2 through l_n and upper bounds u_1, u_2 through u_n and that the array is stored as a contiguous set of elements. Describe how the location of a particular element of the array can be calculated from its subscripts.

Exercise 8.6 *Array Operations*

Consider an extension to Mini-language Type so that arrays are treated as complete objects. That is to say, they may be used in assignments and as operands of operations. Define the changes to the syntax and semantics of this extended version of Type.

Exercise 8.7 *Sets*

From the programming language point of view, a set is a data aggregate that contains an *unordered* collection of *distinct* values. This is in contrast to a single-dimensioned array, which is a data aggregate that contains an *ordered* collection of values, some of which may be repeated. Describe an extension to Mini-language Type that would include sets. To do this, you will have to decide on the operations on sets that will have to be defined. Typically, these will include a membership test, insertion and deletion of single values, and the standard mathematical set operations.

Exercise 8.8 *String Handling*

In Section 8.3, we described how character strings can either be viewed as a primitive type of the language, as in Mini-language Type, or treated as vectors of the primitive type character. By designing additional syntax and semantics, compare two variants of Mini-language Type demonstrating the two methods of character string representation. The comparison should be based on the operations:

Concatenate two strings to form a new string.

Extract a portion of a string.

Search within a string for a given substring.

Obtain the length of a string.

Delete a substring or replace it by another substring, not necessarily of the same length.

Insert a string within another string at a specified point.

Note: To do this exercise well, you will need to think carefully.

Exercise 8.9 *The Mod Operator*

Find out how the mod operator is defined for negative operands in three different languages and compare their usefulness to the programmer.

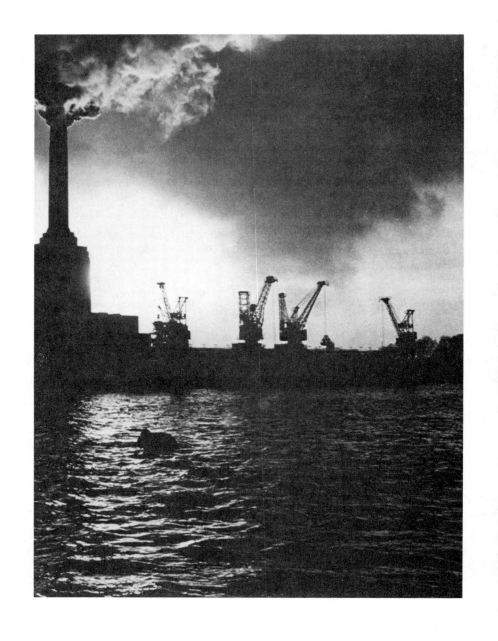

9

Input and Output

Input and output are generally found to be among the least satisfactory aspects of a programming language. This is probably because the clean abstract view of the world presented by a programming language must meet the practical compromises of the real world. In the early days of high-level languages, the compiler generated code that interacted directly with the input-output hardware; as a result, the peculiarities of the hardware were reflected directly in the language.

Currently, many of these rather unpleasant details are screened from the programming language by the operating system. By providing a standard interface between the abstract machine of the language and the abstract machine represented by the operating system, it is possible to achieve a considerable measure of implementation independence.

There seems to be little agreement on standard methods for a programming language to provide facilities for the input and output of data. For example, Fortran uses a format statement approach, Snobol uses a pattern matching operation for input and a special print operation for output, and Modula-2 and Ada use specialized procedures that are not necessarily part of the language for input and output.

The methods mentioned above are used primarily for communication between programs and humans. For example, a user may be entering data from results of tests, or may be reading a report summarizing the test results. A second class of input-output operations takes place when communication is internal to the machine. For example, data may be read from a secondary storage device or may be stored on magnetic tape. This type of transmission is fundamentally different from the first.

Because of the profusion of input-output methods, and the need for standardized, straightforward techniques to specify them, a mini-language devoted exclusively to input-output has been devised. Mini-language Format is based on the familiar format statement in Fortran. This mini-language gives rise to a discussion of methods for human input and output. Finally, we briefly treat methods for machine input and output.

For this mini-language the common definition of input and output statements given for the other mini-languages does not apply.

9.1 Mini-language Format

The syntax of Mini-language Format is given in Table 9.1.

We assume that we have two devices, one for input and one for output. Each of these can be viewed as a device containing an infinitely long piece of paper allowing 60 characters per line and 55 lines per page. For input we shall look at the characters typed, from left to right and line by line. For output, we shall print characters in the same conventional order.

Table 9.1 Mini-language Format

program	::=	`program`
		    variable-declaration. . .
		    format-declaration. . .
		`begin`
		    statement. . .
		`end ;`

variable-declaration	::=	identifier [, identifier]. . . : `integer` ;
format-declaration	::=	identifier : `format` field [, field]. . . ;
field	::=	integer item-specification
item-specification	::=	`B	L	D	C`
statement	::=	assignment-statement | if-statement | loop-statement | input-statement | output-statement
assignment-statement	::=	identifier :`=` expression ;

if-statement	::=	`if` comparison `then`
		    statement. . .
		[`else`
		    statement. . .]
		`end if` ;

The layout of characters on the input or output device is specified through format declarations. Given that the device is positioned at some point on a line, a format declaration specifies the text to follow, on a character by character basis. Actual input-output is initiated with an input or output statement referencing a particular format declaration. During execution of the input-output statement, a correspondence is established between items in the statement and fields in the format declaration.

Consider the following sequence:

```
NEXT_NUM: format 2D;
  . . .
input  N using NEXT_NUM;
output N using NEXT_NUM;
```

When the input statement is executed, a value from the input device is obtained and assigned to the variable N. The value is specified as having the form indicated by 2D. The item specification 2D indicates that the next

Table 9.1 **continued**		
loop-statement	::=	for identifier := expression to expression loop statement. . . end loop ;
input-statement	::=	input [identifier [, identifier]. . .] using identifer ;
output-statement	::=	output [output-item [, output-item]. . .] using identifer ;
output-item	::=	expression | ' character. . . '
expression	::=	[operand arithmetic-operator] operand
comparison	::=	(operand relational-operator operand)
operand	::=	integer | identifier | (expression)
character	::=	letter | digit | special-character
arithmetic-operator	::=	+ | − | * | div
relational-operator	::=	‹ | = | ≠ | ›
special-character	::=	ɓ | + | − | * | / | : | ; | _ | . | , | $ | % | =

two characters are to represent a number having one or two digits. Either, but not both, of the characters may be blank.

Similarly, when the output statement is executed, two characters will be printed on the output device. These characters represent the value of N. If the value of N can be specified with one digit, then the digit is right-justified in the space where the two characters are to be printed.

An input statement generally specifies a list of variables to be input, and the external form of the variables is defined in the named format declaration. Similarly, an output statement usually contains a list of expressions and character strings whose values are to be output, and the printed form of each expression or string is specified in the associated format declaration. The value of an expression in Mini-language Format is always an integer.

For the output of expressions, the integer value is right-justified. For the output of strings, the characters are left-justified. When the value cannot fit within the specified space, an execution error will result.

For example, consider the following output statement and associated format declaration:

```
HEADER: format 25C;
    . . .
output 'HUMAN FACTORS LIMITED' using HEADER;
```

Here a text string HUMAN FACTORS LIMITED is output with a field specification of 25C. The format specification, 25C, indicates that 25 characters are reserved for the output of a string. Since the string is shorter than 25 characters, the string is left-justified within the reserved space. The remainder of the space is filled with blanks.

Aside from the specification of the arrangement of integer and string values, format declarations can also specify the configuration of spaces and empty lines. For example, consider the following statements and associated format declaration:

```
NEXT_LINE: format 1B, 3D, 1B, 3D, 1L;
    . . .
input  A, B using NEXT_LINE;
output A, B using NEXT_LINE;
```

The input statement reads in the values of A and B as follows:

```
1B   -- skip 1 character
3D   -- assign the integer in the next 3 characters to A
1B   -- skip 1 character
3D   -- assign the integer in the next 3 characters to B
1L   -- skip the rest of the line
```

Similarly, the effect of the output statement is:

```
1B   -- print 1 blank
3D   -- print the value of A in the next 3 character positions
1B   -- print 1 blank
3D   -- print the value of B in the next 3 character positions
1L   -- skip to the next line
```

We now summarize the actions to be taken on input and output:

1. For each input or output statement, the named format declaration is examined.

2. If the next field in the format declaration specifies a spacing action, the appropriate spacing action takes place.

3. If the next field specifies a sequence of digits, the corresponding input or output item must be a numeric item, and the input or output of this value takes place.

4. For output statements, if the next field specifies a character string, the corresponding output item must be a character string, and the output action takes place.

5. Input or output terminates when the last field in the format declaration has been processed.

In all cases, the number of items to be input or output must match the number of format fields in the named format declaration.

An input action results in an execution error if a numeric field does not contain an integer. An output action results in an execution error if there is not enough space for an output item. A summary of input and output actions is given in Table 9.2.

Other Features

We now turn to more mundane parts of our mini-language. As in most of our mini-languages, a program consists of a sequence of declarations followed by a sequence of executable statements. All variables used in a program must be declared exactly once, and each format specification named in an input or output statement must also be declared exactly once.

In addition to input and output statements, the executable statements in Mini-language Format include:

- an assignment statement

- an if statement

- a for loop, whereby an enclosed sequence of statements is executed repeatedly

Table 9.2 **Summary of Input-Output Actions**

Let X be the next item on the input or output list, and n be the value of the integer in the corresponding format field.

Format	Action on Input	Action on Output
Spacing		
nB	The next n characters from the input device are skipped, (i.e., treated as blanks).	The next n characters sent to the output device are printed as blanks.
nL	The remaining characters on the current line and the next $(n-1)$ lines from the next $(n-1)$ lines from the input device are skipped.	The remaining characters on the current line and the next $(n-1)$ lines sent to the output device are printed as blanks.
Data		
nD	The next n characters from the input device will be treated as a number and assigned as the value of X. If the next n characters are not a well-formed number, input action is in error. Leading or trailing blanks are allowed; embedded blanks are not.	The digits of the value of X will be printed on the output device. If the value of X can be specified by fewer than n digits, the number will be right-justified with leading zeroes suppressed. If there is not enough space specified for the value of X, the output action is in error.
nC	Not allowed.	The characters of X will be printed on the output device. If X has fewer than n characters, the characters will be left-justified. If X has more than n characters, the output action is in error.

The definition of a for loop specifies a control variable that is to be assigned a sequence of values, starting from the value of one expression and increasing by one at each iteration until the value of a second expression is reached. The control variable in a for loop may not be updated within the loop, and on termination of the loop, the value of the control variable is undefined.

Finally, a few brief notes. Input or output statements need not contain data items, in which case only a spacing action may be specified in the format declaration. The character strings given in an output statement may include letters, digits, blanks, and a number of special characters as defined in Table 9.1.

Examples

In Example 9.1 we see a very simple program in Mini-language Format. Here a single line of text is output, in this case, a sequence of six integer values. The positions of the blanks in the output are shown with the symbol ⊔.

In Example 9.2, if the first line on the input device contains an integer N in its first three characters, and the next N lines contain two (appropriately spaced) columns of integers, then the two columns are printed in reverse order on the output device. Again, the positions of the blanks are shown explicitly.

```
program
    A, B, I: integer;
    TWO_NUMS: format 4D, 4D;
begin
    A := 11;
    B := 22;
    for I := 1 to 3 loop
        output A, B using TWO_NUMS;
    end loop;
end;
```

Output
⊔⊔11⊔⊔22⊔⊔11⊔⊔22⊔⊔11⊔⊔22

Example 9.1 **A Simple Output of a Line of Integers**

```
program
    A, B, NUM_LINES, LINE_COUNT: integer;
    IN_LINE: format 3D, 1L;
    NEXT_LINE: format 2B, 3D, 2B, 3D, 1L;

begin
    input NUM_LINES using IN_LINE;
    for LINE_COUNT := 1 to NUM_LINES loop
        input A, B using NEXT_LINE;
        output B, A using NEXT_LINE;
    end loop;
end;
```

Input

```
3␣␣
␣␣␣␣␣1␣␣␣␣␣2
␣␣␣␣11␣␣␣␣22
␣␣␣111␣␣␣222
```

Output

```
␣␣␣␣␣2␣␣␣␣␣1
␣␣␣␣22␣␣␣␣11
␣␣␣222␣␣␣111
```

Example 9.2 **A Simple Column Reversal Program**

9.2 Varieties of Input-Output Specifications

There appear to be three dominant strategies for handling the formatting of input or output data. These three approaches can be summarized as follows:

1. *Remote format specifications:* Each input or output statement has an associated but separate format declaration. This declaration specifies the layout of data values and the use of spacing in their external representation. A single format declaration can be associated with several input or output statements.

   This method is used in Mini-language Format as well as in Fortran and PL/I.

2. *Picture specifications:* Each piece of data has an associated picture clause describing the form that the character representation of such an item would have on an input or output device. The external character layout of an item is associated with the declaration of the item itself rather than with an actual input or output statement. Thus there is a one-to-one correspondence between data items and their external representation.

This technique is the one used in Cobol and some use of it also appears in PL/I.

3. *Specialized procedures:* The external layout of data values for different kinds of data items is defined through specialized procedures. For example, we may have a procedure to output integers, another procedure to output real numbers, and another procedure to output character strings. There is no analog to the format or picture declaration; the details of spacing and layout are specified entirely by the choice of the procedure invoked and the value of its arguments.

This method is used in Modula-2, Simula 67, and Ada.

Even within these three approaches, there are, of course, considerable differences in language details. Nevertheless, the method for input and output in most programming languages follows one of these three general methods.

In the following discussion, we consider a single problem, the generation of a simple report. Figure 9.1 illustrates a simple price list with two columns of data. The first column indicates the quantity of the item sold, and the second column indicates the price of the corresponding quantity, assuming a fixed unit price. The border, with its marks every five columns and every five lines, is not part of the table but is provided to help the reader account for the spaces. We will compare the generation of this price list, exactly as shown in Figure 9.1 using the three techniques.

Remote Format Specifications

Remote format specifications are based on the idea that the layout of data on an external device can be described separately from the input or output statement initiating the input-output. Typically, such schemes describe not only the form of data but also the configuration of blank spaces and blank lines. To describe the layout, special description characters are introduced and numbers are used to indicate repeated specification characters.

```
                         PRICE LIST
                         ----------



ITEM CODE : 1234
ITEM      : REG. HAND BROOM
UNIT PRICE: $4.36



QUANTITY        PRICE
--------        -----

    1          $ 4.36
    2          $ 8.72
    3          $13.08
    4          $17.44
    5          $21.80

    6          $26.16
    7          $30.52
    8          $34.88
    9          $39.24
   10          $43.60

   11          $47.96
   12          $52.32
   13          $56.68
   14          $61.04
   15          $65.40

   16          $69.76
   17          $74.12
   18          $78.48
   19          $82.84
   20          $87.20
```

Figure 9.1 **A Simple Price List**

For example, in Fortran we can have the format specifications:

I3   —— space for a 3 digit integer, right-justified

2X   —— 2 blank spaces

F6.2   —— space for a 5 digit fixed point number with a decimal
                        —— point 2 digits from the right

A10   —— space for 10 characters

Notice that the letters I (for integers), X (for blanks), F (for fixed point numbers), and A (for characters) indicate the type of the field.

This is the method used in Mini-language Format. Example 9.3 shows a solution to our price list problem using Mini-language Format. A number of comments about this approach are in order.

First, each format statement is associated with a name, which can be referenced by various input and output statements. Thus, unlike Fortran, where format statements can only be referenced by an integer label, it is possible to give some mnemonic significance to a format description.

It is also possible to refer to the same format specification in different input or output statements. In Example 9.3, for instance, the format specification named TITLE_LINE is referenced in two output statements, one giving the title and the other its underline. This kind of reuse of a format specification can enhance both maintenance and readability.

A possible disadvantage of this approach is that the remoteness of the format specifications might cause difficulties in understanding programs with a good deal of input and output. Often, the reader of a program will have to turn to a different section of the program to discover the exact layout of characters. However, the format name serves as an abstraction that points to the details given in the declaration. Thus, it makes the algorithm clearer by leaving it uncluttered with details but, at the same time, showing where the details can be found. An alternative would be to make format declarations into *statements,* which could then be placed near the corresponding input or output statements. This alternative goes away from the format name serving as an abstraction and might, in fact, detract from the readability of the algorithm.

The design of the compiled code for the output of a list of values according to a format list frequently makes use of the idea of *coroutines* (described in section 10.5). This provides a convenient way of stepping through the data item list and the format list in parallel.

One small but interesting problem occurs in Mini-language Format when no data items are printed but some control over blank spacing or blank lines is needed. For example, consider the output statement:

```
output using TRIPLE_SPACE;
```

```
program
   GROUP, UNIT_PRICE, QUANTITY, PRICE, DOLLARS, CENTS: integer;
   LINE_SKIP    : format 1L;
   TRIPLE_SPACE: format 3L;
   TITLE_LINE   : format 24B, 10C, 1L;
   ITEM_INFO    : format 5B, 28C, 1L;
   COL_HEADER   : format 5B, 8C, 6B, 5C, 1L;
   ITEM_LINE_1: format 7B, 2D, 10B, 1C, 2D, 2C, 1D, 1L;
   ITEM_LINE_2: format 7B, 2D, 10B, 1C, 2D, 1C, 2D, 1L;
begin
   output using TRIPLE_SPACE;
   output 'PRICE LIST' using TITLE_LINE;
   output '----------' using TITLE_LINE;

   output using TRIPLE_SPACE;

   output 'ITEM CODE : 1234'              using ITEM_INFO;
   output 'ITEM       : REG. HAND BROOM'  using ITEM_INFO;
   output 'UNIT PRICE: $4.36'             using ITEM_INFO;

   output using TRIPLE_SPACE;

   output 'QUANTITY', 'PRICE' using COL_HEADER;
   output '--------', '-----' using COL_HEADER;

   UNIT_PRICE    := 436;
   for GROUP := 0 to 3 loop
      output using LINE_SKIP;

      for QUANTITY := (GROUP*5) + 1 to (GROUP*5) + 5 loop
         PRICE   := QUANTITY * UNIT_PRICE;
         DOLLARS := PRICE div 100;
         CENTS   := PRICE - (DOLLARS * 100);
         if (CENTS < 10) then
            output QUANTITY, '$', DOLLARS, '.0', CENTS using ITEM_LINE_1;
         else
            output QUANTITY, '$', DOLLARS, '.', CENTS using ITEM_LINE_2;
         end if;
      end loop;
   end loop;

   output using TRIPLE_SPACE;
end;
```

Example 9.3 **Generation of a Price List Using Format Specifications**

This problem can occur in Fortran when READ and WRITE reference format statements appear but have no associated list of statements and expressions. This suggests that the syntax of the input or output statements could be better formulated to avoid the anomaly. For example, we might have adopted a syntax along the lines:

```
output format-identifier [ using output-item-list ];
```

In this case we would have output statements like:

```
output TRIPLE_SPACE;
output TITLE_LINE using 'PRICE LIST';
```

Data Described with Picture Specifications

The central idea behind picture specifications is that the physical layout of the data is described along with other declarative information for the data. For example, in the declaration of an integer variable, one also specifies how the integer variable is to be represented outside the program. Typically, the control of blanks is also associated with data. Thus, the description of data is grouped with corresponding information about leading and trailing spaces.

Picture specifications are best known in Cobol, where input and output is an important application area. In Cobol, the items comprising a unit of printed information are collected into a record-like structure. Each item in the structure is associated with a picture clause describing its external form. Like Mini-language Format, special characters are used to indicate the type of information, and thus a picture clause indirectly defines the type of any variable.

A program along these lines is given in Example 9.4, another solution to our problem of generating a price list. In this program we have altered the syntax of Mini-language Format to present the solution; these changes should cause no problem.

In this example, the basic unit of input or output is assumed to be a *line*. Each line is broken into fields. Each field has a name, as well as a picture clause describing the external appearance of the field.

For example, consider the following:

```
line ITEM_INFO:
    TEXT   : picture 28C;     -- space for 28 characters
    PADDING: picture 32B;     -- 32 remaining blank spaces
end line;
```

Here the line of text named ITEM_INFO is defined as having two fields: TEXT for containing a text string, and PADDING for containing blank spaces. The two fields comprise a complete line.

```
program
   declare GROUP, UNIT_PRICE, QUANTITY;

   line LINE_SKIP:
      FILLER: picture 60B;
   end line;

   line TITLE:
      LEFT_PADDING : picture 25B;
      CAPTION      : picture 10C;
      RIGHT_PADDING: picture 25B;
   end line;

   line ITEM_INFO:
      LEFT_PADDING : picture 5B;
      TEXT         : picture 28C;
      PADDING      : picture 27B;
   end line;

   line COL_HEADER:
      LEFT_PADDING : picture 5B;
      QTY_HEADER   : picture 8C;
      FILLER       : picture 6B;
      PRICE_HEADER : picture 5C;
      RIGHT_PADDING: picture 36B;
   end line;

   line ITEM_LINE:
      LEFT_PADDING : picture 7B;
      QUANTITY     : picture 2D;
      FILLER       : picture 10B;
      PRICE        : picture $DD.DD;
      RIGHT_PADDING: picture 35B;
   end line;
```

Example 9.4 **Generation of a Price List Using Picture Specifications**

```
begin
   write LINE_SKIP;
   write LINE_SKIP;
   write LINE_SKIP;
   TITLE.CAPTION := 'PRICE LIST';
   write TITLE;
   TITLE.CAPTION := '----------';
   write TITLE;
   write LINE_SKIP;
   write LINE_SKIP;
   write LINE_SKIP;
   ITEM_INFO.TEXT := 'ITEM CODE : 1234';
   write ITEM_INFO;
   ITEM_INFO.TEXT := 'ITEM      : REG. HAND BROOM';
   write ITEM_INFO;
   ITEM_INFO.TEXT := 'UNIT PRICE: $4.36';
   write ITEM_INFO;
   write LINE_SKIP;
   write LINE_SKIP;
   write LINE_SKIP;
   COL_HEADER.QTY_HEADER   := 'QUANTITY';
   COL_HEADER.PRICE_HEADER := 'PRICE';
   write COL_HEADER;
   COL_HEADER.QTY_HEADER   := '--------';
   COL_HEADER.PRICE_HEADER := '-----';
   write COL_HEADER;
   UNIT_PRICE := 436;
   for GROUP  := 0 to 3 loop
      write LINE_SKIP;
      for QUANTITY := (GROUP*5) + 1 to (GROUP*5) + 5 loop
         ITEM_LINE.QUANTITY := QUANTITY;
         ITEM_LINE.PRICE    := UNIT_PRICE * QUANTITY;
         write ITEM_LINE;
      end loop;
   end loop;

   write LINE_SKIP;
   write LINE_SKIP;
   write LINE_SKIP;

end;
```

Example 9.4 **continued**

With this scheme, any nonblank item must be assigned a value before printing. In the above case, TEXT must be assigned a string of text, whereas PADDING is assumed to be all blanks. The setting of such values is typically done through assignment statements, for example,

```
ITEM_INFO.TEXT := 'ITEM CODE : 1234';
```

Here we use the notation for assignment to components of records that is used in Mini-language Type. It is assumed that when a character string is assigned to a field of greater length, the string will be padded on the right side with blanks to the correct length.

The actual input or output of data is handled by input-output statements naming only the unit to be input or output, in this case by naming the entire line structure. For example, to output the contents of ITEM_INFO we simply use the statement:

```
write ITEM_INFO;
```

One advantage of the picture specification approach is that all the information about a line of text is contained in a single structure. Since both the type and layout of data are specified together, all that one needs to know about a unit of information can be examined quite simply.

Another advantage of this approach is that "insertion" characters can be included in the description of data. For example, consider the following:

```
PRICE: picture $DD.DD;
```

Here the characters $ and . are considered as insertion characters that are placed within the numeric value as printed. Thus, for example, the number

```
436
```

will be printed as

```
$ 4.36
```

We assume here that numbers with decimal points are treated as exact numeric quantities.

Finally, we note a clear disadvantage with this approach as given: the description of data must often be accompanied by considerable, apparently extraneous, information. For example, in the description of COL_HEADER, we see the need to describe four different fields, two of which are all blank, but all of which must be associated with a name and picture clause. Such descriptions are cumbersome.

Input and Output via Specialized Procedures

The last approach we discuss here is that of using specialized procedures for input and output. This approach has emerged in more recent languages, such as Simula 67, Algol 68, Pascal, Modula-2, and Ada. The general idea is that for each type of data, and thus for each conceptually different layout operation, a dedicated procedure is used. For example, if we wish to output an integer, a procedure for printing integers is invoked. This procedure may have a parameter indicating the character width of the integer. As with all approaches, there are considerable variations within the general theme.

Consider the following sequence of procedure calls:

```
PRINT_STRING('ITEM CODE    : 1234');
ADVANCE_LINE(1);
```

Here the procedure PRINT_STRING takes an argument that is a character string and prints the string on an output device. The following procedure ADVANCE_LINE fills the rest of the printed line with blank spaces and advances to the next line.

The exact control of spacing for data items is usually handled with parameters specifying appropriate field widths. For example, consider the procedure call

```
PRINT_INTEGER(DOLLARS, 2);
```

Here an integer is printed in a two-digit field. In the case where only one digit is required, the digit is right-justified.

Our third program for generating a price list is given in Example 9.5. Again, we have modified the syntax of Mini-language Format to illustrate this technique for input and output.

The use of specialized procedures for input and output has a number of key advantages. Most importantly, we can dispense with explicit format or picture specifications and include input-output within an already accepted feature of programming languages—procedures. Thus, a programmer does not need to learn any additional language features. Furthermore, the details of printing can be summarized in terms of a familiar abstraction, the call to a procedure.

Another advantage with this approach is that the user will generally want to define special input and output procedures particularly suited to an application. Such procedures fit nicely with any that might be predefined in the language.

We observe several problems with the use of this approach in Example 9.5. For one, the sequence of procedure calls to perform a given input or output action is quite lengthy, as compared with the terse forms used with format specifications. While repeatedly calling procedure after procedure

```
program
    GROUP, UNIT_PRICE, QUANTITY, PRICE, DOLLARS, CENTS: integer;
begin
    ADVANCE_LINE(3);
    PUT_SPACES(25);
    PRINT_STRING('PRICE LIST');
    ADVANCE_LINE(1);
    PUT_SPACES(25);
    PRINT_STRING('---------');

    ADVANCE_LINE(4);
    PUT_SPACES(5);
    PRINT_STRING('ITEM CODE  : 1234');
    ADVANCE_LINE(1);
    PUT_SPACES(5);
    PRINT_STRING('ITEM       : REG. HAND BROOM');
    ADVANCE_LINE(1);
    PUT_SPACES(5);
    PRINT_STRING('UNIT PRICE : $4.36');

    ADVANCE_LINE(4);
    PUT_SPACES(5);
    PRINT_STRING('QUANTITY       PRICE');

    ADVANCE_LINE(1);
    PUT_SPACES(5);
    PRINT_STRING('--------       -----');
    ADVANCE_LINE(1);
```

Example 9.5 Generation of a Price List Using Specialized Procedures

can be quite tedious, it may be argued that the intent is just as clear as referring to remote format or picture specifications. However, since the details of the spacing are intermixed with actual output, much of the abstraction advantage of formats is lost.

The subject of specialized procedures brings up two rather interesting extensions to this approach that can add simplicity to the specification of input and output, but at the cost of adding some complexity to the mechanism for procedures. These two extensions are overloading and default parameters.

```
UNIT_PRICE := 436;
for GROUP := 0 to 3 loop
   ADVANCE_LINE(1);

   for QUANTITY := (GROUP*5) + 1 to (GROUP*5) + 5 loop
      PUT_SPACES(7);
      PRINT_INTEGER(QUANTITY, 2);
      PRICE   := QUANTITY * UNIT_PRICE;
      DOLLARS := PRICE div 100;
      CENTS   := PRICE - (DOLLARS * 100);
      PUT_SPACES(10);
      PRINT_STRING('$');
      PRINT_INTEGER(DOLLARS, 2);
      if (CENTS < 10) then
         PRINT_STRING('.0');
         PRINT_INTEGER(CENTS, 1);
      else
         PRINT_STRING('.');
         PRINT_INTEGER(CENTS, 2);
      end if;
      ADVANCE_LINE(1);
   end loop;
end loop;

ADVANCE_LINE(3);

end;
```

Example 9.5 **continued**

Overloading of Subprograms

There are situations where we want to define the same conceptual operation on arguments of different types. A typical case is a print operation for printing different types of values.

Consider the procedure headers

```
PRINT: procedure(X: integer);
```

```
PRINT: procedure(X: real);
```

```
PRINT: procedure(X: string);
```

for printing the string representation of an integer, a floating point number, and a string, respectively.

The actions of each procedure will differ since they are dependent on the format for printing the three kinds of values. The use of two or more subprograms with the same name but different types of parameters is called *overloading* or *generic.*

Overloaded subprograms can be called in the conventional manner, for example:

```
PRINT(I + 1);          -- print an integer
PRINT(SQRT(Y));        -- print a floating point number
PRINT('THIS MESSAGE'); -- print a string
```

The key idea here is that these three subroutine calls are really calls to three different subroutines, each with the name PRINT. The choice of which particular subroutine PRINT is to be invoked by the call is determined by the type of the argument. The subroutine is chosen so that the type of its parameter matches the type of the argument. In most languages, this choice can be made by the compiler.

We note in passing that this use of overloading is similar to the use of + as an operator both for integer addition and floating point addition as discussed in Chapter 8.

Default Parameters

Next consider the following procedure calls:

```
PRINT(I, 3);  -- I is printed with a 3 character field width

PRINT(I);     -- I is printed with a standard field width
```

Here we have two calls to the procedure PRINT, and in each case the value of an integer is printed. In the first case, a three-digit field width is specified. In the second case, no second argument is given and the integer is printed with a standard field width. The field width in the procedure is said to be a *default parameter* in the sense that if it is not provided in the call, a standard value is provided in the body of the procedure.

Default parameters can be handled by the use of overloading. For example, with two procedures defined by the headers

```
PRINT: procedure(X: integer);   -- uses the standard width

PRINT: procedure(X: integer, WIDTH: integer);
```

both of the above calls can be accommodated. Hence, the inclusion of default parameters in a language is questionable.

9.3 Communication with the Outside World

Older programming languages often refer to specific devices, but more modern languages generally deal with the more abstract notion of a *file.* A file can be a source or a sink of data and act as a value in a language just like an array or record. In Pascal there are file variables. The correspondence between the abstract file of a program and the physical file or *data set* of the operating system is established by system control statements outside the language. Since these statements are also outside the program, this correspondence can be changed without recompiling the program. The data set is not always an actual collection of data stored in the system; it can also be a physical device, such as a magnetic tape unit or a typewriter terminal. The system achieves some simplification by treating these devices as though they were data sets.

The actual physical connection between the data set and the file is established only at the time the file is *opened* and is broken when the file is *closed.*

Some languages provide special statements for the opening and closing of files. In others, the file is opened when it is first used and closed when the program terminates. At the time of opening the file, checks are made that ensure that the attributes of the data set connected to the file match the requirements of the program.

The attributes of a file that must be matched include: direction of transfer, type of transfer, and file organization.

Mode of Transfer

The mode of transfer defines the direction in which the data is to be transferred, that is, as input or output. Some files are read only, for example, a card reader; others are write only, for example, a printer. Some can be used for both reading and writing but only in one direction at a time— that is, the operations cannot be mixed—as for example a magnetic tape. Terminals and files on disk or drum can be both written and read. The open operation must ensure that the data set to be associated with the file is capable of transfers in the direction required by the program. If there is a mismatch, it is not necessarily a program error; it may be an error of the control statements that were used to establish the system's invocation of the program.

Type of Transfer

There are two distinct ways in which a program can transfer data to and from a file. One mode of transfer takes place without any conversion; that is, the internal representation of the data in the program is identical with its representation in external storage. This type of storage is not meant for data for human consumption, but is intended as a *backing store* to hold information that will be further processed by a program. Since no conversion is performed as part of the data transfer, the operation is fast.

In the other mode of transfer, there is a conversion of representation, for example from a two's complement binary representation to a string of decimal characters preceded by a sign. This is the mode discussed in the earlier sections of this chapter. This type of transfer is typically used for data that have either been prepared by humans or are to be read by humans. Files of this type are sometimes referred to as *text files.*

File Organization

There are two fundamental forms of file organization. These two methods of organization correspond to the way in which they are to be accessed: *sequential access* and *random access.*

A sequential access file consists of a linear sequence of data items. An input sequential file may be accessed only in the order in which the data were written, from first to last. The basic operation is the *read next* operation, which gives the next data item in order. The files in the earlier part of this chapter are sequential files. An output sequential file is written as a sequence of items, from first to last. Generally, sequential files can only be opened for read mode or for write mode and cannot be used for a mixture of these modes without intermediate closing and reopening. Text files are almost always sequential access files.

Random access files, also referred to as *direct access* files, consist of a set of records that can be accessed in an order that is not only different from that in which they were written but may be unpredictable at compilation time. The analog to this type of organization in program data is the single-dimensioned array or vector. In this type of data organization, a subscript is used to identify the particular element to be accessed. In random access files, the analog of the subscript is the *key,* which can be an integer or an identifier, depending on the support provided by the system. Each statement that accesses a record in a random access file must provide the key to identify the record. A typical statement might be:

```
read MASTER file into(MASTER_RECORD) key(RECORD_ID);
```

where the variable RECORD_ID is the identification of the record to be read and MASTER_RECORD is a record variable to be used as target. Similarly, when a record of a random access file is written, its identification key must be provided. Thus, the write statement might be:

```
write NEW_MASTER file from(MASTER_RECORD) key from(RECORD_ID);
```

Although there are some analogies between the data organizations of an array and a random access file, there are some important differences between the two. A major difference is that with random access files it is generally possible to add records, that is, the file can be enlarged after it has been originally created. Generally, the details of implementation of random access files are part of the operating system and are quite separate from the programming language.

Between these two extreme forms of access, sequential and random, there are many intermediate forms of file organization. As with other topics in this text, a full discussion of the subject of file organization goes beyond the scope of this book. Such topics include the language aspects of dealing with such input-output problems as graphics and real-time data acquisition.

9.4 Where to Look: Fortran, Cobol, Ada

The languages Fortran, Cobol, and Ada provide examples of the three types of data format control described in the earlier part of this chapter.

Fortran

Fortran supports both sequential and random access files. This support may be summarized as follows:

1. Transfer of data is specified by READ, WRITE, and PRINT statements.
2. The OPEN, CLOSE, and INQUIRE statements allow the attributes of the file to be specified or queried.
3. The external format of data items can either be defined by the system, for example with the statement

   ```
   READ *, I, J, K
   ```

   or it can be defined explicitly by means of a format specification

   ```
        WRITE (6, 17) NO1, NO2, ISUM
   17   FORMAT(5X, I4, 6X, I5, 4X, I6)
   ```

   where the (6, 17) specifies the file unit number and the numeric statement label of the format specification.

Cobol

Cobol provides a very simple set of input and output facilities:

1. READ and WRITE statements are available for the input and output of sequential files.

2. The form of a file is defined in a separate part of the program, the FILE SECTION of the DATA DIVISION.

The declaration of an external file defines, beyond its major characteristics, the format of each record of the file. The form of this definition resembles the picture specifications that are discussed earlier in this chapter, for example:

```
01 OUTPUT-LINE.
   02 ITEM-NAME PICTURE X(30).
   02 FILLER VALUE 'ITEM PRICE =' PICTURE X(15).
   02 PRICE-OUT PICTURE $$,$$$,$$9.99.
   02 FILLER PICTURE X(44).
```

The picture for PRICE-OUT contains a special insertion character, called a *floating* or *drifting dollar sign,* that causes the dollar symbol to drift to the right until a nonzero digit is reached. This prevents a large gap between the dollar symbol and the start of the amount. In addition, the commas are only inserted if there are digits printed to the left of them. The 9 characters cause digits to be printed, whether they are zero or not. Thus, the printed value corresponding to the PRICE-OUT field might be

```
$27,947.23
```

Ada

In Ada, input and output are handled by the third of the methods described in this chapter, special purpose subroutines. These are chosen from *packages* of subroutines designed for particular purposes. For example, there is a package of subroutines for sequential input-output, another for direct input-output, and a third for text input-output. The last of these contains subroutines for handling the data transfer and the format conversions for the different data types.

Before each separately compiled unit there must be a clause specifying the appropriate package, for example:

```
with TEXT_IO;
```

For the program to get access to the subroutines for performing the format conversions for particular data, types they must be declared inside the compilation unit.

```
package INT_IO is new TEXT_IO.INTEGER_IO(INTEGER);
```

INTEGER_IO is a package template defined within the TEXT_IO package. The above declaration causes the compiler to select this template for use in the procedure. Finally, an actual data transfer with format conversion in the procedure is specified with a statement such as:

```
GET(K);
```

Since this call has an integer argument, the version of GET in the INT_IO package is selected by the compiler to perform the operation.

The subject of packages is dealt with in greater detail in Chapter 17.

Further Reading

Of all of the topics in this text, the topic of input-output has received least attention. Works devoted primarily to this area are particularly sparse.

As typical language examples, format statements are described in Fortran and PL/I, picture clauses in Cobol, and specialized procedures in Algol 68, Modula-2, and Simula 67. The references for these languages cited in the bibliography provide detailed descriptions of the various techniques.

The use of specialized procedures for input-output as used in Ada is described in [Ichbiah et al. 1979]. Here, extensive use is made of overloading and default parameters.

Exercises

Exercise 9.1 *Price List*

To compare the relative ease of modification afforded by the three methods of output specification described in this chapter, you are to modify the programs shown in Examples 9.3, 9.4, and 9.5 to produce a different version of the table shown in Figure 9.1. This table, of which the top portion is shown below, has the information arranged in two columns. Your modified versions of the programs should produce the full table.

```
                         PRICE LIST
                         ----------


                ITEM CODE : 1234
                ITEM      : REG. HAND BROOM
                UNIT PRICE: $4.36


        QUANTITY      PRICE       QUANTITY      PRICE
        --------      -----       --------      -----

               1      $ 4.36         21         $ 91.56
               2      $ 8.72         22         $ 95.92
               3      $13.08         23         $100.28
               4      $17.44         24         $104.64
               5      $21.80         25         $109.00

               6      $26.16         26         $113.36
               7      $30.52         27         $117.72
               8      $34.88         28         $122.08
               9      $39.24         29         $126.44
              10      $43.60         30         $130.80
```

Exercise 9.2 Table Generation

The object of this exercise is to compare the three methods of output specification described in this chapter. Write three versions of a program defined below using the output specification techniques shown in Example 9.3, 9.4, and 9.5 to print the temperature conversion table defined below. When you have completed the three programs, compare their clarity and ease of writing.

The program is to output a simple table. The table consists of two columns labeled Fahrenheit and Celsius. The Fahrenheit temperatures are listed for every degree from 32 through 212. The corresponding Celsius temperatures are printed as integers. There is a blank line left after every five degrees. After every 50 degrees, 10 blank lines are output and the column headings are repeated. The Celsius equivalent of t degrees Fahrenheit is $5(t-32)/9$. The first few lines of the table are:

```
Fahrenheit        Celsius
----------        -------

       32         0
       33         1
       34         1
       35         2
       36         2

       37         3
       38         3
```

Exercise 9.3 Programming in Mini-language Format

Write a program in Mini-language Format that reads a number N from the input device and then prints a pattern of the form shown below.

```
       1
      2 2
     3   3
     .     .
    .       .

   .         .
   N         N
```

The pattern should be centered on the output device. You may assume that the value of N will be less than 20.

Exercise 9.4 *Programming in Mini-language Format*

Printing tables and reports is certainly one of the most important applications of input-output. Write a program to solve the following problem. January 1, 1901 was a Tuesday. Write a Mini-language Format program that takes as input the number of a month (from 1 to 12) and the number of a year (from 1901 to 2000), and prints a calendar for the month. For example:

```
        JANUARY
    S   M   T   W   T   F   S
    --------------------
                1   2   3   4   5
    6   7   8   9  10  11  12
   13  14  15  16  17  18  19
   20  21  22  23  24  25  26
   27  28  29  30  31
```

Exercise 9.5 *Printing Pictures*

Suppose that output consists of pictures printed on a two-dimensional coordinate system. If the pictures are limited to straight lines, circles, and arcs of circles, define a set of formatting features for a programming language suitable for drawing pictures.

Exercise 9.6 *Backing Storage*

Design additional syntax and semantics for Mini-language Format for input and output of data on a file that is to serve as a backing store for temporary results. Such transmission is to take place without any conversion, and the data are represented in the file in the same way that they are represented in machine storage during execution. The new facilities should allow both sequential and random order access to the data.

Exercise 9.7 *Using Money*

Examples 9.3, 9.4, and 9.5 use three basic approaches for reading and writing data: format specifications, picture specifications, and specialized procedures.

Suppose that input and output of amounts of money were important enough in the design of a special purpose language that they should be built into the language. Describe a *good* set of primitives for this, using each of the three approaches. You will need to handle dollar signs, commas in numbers, and decimal point notation for cents.

Exercise 9.8 *Interactive Input and Output*

Design additional syntax and semantics for Mini-langauge Format for interactive input and output through a terminal. There must therefore be a means of displaying information on the screen and reading what the user has typed. In addition, it must be possible for the user to indicate when the current sequence of input data, which might span several lines, is terminated. You should also consider how you will handle characters for which there is no printable equivalent that can be built into a character string.

Exercise 9.9 *Formatting subroutines*

In Example 9.5, we presented the use of special purpose subroutines to handle the formatting of input and output. Define a complete set of such routines for a programming language. Pay particular attention to the way in which you define the parameters to the routines.

10
Procedures and Parameters

The use of subprograms is a familiar programming concept. Charles Babbage's Analytical Engine in 1840 already had provision for the use of a group of punched cards for performing a frequently used part of a larger calculation. Now, it is hard to imagine a programming language that does not offer a subprogram facility in some form.

Subprograms allow the programmer to package computations and parameterize their behavior. There are two forms of subprograms, procedures and functions. A procedure subprogram is a sequence of actions that is invoked as though it were a single statement. A function subprogram is a sequence of computations that results in a single value and is invoked from within an expression. Usually, control returns to the point of invocation after execution of the subprogram, thus forming another one-in, one-out control structure.

Both forms of subprogram invocation represent operational abstractions that simplify the programs that contain them. Subprograms provide one of the most powerful abstraction mechanisms offered by programming languages. In many recent languages, the invoking statement consists only of the name of the called subroutine and an argument list. Thus, it amounts to a language extension that provides a new statement. For example, a call to a sort routine of the form

```
SORT_LIST(ADDRESS_LIST);
```

has the effect of extending the language by adding a sort-list statement.

There must be some means of passing data between the subprogram and the program that calls it. The usual method of passing data is through parameters in the subprogram and through global variables. In this chapter, we use a mini-language to provide a basis for discussing procedures and the various mechanisms used for passing data. Global variables are discussed in Chapter 11. The special properties of functions are described in Chapter 14.

Before describing the mini-language, there is a question of terminology that must be clarified. In different languages, various terms are used to refer to the data passed between procedures. For example:

- The information that is *passed to* a subprogram by a caller is termed the argument in Fortran and PL/I. In Ada, Pascal, and Algol, it is called the actual parameter. We will use the term *argument.*

- The information that is *received from* a caller by a subprogram is termed the dummy argument in Fortran; the formal parameter in Ada, Pascal, and Algol; and parameter in PL/I. We will use the term *parameter.*

10.1 Mini-language Procedures

We begin with our mini-language, as described in Table 10.1.

A program in Mini-language Procedures consists, as usual, of a set of declarations followed by a sequence of statements. There are two types of declarations, for variables and for procedures.

Variable declarations introduce simple variables and arrays that take integer values. Array variables contain an unspecified number of components. For example, we may have:

```
X, Y, TOTAL: integer;   -- three integer-valued variables
A, B: integer array;   -- two arrays with integer components
```

All variables used in the statement part of a program must be declared exactly once.

A procedure declaration defines a subprogram and contains the following parts:

- an identifier that is the name of the procedure,
- the names of the parameters and their modes,
- the declaration of any variables local to the procedure,
- a sequence of statements comprising the body of the procedure.

Table 10.1 **Mini-language Procedures**

program	::=	program
		   variable-declaration. . .
		  [procedure]. . .
		begin
		   statement. . .
		end ;

variable-declaration	::=	identifier [, identifier]. . . : integer [array] ;

procedure	::=	identifier : procedure (parameter-list)
		  [variable-declaration. . .]
		begin
		   statement. . .
		end ;

parameter-list	::=	parameter [, parameter]. . .
parameter	::=	identifier : parameter-mode
parameter-mode	::=	value | result | value_result | location | name
statement	::=	assignment-statement | call-statement | input-statement | output-statement
assignment-statement	::=	variable := expression ;
call-statement	::=	identifier ; | identifier (expression [, expression]. . .) ;
input-statement	::=	input variable [, variable]. . . ;
output-statement	::=	output variable [, variable]. . . ;
expression	::=	[expression +] operand
operand	::=	integer | variable | (expression)
variable	::=	identifier | identifier [expression]

For example, consider the procedure declaration:

```
SUM_FIVE_TIMES: procedure(I: value, J: value, SUM: result)
   TEMP: integer;
begin
   TEMP := I + J;
   SUM  := TEMP + TEMP + TEMP + TEMP + TEMP;
end;
```

This procedure has the following characteristics:

1. Its name is SUM_FIVE_TIMES.

2. It has two parameters I and J of mode value, and another parameter SUM of mode result.

3. There is one local variable named TEMP.

4. The body contains two assignment statements.

In Mini-language Procedures, all variables used within the body of a procedure must either be declared in the procedure or be parameters. The names of all local variables must be different from those of the containing program and from those of local variables and parameters in other procedures. In other words, no identifier may be used for more than one purpose. The meaning of the different parameter modes will be discussed below.

There are four kinds of statements in Mini-language Procedures. An assignment statement causes the value of an expression to be assigned to an integer variable or to a component of an array. Input statements allow integer values to be read into a variable. Output statements allow the values of variables to be printed. Finally, a call statement, which consists of the name of a declared procedure and arguments corresponding to each parameter associated with the procedure, causes execution of the named procedure as described below. The number of arguments must equal the number of parameters declared in the procedure. For example, we may have:

```
X   :=  7;
Y   :=  9;
SUM_FIVE_TIMES(X, Y, TOTAL);
output TOTAL;
```

The third statement invokes the procedure SUM_FIVE_TIMES. When control returns from executing the procedure, the value of the variable TOTAL is five times the sum of the values of X and Y, that is, 80. The next statement to be executed is the output statement.

Note that, since TEMP is a local variable belonging to the procedure SUM_FIVE_TIMES, this variable cannot be referred to by any statement outside the body of the procedure. Also, the rules of the mini-language prohibit any reference from the body of a procedure to variables declared outside the procedure except through the argument parameter correspondence.

We now turn to the exact mechanism by which procedures are invoked. A call statement consists of the name of the procedure to be invoked followed by a parenthesized list of expressions, the argument list. During the execution of a call statement, two things take place:

1. A correspondence between the arguments and the parameters is established in left-to-right order. The i-th argument corresponds to the i-th parameter. The rules for passing the argument to the procedure being called are then applied to each separately.

2. Control is transferred to the first executable statement of the body in the invoked procedure.

When the last statement in the called procedure has been executed, control is returned to the statement following the call statement.

The way in which the argument is passed to its corresponding parameter depends on the mode of the parameter. Since the rules are applied to each parameter separately, we will describe the rules by assuming that a procedure has only one parameter. Where there is the possibility of interaction among several parameters, this will be discussed.

We use the terms *pass by value, pass by result,* and so on to indicate the way in which information passes between argument and parameter. Sometimes the terms *call by value, call by result,* and so on are used for the same concept. We prefer to reserve *call* for the actual invocation of a procedure.

Pass by Value

Here the parameter acts as a local variable belonging to the procedure. This local variable is initialized with the value of the corresponding argument. Since the parameter is purely a local variable, any change of its value during execution of the procedure can have no effect on the corresponding argument. An argument passed by value can be an integer-valued expression.

Pass by Result

In this case the parameter again acts as a local variable, but its value must be initialized locally within the procedure body. After the statements of the body have been executed, the value of the parameter is assigned to the corresponding argument. In this case, of course, the argument must be a variable.

We see here the dual roles of pass by value and pass by result. Arguments passed by value are expressions that provide *inputs* to a procedure; arguments passed by result are variables that receive *outputs* from a procedure.

Pass by Value-Result

Pass by value-result combines the effects of pass by value and pass by result. The parameter is considered as a variable local to the procedure: its initial value is given by the value of the corresponding argument, and the final value of the parameter is assigned to the argument on completion of execution of the procedure. This is another case where the corresponding argument must be a variable.

Pass by Location

Here again, the argument must be a variable. The parameter is considered as a local variable of the procedure, but its location is the location of the argument. Thus, any reference to the value of the parameter is considered to be a reference to the value of the argument, and any assignment to the parameter is an assignment to the location of the corresponding argument, thus changing the argument's value.

Pass by Name

This case is the most difficult to understand. The argument must be a variable if an assignment to the parameter is made inside the procedure; otherwise, it can be any expression. A reference to a parameter that is passed by name is a *direct* use of the corresponding argument exactly as it appears in the argument list.

The pass by name mechanism in Mini-language Procedures can be modeled as a textual modification to the procedure at the time of invocation. In this model, each reference in a statement to the parameter is replaced by the actual text of the argument. This is accompanied by a relaxation of the rule against referring to variables that are neither parameters nor local variables. For example, in the procedure:

```
ADD_ONE: procedure(X: name)
begin
    X := X + 1;
end;
```

execution of the call

```
ADD_ONE(V);
```

results in executing the procedure body with the identifier X replaced by the identifier V from the argument list. Thus, the call to the procedure is equivalent to executing the assignment

```
V := V + 1;
```

Similarly, execution of the call

```
ADD_ONE(COUNT);
```

is equivalent to executing the assignment

```
COUNT := COUNT + 1;
```

For arguments that are scalars, such as V and COUNT, pass by name has the same effect as pass by location. However, if the argument is a reference to an array component, the effect is somewhat different. Execution of the call

```
ADD_ONE(A[COUNT]);
```

is equivalent to executing the assignment

```
A[COUNT] := A[COUNT] + 1;
```

and the component of the array A that is incremented depends on the value of COUNT *at the time the statement is executed.*

Some Examples

To clarify the issues of parameter passing in Mini-language Procedures, we now present a series of small examples.

Consider the following simple procedure:

```
program
    A, B, SUM: integer;

    ADD: procedure(X: value, Y: value, R: result)
    begin
        R := X + Y;
    end;

begin
    A := 2;
    B := 3;
    ADD(A, B, SUM);
    output A, B, SUM;
end;
```

```
program
   I: integer;
   A: integer array;

   SWAP_BY_VALUE: procedure(X: value, Y: value)
      TEMP: integer;
   begin
      TEMP := X;
      X    := Y;
      Y    := TEMP;
   end;

begin
   I    := 3;
   A[I] := 6;
   output I, A[3];
   SWAP_BY_VALUE(I, A[I]);
   output I, A[3];
end;
```

Output
```
   I = 3    A[3] = 6
   I = 3    A[3] = 6
```

Example 10.1 **Pass by Value**

Here the procedure ADD takes two input values, named X and Y, and has a single output named R. The net effect of the procedure is simply to add X and Y and return the value through R.

The statement part of the main program calls the procedure ADD with two input arguments A and B, and another variable SUM intended to store the result of calling the procedure ADD. The final values of A, B, and SUM are then printed. These are 2, 3, and 5.

To illustrate the effects of parameter passing modes we use a rather well-known example, that of swapping the values of two variables passed as arguments. Examples 10.1 through 10.4 are identical except for the modes in which the arguments are passed. In each example, a variable I is set to 3, a variable A[I] is set to 6, and a procedure to swap the values of the two variables is invoked. Finally, the values of I and A[I] are printed.

In Example 10.1 the parameters of the swapping procedure are passed by value. For value parameters, the corresponding arguments are used solely as initial values. As a result, the assignments to the parameters X and

```
program
    I: integer;
    A: integer array;

    SWAP_BY_LOCATION: procedure(X: location, Y: location)
        TEMP: integer;
    begin
        TEMP := X;
        X    := Y;
        Y    := TEMP;
    end;

begin
    I    := 3;
    A[I] := 6;
    output I, A[3];
    SWAP_BY_LOCATION(I, A[I]);
    output I, A[3];
end;
```

Output
```
    I = 3    A[3] = 6
    I = 6    A[3] = 3
```

Example 10.2 **Pass by Location**

Y in the procedure have no effect on the arguments. Thus, the procedure does not perform the desired action. Execution of the procedure has left the values of I and A[I] unchanged.

In Example 10.2 the parameters are passed by location. Thus, any assignment to X and Y results in assigning the values to the corresponding location of the variables given as arguments, in this case the locations in which I and A[I] are stored. Thus, this procedure has the desired effect, as shown by the output of the program. Note that it is the value of I at the time the call statement is executed that determines the component of A referenced by Y. That is, the location that is passed is evaluated at the time the procedure is invoked and before the first statement in the body is executed.

In Example 10.3 where the parameters are passed by name, we have a rather surprising result. The values of I and A[3] are set to 3 and 6, re-

```
program
   I: integer;
   A: integer array;
   SWAP_BY_NAME: procedure(X: name, Y: name)
      TEMP: integer;
   begin
      TEMP := X;
      X    := Y;
      Y    := TEMP;
   end;

begin
   I    := 3;
   A[I] := 6;
   output I, A[3];
   SWAP_BY_NAME(I, A[I]);
   output I, A[3];
end;
```

Output
```
   I = 3    A[3] = 6
   I = 6    A[3] = 6
```

Example 10.3 **Pass by Name**

spectively, as before. The procedure call SWAP_BY_NAME(I, A[I]) is then executed. This is equivalent to executing the statements:

```
TEMP := I;
I    := A[I];
A[I] := TEMP;
```

This execution results in 3 being assigned to TEMP, 6 to I, and then 3 to A[6]! The value of A[3] is left unchanged.

In Example 10.4, the arguments are passed by result. Since result parameters can only provide return values to their corresponding arguments, and must be given initial values by statements in the procedure, execution of this program will result in a run-time error. The error will occur when the assignment of the value of X to the local variable TEMP is attempted, since X is given no value within the body of the procedure. Notice that this error occurs despite the fact that the argument corresponding to X has a value.

```
program
   I: integer;
   A: integer array;
   SWAP_BY_RESULT: procedure(X: result, Y: result)
      TEMP: integer;
   begin
      TEMP := X;
      X    := Y;
      Y    := TEMP;
   end;

begin
   I    := 3;
   A[I] := 6;
   output I, A[3];
   SWAP_BY_RESULT(I, A[I]);
   output I, A[3];
end;
```
Output
```
   I = 3    A[3] = 6
   *** ERROR: ATTEMPT TO EVALUATE AN UNDEFINED VARIABLE X
```

Example 10.4 **Pass by Result**

10.2 Procedures as Abstractions

The procedure facilities in a programming language can be a powerful tool for writing clear, modular programs. Not only do these facilities allow the programmer to factor out frequently executed sections of code but, more importantly, they provide a basic unit for abstraction of program modules. This abstraction can have a great effect on program readability by exposing the program's logical structure.

When procedures are used effectively, they allow the program to be presented in levels of abstractions. The top-most level, the main program, defines the outer structure of the program. The successive lower levels give increasing details about the computations needed to obtain the desired result.

Perhaps the most primitive facility for procedures is evident in Basic and Cobol. In these languages, procedures have no parameters and must rely on global variables, but still units of computation can be grouped into modules and invoked through some form of procedure call. The Basic programmer is denied even the mnemonic power of a subroutine name since subroutines are referenced by line number.

Example 10.5 shows the original use of procedures in Cobol. The names of procedures are given as paragraph headers and procedures are invoked using a *perform* statement, such as

```
PERFORM PRODUCE-PAGE-EJECT.
```

This perform statement invokes the paragraph named PRODUCE-PAGE-EJECT, and after execution of this paragraph control returns to the calling sequence. More modern versions of Cobol have a call statement that can pass arguments to an external procedure.

Even with this simple scheme, we see a basic value in providing procedures in a programming language. In particular, they allow named units of computation to be extracted from the program text and to be invoked when needed. The simple procedure facility of Cobol brings up an important issue not present in Mini-language Procedures. Notice that in the Cobol program of Example 10.5, execution of the procedure takes place as if the procedure were inserted in place at the point of call. As a result, the effect of the procedure takes place directly upon the variables that can be referenced at the point where the procedure is invoked. This is in sharp contrast to Mini-language Procedures, where all variables in a procedure are local and the effect of the procedure takes place only by assignment to arguments of the call. However, the Cobol syntax gives the reader no clue as to the variables that will be modified by executing the procedure. Passing all data through arguments makes this clear.

In most programming languages, procedures may achieve an effect by both methods. That is, a procedure may affect its arguments or may affect variables that can be referenced at the point where the procedure is called. This brings up the whole idea of global variables, as well as the concepts of block structure and the nesting of procedures. These topics are saved for treatment in Chapter 11. Our intent here is to present procedures in their simplest form, without these additional complexities.

Procedures have one clear and strong advantage from our point of view. In our discussion of control structures, we noted the simplicity gained if the flow of control in a program followed a one-in, one-out strategy. Procedures fit perfectly within this scheme. Even with the somewhat simple procedure structure in Cobol, we see the value of using these one-in, one-out abstractions.

To follow a strict one-in, one-out structure, procedures can have only a single entry point and a single exit. In Mini-language Procedures, the programmer is not allowed any choice in this matter. In other languages it can be different. PL/I, for example, permits a procedure to have several entry points, each with its own name that can be called separately. Ada, Fortran, and PL/I also allow the programmer to use a return statement to specify that control is to return to the calling procedure. Thus, it is possible to construct a procedure that is no longer a one-in, one-out structure.

```
PREPARE-ACTION-RPT.
    PERFORM    PRODUCE-PAGE-EJECT.
    PERFORM    PRODUCE-ACTION-RPT-HEADER.

INCORPORATE-NEXT-TRANSACTION.
    PERFORM GET-NEXT-TRANSACTION-REC.
    IF (NOT EOF-SALE-TRANSACTION-FILE)
        PERFORM GET-MATCHING-MASTER-REC
        IF (MATCHING-MASTER-REC-OBTAINED)
            PERFORM UPDATE-MASTER-REC
            ADD 1 TO NUM-OF-UPDATES
        ELSE
            PERFORM HANDLE-UNMATCHED-TRANSACTION.

    . . .


PRODUCE-PAGE-EJECT.
    MOVE SPACES TO RPT-LINE.
    WRITE RPT-LINE BEFORE ADVANCING PAGE.

PRODUCE-ACTION-RPT-HEADER.
    ACCEPT TODAYS-DATE IN ACTION-RPT-HEADER FROM DATE.
    MOVE ACTION-RPT-HEADER TO RPT-LINE.
    PERFORM FREE-RPT-LINE.

GET-NEXT-TRANSACTION-REC.
    READ SALE-TRANSACTION-FILE
        AT END MOVE 1 TO SALE-TRANSACTION-FILE-STATUS.

GET-MATCHING-MASTER-REC.
    MOVE SALESPERSON-ID-NUM IN TRANSACTION-REC
        TO ID IN MASTER-REC.
    MOVE 0 TO MATCHING-MASTER-REC-STATUS.
    READ SALESPERSON-MASTER-FILE
        INVALID KEY MOVE 2 TO MATCHING-MASTER-REC-STATUS.

HANDLE-UNMATCHED-TRANSACTION.
    IF (NUM-OF-UNMATCHED-TRANSACTIONS = 0)
        PERFORM PRODUCE-LINE-SKIP
        PERFORM PRODUCE-UNMATCH-IST-HEADER.
    PERFORM LIST-UNMATCHED-TRANSACTION.

    . . .
```

Example 10.5 **Use of Procedures in Cobol**

It is clear that these extra facilities add complexity to programs. What is not so clear is whether this added complexity gives the reader an equivalent simplification.

10.3 Arguments and Parameters

Of course, procedures cannot exist in isolation. They must have some form of data communication with the point at which they are called. Parameters are an important part of almost every facility for procedures, for it is through parameters that we generalize the action of a procedure.

The identifiers used for the parameters of a procedure have no effect on its meaning. Thus, the effect of

```
ADD: procedure(X: value, Y: value, R: result)
begin
   R := X + Y;
end;
```

is precisely the same as the effect of

```
ADD: procedure(ITEM_A: value, ITEM_B: value, SUM: result)
begin
   SUM := ITEM_A + ITEM_B;
end;
```

where the identifiers have been changed. Parameter identifiers are purely local to the procedure and have no connection with any identifiers used outside the procedure. Because Mini-language Procedures has a rule against declaring an identifier more than once, there is no chance of a parameter identifier being the same as a locally declared variable. If this rule were relaxed, then it would be possible for a parameter identifier to be the same as an identifier used for a variable elsewhere in the procedure. Nevertheless, the two uses of the identifier are quite separate, and a call statement such as

```
ADD(SUM, ITEM_A, ITEM_B);
```

would invoke the procedure ADD, using the values of the variables SUM and ITEM_A and assign the result to the variable ITEM_B. This independence between the two sets of identifiers is essential to the procedure's role as an abstraction. The user does not need to be aware of the internal details of the procedure to be able to use it.

Conceptually, we may view a procedure in rather simple terms. In particular, parameters may be classed as:

- *Inputs:* The inputs provide values from the caller that are to be used within a procedure. If we view a procedure like a function, inputs are arguments in the traditional sense.

- *Outputs:* The outputs of a procedure convey the values returned to the calling environment. Again, if we view a procedure as a function, outputs correspond to the value computed by a function. While normally a function may return only a single value, with procedures several outputs may be computed.

- *Updates:* The updates characterize those objects in a calling environment that are used both as inputs and as outputs by a procedure. Because of the use of assignment in programming languages, it is frequently the case that an object, for example an array or variable, will need to be modified by a call to a procedure.

This rather simple view of procedures is illustrated as follows:

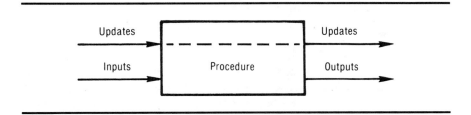

Generally speaking, each parameter mode of Mini-language Procedures models one of these three types of parameters. Unfortunately, it is the nature of programming languages that such a simple view of parameter passing is often not sufficient to characterize their behavior. We now turn to the various methods by which arguments are passed.

Passing by Value

Argument passing by value is used in many computer languages, for example, Modula-2, Pascal, Algol 68, and Snobol. The reason for the popularity of this method is its analogy to the arguments of a function, where values are provided in order to compute the result.

The simple description of passing by value is that the parameters are treated as local variables. Initial values are provided by copying the values of the corresponding arguments. However, all is not quite so easy.

One of the debits of pass by value is that the operation of copying the value of an argument into the location used for the corresponding parameter may be an expensive operation. This is especially true when *large* objects are passed. Imagine for the moment a procedure with two parameters, the first being a thousand-element array and the second being an integer-valued variable. Assume that the first parameter is called by value, and the second by result. The body of the procedure simply sums all of the elements in the array and passes the result back to the calling environment via the second variable.

Although copying such a large array is expensive, the operation is necessary. In general, a value parameter may be modified in the body of the procedure, and thus a local copy of the array is needed.

This problem is nicely solved in Ada by *in* parameters. Such parameters are similar to *value* mode parameters but may not be targets of assignments. Thus, the value of such a parameter acts as a local constant whose value is initialized by the procedure call. There is no need to copy the values supplied as an argument when the procedure is invoked. The compiler is able to check that no in parameter occurs in a position where it may have a value assigned to it. Once this check has been made, there is no longer a need to make a copy of the argument's value since it is quite safe to reference the argument directly.

Passing by Result

Passing by result is a relatively rare method of argument passing, but exists in Algol W and Ada. In a sense, passing by result is the converse of passing by value, in that the values of the corresponding arguments are set on completion of the execution of the procedure body. Passing by result thus directly models the principle of outputs mentioned above. Of course, the arguments corresponding to a parameter passed by result must be variables.

There are two potential problems with result parameters that can only be resolved by careful language design and definition. If a procedure has more than one result parameter, there is the possibility that it will be invoked by a call statement that associates two of them with the same variable, for example a call statement such as P(I, I);. If, after execution of the procedure, the two parameters have different values, the question of the order in which these two values are assigned to I arises.

Mini-language Procedures does not specify this ordering; it is left to the decision of the implementor. For this reason, a call statement like this is generally regarded as a programming error or at least as poor programming practice. Indeed, some languages specifically forbid such calls because the results are indeterminate.

The second problem arises where an argument passed by result is a subscripted variable whose subscript depends on other arguments in the same call. For example, if the procedure Q has two result parameters and it is invoked by the call statement

```
Q(A[I], I);
```

then its effect may depend on the order in which the two result values are assigned to their corresponding arguments. Here, the language definition must specify carefully whether the location of the first argument is evaluated before or after the procedure Q is executed. The effect of the procedure can be quite different in these two cases. In this particular example, the effect of the procedure will also depend on the solution taken in the first problem. In languages where global variables exist, the situation is more complex.

Perhaps the reason for the general lack of passing by result in programming languages is that the same effect can usually be achieved with passing by location. However, in general we feel that the notion of outputs of a procedure is so important that a parameter passing convention strictly for this case is well justified.

Passing by Location

Passing by location, sometimes known as *passing by reference,* is a popular method of argument passing. This method exists in Fortran, Cobol, Modula-2, Pascal, PL/I, and Algol 68. The popularity of this method must be due to its simplicity and its direct analogy with the idea that variables have a location from which their values can be obtained or updated. Passing by location models update parameters for a procedure.

Pass by location can be implemented efficiently, for its implementation only requires the computation of the address of each argument, which is then associated with the corresponding parameter.

As with passing by result, there are two areas where careful attention to the details of the design must be given. Again, the first one concerns the same variable being used as two arguments and thus associated with two different parameters. That is, both parameters are associated with the same location. The two parameters are said to be *aliases.* Generally, the term is used to cover the situation where two different identifiers in a segment of a program refer to the same location. There are other ways in which this can occur as we shall see in Chapter 11.

Procedures in which there are aliases are difficult to understand. In addition, when there is a potential for aliasing, there are certain optimizations that cannot be performed for fear of changing the meaning of the program. In PL/I, where arguments are passed by location, procedures are often compiled separately from the call statements that invoke them. In these circumstances, it is impossible for the compiler to determine whether any aliasing exists; the conservative approach must be taken, by omitting the optimization.

The second area of design concerns the restriction that arguments that are passed by location must be variables. Certainly, if an argument were an expression, its value could be stored in a temporary location and this passed to the corresponding parameter. This would then mean that an assignment in the procedure to the parameter would be an assignment to the temporary value. This would allow the parameter to continue in its role as one of the procedure's local variables. Such an assignment would have no effect in the calling environment. It is an open question of language design whether passing arguments that are expressions by location should be allowed.

Passing by Value-Result

In spirit, this method of passing arguments is similar to passing by location. The value of the argument, which must be a variable, is assigned as the initial value of the corresponding parameter. When the procedure completes execution, the final value of the parameter is assigned to the argument variable. Like passing by result, passing by value-result is rare, but it does exist in Algol W.

Because of the copying of values that is required, this method of passing arguments is less efficient than passing by location. However, since the parameter is a variable in its own right, there can be no danger of aliasing. Thus, there is a greater potential for optimization than there is with location mode parameters.

A sharp difference between passing by location and passing by value-result occurs in cases where an *exception* condition arises during execution of the procedure. Exception conditions are discussed in Chapter 15, but a brief point will be made here.

Consider a procedure with one value-result parameter. Let us assume that arithmetic is performed on the parameter and that during the arithmetic computation, a value is computed that lies beyond the maximum numeric value handled by the implementation. This is an *overflow* condition. In this case, a program will usually terminate abnormally, and then the values of variables can often be inspected.

With passing by value-result, inspection of the corresponding argument will reveal that the value is the same as that obtained when the procedure was invoked, as no change to the value of this variable is performed during execution of the procedure body. With passing by location, however, the value stored in the location may be altered. Inspection of the value of the variable given as an argument will show such a change. Thus, the two methods of parameter passing may differ under abnormal termination conditions.

Passing by Name

Historically, passing by name has received much attention in the literature. Yet its use is very rare and, to our knowledge, exists only in Algol 60.

The relative unpopularity of this method is due to the surprises it can give the programmer and to its inefficiencies. This method of passing arguments stems directly from the Lambda Calculus [Church 1941].

The characteristic of passing by name is the *deferred evaluation* of the argument. In the other modes of argument passing, the argument is evaluated *before* the body of the called procedure is executed. Instead of passing a value or location to a name parameter, a rule for evaluating the argument is passed. This rule is used whenever the argument is referenced. In Section 10.1, we described this process through the metaphor of textual substitution. This metaphor works well for a small language like Mini-language Procedures; however, in a more complex language, it soon loses its simplicity if it is to remain accurate.

Suppose the Mini-language Procedures rule that the name of all identifiers must be different were relaxed. It would then be possible to have a local variable in a procedure whose name was the same as the name of a variable in the containing program. The following version of SWAP_BY_NAME would then be a valid program:

```
program
    I: integer;
    A: integer array;

    SWAP_BY_NAME: procedure(X: name, Y: name)
        I: integer;
    begin
        I := X;
      . X := Y;
        Y := I;
    end;

begin
    I    := 3;
    A[I] := 6;
    output I, A[3];
    SWAP_BY_NAME(I, A[I]);
    output I, A[3];
end;
```

If we then follow the metaphor of textual substitution described earlier, the body of SWAP_BY_NAME would become

```
I    := I;
I    := A[I];
A[I] := I;
```

There is clearly a problem with the identifier I. Some of its occurrences in this sequence refer to the I in the containing procedure and some refer to the local variable I in SWAP_BY_NAME. This is a *name* or *identifier clash*. Our model has broken down. If we are to define the model precisely, we must give rules that will avoid the clash. Informally, the names of any local variables that clash with the names contained in any of the substituting arguments must be changed consistently to new names that will not clash. To make this rule in a precise, unambiguous way is rather complicated. For our purposes, the informal rule will be satisfactory.

The real point is that the deferred evaluation of the arguments must take place using the identifiers that are current at the place where the call statement occurs. This is said to be the *environment* of the call. An environment provides the mapping between identifiers and values at a point in a program. We return to this concept in several later chapters.

10.4 Value-Returning Procedures

A value-returning procedure is one that is invoked as a function reference in an expression. The value that it computes is "returned" to the point of its invocation and is used in the next stage in evaluation of the expression. Value-returning procedures are also known as function procedures or function subprograms.

This could be illustrated by extending Mini-language Procedures to include a return statement with the syntax:

```
return expression ;
```

This statement would only be permitted in a procedure. Its execution would cause evaluation of the expression followed by return of control to the point at which the procedure was invoked. The value obtained from evaluating the expression would be the value of the reference to the procedure. To invoke a procedure containing a return statement by a call statement would be meaningless since there would be no way of using the returned value. The mini-language extension would therefore require a rule that restricted reference to a procedure containing return statements to expressions.

Consider the following simple example of a value-returning procedure:

```
DOUBLE: procedure(V: value)
begin
   return V + V;
end;
```

Such a procedure must be invoked in an expression such as

```
X := A + DOUBLE(A) + 3;
```

If the value of A were 3, then 12 would be assigned to X.

The expression containing function references of this sort could also be nested, for example:

```
X := DOUBLE(A + DOUBLE(A + 5)) + 3;
```

which would lead to the value 41 being assigned to X.

A completely equivalent way of writing the value-returning procedure DOUBLE would be:

```
DOUBLE: procedure(V: value)
begin
   V := V + V;
   return V;
end;
```

This is equivalent because the parameter is declared with value mode and thus behaves as a local variable. The assignment to it cannot change the value of the corresponding argument. Had the parameter been declared with *location* mode, the assignment to V would double the value of the argument. This is known as a *side effect*. The actual result assigned to X when

```
X := A + DOUBLE(A) + 3;
```

is executed would be difficult to understand. Since evaluating DOUBLE(A) causes the value of A to be doubled as a side effect, it will depend on the details of the expression evaluation implemented by the compiler. If the values are obtained in left-to-right order, then the expression

```
A + DOUBLE(A) + 3
```

would be equivalent to

```
3 + 6 + 3
```

However, if DOUBLE(A) is evaluated first, it would be equivalent to

6 + 6 + 3

For a programmer to have to understand such implementation details in order to understand the program is an unreasonable burden and is also likely to reduce the machine independence of the program. Thus, the use of value-returning procedures that have side effects can have implementation defined results and is bad programming practice.

10.5 Coroutines

The invocation and execution of procedures described in this chapter are the classical form common to most standard programming languages. Another form, known as *coroutines,* is much less common and will be described in this section.

The relationship between the part of a program that contains a call statement, often called the *main procedure,* and the subroutine is asymmetric. The flow of control that characterizes this relationship is shown in Figure 10.1. The asymmetry is shown by the fact that the called procedure is always entered at its first statement, but when control returns to the main procedure, execution is *resumed* at the point following the call. Thus, the subprocedure is in a subservient role to the main procedure.

Coroutines have a more symmetric relationship between the calling and called parts of the program. In normal use, a pair of procedures work together as coroutines. When they are invoked, they do not execute to completion as in normal procedures, but return control after partial execution. At this point, execution of one coroutine is suspended, and the execution of the other is resumed from the point at which its execution was suspended. This sequence of suspensions and resumptions of control continues as the coroutines work together, as shown in Figure 10.2. In this arrangement, the two coroutines are on the same level, and there is no master-slave relationship as there is in normal calling mechanisms.

Coroutines allow programs with complex sequencing logic to be simplified by allowing the details of the sequencing structure to be separated into separate modules. It is difficult to find an illustrative example that is short enough that it does not hide the principle being illustrated under a mass of detail describing the problem.

An Example

The following highly contrived example is based on one given in [Grune 1977]. We wish to copy integers from input to output with the rule that when the input contains two successive occurrences of the integer 1, a 2

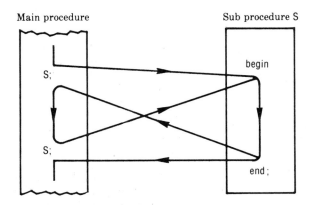

Figure 10.1 **Control Flow Relationship between Main Procedure and Subprocedure**

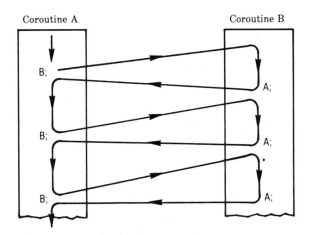

Figure 10.2 **Flow of Control between a Pair of Coroutines**

will be substituted. In addition, after a possible substitution according to this rule, if there are two successive occurrences of the integer 2, a 3 will be substituted. To make things simpler, we will assume that the stream of input never ends. See Exercises 10.6 and 10.7.

If we try to implement this using two procedures, ONES_TO_TWO and TWOS_TO_THREE, we run into the problem that TWOS_TO_THREE needs to keep account of what it has received. This makes its logic very difficult to

```
program
   ONES_TO_TWO: procedure
      IN: integer;
   begin
      input IN;
      while(1 = 1) loop
         if (IN = 1) then
            input IN;
            if (IN = 1) then
               resume TWOS_TO_THREE(IN);
            else
               resume TWOS_TO_THREE(1);
               resume TWOS_TO_THREE(IN);
            end if;
         else
            resume TWOS_TO_THREE(IN);
         end if;
         input IN;
      end loop;
   end;

   TWOS_TO_THREE: procedure(NEW_IN: value)
   begin
      while(1 = 1) loop
         if (NEW_IN = 2) then
            resume ONES_TO_TWO
            if (NEW_IN = 2) then
               output 3;
            else
               output 2;
               output NEW_IN;
            end if;
         else
            output NEW_IN;
         end if;
         resume ONES_TO_TWO;
      end;
   end;
begin
   A;
end;
```

Example 10.6 **A Program That Uses Coroutines**

understand. The program shown in Example 10.6 is a solution to this problem using coroutines. It uses a resume statement instead of a call statement. The semantics of this statement are that the resumed procedure continues from its own last resume statement or, if it has not yet been invoked, from the beginning. The condition (1 = 1) on the loops in the two coroutines makes them into infinite loops. The symmetry between the two coroutines can be seen in the example.

Coroutines are of use in complex searching processes and in simulation of multiprocessing, discussed in Chapter 16, as well as in the handling of interleaved lists. A particular example of interleaved lists where the idea of coroutines is often used in machine code is the output of values from a data list using a format list to specify the form of the output as we did in Chapter 9. In Mini-language Format, the implementation would be fairly easy since it was always certain during compilation which format definition would be paired with which data value. In a more general language, such as PL/I, this cannot always be determined during compilation because the number of elements in an array can vary and there can be repetition expressions in the format list that are evaluated at execution time. Thus, it is impossible for the compiler to determine the pairing between data values and formats. The machine code generated by the compiler to achieve this pairing is generally in the form of coroutines.

10.6 Where to Look: PL/I, Ada

PL/I

PL/I provides procedures that can optionally be defined to be value-returning procedures. A synopsis of the facilities is as follows:

1. A procedure declaration starts with the name of the procedure followed by a colon and the keyword PROCEDURE. It is terminated by the symbol END. Following the keyword PROCEDURE is a parameter list giving the names of the parameters but not their type. In the case of function procedures, the argument list is followed by the keyword RETURNS and the type of the returned value in parentheses, for example

   ```
   X: PROCEDURE(I, J) RETURNS(FLOAT);
   ```

2. All arguments are passed by location. If the argument is a constant, expression, or requires a value conversion before being passed, the value is placed in a compiler-assigned temporary location and a reference to that location is passed. When this is done, the effect is that of passing by value.

3. Procedures are invoked by writing the keyword CALL and the procedure name followed by the argument list. Value-returning procedures are invoked by referencing the function name followed by the argument list at the point at which the value is needed, generally in an expression.

4. Values are returned from procedures by a return statement containing an expression that evaluates to the value to be returned.

Ada

Ada also provides both procedures and functions. An outline of these facilities is:

1. A procedure has the heading

   procedure identifier (parameter-list) is

2. A function has the heading

   function   identifier (parameter-list) return type is

3. There are three ways of passing information between arguments and parameters:
   a. in: the parameter is a named constant whose value is the value of the corresponding argument. Its action is thus equivalent to passing by value in Mini-language Procedures, with the restriction that the parameter may not be assigned to.
   b. out: the parameter is a variable whose value is not initialized but is assigned to the corresponding argument on exit from the procedure. This corresponds to passing by result in Mini-language Procedures.
   c. in out: this method of transmission corresponds either to value-result or location in Mini-language Procedures depending on the implementation of Ada.

4. Arguments are associated with parameters either by their position in the argument list, as in Mini-language Procedures, or by specifying in the argument list the name of the parameter with which the argument is to correspond. For example, with the procedure header

   procedure PLOT(X, Y: in REAL; PEN_UP: in BOOLEAN);

where in denotes an input parameter, we may have the calls:

```
PLOT(0.0, 0.0, TRUE);                        -- positional
PLOT(X => 0.0, Y => 0.0, PEN_UP => TRUE); -- named
PLOT(PEN_UP => TRUE, X => 0.0, Y => 0.0); -- named reordered
PLOT(0.0, 0.0, PEN_UP => TRUE);              -- combination
```

5. A procedure may give default values to be given to parameters if values are not provided in the argument list.

Further Reading

There are several further readings that deserve special note here. Of importance is [Jones and Muchnick 1978]. This discusses the general concept of binding time and the methods of parameter passing in programming languages. It treats most of the issues covered in this chapter and presents the concepts in a clear and effective way. Readers who wish to explore the origins of pass by name may refer to the classic work [Church 1941]. The use of this parameter passing mechanism in Algol 60 is described in [Rutishauser 1967].

Traditionally, as well as in the presentation given above, the arguments of a procedure are always passed in positional order. That is, the arguments given in a procedure call correspond one by one to the corresponding position of the parameters given in the declaration of the procedure itself. An interesting variation of this method of parameter passing is described in [Ichbiah et al. 1979]. This work describes an alternative mechanism for stating the correspondence between arguments and parameters through the use of a keyword notation, in which the procedure call explicitly names the association between arguments and parameters.

Coroutines were introduced in [Conway 1963]; this paper serves as a good introduction to the use of coroutines in the compiling process.

Exercises

Exercise 10.1 *Methods of Passing Parameters*

Suppose Mini-language Procedures were modified so that a variable declared outside a procedure could be referenced and modified from within the procedure. Consider the following program, written in this variant of Procedures where a parameter mode has been omitted.

```
program
    I: integer;
    B: array;

    Q: procedure(X:     ...    )
    begin
        I    := 1;
        X    := X + 2;
        B[I] := 10;
        I    := 2;
        X    := X + 2;
    end;

begin
    B[1] := 1;
    B[2] := 1;
    I    := 1;
    Q(B[I]);
    output B[1], B[2];
end;
```

Consider the mode of the parameter X of procedure Q to be (1) value, (2) result, (3) value result, (4) location, and (5) name. Execute the program for each argument passing convention and determine the values output.

Note: One of the executions terminates abnormally; in all others, the results are different.

Exercise 10.2 *Pass by Name versus Pass by Value*

The short program below incorporates most of the basic pass by name and pass by value problems. The value-returning procedures, INCREMENT_BY_VALUE and INCREMENT_BY_NAME, differ in that their argument is passed by value versus by name. That is the only difference. ADD_BY_VALUE and ADD_BY_NAME differ similarly.

The problem is to determine the values printed in each output statement. This exercise is adapted from [Weil 1965].

```
program
    A, B: integer;

    INCREMENT_BY_VALUE: procedure(X: value)
    begin
        X := X + 2;
        return X;
    end;

    INCREMENT_BY_NAME: procedure(X: name)
    begin
        X := X + 2;
        return X;
    end;

    ADD_BY_VALUE: procedure(X: value)
    begin
        return X + X;
    end;

    ADD_BY_NAME: procedure(X: name)
    begin
        return X + X;
    end;

begin
    A := 3;
    B := ADD_BY_VALUE(INCREMENT_BY_VALUE(A));
    output A, B;
    A := 3;
    B := ADD_BY_VALUE(INCREMENT_BY_NAME(A));
    output A, B;
    A := 3;
    B := ADD_BY_NAME(INCREMENT_BY_VALUE(A));
    output A, B;
    A := 3;
    B := ADD_BY_NAME(INCREMENT_BY_NAME(A));
    output A, B;
end;
```

Exercise 10.3 *Jensen's Device*

Passing parameters by name may be used in a programming strategem known as Jensen's Device. To use the technique, a procedure has two or more parameters that are passed by name. During execution, the value of one or more of these parameters is changed. If one of the arguments is an expression that involves the variable that is updated during execution, the expression may be evaluated for many different values of its variables.

A simple example of this procedure is the function procedure:

```
SUM: procedure(L_BOUND: value, U_BOUND: value, INCREMENT: value,
               TERM: name, EXPRESSION: name)
   TOTAL: integer;
begin
   TOTAL := 0;
   TERM  := L BOUND;
   while (TERM <= U_BOUND) loop
      TOTAL := TOTAL + EXPRESSION;
      TERM    := TERM + INCREMENT;
   end loop;
   return TOTAL;
end;
```

The invocation of the procedure SUM by

```
SUM(1, 25, 1, I, A[I]);
```

will produce the sum of the first 25 elements of the array A. The invocation

```
SUM(1, 25, 1, I, 1/A[I]);
```

will compute the sum of the inverses of the elements.

1. Write an invocation of SUM that will give the sum of the first five powers of three.

2. Write a general purpose routine that will find the maximum value from a set of values obtained by evaluating an arbitrary expression containing a variable that ranges from a given lower bound to a given upper bound with a given step size.

3. Describe the limitations of this technique.

Exercise 10.4 Aliasing

The term *aliasing* is used to describe the situation where a single location, and hence its value, may be accessed through more than one name. Describe:

1. The ways in which aliasing can occur.
2. The implementation problems that aliasing can cause.
3. Some rules for a language without pointers that attempt to prevent aliasing.

Illustrate your answer with examples.

Exercise 10.5 Coroutines

Devise some additional syntax and define the corresponding semantics for the extension of Mini-language Procedures to include coroutines. How could your proposal be generalized to allow any number of intercommunicating coroutines?

Exercise 10.6 Programming without Coroutines

Program the problem discussed in Section 10.5 without the use of coroutines. The problem is stated as:

We wish to copy integers from input to output with the rule that when the input contains two successive occurrences of the integer 1, a 2 will be substituted. In addition, after a possible substitution according to this rule, if there are two successive occurrences of the integer 2, a 3 will be substituted. To make things simpler, we will assume that the stream of input never ends.

Exercise 10.7 Programming with Coroutines

In Example 10.6 we showed a program written using coroutines to solve the problem restated in Exercise 10.6. In that program we assume, to make things easier, that the input stream never ends. Suppose the problem is changed so that the input stream is terminated when the integer value zero is encountered. Reprogram the solution to the problem to meet this new condition. Remember that the coroutine TWOS_TO_THREE also needs to be informed when input has terminated in case it still has a character that must be output.

Exercise 10.8 *Named Parameters*

In Ada, as described in Section 10.6, the arguments to a subroutine can be given in positional order or by naming the parameters associated with the arguments, or in combination. Named parameters can be given in any order.

There are basically two positions on this feature:

1. Such a feature is useful and highly reliable. The programmer does not have to remember the order of parameters. With long parameter lists, the feature is almost indispensable.

2. Such a feature is of dubious importance. The desired effect on readability can be achieved in other ways; for example, writing procedures with fewer arguments or giving mnemonic names to arguments. Furthermore, a change to the names of parameters forces the calls to be changed.

Make your choice, and write a one- to three-page position paper on your choice.

Exercise 10.9 *Parameter Passing Efficiency*

Ada leaves it to the implementor to decide whether composite parameters should be passed by value-result (i.e., by copying values twice) or by location, which does not involve copying but means that references must pass through an extra level of indirection. Derive the criteria on which a compiler could make the choice of which kind of code to generate.

Exercise 10.10 *Ada Parameters Again*

Although Ada leaves it to the implementor to decide whether composite parameters should be passed by value-result or by location, the language definition stipulates that Ada programs that would produce different results under the two implementations are "erroneous." Write a subprogram in either Ada or Mini-language Procedures with suitable modifications that would give differing results under the two implementations.

11
Nesting and Scope

The association between a parameter and its value holds only within the procedure. We say that the identifier is *local* to the procedure. Outside the procedure, either the identifier has no meaning, or it is associated with some other object.

Identifiers are used in programs to refer to many different kinds of entities. In a large program there can be hundreds, if not thousands, of such identifiers. Since a large program is likely to be the work of many programmers, there must be some method of avoiding incompatible uses of the same identifier without onerous bookkeeping. Identifiers introduced by a programmer should not be required to have the same meaning over the complete program. It must be possible to limit the area of a program in which a particular identifier is associated with a specific entity.

The part of the program over which an identifier refers to the value defined in a declaration is the *scope* of the declaration. The process of matching an identifier reference to its defining declaration is the *resolution* of the reference. An identifier is said to be *known* within the scope of its declaration.

Mini-language Scope introduced here has rules based on those of Algol and Pascal.

11.1 Mini-language Scope

As with most of our mini-languages, the program consists of one or more declarations followed by a sequence of statements, as shown in Table 11.1. There are two kinds of declarations: variable declarations and procedure

Table 11.1 **Mini-language Scope**

program	::=	`program`
		    declaration-section
		`begin`
		    statement. . .
		`end` ;

declaration-section	::=	variable-declaration. . . [procedure-declaration. . .]
variable-declaration	::=	identifier [, identifier]. . . : `integer` ;
procedure- declaration	::=	identifier : `procedure` [declaration-section] `begin` statement. . . `end` ;
statement	::=	assignment-statement | call-statement | input-statement | output-statement
assignment-statement	::=	identifier := expression ;
call-statement	::=	identifier ;
input-statement	::=	`input` identifier [, identifier]. . . ;
output-statement	::=	`output` identifier [, identifier]. . . ;
expression	::=	[operand +] operand
operand	::=	integer | identifier | (expression)

declarations. In any declaration section, a name may be declared only once.

A variable declaration introduces one or more integer variables. All variables in a program must be declared.

A procedure declaration introduces a named procedure. A procedure consists of zero or more declarations followed by a sequence of statements. All identifiers used within a procedure must also be declared, either in the declarations given with the procedure or in an outer program unit. A program unit is either a procedure (that is, bracketed by the keywords procedure and end) or a main program (that is, bracketed by the keywords program and end).

Mini-language Scope has assignment, call, input, and output statements, all of the familiar form that we used in previous mini-languages. The expressions that can be used in an assignment statement are extremely simple, and can only consist of operands or the addition of operands.

Scope Rules

A declaration associates certain properties with an identifier; in this mini-language it defines whether an identifier is an integer variable or a procedure. The region of a program over which a particular declaration of an identifier is in effect is the *scope* of the declaration.

A program in Mini-language Scope is made up of blocks. The complete program is itself a block. The part of a procedure declaration from the symbol procedure to the end symbol that terminates the procedure is also a block. Except for the outermost block, all blocks are contained in at least one other block. The scope of a declaration consists of the block in which it occurs and all contained blocks that do not have a redeclaration of the same identifier.

Within any block, excluding any contained blocks, a particular identifier may only be declared once. A reference to an identifier in a statement sequence must be within the scope of the declaration of that identifier. Although a particular identifier may not be declared more than once in any block, it may be declared in other blocks. Each such declaration can associate the identifier with different properties. Each declaration has its own scope, which is disjoint from the scopes of all other declarations of the same identifier.

The following program fragment shows how the scopes of different declarations of the same identifier cover different parts of the program:

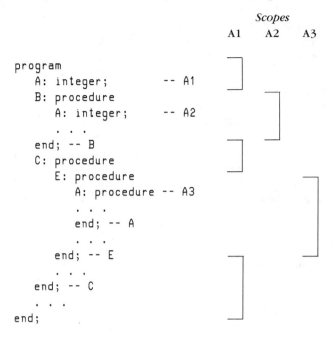

```
                            Scopes
                        A1    A2    A3

program
    A: integer;      -- A1
    B: procedure
        A: integer;  -- A2

        . . .
    end; -- B
    C: procedure
        E: procedure
            A: procedure  -- A3

            . . .
            end; -- A

        . . .
        end; -- E

    . . .
    end; -- C

    . . .
end;
```

The outer declaration of A has a scope that consists of the outermost block and the procedure C; however, it includes neither the procedure B, where it is redeclared as an integer variable, nor the procedure E, where it is redeclared as a procedure. The gaps corresponding to parts of the text where the identifier has been redeclared are known as *holes in the scope*.

An identifier declared in a block is said to be *internal* or *local* to the block in which it is declared, and *external* or *global* to all inner blocks that do not contain redeclarations of it.

When an identifier is used within a statement sequence, the declaration that defines the identifier can be determined as follows:

- If the declaration section of the block that contains the statement sequence has a declaration of the identifier, then this is the defining declaration.

- Otherwise, the blocks enclosing the sequence of statements are examined, and the most local enclosing block containing a declaration of the identifier defines the given identifier.

A procedure's local variables do not exist until the procedure is invoked. At that time, the variables are created with undefined values. The variables continue to exist until execution of the procedure is completed, at which point they cease to exist.

Examples

Example 11.1 shows the use of nesting and the redeclaration of identifiers. Here a variable named A is declared within the procedure PURELY_ LOCAL. Its scope thus consists only of the procedure itself. The variable A is also declared in the main program; its scope does not include the procedure PURELY_LOCAL.

When the program of Example 11.1 is executed, the value of A will be set to 1, and this value will be output. The procedure PURELY_LOCAL is then called; this procedure sets the local variable to 5 and outputs its value. It thus has no effect on the containing program unit. Finally, the value of A in the main program unit is again printed. Since the value associated with this identifier has not been changed by the call of PURELY_ LOCAL, the value 1 will again be printed for the variable A.

```
program
    A: integer;

    PURELY_LOCAL: procedure
        A: integer;
    begin
        A := 5;
        output A;
    end;

begin
    A := 1;
    output A;
    PURELY_LOCAL;
    output A;
end;
```

Output

```
A = 1
A = 5
A = 1
```

Example 11.1 **Use of a Local Variable**

Example 11.2 shows a program similar to that of Example 11.1, except that the variable A is not declared as local to the procedure. The effect of the procedure PURELY_GLOBAL in Example 11.2 will be to change the value of A declared in the main program. Thus, when this program is executed, the first output statement will print the value 1 and the second output statement will print the value 5. However, in this example, the third output statement will also print the value 5, since the call to PURELY_GLOBAL changes the value of A.

Example 11.3 illustrates the full complexities of Mini-language Scope. The main program unit introduces three variables A, B, and C. Three procedures Q, R, and S are also defined within the main program unit. Furthermore, procedure R introduces a local declaration of the variable C, and procedure S introduces local declarations of B and C, as well as an inner declaration of procedure Q.

The way in which this program executes is shown in Table 11.2. The statement numbers correspond to those shown in comments in the program. To distinguish the separate uses of the same identifier, the variables are distinguished in Table 11.2 by prefixing their names with the name of the procedure in which they are declared. For example, S.C is the variable

```
program
   A: integer;

   PURELY_GLOBAL: procedure
   begin
      A := 5;
      output A;
   end;

begin
   A := 1;
   output A;
   PURELY_GLOBAL;
   output A;
end;
```

Output

```
   A = 1
   A = 5
   A = 5
```

Example 11.2 **Use of a Global Variable**

```
program
    A, B, C: integer;              -- variables A, B, and C

    Q: procedure
    begin                          -- line 1
        A := A + 2;                -- line 2
        C := C + 2;                -- line 3
    end;

    R: procedure
        C: integer;                -- variable R.C
    begin                          -- line 4
        C := 2;                    -- line 5
        Q;                         -- line 6
        B := A + B;                -- line 7
        output A, B, C;            -- line 8
    end;

    S: procedure
        B, C: integer;             -- variables S.B, and S.C
        Q: procedure
        begin                      -- line 9
            A := A + 1;            -- line 10
            C := C + 1;            -- line 11
        end;
    begin                          -- line 12
        B := 3;                    -- line 13
        C := 1;                    -- line 14
        Q;                         -- line 15
        R;                         -- line 16
    end;

begin                              -- line 17
    A := 1;                        -- line 18
    B := 1;                        -- line 19
    C := 1;                        -- line 20
    R;                             -- line 21
    S;                             -- line 22
end;
```

Example 11.3 **The Joys of Scope**

Table 11.2 **Execution of Example 11.3**

line	A	B	S.B	C	R.C	S.C	Notes
17	?	?	—	?	—	—	The three local variables of the outermost block have no defined value. No other variables exist.
18	1	?	—	?	—	—	A is assigned 1.
19	1	1	—	?	—	—	B is assigned 1.
20	1	1	—	1	—	—	C is assigned 1.
21	1	1	—	1	—	—	The procedure R is invoked.
4	1	1	—	1	?	—	R's local variable C is created.
5	1	1	—	1	2	—	R's local variable C is assigned 2.
6	1	1	—	1	2	—	The procedure Q is invoked.
1	1	1	—	1	2	—	
2	3	1	—	1	2	—	A is incremented by 2.
3	3	1	—	3	2	—	C is incremented by 2, Q is completed.
7	3	4	—	3	2	—	
8	3	4	—	3	2	—	A=3, B=4, C=2 is printed. R is completed. R's local variable C ceases to exist. Control returns to the main program.
22	3	4	—	3	—	—	Procedure S is invoked.
12	3	4	?	3	—	?	S's local variables B and C are created.
13	3	4	3	3	—	?	S's local variable B is assigned 3.
14	3	4	3	3	—	1	S's local variable C is assigned 1.
15	3	4	3	3	—	1	Procedure Q contained in S is invoked.
9	3	4	3	3	—	1	
10	4	4	3	3	—	1	A is incremented.
11	4	4	3	3	—	2	S's local variable C is incremented. Q is completed.
16	4	4	3	3	—	2	Procedure R is invoked.
4	4	4	3	3	?	2	R's local variable C is created.
5	4	4	3	3	2	2	R's local variable C is assigned 2.
6	4	4	3	3	2	2	The procedure Q is invoked.
1	4	4	3	3	2	2	
2	6	4	3	3	2	2	A is incremented by 2.
3	6	4	3	5	2	2	C is incremented by 2. Q is completed.
7	6	10	3	5	2	2	
8	6	10	3	5	2	2	A=6, B=10, C=2 is printed. R is completed. Control returns to S. S is completed. Control returns to main program, which is completed.

C declared in the procedure S. Execution begins at the first statement in the statement sequence of the outermost program unit, line 17.

Where the same identifier is used for more than one object in a program and the rules of scope must be used to determine which object is being referenced, the names of the objects are said to *clash*. The many clashes illustrating the rules of Scope in Example 11.3 make the program difficult to understand and are best avoided.

11.2 The Idea of Scope

In mathematical writing, the concept of scope is used extensively. It is common to introduce local definitions to give the current meaning of a symbol. For instance, we may write, "let N be . . . ." Such definitions are usually local to a section of text and have no connection to other uses of the symbol N elsewhere in the text. Although there are no formal rules that define the scope of such textual declarations, in a clearly written document there will be no difficulty in understanding the meaning. In programming languages, since compilers have no intuition to rely on, we must be more precise in our definition of scope. Hence, for example, we have the scope rule given for Mini-language Scope.

The idea of a declaration having a scope that is less than the complete program allows the same identifier to be used for different purposes in separate parts of a program. Consider the program fragment of Example 11.4. We assume that we are writing a program that processes text. This program contains two procedures, GET_SYMBOL and MOVE_LINE_ POSITION. Within these procedures a number of variables are declared, and these declarations are assumed to hold for the procedure in which

```
program
    . . .
    GET_SYMBOL: procedure
        INDEX, LENGTH, SYMBOL_CODE: integer;
    begin
        -- statements for obtaining the next symbol code;
    end;


    . . .
    MOVE_LINE_POSITION: procedure
        INDEX, LENGTH, TEMP_POSITION: integer;
    begin
        -- statements for advancing the current line position;
    end;


    . . .
begin
    -- statements for main program
end;
```

Example 11.4 **Reuse of Local Variable Names**

they are given. Notice that two variables, INDEX and LENGTH, happen to have the same identifier in both procedures, although they represent different entities.

The value of such an idea is immediate. When writing a procedure, a programmer can devise names that are suitable for the computation at hand, without regard to other portions of the program. In a program with a large number of procedures written by several programmers, the programmers can choose names quite freely.

Some languages, for instance, Basic and Cobol, do not have the concept of scope. Whenever a new entity must be declared, the programmer is forced to devise a unique name for the entity. Even in relatively small programs, this forces somewhat awkward naming conventions. Perhaps even more important, the declaration and use of the name may be quite distant. Thus, the programmer may have no clear way of showing the locality of effects on the various components of the program. For these reasons, almost all recently designed programming languages have some notion of scope.

Block Structuring

Mini-language Scope is modeled on the idea of block-structured languages, originally introduced with Algol 60. Similar directions have been taken in many other languages, for example, PL/I, Pascal, Algol 68, and Ada.

The essential features of block structure are a system of program units that delimit the regions of program text and a method for specifying the names that belong to these regions. In Mini-language Scope, we use program or procedure as the opening bracket of a unit and end as the closing bracket. Note that blocks can be nested one inside another.

There are, in general, two sets of rules for the resolution of name references. These rules correspond to the static and the dynamic structure of the program. We will first discuss the set that corresponds to the static structure of the program; this is sometimes called *lexical scoping*. The term *lexical* refers to the fact that all references can be resolved from the text of the program. The term *static binding* is also used; this indicates that the connection between the declaration and the reference does not change during the execution of the program.

The conventional rules of lexical scoping are:

- The scope of a declaration includes the block in which it occurs but excludes any block surrounding it.

- The scope of a declaration includes any block contained within the block in which the declaration occurs but excludes any contained block in which the same identifier is redeclared.

One effect of these rules is to prevent access to variables and procedures declared within a procedure from outside the procedure. For example, consider the fragment:

```
. . .
P: procedure
    B: integer;
    C: procedure
        . . .
    end;
begin
    -- statements for P
end;
. . .
```

The variable B cannot be referenced outside the procedure P nor can the procedure C be invoked from outside the procedure P.

Another consequence is that the redeclaration of an identifier prevents reference to the original entity. For example, consider the fragment:

```
X: integer;      -- outer X
A: procedure
    X: integer; -- inner X
    B: procedure
        . . .
    begin
        . . . -- the outer X cannot be referenced here
    end;
begin
    . . .
end;
```

PL/I provides an escape from this situation by using external names. External variables behave as though they were declared in a conceptual block that contains all the separately compiled procedures of the program. An external name may be referenced within the scope of any declaration of the same identifier with the attribute EXTERNAL, as in the following fragment:

```
DECLARE X FIXED EXTERNAL;      /* outer variable X */
A:
PROCEDURE;
   DECLARE X FIXED;            /* inner variable X */
   B:
   PROCEDURE;
      DECLARE X FIXED EXTERNAL;
      X = 5;                   /* reference to outer variable X */
   END B;
   X = 5;                      /* reference to inner variable X */
END A;
X = 5;                         /* reference to outer variable X */
```

Block structure permits efficient use of storage. Since a variable only comes into existence at the time the procedure that declared it is invoked, storage may be shared among local variables of procedures declared at the same level. This is the reason that a Pascal program, for example, frequently requires less storage than the equivalent Fortran or Cobol program. The Pascal program only requires storage for the data associated with active procedures, whereas Fortran and Cobol generally require storage for data associated with all procedures all the time.

There are also severe disadvantages to nesting and block structure. It promotes programs that are difficult to read. This is because of the physical separation of procedure headings that contain the declarations of variables from the use of the variables in the body of the procedure. Although variables are declared within the procedures in which they are used, the procedure headings contain declarations of all the contained procedures. In a deeply nested set of procedures, there can be a great amount of text between the variable declarations and the executable statements of the procedure. Something of this can be seen in Example 11.3. The variables A, B, and C of the outermost procedure are declared in the second line of the program but they are not referenced until line 18.

There is a temptation to treat the variables in the containing blocks as global variables. As we shall see shortly, global variables greatly increase the complexity of a program.

Global Variables

The use of even a few global variables in a block increases the complexity of the block considerably. An understanding of the computation performed by the block involves considering the use that is made of the global variables in the larger context of the complete program. Changes made to global variables outside the block can affect the correctness of the block itself.

With blocks that are procedures, the dangers of global variables can be seen quite dramatically. Consider the program of Example 11.2. Here we have the sequence of statements:

```
output A;
PURELY_GLOBAL;
output A;
```

Notice that the same output statement appears twice, but the value output by each statement is different. The problem here is caused by the invocation of the procedure PURELY_GLOBAL. The call statement does not even mention the variable A, yet the invocation of the procedure changes the value of this variable. This is known as a *side effect* or a *context effect.*

The problems associated with global variables were the subject of a paper [Wulf and Shaw, 1973]. These problems can be summarized as:

- *Context effects.* We gave a small example of this problem earlier in this section. In a small program like Example 11.2, the danger of side effects may not appear to be particularly serious. But imagine a program with hundreds of statements and many procedure calls, where each procedure exhibits some context effect. Keeping track of the dynamic behavior of such a program is often almost impossible.

- *Aliasing.* The side effects problem is compounded when the use of global variables is combined with passing parameters by location. Then, if a global variable is passed as an argument to a procedure, there are two separate ways in which the procedure may reference the variable: as the global variable, and as the parameter. Thus, to the reader of the procedure, it will appear as though two different variables have been referenced whereas, in fact, only one variable is involved. The two different names are *aliases.* This is not only confusing to the programmer but also makes it impossible for certain optimization processes to be performed.

- *Public Access.* The variables A, B, and C declared at the beginning of the program in Example 11.3 are global to the procedures Q, R, and S. There is no way of restricting their access. Although some procedures, through redeclaration of the same identifiers, are not able to reference them, this is a choice made during the programming of the procedures. There is no way that the programmer of the outer procedure can prevent these variables being referenced by the inner procedures. This makes the maintenance of the program much more difficult since the programmer making the modifications must be aware of the access patterns of all the procedures to understand the usage of the global variables.

■ *Screening.* This is the converse of the public access problem. Where procedures are deeply nested, the addition of a new declaration of a local variable to a procedure may screen the access of an inner procedure to a global variable declared at an outer level. For example, in Example 11.3, the addition of a declaration of A in the procedure S would prevent the access in the inner procedure Q to the outermost global variable A in the statement in line 10. This is another problem that makes the maintenance of large block-structured programs difficult.

Our view of block structuring is adequately summed up by the title of a paper, *Nesting in Ada Is for the Birds* [Clark et al. 1980].

11.3 Storage Allocation

In addition to the use of block structure as a means of controlling the scope of declarations, it is also of significance at execution time. As was mentioned in the previous section, block structuring allows for the dynamic sharing of storage and thus its efficient use. It may be argued that, with the development of inexpensive storage on modern computers, this gain in efficiency may be dubious.

The fact that a variable is not known outside the block in which it is declared means that storage for variables in a block need only be allocated during the execution of the block. Thus, storage for the variables is obtained when the block is entered and released when the block is completed. This provides a basis for the sharing of storage between blocks in an easily controlled and well-defined way. This form of storage management is known as *dynamic storage allocation.* It was originally developed for the implementation of Algol 60 and has since been adapted for other block-structured languages.

The acquisition of storage on block entry is handled by a special sequence of instructions, known as the *prologue,* generated by the compiler. Corresponding to the prologue, there is an *epilogue* that is executed as the block terminates. The epilogue handles the release of storage that is no longer required. Generally, the simplest way to manage dynamic allocation is through the use of a stack.

The Run-Time Stack

The basic idea is to use a region of consecutive locations of storage as a stack. That is, allocated storage will always be added to the top of the stack by incrementing a stack pointer, and released storage will always be removed from the top of the stack by decrementing the pointer. Although this kind of management technique is unable to handle arbitrary allocation and release of storage, the last-in, first-out mode of operation corresponds precisely to the storage requirements of a block-structured language.

All the storage required for the fixed-size variables of a block is collected together into a single area of storage called an *activation record* or a *stack frame*. In addition to the storage for variables, an activation record will contain other items concerned with the control of the execution of the program. Such items include:

- Information about parameters
- Information about local variables that cannot be determined during compilation, for example, when the bounds of a local array are calculated from the parameters
- Temporary storage for expression evaluation
- Addressing information for nonlocal variables
- The return address, that is, the point in the calling block to which control returns when the current block terminates
- A pointer to the activation record of the caller

The prologue manipulates the stack pointer and then initializes the newly created activation record on the stack. Upon termination, the pointer is reset to its position before the block's invocation and returns control to the caller. Thus, at any time during execution, the run-time stack consists of activation records for all those blocks that have been invoked but have not yet terminated.

As an illustration of the use of the run-time stack, we trace block entries and exits (with their corresponding effects on the run-time stack) of Example 11.3, as shown in Table 11.3.

The rules of scope define a mapping from an identifier reference to a declaration. The environment of a block provides the mapping from the declarations to locations and thus values. An environment must be associated with the kinds of objects treated by the programming language. In Chapter 10, we discussed the concept of passing arguments by name and the problem of name clashes. The actual technique used for passing an expression is generally through the construction of a small procedure that calculates the value of the expression being passed as argument. Such procedures, named "thunks" in [Ingerman 1961], must be associated with the environment of the call statement if they are to calculate the correct value of the expression. Other examples of objects that require an environment are format descriptors that are passed as arguments to procedures, label variables, and procedures themselves, if they are treated as objects. We will discuss this latter question in Chapter 14.

Table 11.3 Stack Execution of Example 11.3

[SP denotes the stack pointer]

Line 17: The main program is entered. An activation record containing locations for variables A, B, and C is created.

Line 21: Procedure R is invoked.
Line 4: Procedure R is entered. An activation record containing a location for variable C is created. This new activation record contains a pointer to the activation record of the caller. A reference to the identifier C in this block is a reference to the current activation record. However, references to the identifiers A and B are references to these variables in the previous activation record labeled MAIN. The use of the ENV pointer is explained below.

Line 6: Procedure Q is invoked.
Line 1: Procedure Q is entered. An activation record for this block is obtained. Since this block does not have any local variables, there is no need for any storage for them. However, space for control information such as the return address is still needed. References to the identifiers A and C are references to the activation record of the main program. A simple pointer to the activation record of the caller does not provide the necessary information and an additional pointer, labeled ENV, is needed. This is the *environment* pointer and is used when the calling procedure does not contain the called one, for example, when S invokes R.

Line 3: Execution of Q completes and control returns to line 7. The activation record for Q is removed from the stack.

Table 11.3 **continued**

Line 8: Execution of R is completed and control returns to line 22. The activation record for R is removed from the stack.

Line 22: Procedure S is invoked.
Line 12: Procedure S is entered. An activation record
containing locations for variables B and C is created.
The storage used for this activation record is the
space just released from the activation record of procedure R.

Line 15: Procedure Q internal to S is invoked.
Line 9: Procedure Q is entered. An activation record
for this block is obtained. The environment for this
block consists of the activation record for S for references to the identifiers B and C and the activation record for MAIN for references to the identifier A. Thus
two environment pointers are provided in the activation record for procedure Q.

Line 11: Execution of procedure Q is completed and
control returns to line 16. The activation record for
procedure Q is removed from the stack.

Table 11.3 **continued**

Line 16: Procedure R is invoked.
Line 4: Procedure R is entered. An activation record containing a location for the variable C is created. The environment pointer permits references to A and B in the main program.

Line 6: Procedure Q is invoked.
Line 1: Procedure Q is entered. An activation record for this block is obtained. This activation record is at a different place on the run-time stack from the previous activation record for this block. Since procedures Q, R, and S are all immediately contained in the main procedure, the activation record for the main procedure is the environment for each of these blocks.
Line 3: Execution of Q is completed and control returns to line 7. The activation record for Q is removed from the stack.

Line 8: Execution of R completes and control returns to the end of procedure S. This terminates S and returns control to the end of the main procedure, which also terminates. As each terminates, its activation record is removed from the stack. The stack is left empty.

The mechanism of providing one or more environment pointers in an activation record is not the only possible implementation. A full discussion of these techniques is beyond the scope of this text; for further information the reader is referred to a compiler text such as [Aho and Ullman 1977].

Arrays and structures whose sizes are unknown during compilation can also be handled on the run-time stack. The technique generally employed is to allocate first the part of the activation record whose size is known during compilation. Once this has been done, the size of the array can be calculated, and the size of the activation record can be increased by advancing the stack pointer. A pointer to the array is then inserted into the fixed part so that it can be accessed through an address calculated during compilation. For the size of an array to be calculated during a prologue, there must be sufficient information available when the prologue is executed. Thus, the data from which the size of the array is calculated must be available either in parameters or global variables that can be accessed by the prologue.

A recursive procedure is one that can have more than one activation record on the run-time stack at some point during execution. Each of these activation records is distinct, and each can contain locations for different generations of the local variables. It is of particular importance in dealing with recursive invocations that questions of environment be carefully defined. We shall also return to this question in later chapters.

Some languages permit goto statements that will transfer control out of the current block into another block that is currently active—that is, a block that has a stack frame. The label value in the goto statement can either be a constant or a label variable. In the case of the constant, the goto statement must be within the scope of the label constant declaration. In this case, the most recent stack frame belonging to the block containing the label constant declaration is made the current stack frame. To do this, the current stack frame and all stack frames between it and the new current stack frame must be removed from the run-time stack. In the case of label variables, its label value must contain an environment component that defines the new current stack frame. The identity of this stack frame is determined at the time the label value is assigned to the label variable. For the program to execute correctly, that stack frame must still exist on the run-time stack at the time the goto statement is executed.

Other Kinds of Storage Management

A block-structured language allocates storage for variables as each block is invoked. This is, however, not true of all languages; there are essentially three different times at which storage can be allocated:

1. When the complete program is loaded into storage. This is the case in Fortran and Cobol, the PL/I storage class STATIC, and Algol *own* variables. PL/I static storage and Algol own variables differ from normal block-structured storage in that they are preserved when control leaves a block containing them and their values are made available on reentry. This permits values to be retained from one invocation to another without the use of global variables. Own variables have the advantage over global variables that they are private to the procedure that declares them. Global variables can be accessed by any procedure within their scope. Generally, the bounds of own variables must be determined during compilation and cannot change during execution.

2. When the block is invoked. This is the type of storage management that we have described in detail in this section. The allocation and release of storage is tied directly to the block structure of the program.

3. Under the direct control of the programmer. This is achieved through the execution of special statements. This case is discussed in Chapter 13.

11.4 Dynamic Scope

In addition to the more common static rules of scope that we have defined and demonstrated through Mini-language Scope, there are some languages where the resolution of an identifier reference to the defining declaration must be performed dynamically. That is to say, the region of the program over which a particular declaration applies varies during the execution of the program.

The scope rules used by Snobol, APL, and Lisp are essentially the same. These require that a reference to an identifier be resolved to the declaration of that identifer in the most recently invoked, but not yet terminated, block that contains a declaration of the identifier. Thus, the resolution of a nonlocal reference will depend on the sequence of invocations, and the resolution can change during execution.

The implementation of this type of scope rule can be achieved with a run-time stack by including in the activation record a list of all identifiers declared in the block. Resolution is performed by searching the stack for the most recent activation record that contains the desired identifier. In practice, this can be time-consuming and more efficient implementations are available. However, it serves well as a model of the process.

Some surprising effects can result from this kind of scope rule. In particular, an assignment statement does not always change the same variable, and a call statement may invoke a different procedure depending on the state of the run-time stack.

For example, suppose that the rules of Mini-language Scope were changed so that name resolution had to be performed dynamically. The execution of Example 11.3 would then proceed differently. In particular, procedure R is invoked both from the main procedure and from procedure S. When R is invoked from the main procedure, the reference to B in line 7 is to the variable B in the main procedure, and the invocation of Q in line 6 is an invocation of the procedure Q that includes lines 1 through 3. When R is invoked from procedure S, the reference to B in line 7 is resolved to a reference to the variable S.B, and the invocation of Q in line 6 is an invocation of the procedure Q that includes lines 9 through 11. This is because S's activation record is more recent than that of the main procedure.

A consequence of this kind of behavior is that it is impossible to protect the variables of a block against access by a subroutine. In a statically scoped language, such protection exists where the subroutine is not contained inside the calling block. This danger with dynamic scoping brings into serious question the applicability of dynamically scoped languages to the production of large reliable programs.

A second consequence of dynamic scoping is that it entails typing. Since the resolution of a reference to a declaration is performed during execution, it is impossible to perform type checking during compilation. Thus, in addition to the overhead of resolving the reference dynamically, there is the overhead of type checking so that this kind of scope rule really implies an interpretive execution.

As we mentioned earlier, the major purpose of block structure is to localize the use of data, to hide the information about a process within the procedure that performs it. This is of great advantage since it localizes the changes that must be made to a program during later modifications. However, block structuring is an inadequate mechanism for achieving this information hiding. The visibility rules are implicit and based only on nesting. It is now recognized that there is a need to make the visibility explicit and to divide a program into separately compiled modules. Identifiers that are to be visible outside a module must be explicitly declared as *exported identifiers*. Similarly, identifiers defined in another module must be explicitly declared as *imported identifiers* before they can be referenced. The visibility of all other identifiers is restricted to the module in which they are declared. There are no implicit visibility assumptions. The subject of separately compiled modules is treated in Chapter 17.

11.5 Where to Look: `Pascal`, `PL/I`, `APL`

Pascal

Both Pascal and PL/I are block-structured languages. However, there are numerous differences in both overall structure and detail. A Pascal program is always formed from a single main program block that contains internal subprograms that can be at a single level or nested. A Pascal program has the same general form as a Mini-language Procedures program. The syntax of a program is

```
program identifier ( program-parameters ) ;
    block .
```

where the structure of a block is

```
[label-declarations]
[constant-declarations]
[type-declarations]
[variable-declarations]
[subprogram-declarations]
begin
    statement. . .
end
```

A subprogram declaration has the form

```
subprogram-type identifier [ ( parameter-list ) ] [ : type-identifier] ;
    block
```

where a subprogram-type is either `procedure` or `function`. The type-identifier is used only on function-subprocedure declarations to indicate the type of the value to be returned. The scope rules of Pascal match those of Mini-language Procedures. All variables in Pascal have a lifetime of the procedure that declares them; that is, they are created when the procedure is invoked and destroyed when the procedure completes.

PL/I

The general form of a PL/I program consists of one or more separately compiled block-structured procedures combined to form a program by incorporating them into one all-encompassing nameless block. One of the incorporated procedures is designated as the entry procedure for the whole program. The syntax of a procedure is

identifier : PROCEDURE [(parameter-list)]
                                        [RETURNS (attribute-list)] ;
    [declaration]. . .
    [procedure]. . .
    [statement]. . .
END ;

Although PROCEDURE, RETURNS, and END have been shown as special symbols, PL/I does not distinguish between identifiers and keywords except by the context in which they occur. Further, PL/I does not predefine the order in which declarations, procedures, and statements appear in a procedure.

In addition to the block structure formed from the nesting or procedures, there are also blocks delimited by BEGIN and END; that can be nested within procedures and themselves. The scope rules are again the same as those in Mini-language Procedures with the addition of the ability to declare an identifier to have the attribute EXTERNAL. An external identifier has global scope; it is as if the declaration had been written in the outermost, all-encompassing block. However, access to external identifiers can always be established in a block by declaring the identifier with the attribute EXTERNAL. Thus, it is impossible to screen access by an inner procedure by redeclaring the identifier in a procedure at an intervening nest level.

In addition to variables known as automatic variables, whose lifetime corresponds to the lifetime of the declaring procedure, PL/I variables can be given other storage attributes. The PL/I equivalent of own variables are static variables. These can be external, as we described in the previous paragraph, or internal, in which case they behave in the same manner as own variables. Their lifetime is that of the program; they are created when the program is invoked by the operating system and continue to exist until the program terminates. There are also two other classes of variables, controlled and based, whose lifetime is directly controlled by the programmer through allocate and free statements. The allocate statement creates such a variable and a free statement destroys it. The difference between the two is that based variables must be referenced through a pointer value whereas a controlled variable is referenced by name in the normal way.

APL

APL is designed to be executed interactively. That is to say, it is possible to enter assignments containing expressions that are evaluated immediately with the value being assigned to global variables. In addition, the programmer can define subprograms for execution during evaluation of immediate expressions.

APL is not a block-structured language; however, APL subprograms can define local variables and can reference global variables. Subprograms may have zero, one, or two arguments and may or may not return a value. The first line of a subprogram defines the name of the subprogram, the names of its parameters, its return value parameter, if any, and the names of its local variables. For example, the header:

∇ PAY ← RATE OVERTIME HOURS; TIME

defines the subprogram OVERTIME as having two parameters, RATE and HOURS, a result parameter PAY, and a local variable TIME.

The names of subprograms in APL are automatically global identifiers. Global variables are defined implicitly by the appearance of an assignment to an identifier that has not been used before or defined as a parameter or local variable. References to nonlocal variables in a subprogram are resolved dynamically according to the rule described in Section 11.4. That is, if during execution a subprogram references a nonlocal variable X, the calling stack is searched backwards for the most recent subprogram that has a definition for X. If no such resolution is possible, then the set of global variables is searched. If it is still impossible to make a name resolution, then a referencing error is signaled.

Further Reading

Certainly the most complete reference on the topics treated in this chapter is given in [Schwenke 1978]. This rather lengthy paper outlines the area traditionally associated with scope, surveys the various mechanisms required in a number of contemporary programming languages, and studies the impact of many of these issues on implementation.

An earlier article [Wulf and Shaw 1973] summarizes the dangers associated with the use of global variables. Another early work [Johnston 1971] discusses a model in which block-structured languages with scope rules may be viewed.

An additional work in this area is [Jones and Muchnick 1978]. This short text defines a small language called Tempo; this language and the authors' treatment present an overall view of argument passing and scope, with particular emphasis on the notion of binding times (see Exercise 11.5).

Exercises

Exercise 11.1 *Static Scope*

Trace the execution of the following program written in Mini-language Scope.

```
program
   A, B, C: integer;

   Q: procedure
   begin
      B := B + 2;
      C := C + 2;
      output A, B, C;
   end;   -- Q

   R: procedure
      A: integer;
   begin
      C := 2;
      Q;
      B := A + C;
      output A, B, C;
   end;   -- R

   S: procedure
      A, C: integer;
      Q: procedure
         C;
      begin
         A := A + 1;
         C := B + 1;
         output A, B, C;
      end;
   begin
      B := 3;
      C := 1;
      Q;
      output A, B, C;
      R;
      output A, B, C;
   end;   -- S
```

```
begin
   A := 1;
   B := 1;
   C := 1;
   R;
   output A, B, C;
   S;
   output A, B, C;
end;
```

Exercise 11.2 *Revisiting the Joys of Scope*

This is more difficult than Exercise 11.1. Trace the execution of the
following program:

```
program
   A, B, C: integer;

   P: procedure
      C;

      Q: procedure
         A, B: integer;
      begin
         A := 3;
         B := C + A;
         output A, B, C;
         R;
         ouput A, B, C;
      end;   -- Q

      S: procedure
         C, D: integer;
         R: procedure
         begin
            C := A + (B + 3);
            A := B + D;
            output A, B, C;
         end;   -- R
   begin
      A := A + 3;
      C := 5;
      D := 2;
      Q;
      output A, B, C;
      R;
      output A, B, C;
   end;   -- S
```

```
begin
   C := 2;
   A := A + 1;
   B := A + C;
   output A, B, C;
   R;
   output A, B, C;
   S;
   output A, B, C;
end;   -- P

R: procedure
   A: integer;
begin
   A := B + 2;
   B := B + C;
   C := C + 5;
   output A, B, C;
end;   -- R

begin
   A := 1;
   B := 2;
   C := 3;
   P;
   output A, B, C;
end;
```

Exercise 11.3 *Avoiding Side Effects in Functions*

Consider a programming language having the usual rules of scope, that is, a block-structured language. There are two types of internal subprograms allowed in the language: *functions,* which return a value to the point of invocation, and *procedures,* which do not. The language is defined so that function invocation cannot cause any side effects.

If you were implementing the compiler, how would you make sure that this rule is enforced?

Note: It may be necessary to restrict the types of statements that can appear within the body of a function, either to enforce the rule or to warn programmers who apparently do not understand the rule.

Exercise 11.4 *Reaching above a Local Scope*

In accordance with the usual block structure rules of scope, a declaration causes a declared identifier to have local scope. The use of an identifier yields a reference to the innermost containing procedure or block in which the identifier is declared.

Suppose we wish to retain these rules but add some way of allowing identifiers to be declared so that they have a nonlocal scope that is derived from a containing block, but not necessarily the innermost containing block. For example, with the structure

```
A: procedure
   X: integer;

   B: procedure
      X: integer;

      C: procedure
         X: integer;
         . . .      -- use of X
      end;  -- C
   . . .
   end;  -- B
. . .
end;  -- A
```

we would like some way for the use of X in procedure C to refer to the X in procedure A, rather than be local as it is now, or refer to the X in procedure B as it would if it were not redeclared in procedure C.

1. Suggest an extension or modification to the declaration syntax to accommodate the revised scope rules.
2. What problems, if any, would this extension cause if run-time references were resolved using the usual simple symbol table?
3. Offer arguments for or against the use of these revised scope rules in a programming language.

Exercise 11.5 Binding Time

The term *binding* is used to denote the association of an identifier with a value. Basically, there are six times at which binding can occur:

1. Writing of program text

2. Compilation of program text

3. Linking together of separately compiled modules to form a complete program

4. Loading of a complete program into machine storage

5. Invocation of a subprogram

6. Execution of a statement

Give an example of a binding that can occur at each of these times.

Exercise 11.6 *Recursive Invocation*

Trace the execution of the following program showing the layout of the run-time stack.

```
program
    A: integer;

    P: procedure
        X: integer;
        Q: procedure
        begin
            output X;
        end;
    begin
        if (A = 1) then
            A := 2;
            X := 5;
            R;
        else
            X := 11;
            Q;
        end;
    end;

    R: procedure
    begin
        S;
    end;

    S: procedure
    begin
        P;
    end;

begin
    A := 1;
    P;
end;
```

What other static nestings are possible for the procedures P, Q, R, and S? For three of these nestings, show the dynamic stack during execution.

Exercise 11.7 *Dynamic Scope*

Trace the execution of Exercise 11.2 under the rule of dynamic scope as described in Section 11.4.

Exercise 11.8 *Aliasing*

Construct an example of a program fragment where an optimizing compiler would be unable to perform an optimization due to the possibility of aliasing.

Exercise 11.9 *Global versus Local Variables*

[Fisher 1983] advocates the use of global variables in all programs and suggests abandoning the use of local variables altogether. In support of this position, the following arguments are offered:

1. The use of local variables does not save very much storage, especially when execution reaches the innermost blocks.

2. The use of the same identifier names with different scopes creates confusion in reading programs.

3. The use of global variables can significantly reduce the number of parameters to be passed to procedures.

4. If all global variables are placed in a common area, then the problem of checking type consistency between arguments and parameters for separately compiled procedures is avoided.

5. If all variables are made global as in argument 4, then programs are easier to maintain and modify than otherwise.

Write a position paper that either points out fallacies in these arguments or supports them.

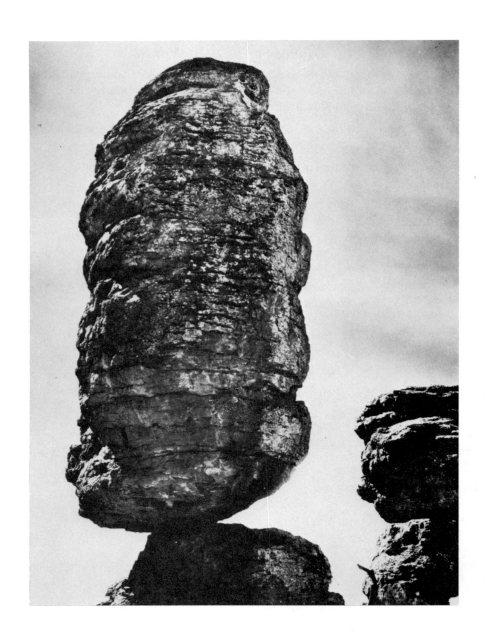

12

Definition of New Data Types

A high-level programming language seeks to develop tools that represent the objects and operations of an application properly. Different areas of application, for example, data processing, graphics, operations research, or text preparation, require abstractions through data types that are not directly available in general-purpose languages like Fortran, PL/I, or Basic. With these languages, the programmer must make *mental* associations between the objects and operations in the real world of the application and the structured data objects that represent them in the program.

To make application programming easier, special-purpose languages have often been developed to suit some well-defined application area, for example, machine tool control. This approach has the drawback that, because of limitations on the size of a language, not all the objects and operations that would be potentially useful in writing programs for a single application area can be included in the language. As applications become more sophisticated, they need to draw on wider domains. Planning to live with any predetermined number of special-purpose features will restrict the usefulness of the language.

Another approach has been taken in the more recent languages such as Pascal, Simula 67, Algol 68, Euclid, Modula-2, Alphard, Clu, and Ada. To various extents, these languages enable the application programmer to define particular abstract objects and operations, that is, to define new data types. The application program can then be written using newly defined types and their operations. In essence, the programmer can create a dialect of the original language that more closely matches the application.

In this chapter, the beginnings of a user-defined type mechanism is explored using Mini-language Typedef. This mechanism goes beyond that

359

provided in Pascal since it provides for the definition of operators as well as for classes of values. Important extensions of this facility available in other languages are then discussed.

12.1 Mini-language Typedef

The syntax of Mini-language Typedef is given in Table 12.1. Mini-language Typedef has many features similar to the mini-languages presented in previous chapters. As with previous mini-languages, a program in Typedef consists of a declarative part followed by a sequence of statements.

Table 12.1 **Mini-language Typedef**

program	::=	`program`
		[type-declaration. . .]
		[operator-declaration. . .]
		variable-declaration. . .
		`begin`
		statement. . .
		`end` ;
type-declaration	::=	identifier : `type` type-definition ;
operator-declaration	::=	operator : `operator` operator-type
		[variable-declaration]. . .
		`begin`
		statement. . .
		`return` expression ;
		`end` ;
operator-type	::=	(identifier : type , identifier : type) `=>` type
variable-declaration	::=	identifier [, identifier]. . . : type ;
type	::=	`integer` | `boolean` | identifier
type-definition	::=	enumerated-type | sub-type | array-type
enumerated-type	::=	(identifier [, identifier]. . .)
sub-type	::=	type range
range	::=	value . . value
value	::=	integer | identifier
array-type	::=	`array [ range ] of` type

All identifiers in a Typedef program must be declared exactly once. There are three kinds of declarations: type declarations, operator declarations, and variable declarations. A variable declaration associates one or more identifiers with the type integer or with a type that has been defined in a type declaration. Integers have the usual meaning and operations.

With the exception of the loop statement, to be described later, the statements in Mini-language Typedef are conventional. In an assignment statement, the variable and the expression must have the same type.

Table 12.1 **continued**

statement	::=	assignment-statement | if-statement
	|	loop-statement | input-statement
	|	output-statement
assignment-statement	::=	variable := expression ;
if-statement	::=	if expression then
		statement. . .
		[else
		statement. . .]
		end if ;
loop-statement	::=	for identifier := range loop
		statement. . .
		end loop ;
input-statement	::=	input variable [, variable]. . . ;
output-statement	::=	output variable [, variable]. . . ;
expression	::=	[operand operator] operand
operand	::=	integer | identifier | variable
	|	(expression) | boolean
variable	::=	identifier
	|	identifier [expression [, expression]]
operator	::=	< | = | ≠ | > | + | - | * | div
boolean	::=	true | false

Declaration of New Types

The major item of interest in Mini-language Typedef, however, lies in the declaration of new types and operations. For example, we may have:

```
DAY: type (MON, TUE, WED, THU, FRI, SAT, SUN);
SUIT: type (CLUBS, DIAMONDS, HEARTS, SPADES);
```

The first declaration introduces a type named DAY. Just as we can say

```
COUNTER: integer;
```

to declare a variable COUNTER of type integer, we can say

```
TODAY: DAY;
TRUMPS: SUIT;
```

to declare a variable TODAY of type DAY and a variable TRUMPS of type SUIT.

Just as a variable of type integer can only take integer values, a variable of type DAY can only take one of the seven values MON through SUN. In this language, type describes a class of values. The two types introduced above are called *enumerated types* since the type declarations explicitly enumerate the class of values.

For simplicity, an identifier can only appear in one enumerated type. Thus, the pair of declarations

```
TRAFFIC_LIGHT: type (RED, AMBER, GREEN);
FLAG_COLOR:    type (RED, WHITE, BLUE);
```

is not allowed.

Variables declared with the new types behave much like variables declared of type integer. They can be assigned to variables of the same type and have values assigned to them from constants belonging to that class of values. For example, we may have

```
TODAY    := MON;
NEW_COIN := NICKEL;
```

but not:

```
SUN   := MON;      -- only variables can be assigned values
TODAY := 1;        -- types do not match
TODAY := NICKEL;   -- types do not match
```

The input and output facilities of Mini-language Typedef also apply to values of enumerated types. When applied to an enumerated variable, an input statement gets the next item in the input stream, checks that it is the character representation for a value of the enumerated type of the variable, and sets this value to the corresponding variable. Similarly, an output statement prints the character representation corresponding to the enumerated value of the variable.

Sub-Types

Restricted sequences or subranges of both integer and enumerated types can be defined by a *sub-type*. A sub-type is specified by its parent type and its *bounds,* its first and last values. The purpose of a sub-type is to control the set of values that a variable may take during execution. For example, we may have:

```
YEAR_NUM   : type integer 1776..2001;
COLUMN_POS: type integer 1..72;
WEEKDAY    : type DAY MON..FRI;
WEEKEND    : type DAY SAT..SUN;
```

Both the first and last bounds of a range must be of the same type as the parent type and must be stated in the same order as they are declared— in the case of integers, in increasing order. For example, the following range definitions are illegal:

```
A: SUIT 1..HEARTS; -- bounds not of the same type
B: DAY FRI..TUE;   -- bounds not in enumeration order
C: integer 17..12; -- integer bounds not in increasing order
```

A sub-type is thus characterized by two properties:

- **The parent type:** For instance, the parent type of YEAR_NUM is integer; the parent type of WEEKDAY is DAY.
- **The bounds of the range:** For instance, 1776 and 2001 are the bounds for the type YEAR_NUM. The bounds determine the *range size,* which is the number of elements in the range type. For instance, the range size of WEEKDAY is 5.

Variables of a sub-type are declared just as variables of other types. Examples are:

```
WORK_DAY:  WEEKDAY;
THIS_YEAR: YEAR_NUM;
```

A sub-type variable behaves like a variable of the parent type. The only difference is that a range variable is constrained during execution to hold only scalar values that belong to the range.

Array Types

Finally, the types definable in Mini-language Typedef include array types. For example, we may declare the array variables

```
INPUT_VALUE:  array [1..72] of integer;
HOURS_WORKED: array [MON..FRI] of integer;
JANUARY:      array [1..31] of DAY;
```

or alternatively, use:

```
INPUT_LINE:    type array [1..72] of integer;
WEEKS_VALUES:  type array [MON..FRI] of integer;
CALENDAR:      type array [1..31] of day;

INPUT_VALUE:   INPUT_LINE;
HOURS_WORKED:  WEEKS_VALUES;
JANUARY:       CALENDAR;
```

The second form is to be preferred. As for sub-types, the bounds of an array type must belong to a declared enumerated type or to the predefined type integer.

The components of an array are denoted by naming the array and giving an expression specifying an individual element. For example, we may have:

```
INPUT_VALUE[2]     -- the second input value
INPUT_VALUE[I]     -- the I-th input value
HOURS_WORKED[WED]  -- the number of hours worked on Wednesday
```

Any attempt to use a subscript outside the bounds declared for the array variable results in an execution error.

Loop Statements

The loop statement in Mini-language Typedef is designed to work with ranges of values. The statement at the head of the loop defines a range of values that are to be assigned to a control variable. For each value in the range, the sequence of statements that form the body of the loop will be executed with the control variable having one of the values of the specified range. Thus, in the loop

```
for DAY := MON..FRI loop
   TOTAL_HOURS := TOTAL_HOURS + HOURS_WORKED[DAY];
end loop;
```

the loop will be executed five times with the control variable taking the values MON through FRI in sequence.

Declaration of Operations

As emphasized in Chapter 8, a data type implies more than just a class of values. There must also be a class of operations that can be performed on the values. In Mini-language Typedef, the symbols ‹, =, ≠, ›, +, -, *, and div denote operators. The operators = and ≠ are defined for all types and can be used to compare the values of variables for equality with others of the same type. Thus, if TODAY has the value MON, we may have the following comparisons:

```
(TODAY = TUE)   -- comparison is false
(TODAY ≠ FRI)   -- comparison is true
```

The operators = and ≠ are the only overloaded operators in the mini-language; all the rest of the operators are only defined for integers. The operators +, -, and * are conventional arithmetic operators, and the div operator provides integer division.

While the value of a sub-type is a subset of the parent type, the operations of a sub-type are those that are applicable to the containing type. For sub-types whose parent type is integer, the arithmetic operators apply as well.

In Typedef, expressions including variables and constants of various types are allowed, provided that operations are applied only to values for which the operation is defined. For instance, consider the following:

```
(TODAY = MON)   -- valid only if TODAY is of type DAY
X + Y           -- valid only if X and Y are of type integer
```

The context in which expressions may appear may require the result value to be restricted to a specified range. For example, the left side of an assignment statement may be a variable declared with a given range. In such assignments, the evaluation of the expression on the right must yield a value within the range of the variable. Any attempt to assign a value that lies outside of the declared range will result in an execution error. Examples of range variable assignments in Mini-language Typedef are:

```
WORK_DAY  := TUE;           -- always valid
THIS_YEAR := THIS_YEAR + 50; -- can lead to execution error
```

In general, exceeding a declared range can only be detected during execution. However, it is important to note that sensible use of ranges allows system detection of range errors. Without a range specification, there would be no hint of wrongdoing until some doubtful results appear in the program output.

For the operators ‹, ›, +, -, *, and div to be applied to the values of enumerated types, their meaning must be defined through operator declarations. These new operator definitions overload the operators with new meanings outside those predefined in Mini-language Typedef. For example, given the type SUIT, we can define the comparison operator ‹ as follows:

```
‹: operator(LEFT_OPERAND: SUIT, RIGHT_OPERAND: SUIT) => boolean
   RESULT: boolean;
begin
   if (LEFT_OPERAND = RIGHT_OPERAND) then
      RESULT := false;
   else
      if (LEFT_OPERAND = CLUBS) then
         RESULT := true;
      else
         if (RIGHT_OPERAND = CLUBS) then
            RESULT := false;
         else
            if (LEFT_OPERAND = DIAMONDS) then
               RESULT := true;
            else
               if (RIGHT_OPERAND = DIAMONDS) then
                  RESULT := false;
               else
                  if (LEFT_OPERAND = HEARTS) then
                     RESULT := true;
                  else
                     RESULT := false;
                  end if;
               end if;
            end if;
         end if;
      end if;
   end if;
   return RESULT;
end;
```

The heading of the operator definition,

```
‹: operator(LEFT_OPERAND: SUIT, RIGHT_OPERAND: SUIT) => boolean
```

shows that there are two operands of type SUIT and the type of the value produced by the operation will be boolean. The value returned by the operation is specified in the return statement at the end of the operation specification.

As another example of the definition of operations, the Mini-language Typedef can be extended to include logical operators by the following operator definitions, which define the operators + and * with two boolean operands to be the logical *or* and *and* operators respectively:

```
+: operator(LEFT_OPERAND: boolean, RIGHT_OPERAND: boolean) => boolean
   RESULT: boolean;
begin
   if (LEFT_OPERAND) then
      RESULT := true;
   else
      if (RIGHT_OPERAND) then
         RESULT := true;
      else
         RESULT := false;
      end if;
   end if;
   return RESULT;
end;

*: operator(LEFT_OPERAND: boolean, RIGHT_OPERAND: boolean) => boolean
   RESULT: boolean;
begin
   if (LEFT_OPERAND) then
      RESULT := RIGHT_OPERAND;
   else
      RESULT := false;
   end if;
   return RESULT;
end;
```

The types of the two operands for operations declared in this way do not need to be of the same type. Consider, for example, the following operator declaration for adding an elapsed number of days to a DAY value to obtain a new DAY value:

```
+: operator(LEFT_OPERAND: DAY, RIGHT_OPERAND: integer) => DAY
   I, DAY_INDEX: integer;
   DAY_VALUES:   array[1..7] of DAY;
```

```
begin
   DAY_VALUES[1] := MON;
   DAY_VALUES[2] := TUE;
   DAY_VALUES[3] := WED;
   DAY_VALUES[4] := THU;
   DAY_VALUES[5] := FRI;
   DAY_VALUES[6] := SAT;
   DAY_VALUES[7] := SUN;
   for I := 1..7 loop
      if (LEFT_OPERAND = DAY_VALUES[I]) then
         DAY_INDEX := I;
      end if;
   end loop;
   DAY_INDEX := DAY_INDEX + RIGHT_OPERAND;
   DAY_INDEX := DAY_INDEX - (((DAY_INDEX - 1) div 7) * 7);
                            -- reduce DAY_INDEX modulo 7
   return DAY_VALUES[DAY_INDEX];
end;
```

One operator declaration is able to refer to already defined operators. Thus, the converse version of the above operator, adding an integer to a DAY, can be defined as:

```
+: operator(LEFT_OPERAND: integer, RIGHT_OPERAND: DAY) => DAY
begin
   return RIGHT_OPERAND + LEFT_OPERAND;
end;
```

An Example

As a simple illustration of the power of user-defined types, we present Example 12.1. This example illustrates the basic idea that a program can introduce a type to describe a class of values needed for an application. The program reads in an initial compass direction followed by a sequence of course changes and computes a final course direction. The body of the program is very simple. The computation is expressed in terms of adding a change to a course to get a new course and is thus natural to the problem being solved. In addition, the input is expressed in natural values such as NORTH and REVERSE.

To solve the same problem in a language whose sole type is integer and where it is not possible to define new types or operations would be more difficult. Directions and headings would have to be encoded into integers and the logic would be more difficult to understand. Even if a look-up table were used, checking the correctness of the program would be more difficult than the one shown in Example 12.1.

```
program

    -- This program reads in a compass direction followed by
    -- a sequence of 20 course changes.
    -- The program outputs the final course direction.

    HEADING: type (NORTH, EAST, SOUTH, WEST);
    TURN:    type (RIGHT, REVERSE, LEFT);

    COURSE:  HEADING;
    CHANGE:  TURN;
    COUNTER: integer;

    +: operator(DIRECTION: HEADING, ALTERATION: TURN) => HEADING

       DIRECTION_VECTOR: type array[RIGHT..LEFT] of HEADING;
       LOOK_UP_TABLE:    array [NORTH..WEST] of DIRECTION_VECTOR;

    begin
        LOOK_UP_TABLE[NORTH, RIGHT]   := EAST;
        LOOK_UP_TABLE[NORTH, REVERSE] := SOUTH;
        LOOK_UP_TABLE[NORTH, LEFT]    := WEST;
        LOOK_UP_TABLE[EAST, RIGHT]    := SOUTH;
        LOOK_UP_TABLE[EAST, REVERSE]  := WEST;
        LOOK_UP_TABLE[EAST, LEFT]     := NORTH;
        LOOK_UP_TABLE[SOUTH, RIGHT]   := WEST;
        LOOK_UP_TABLE[SOUTH, REVERSE] := NORTH;
        LOOK_UP_TABLE[SOUTH, LEFT]    := EAST;
        LOOK_UP_TABLE[WEST, RIGHT]    := NORTH;
        LOOK_UP_TABLE[WEST, REVERSE]  := EAST;
        LOOK_UP_TABLE[WEST, LEFT]     := SOUTH;

        return LOOK_UP_TABLE[DIRECTION, ALTERATION];
    end;

begin
    input COURSE;

    for COUNTER := 1..20 loop
        input CHANGE;
        COURSE := COURSE + CHANGE;
    end loop;

    output COURSE;
end;
```

Example 12.1 **Plotting the Course**

12.2 Type Definitions

In Mini-language Typedef, all programmer-defined types are introduced by type declarations of the form

    identifier : type type-definition ;

The identifier specifies a name for the type. The type-definition specifies the class of values. Except for sub-types of other defined types, every type definition introduces a distinct type. Separate declarations define operations that can manipulate the values of a type.

With this discussion in mind, we recall the basic definition of a type given earlier:

A type characterizes a set of values *and* the set of operations that are applicable to the values.

The type declarations of values together with the definition of operations given in Mini-language Typedef allow the specification of both components of a type. In programs written in statically typed languages, like Typedef, all variables have an associated type that is specified when the variable is declared.

One of the key issues in programming is the certainty with which we can draw conclusions about a program. Consider the following declarations:

```
TODAY:   DAY;
TRUMPS:  SUIT;
COUNTER: integer;
```

It would be meaningful to have the statements:

```
TODAY   := TUE;
TRUMPS  := HEARTS;
COUNTER := COUNTER + 1;
```

but not meaningful to have the statements:

```
TODAY   := SPADES;     -- SPADES is not a day
TRUMPS  := TUE;        -- TUE is not a suit
COUNTER := TODAY + 1;  -- value of expression is not an integer
```

In the last case, we have defined through an operator declaration that the result of adding an integer to a DAY is a DAY. We cannot assign a DAY value to an integer.

As a result of the use of the types DAY and SUIT, the compiler can enforce more restrictive checking than is possible with only the primitive types of a language. There is thus a greater certainty that the program is correct—there will be no violation of type properties during execution.

Enumerated Types

As mentioned earlier, an enumerated type is defined by enumerating its values. Such types can be used as freely as integers, and often with greater clarity. For example, we may declare a table itemizing the number of hours worked on each day of the week as:

```
HOURS_WORKED: array[MON..FRI] of integer;
```

Furthermore, we may have a loop iterating over Monday through Sunday, as in:

```
for CURRENT_DAY := MON..SUN loop
-- what to do for each value of CURRENT_DAY
end loop;
```

Note the clarity of this loop compared with the following:

```
DAY_INDEX := 1;
for DAY_INDEX := 1..7 loop
    -- what to do for each value of DAY_INDEX
end loop;
```

Unless we are extremely careful, when we come to look at the program containing this encoding in the future, we will have difficulty in remembering how we represented days. We will wonder whether we started numbering the days of the week from Monday, because that is the first working day, or from Sunday, because that is what the calendar shows as the first day of the week.

Table 12.2 shows the definition of a number of enumerated types. The use of such types can add considerably to the clarity of a program.

Table 12.2 **A Sampler of Enumerated Types**

DAY:	type (MON, TUE, WED, THU, FRI, SAT, SUN);
COIN:	type (PENNY, NICKEL, DIME, QUARTER, HALF_DOLLAR, DOLLAR);
DIRECTION:	type (NORTH, EAST, SOUTH, WEST);
OP_CODE:	type (ADD, SUB, MUL, LDA, STA, STZ);
HALF_DAY:	type (AM, PM);
FILE_STATUS:	type (OPEN, CLOSED);
ARMY_RANK:	type (PRIVATE, CORPORAL, SERGEANT, LIEUTENANT, CAPTAIN, MAJOR, COLONEL, GENERAL);
CONTROL_CHAR:	type (NULL, END_OF_TRANSMISSION, ENQUIRE, BELL, BACKSPACE, LINE_FEED, CANCEL, ESCAPE);
PEN_STATUS:	type (DOWN, UP);
SHAPE:	type (TRIANGLE, QUADRANGLE, PENTAGON, HEXAGON);
DRIVING_CODE:	type (NORMAL, LIMITED, SPECIAL, VIP);
COLOR:	type (RED, BLUE, GREEN, BROWN);

Undefined Values

Our definition in Section 12.1 of the operator + between values of type DAY and integers made use of the fact that the set of DAY values was circular. That is, MON followed SUN just as TUE followed MON. As a result, it is always possible to generate a value that is a result of the operation. What should be done if this is not the case? Consider the operator + defined for ARMY_RANK as follows:

```
+: operator(LEFT_OPERAND: ARMY_RANK, RIGHT_OPERAND: integer)
                                              => ARMY_RANK
   I, RANK_INDEX: integer;
   RANKS:    array[1..8] of ARMY_RANK;
```

```
begin
   RANKS[1] := PRIVATE;
   RANKS[2] := CORPORAL;
   RANKS[3] := SERGEANT;
   RANKS[4] := LIEUTENANT;
   RANKS[5] := CAPTAIN;
   RANKS[6] := MAJOR;
   RANKS[7] := COLONEL;
   RANKS[8] := GENERAL;
   for I := 1..8 loop
      if (LEFT_OPERAND = RANKS[I]) then
         RANK_INDEX := I;
      end if;
   end loop;
   RANK_INDEX := RANK_INDEX + RIGHT_OPERAND;
   return RANKS[RANK_INDEX];
end;
```

The problem with this definition is that there is no provision for the case where, for example, we try to evaluate the expression MAJOR + 3. This will lead to an error in executing the return statement since the value of RANKS[9] is not defined. One possible solution to this problem is to implement an idea we have discussed briefly in chapters 4 and 8. This is the concept of undefined values.

Suppose that we changed the definition of the type of ARMY_RANK to be:

```
ARMY_RANK: type (PRIVATE, CORPORAL, SERGEANT, LIEUTENANT,
                 CAPTAIN, MAJOR, COLONEL, GENERAL,
                 UNDEFINED);
```

so that we have an additional value, UNDEFINED, that signifies that some operator was not able to generate a value within the set of defined values. We could take advantage of this by redefining the + operator as:

```
+: operator(LEFT_OPERAND: ARMY_RANK,
                          RIGHT_OPERAND: integer) => ARMY_RANK
   I, RANK_INDEX: integer;
   RANKS:        array[1..8] of ARMY_RANK;
   RESULT:       ARMY_RANK;
```

```
begin
   if (LEFT_OPERAND = UNDEFINED) then
      RESULT := UNDEFINED;
   else
      RANKS[1] := PRIVATE;
      RANKS[2] := CORPORAL;
      RANKS[3] := SERGEANT;
      RANKS[4] := LIEUTENANT;
      RANKS[5] := CAPTAIN;
      RANKS[6] := MAJOR;
      RANKS[7] := COLONEL;
      RANKS[8] := GENERAL;
      for I := 1..8 loop
         if (LEFT_OPERAND = RANKS[I]) then
            RANK_INDEX := I;
         end if;
      end loop;
      RANK_INDEX := RANK_INDEX + RIGHT_OPERAND;
      if (RANK_INDEX > 8) then
         RESULT := UNDEFINED;
      else
         RESULT := RANKS[RANK_INDEX];
      end if;
   end if;
   return RESULT;
end;
```

Note that, if the value of LEFT_OPERAND is UNDEFINED on entry to this operation, the result will also be UNDEFINED. Thus, the undefined value can take part in the computation and its results are always defined. In a more extensive language than Typedef, it would be possible to use the value UNDEFINED for all programmer-defined types for this purpose.

12.3 Definition of Structured Types

The type definition mechanism for array types in Mini-language Typedef can be readily extended to include the type definition of record structures like those in Mini-language Type.

Record Types

Record types are similar to record structured variables in Mini-language Type, in that records are used to model some composite entity. The important difference is that record types enable the programmer to separate the abstraction process of representing a real-world object by a collection of data items from the declaration of variables that reference the abstraction.

A record type can be defined by associating a new type name with a description of the fields in the record structure. A simple record type definition is given below:

```
COMPLEX: type record
                REAL_PART: integer;
                IMAG_PART: integer;
         end record;
```

The component types need not be restricted to the predefined types, such as integer, but may be any other type defined in a program. The following sequence of declarations is thus perfectly acceptable:

```
MONTH_NAME:  type (JAN, FEB, MAR, APR, MAY, JUN,
                  JUL, AUG, SEP, OCT, NOV, DEC);

YEAR_NUMBER: type integer 1776..2001;

DAY_NUMBER:  type integer 1..31;

DATE:        type record
                MONTH: MONTH_NAME;
                DAY  : DAY_NUMBER;
                YEAR : YEAR_NUMBER;
             end record;
```

This set of declarations provides the basis on which the following are built:

```
EMPLOYEE_NUM:  type integer;

MARITAL_STATUS: type (SINGLE, MARRIED, DIVORCED, WIDOWED);

EMPLOYEE:      type record
               ID    : EMPLOYEE_NUM;
               STATUS: MARITAL_STATUS;
               BORN  : DATE;
               HIRED : DATE;
             end record;
```

Note that in the last record type definition, the two fields BORN and HIRED are actually two record components of type DATE.

Just as for other types, variables may be declared as having a record type. Example record variable declarations are:

```
PERSON: EMPLOYEE;
BIRTH_DATE, TODAY: DATE;
```

One advantage of record type definitions, in this case, is that it is clear to the user that the variables BIRTH_DATE and TODAY have identical types, that is, identical structure and component types.

The components of record type variables may be selected in the same way as the components of records. Thus TODAY.MONTH refers to the MONTH component of TODAY. In some languages, global operators, that is, operators that apply to the entire structure, are allowed. For example, if E and F have the same record type,

```
(E = F)
```

will be true only if all corresponding components in E and F have identical values, and

```
E := F;
```

will assign the value of F to E.

Type Equivalence

In the previous paragraph we used the phrase "if E and F have the same record type." However, we have not yet defined the conditions for two record types to be equivalent. There are two ways in which record type equivalence can be defined:

- **Structural Equivalence.** Two objects are said to be of equivalent types if they have the same internal structure; that is, the objects are represented in the same way in storage.

- **Name Equivalence.** Two objects are said to be of equivalent types only if their types have the same name.

Structural Equivalence

Under the rule of structural equivalence, the declarations:

```
DIMENSIONS: type record
                  BREADTH: integer;
                  LENGTH:  integer;
              end record;

COMPLEX:    type record
                  REAL_PART: integer;
                  IMAG_PART: integer;
              end record;
```

define equivalent types. Thus the two variables declared

```
SIZE: DIMENSIONS;
ROOT: COMPLEX;
```

may be assigned to each other. The problem here is that, if the programmer declared two separate types, it was probably because they were intended to represent different kinds of real-world objects. The fact that they have the same internal representation structure is probably a coincidence. For the language to consider them to be of equivalent types is to severely reduce the power of type checking and to lose a lot of its ability to detect errors.

In addition to the problem that structural equivalence has of being too lenient in its checking, there are some subtle questions in determining exactly what constitutes structural equivalence. Examples of these questions are:

1. Should the names of the components in record types be taken into account? In our declarations of DIMENSIONS and COMPLEX, we did not make use of the component names. However, a more restrictive version of structural equivalence might require that the names of the components be identical.

2. If component names are taken into account, must the components be in the same order? For example, given the declarations:

```
A: type record
          X: integer;
          Y: integer;
      end record;

B: type record
          Y: integer;
          X: integer;
      end record;
```

   should types A and B be equivalent?

3. Structural equivalence also applies to arrays. For array type equivalence, is it sufficient for the number of elements to be the same or must the subscript bounds be identicial?

4. For enumerated types, is it sufficient for the number of possible values to be the same or must the names of the values be identical? In which case, must the enumeration of the values be in the same order?

Name Equivalence

With name equivalence, our two types DIMENSION and COMPLEX are certainly different and there is no danger of type mismatches being missed. However, there are still difficulties because we can have unnamed types, referred to as anonymous types. These arise when variables are declared as records or arrays, for example:

```
X: record
       VALID: boolean;
       COUNT: integer;
    end record;

Y: record
       VALID: boolean;
       COUNT: integer;
    end record;
```

Should X and Y be considered to be of the same type? If not, what of the declaration:

```
A, B: record
         VALID: boolean;
         COUNT: integer;
      end record;
```

An argument often advanced is that the compiler generates internal names for anonymous types and different names will be generated for the types of X and Y. However, the same type name will be given to A and B.

With name equivalence, type names must be global so that the same types can be used throughout a program. This may require special scope rules for type names, which may mean that type names are treated differently from other kinds of names. This is unfortunate since it will provide another exception that the programmer will have to remember.

To summarize:

1. Structural equivalence is more flexible; however, it is not as safe or clean as name equivalence.

2. Name equivalence is easier to implement in a compiler.

We support name equivalence, and believe that all types should be named.

12.4 User-Defined Operators

Mini-language Typedef embodies several of the basic ideas for a data type definition mechanism. However, the mini-language lacks some important features that are available in several languages. These allow the programmer to exercise the full power of a type definition mechanism. They include the ability to define operations as part of the type definition and to make the type definition into a module that is separate from the program. This technique is discussed in detail in Chapter 17.

Consider a program that is manipulating data of the type DATE, defined in the previous section. Although the declaration part of the program shows that the program concerns *dates,* the executable part may contain statements such as

```
TOMORROW.DAY := TODAY.DAY + 1;
```

and much of the abstraction is lost because it is written, not in terms of dates, but in terms of fields or components of a type named DATE. It is not clear to the reader that TOMORROW gets the right value during execution; all assignments to the individual fields of TOMORROW must be inspected. If for any reason the definition of the type named DATE has to be changed, the entire executable part of the program must be scanned for further changes. For large programs, this process is unreliable.

Suppose we want to rewrite this program in a manner that better emphasizes the abstraction of a *date.* What we would like to write is something like

```
input TODAY;
TOMORROW := NEXT_DATE(TODAY);
output TOMORROW;
```

To write such a program we need to be able to define a new operation, the function NEXT_DATE for a type DATE. This is not possible in Mini-language Typedef, where all operator definition is by overloading predefined operators. Instead, we need to program new operators for user-defined types. In our case, we need to be able to write a function that takes a DATE as an argument and returns a DATE as a result.

A function implementing the NEXT_DATE operator for DATE might read:

```
NEXT_DATE: function(D: DATE) DATE:
   NEXT: DATE;
begin
   NEXT.DAY := NEXT_DAY(D);
   if (NEXT.DAY < D.DAY) then
      NEXT.MONTH = NEXT_MONTH(D.MONTH);
   else
      NEXT.MONTH = D.MONTH;
   end if;
   if (NEXT.MONTH < D.MONTH) then
      NEXT.YEAR := D.YEAR + 1;
   else
      NEXT.YEAR := D.YEAR;
   end if;
   return NEXT;
end;
```

It is only during the writing of an operator such as this that the actual structure of the type DATE needs to be defined. The operator NEXT_DATE is defined through the use of the operators NEXT_DAY, NEXT_MONTH, and the operator < overloaded to operate on values of type MONTH, over the field types. The definition of the structure of DATE is paralleled by the definition of its NEXT_DATE operator.

By careful programming, knowledge of a type representation can be restricted to its own operators, as indicated above. Such practice makes a program easier to understand and maintain.

Although use of functions and procedures can provide good facilities for abstractions, it does not guarantee the integrity of these abstractions. Nothing prevents a main program from accessing the fields of a DATE and changing them arbitrarily. This may be convenient, but it may also lead to serious troubles. For instance, the main program could set a date variable to the thirty-first day of February, which is not a valid date. Furthermore, it is not known how the operations over a date would behave on such data, since they were written with real dates in mind. Programming errors of this kind can be especially difficult to correct. Thus, some safeguards are needed to preserve the integrity of these abstractions.

Realization in Languages

In Ada (most notably), Modula-2, Alphard, Euclid, and Clu, the definition of a data representation for a new type and the definition of new operations are grouped in a program module. This module can be separated from the main program, and thus the representation can be hidden from the main program. The module includes specifications of what can be known about itself from outside of the module. Some parts of the data type representation may remain private to the module and be used exclusively for internal computations needed to implement the operations. Similarly, operations needed to implement the visible operations may be hidden from the user. This idea is one of the main themes of Chapter 17.

The preceding paragraphs have sketched a type definition mechanism combining the type definition facility of Typedef, a function and procedure facility, modular grouping, and information hiding mechanisms. Some languages implement this scheme to various degrees. Pascal and Algol 68 lack the module and information control facilities. Pascal lacks the means of defining operators. Simula 67 provides a powerful modular facility called a class, but access to module components cannot be restricted. Alphard, Clu, Euclid, Modula-2, and Ada offer all the abstraction mechanisms described above. However, these languages differ in the extensions and complexities of the basic mechanism.

Type definition mechanisms enable the user to bring the programming environment closer to the application than many languages usually allow. The early stages of program design may require more effort and discipline to select the abstractions that need to be implemented to solve the application problem. However, when compared to other languages, languages with type definition mechanisms promote the development of self-documenting code and security. The clear separation between the definition and use of a type facilitates validation and maintenance of programs.

12.5 Where to Look: Pascal, Algol 68

Pascal

The model for enumerated types and subranges shown in Mini-language Typedef comes from Pascal, though the form is slightly different.

Types are defined in a special section of the header of a program, procedure, or function, introduced by the keyword type. Types can be enumerated types, subranges, records, or arrays. Examples of these type declarations are:

```
type
    DAY     = (MON, TUE, WED, THU, FRI, SAT, SUN);
    WEEKDAY = MON..FRI;
    HOURSWORKED = array[DAY] of integer;
    TOTALRECEIPTS = record
                    DATE:   DAY;
                    AMOUNT: real;
                end;
```

The relational operators =, <>, <, >, <=, and >= are defined for enumerated types. In addition the successor and predecessor operators, succ and pred, which give the next and previous values in an enumeration sequence, are defined. The assignment operator is defined for identical types. The definition document [Jensen and Wirth 1975] does not specify precisely what it means for two types to be identical, and different implementations have interpreted this in different ways. Generally, structural equivalence has been used but some implementations use the stricter name equivalence.

Pascal does not permit the user to overload any of the standard operators for use with user defined types.

Algol 68

In Algol 68, the mechanism for the definition of new types—"modes"—has a different bias from that in Pascal. While Pascal concentrates on the definition of a class of values and does not allow the definition of new operators, the emphasis in Algol 68 is in the counter direction. New modes can be constructed as records and arrays, for example:

```
mode rational = struct(int numerator, int denominator);
mode matrix   = [1 : n, 1 : n] real;
```

However, there is no way to construct enumerated types or sub-types.

The mechanism for defining operators is similar to that in Typedef, with the extension that any symbol such as:

```
+ - = ‡ ÷  ↓  >= +x /x -:= /:=
```

or an identifier can be defined as an operator. There are two kinds of operators, monadic that are applied to the operand on its right, and dyadic that are placed between two operands. An example of a group of boolean operators, the first monadic and the other two dyadic, defined in Algol 68 are:

```
op ^    = (bool a) bool: if a then false else true fi;
op &    = (bool a, bool b) bool: if a then b else false fi;
op impl = (bool a, bool b) bool: (a & b);
```

Since the impl is not a standard operator with a built-in precedence, one must be defined for it:

```
prio impl = 5;
```

The core of Algol 68 is relatively small, and this mechanism for defining operators is used in a "standard prelude" to define many of the operators that most users would take for granted in a language of its power.

Further Reading

Of the topics treated in this text, few have received more attention in the literature than the idea of abstract data types and the definition of new types.

[Hoare 1972], a key work in this area, discusses both the notion of simple types as well as composite types. The properties of types are well expressed in the work [Guttag 1977].

In the area of type definition facilities, there are numerous relevant works. One early work [Liskov and Zilles 1974] discusses a model for the process. Other related works are [Mailloux and Peck 1969] and [Demers et al. 1977]. A good discussion of some of the problems in the area of data abstraction can be found in [Gries and Gehani 1977].

Exercises

Exercise 12.1 *The Stack Data Type*

Define an extension to Mini-language Typedef that adds a stack structure to the base language in the same way that an array is part of the language. This definition should include the operations that are to be available in the language for the access and manipulation of stacks.

Exercise 12.2 *Enumerated Types*

In Pascal, the functions succ and pred are predefined operations that apply to enumeration values. They yield respectively the next and previous values of an enumeration value in the declared ordering. For a given enumeration type, the first value in the type definition has no predecessor, and the last value has no successor. The following is a program fragment in an extension to Typedef. It contains the two functions for performing a computation by iterating over the days of the week:

```
CURRENT_DAY  := MON;
while (CURRENT_DAY ≠ SAT) loop
   -- what to do for each value of CURRENT_DAY
   CURRENT_DAY  := succ(CURRENT_DAY);
end loop;
```

If we attempt to modify this program to iterate over Monday through Sunday, a problem arises. Describe this problem. Propose changes to the language that would avoid this problem entirely.

Exercise 12.3 Definitions of Record Types

Write down the context-free productions needed to add the record type definitions like those given in Section 12.3 to Mini-language Type-def.

Exercise 12.4 Extensible Languages

Opinions differ on what *extensible* means when applied to programming languages. At the trivial level only simple text substitution is allowed, while the very ambitious allow elaborate new data types and operations on them to be defined.

Describe what you feel an extensible language should offer. Aim for an intermediate level of complexity between the two extremes: simple enough for competent programmers to understand and use without heroic efforts, yet complex enough to add nontrivial power and capability to the language.

Illustrate your ideas with examples showing the syntax and semantics of your extensions. Your ideas must be implementable without recourse to magic, but do not describe implementation strategy. You may assume that the base language has a reasonable assortment of data types and control structures, that is, that one can write nontrivial programs in the base language without extending it.

Exercise 12.5 Structural Equivalence

Write a precise definition of structural equivalence of types. Embody this definition in an algorithm to determine whether two types are structurally equivalent.

Exercise 12.6 By Name Assignment

Cobol and PL/I have a form of record access in which the fields accessed depend on the names of the variables. In Cobol, this type of access occurs in the CORRESPONDING forms of the MOVE, ADD, and SUBTRACT statements. In PL/I, it appears in the BY NAME option on the assignment statement. Simply stated, the operation is only performed between those components of the operands that have the same name. Define the rules that determine which elements are to be selected to take part in the operation.

Exercise 12.7 *Boolean Operators*

In Section 12.1, we defined the boolean operator corresponding to the logical *and*.

```
*: operator(LEFT_OPERAND: boolean, RIGHT_OPERAND: boolean)
                                                    => boolean
   RESULT: boolean;
begin
   if (LEFT_OPERAND) then
      RESULT := RIGHT_OPERAND;
   else
      RESULT := false;
   end if;
   return RESULT;
end;
```

Under what conditions would this operator behave in the same way as the short-cut logical operator defined in Chapter 8?

13
Dynamically Varying Structures

One area of programming languages with many divergent views is the area generally included under the term *data structures*. By a data structure we mean a collection of data that bear some relation to each other and are organized so as to represent these relationships. The organization reflects real-world relationships and thus must be able to change dynamically. For example, we may describe the nodes in a network, the components of a data base, the items in a linked list, or the members of a family tree.

The naming, searching, deleting, sharing, and updating of items in a data structure are all critical issues. Mini-language Structures is an attempt to deal with some of these issues. In our opinion, the concept of a data structure is still quite vague, and none of the existing facilities for data structures is satisfactory. A good attempt to provide such a facility has been made in the language Ada, and Mini-language Structures is based on this work.

13.1 Mini-language Structures

Along with integers and strings, the types in Mini-language Structures include classes of objects called *structures*. A *structure type* is declared by a structure declaration that gives the name of the type being declared as well as the name and type of each structure component. All structure types must be declared, and interdependent definitions are allowed. The syntax of Mini-language Structures is given in Table 13.1.

Table 13.1   **Mini-language Structures**

---

program	::=	`program`
		structure-declaration. . .
		variable-declaration. . .
		`begin`
		statement. . .
		`end` ;

structure-declaration	::=	identifier : `structure`
		    identifier : type ;
		    [identifier : type ;]. . .
		`end structure` ;

variable-declaration	::=	identifier [, identifier]. . . : type ;
type	::=	identifier | `string` | `integer`
statement	::=	assignment-statement | loop-statement | if-statement | input-statement | output-statement
assignment-statement	::=	variable `:=` expression ; | variable `:=` `new` identifier (expression [, expression]. . . **)** ;

if-statement	::=	`if` comparison `then`
		    statement. . .
		[`else`
		    statement. . .]
		`end if` ;

Declarations

For example, we may have the structure declarations:

1. `COMPLEX_NUM: structure`
`    REAL_PART:  integer;`
`    IMAG_PART:  integer;`
`end structure;`

2. `PERSON: structure`
`    NAME       :  string;`
`    SS_NUM     :  string;`
`    NEXT_OF_KIN:  PERSON;`
`end structure;`

Table 13.1 **continued**		
loop-statement	::=	while comparison loop statement. . . end loop ;
input-statement	::=	input variable [, variable]. . . ;
output-statement	::=	output variable [, variable]. . . ;
comparison	::=	(operand comparison-operator operand)
expression	::=	[expression +] operand
operand	::= |	null | integer | string (expression) | variable
variable	::=	identifier | variable . identifier
string	::=	' character. . . '
character	::=	letter | digit | ₿
comparison-operator	::=	⟨ | = | ≠ | ⟩

```
3. LIST: structure
      HEAD:  integer;
      TAIL:  LIST;
   end structure;
4. COMPLEX_NUM_LIST: structure
      HEAD:  COMPLEX_NUM;
      TAIL:  COMPLEX_NUM_LIST;
   end structure;
```

Examples of each of these structures are shown in Figure 13.1. Here an arrow is used to refer to a component that is itself a structure.

The first declaration above declares a very simple structure with two integer components. This structure is analogous to a record structure in Mini-language Type. The essential difference is illustrated in the second example. Here we see a structure named PERSON, which has two string components and a component that is the structure PERSON itself. This is a recursive definition and defines an infinite class of objects. One member of this class is illustrated in Figure 13.1. The apparent infinite recursion is handled in Mini-language Structures by a special object called null. The

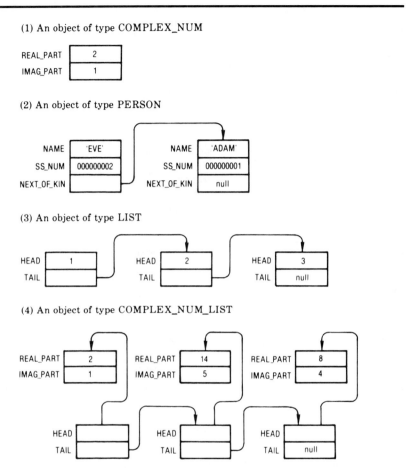

(1) An object of type COMPLEX_NUM

(2) An object of type PERSON

(3) An object of type LIST

(4) An object of type COMPLEX_NUM_LIST

Figure 13.1 **Illustrations of Structures**

value of null designates an object with no components. Each defined structure type includes the null object as one of its values.

The third structure declaration defines a type called LIST. A list denotes a series of objects, each with a head and a tail component, terminated by the null object.

The fourth structure declaration defines another class of lists called COMPLEX_NUM_LIST. The HEAD of each component of such a list is a COMPLEX_NUM object. This structure declaration illustrates the definition of structures that require more than one structure declaration for their specification. One member of this class of objects is illustrated in Figure 13.1.

All variables used in a program must be declared and their types specified as either integer, string, or by a previously declared structure type identifier. Some examples are:

```
HIS_NAME:    string;
NUM_HITS:    integer;
NODE_VALUE:  integer;
ADAM:        PERSON;
EVE:         PERSON;
LAST_BORN:   PERSON;
L:           LIST;
NEXT_NUM:    COMPLEX_NUM;
ITEM:        COMPLEX_NUM_LIST;
```

There are important semantic differences between these declarations of structure variables and declarations of record variables in Mini-language Type. In Type, an identifier that is declared to be of a record type x has the mode reference-to-x and is identically equal to a location that can contain record objects of type x. This meaning of declarations was discussed in Chapter 6. In Mini-language Structures, an extra level of referencing is inserted. The identifier ADAM declared above is not identically equal to a location that can contain a PERSON object, but to a location that can contain a reference to a PERSON object. This object does not exist until it is constructed, as described below. The contents of the location associated with ADAM are initially undefined.

Components of structure variables can be designated by naming the variable itself, followed by a dot and the name of one of its components. As nested structures are allowed, nested components are designated by giving the name of the appropriate component at each level of nesting. For example, we may have the variables:

```
ADAM.SS_NUM          -- a component of type string
ADAM.NEXT_OF_KIN     -- a component of type PERSON
ITEM.HEAD.REAL_PART  -- a component of type integer
```

Assignments

Several kinds of assignment statements are allowed in Mini-language Structures. The first is the simple assignment of an arithmetic or string value, for example:

```
NUM_HITS := NUM_HITS + 1;
HIS_NAME := 'GEORGE WASHINGTON';

NEXT_NUM.REAL_PART := 2;
NEXT_NUM.REAL_PART := NEXT_NUM.REAL_PART + 1;
```

All values assigned to a variable must be of the same type as that declared for the variable.

Of more interest to us here is the assignment of structure objects to structure variables. A null value can be assigned to a structure variable by simply giving null as the assigned expression, as in:

```
LAST_BORN          := null;
ADAM.NEXT_OF_KIN := null;
L.TAIL             := null;
```

A special kind of assignment is used to create a structure object. The assigned expression is prefixed by the symbol new followed by the name of the structure type and a parenthesized list of expression values, one for each component of the structure. For example, we may have:

```
NEXT_NUM := new COMPLEX_NUM (2,1);
ITEM     := new COMPLEX_NUM_LIST (NEXT_NUM, null);
ADAM     := new PERSON ('ADAM', '000000001', null);
```

Such statements specify the dynamic creation of an object of the type defined by the structure identifier and assign this value to the variable given on the left side of the assignment. The assigned value is a *reference* to the dynamically created object.

During the creation of a structure object, the components of the object are given values from the parenthesized list of expressions following the symbol new. If any of these expressions refers to a previously created object, the value of the expression is a reference to the previously created object. For example, the variables NEXT_NUM and ITEM created above may be represented as in:

Assignment of one structure variable to another structure variable is also allowed. In this case, after the assignment, both variables will refer to the same dynamically created object. For example, if the above sequence were followed by the assignment:

```
LAST_BORN := ADAM;
```

then both ADAM and LAST_BORN would refer to the same object, as illustrated in:

Statements

Finally, Mini-language Structures includes the following more traditional statements:

- If statements
- Loop statements
- Input statements
- Output statements

The input and output statements handle only integer and string values.

Examples

Consider Example 13.1. The first statement

```
LAST_BORN := null;
```

sets the value of the variable LAST_BORN to reference a null object. The birth of the first member of our family is accomplished with the operation new:

```
ADAM      := new PERSON ('ADAM', '000000001', null);
LAST_BORN := ADAM;
```

The first statement above creates a new object with three components, and the variable ADAM is set to reference this new object. The second statement assigns a reference to the same newly constructed object to LAST_BORN. Notice that the third component of the object referenced by ADAM is null.

```
program
   PERSON: structure
          NAME      :  string;
          SS_NUM    :  string;
          NEXT_OF_KIN:  PERSON;
      end structure;

   ADAM, EVE, LAST_BORN: PERSON;
begin
   -- initial state, no one on earth
   LAST_BORN := null;

   -- birth of Adam
   ADAM      := new PERSON ('ADAM', '000000001',  null);
   LAST_BORN := ADAM;

   -- birth of Adam's spouse
   EVE := new PERSON ('EVE', '000000002', ADAM);
   ADAM.NEXT_OF_KIN  := EVE;
   LAST_BORN         := EVE;
end;
```

Example 13.1 **The Beginning of a Genealogy**

Next, consider a new birth given in the statements:

```
EVE              := new PERSON ('EVE', '000000002', ADAM);
ADAM.NEXT_OF_KIN := EVE;
LAST_BORN        := EVE;
```

The first statement creates a new object with three components, and the variable EVE is set to reference this new object. The second statement results in setting the third component of the object associated with ADAM as a reference to EVE. The third statement updates the value of LAST_BORN.

Now that we have two persons in the family, we can see the development of dynamic relationships during program execution. The third components of ADAM and EVE now refer to each other and LAST_BORN has been maintained as a reference to the person who was last born.

Next, consider Example 13.2. After execution of the first six statements, the structure of Figure 13.2 is obtained. The remaining statements read in an integer representing a node value and then print the number of times the node value occurs in the tree list.

```
program
   TREE: structure
         NODE: integer;
         LB  : TREE;
         RB  : TREE;
      end structure;

   TREE_LIST: structure
         HEAD: TREE;
         TAIL: TREE_LIST;
      end structure;

   NODE_VALUE, NUM_HITS: integer;
   A, B, C:              TREE;
   L, P:                 TREE_LIST;

begin
   A := new TREE (1, null, null);
   B := new TREE (2, null, null);
   C := new TREE (3, null, null);

   L := new TREE_LIST (C, null);
   L := new TREE_LIST (B, L);
   L := new TREE_LIST (A, L);

   input NODE_VALUE;
   P := L;

   NUM_HITS := 0;
   while (P ≠ null) loop
      if (P.HEAD.NODE = NODE_VALUE) then
         NUM_HITS := NUM_HITS + 1;
      end if;
      P := P.TAIL;
   end loop;

   output NUM_HITS;
end;
```

Example 13.2 **Searching a Linked List**

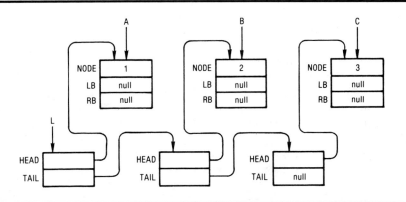

Figure 13.2 **Development of a Tree List**

13.2 Dynamically Varying Data Structures

The general concept of data structures is quite diffuse and almost impossible to treat with a single mini-language.

Often we need to model large amounts of data and to express quite complex relationships between the data items. Whether it be the symbol table of a compiler, the connections in a rail network, the accounting system in an organization, Census Bureau information, or, simply, a binary tree of alphabetically ordered keys, there is an inherent variety and complexity in the kinds of problems that data structures are meant to solve. To deal with this complexity, programmers should be able to work at a very high level of abstraction, generally far removed from the details of a machine implementation.

From a language viewpoint, the concept of such data structures brings in some critical new issues. The first is that the storage requirements for a program cannot be determined simply from the number of variables and the nature of their types. For example, consider the following sequence:

```
L := new LIST (1, null);
L := new LIST (2, L);
L := new LIST (3, L);
L := new LIST (4, L);
```

Here we see the development of a single list structure named L. Over the course of execution, the size of L grows. Generally, the actual number of elements cannot be predicted until execution is completed. Thus, we see a need to allocate storage dynamically. This is in sharp contrast with the variables introduced in previous mini- languages.

```
program
   LIST: structure
         HEAD: integer;
         TAIL: LIST;
      end structure;
   L, M: LIST;
begin
   L := new LIST (1, null);
   L := new LIST (2, L);
   M := new LIST (3, L);
   L := new LIST (4, M);
   output L.TAIL.HEAD, M.HEAD;   -- values are 3 and 3
end;
```

Example 13.3 Building a List in Mini-language Structures

A second issue with such structures is that the components of a structure may relate to previously defined structures, and these relationships may themselves change during program execution. In the above sequence of statements, the interrelation of the list elements changes as each statement is executed.

Perhaps the central issue in the use of data structures is the sharing of information. For example, consider the program of Example 13.3. The structure set up by this program is shown in Figure 13.3. Here both L and M are lists, some of whose components are identical. In particular, both

```
L.TAIL.HEAD
M.HEAD
```

denote the same value, the integer 3. Finally, note that even if the list L is assigned a completely new value, as with the statement

```
L := new LIST(5, null);
```

some of the elements originally in L will still be accessible via the list named M. This brings up another difficult issue, namely, when do the objects of a structure become inaccessible? In order for this to be determined automatically, the implementation must maintain extra information such as reference counts or chaining pointers together. This of course requires extra overhead in both execution time and storage.

Figure 13.3 **A List Structure with Shared Components**

13.3 Pointers

In many higher-level languages (and in most lower level languages) data structures are developed with some kind of mechanism for pointers. A *pointer* is an object that gives the address of, or refers to, another object. The value of a pointer is a location.

Working with pointers is full of hazards for the unwary. The object associated with a pointer may change during program execution. Although complex structures may be developed, the programmer must always keep in mind whether a variable refers to an object directly or indirectly through a pointer. When a complex data structure is involved, a clear understanding of a program that uses pointers is difficult to obtain. The complex relationships that pointers are intended to represent are often very difficult to fathom.

There is a strong analogy between pointer values and label values. That is, pointer values are to data structuring what label values are to flow of control. Both are very primitive concepts and their application through dereferencing, or goto statements, can be very difficult to understand.

Nevertheless, there is still a fundamental question: do we need the notion of a pointer to understand the use of data structures? For example, consider the statements that establish the list structure illustrated in Figure 13.3. Here the value of M.HEAD is 3. Now suppose we execute the statement:

```
L.TAIL.HEAD := 6;
```

The value of M.HEAD will now be 6. Notice that M does not appear in this assignment statement, but its value is changed nevertheless.

This is a situation in which the program behavior can be readily understood in terms of the concepts of a pointer. This is especially true when we have the sharing of structure information. Thus, we see that even in Mini-language Structures, in which pointers are not explicit, the idea of a pointer is quite central to understanding actions performed in the language.

Use in Pascal

Many programming languages make the notion of a pointer explicit. For example, consider the following Pascal declarations:

```
type ITEM =  ↑LIST;
     LIST = record
                HEAD: INTEGER;
                TAIL: ITEM
            end;

var  L, M, NEXT: ITEM;
```

Here a pointer type is explicitly indicated with an ↑. In Pascal, the type of object to which a pointer points must be explicitly indicated, in this case a list. The Pascal statements corresponding to the structures of Figure 13.3 are given in Example 13.4.

Each call to the procedure NEW allocates space for the type of object referenced by the pointer given as an argument and assigns a reference to the new object to the pointer. In subsequent statements, all references to the objects pointed to by L or M must be explicitly indicated. For example, we have:

```
L          -- denotes the pointer value of L
L↑         -- denotes the object pointed to by L
```

In comparison with Mini-language Structures, we see here a very straightforward set of conventions in which pointers are explicitly identified. Unlike Mini-language Structures, however, the Pascal programmer must always be aware of the notion of a pointer, even in the case where knowledge that a value is a pointer is somewhat superfluous. While both views are valid and a final resolution of this issue is not clear, we generally support the suppression of pointers.

```
program BUILDLIST (INPUT, OUTPUT);

    type ITEM = ↑LIST;
         LIST = record
                    HEAD: INTEGER;
                    TAIL: ITEM
                end;

    var L, M, NEXT: ITEM;

begin
    NEW (L);
    L↑.HEAD := 1;
    L↑.TAIL := nil;
    NEXT     := L;

    NEW (L);
    L↑.HEAD := 2;
    L↑.TAIL := NEXT;
    NEXT     := L;

    NEW (M);
    M↑.HEAD := 3;
    M↑.TAIL := NEXT;
    NEXT     := M;

    NEW (L);
    L↑.HEAD := 4;
    L↑.TAIL := NEXT;

    WRITE (L↑.TAIL↑.HEAD, M↑.HEAD)
      { output values are 3 and 3 }
end.
```

Example 13.4 **Building a List Structure in Pascal**

13.4 Design Criteria for Data Structures

Facilities for defining dynamically varying collections of data are not a part of every language. For example, neither Fortran nor Basic has a facility corresponding to that given in Mini-language Structures. With such languages, the reader is forced to use alternative constructs to deal with structured data. Typically, arrays are used with indices to simulate pointers. Clearly, if the development of dynamically varying data structures is an important application domain, such languages are difficult to use.

To discuss the various design issues in data structures, we will compare the facilities given in Mini-language Structures with those in Pascal. This is taken further in Examples 13.3 and 13.4.

Definition of Data Structures

A definition of a data structure defines the objects to be manipulated and, implicitly, the ways in which they can be referenced.

In Mini-language Structures, the definition of data structures is handled by a structure declaration in which each of the components of the structure is identified. This requires that the structure be defined to have a specific form since arbitrarily connected structures are prohibited. The development of chained structures is handled by the use of recursion in the definition of the structure. The apparent infinite recursion indicated in Example 13.3 is prevented by associating a null object with each defined structure.

In Pascal, the mechanism for defining structures is analogous to that of Mini-language Structures. Here, however, an intermediate type must be used to indicate a pointer to another structure, which is in fact the normal record structure in Pascal. This intermediate type slightly obscures the definition of the object being defined, but makes the existence of pointers explicit, as well as clearing up any ambiguity about possible infinite recursion.

Operations over Structures

There are two general kinds of operations relevant to the use of structures. First are those provided within the language. Second are the higher-level operations more suitable to the domain that these structures are intended to represent.

In Mini-language Structures, the primitive operations over structures are basically those of creation, assignment, and component selection. Assignment of structures is handled just as assignment of variables that can take single values. References to components of structures are specified by the dot notation used for record structures. With the dot notation the use of pointers is suppressed and the dereferencing operation is implicit. Consider the variable M.HEAD in Example 13.3. Here, although M can be viewed as a pointer to a structure, if a component of that structure, HEAD, for instance, is referenced, it is as if M points to the component instead of the whole structure. This implicit dereferencing appears to be generally what is meant when the components of the structure are referenced. Thus, Mini-language Structures presents a conceptually simple mechanism for handling the components of structures.

In Pascal, on the other hand, the use of pointers is made explicit. Each reference to the component of a structure must be handled by giving an up-arrow explicitly dereferencing the pointer to the named structure to one of its components. The extensive use of the up-arrow in Pascal is somewhat annoying. While it does make explicit the fact that an object is really a reference to a structure, the repeated use of the up-arrow somewhat detracts from the readability of the intended operations.

For higher-level operations, for example, a subprogram to reorder the components of a list, Mini-language Structures and Pascal both require the use of functions and procedures. Thus, the user has no way of explicitly defining higher-level operations on the structures other than through the mechanism of subprograms. The general issue of defining such operations is treated in Chapter 12 on type definitions.

Construction of Data Structures

In Mini-language Structures, the construction of new structures is handled with the new operation. Values must be given for each component of a structure, and the component type must be stated. Notice that only one instance of a structure can be generated by a single statement. More complex structures must be built via repeated assignment statements, each with a new operation.

In Mini-language Structures, both the allocation of space for the structure and the setting of the pointer value are handled implicitly. Thus, the user can think more directly in terms of the actual kinds of objects being generated.

In Pascal, on the other hand, objects of structures are not created directly. The Pascal procedure NEW must be applied to an object with a pointer type. This procedure call allocates the space for the object and sets a pointer value to this storage area. The actual setting of components of structures must be handled via direct record assignment to each component. This method suffers from the fact that objects are not treated as a whole, but only on a component-by-component basis. Furthermore, the pointer set by the procedure NEW must be explicitly dereferenced when any component of the structure is initialized.

Both languages treat the selection of components of structures in a manner analogous to that of selecting the components of a record valued variable. Pascal, however, has a drawback from our point of view, in that the pointer to the structure object must always be explicitly dereferenced before a component can be selected.

When dealing with data structures, especially large ones, it is frequently the case that different types of objects must be connected into the structure at a particular point. There is thus a need for *union* types as described in Section 8.5. Furthermore, there will be a need to make a test of the type of a given object. That is, it must be possible to define predicates that test the type to which the current value of a union variable belongs. Union types and such tests are still very uncommon in modern programming languages.

In Pascal, for example, the type of an object is part of the specification of a procedure. Procedures that operate on multiple types are not allowed, except as permitted through variant records, and thus the writing of any generalized procedures is prohibited.

The development of data structures is becoming an increasingly important application domain for computers. Development of large information bases and the applications of computers to much more sophisticated information processing areas are becoming more and more widespread. The issue of dynamically varying data structures as discussed here is only a part of the problem. In this chapter in particular, we have barely scratched the surface.

13.5 Dynamic Allocation of Storage

In Mini-language Structures, storage is allocated for structure objects through a special form of the assignment statement. It is thus under the direct control of the programmer. This differs from the allocation pattern for variables in block-structured languages, where the activation record forms the model. This pattern was described in Section 11.3.

The space for variables of a block-structured language is created when the block is invoked and destroyed when the block terminates. The lifetime of an object thus directly follows the dynamic block structure of the language and may be implemented with an execution stack. The lifetime of an object that is created explicitly by the execution of a special statement does not follow the block invocation pattern. A structure object can exist from one block invocation to the next. Thus, a method of storage management that is separate from the execution stack is required for languages where the programmer has explicit control of storage allocation.

In some languages, such as Pascal and PL/I, specific statements are provided for the release of storage allocated for an object. Suppose a destroy statement were added to Mini-language Structures, where the form of the statement is:

```
destroy identifier ;
```

Execution of the statement would have the effect of destroying the object referenced by the identifier and setting the value of the identifier to undefined. The problem here is exemplified by the statement sequence:

```
L := new LIST(1, null);
L := new LIST(2, L);
M := new LIST(3, L);
L := new LIST(4, M);
destroy L;
```

The complete list referenced by L has now been destroyed and the value of L is undefined. However, the variable M now references a location that no longer exists. It has become a *dangling reference*. While it is easy to see what is happening in this short fragment, in a larger program invalid references of this sort are very difficult to detect.

An alternative is, as in the original definition of Mini-language Structures, to provide no explicit means for the destruction of an object. Then, for example, if the statement

```
L := new LIST(1, null);
```

which creates a new object and assigns a reference to L, were immediately followed by the statement

```
L := new LIST(2, null);
```

this would create a second LIST object and supplants the reference to the first object by a reference to the second one. The original object can no longer be referenced, and there is no way of regaining access to it. The storage occupied by the object is no longer usable and can be returned to the system for potential reallocation. In some languages, such as Lisp and Algol 68, this is done by a special support routine, known as a *garbage collector*. This routine searches currently allocated storage for objects that are no longer accessible and destroys them. Such support can require a considerable execution overhead.

13.6 Where to Look: PL/I, Pascal, Ada

PL/I

PL/I provides the programmer with control over the creating and destruction of data records. A record can be created, with bounds determined at the time of creation, by means of an allocate statement, which provides the program with a pointer value that can be used to reference the newly created record. There is no facility for defining data structures recursively. To build a data structure such as a list or tree, the elements must be created individually through separate allocate statements and interconnected explicitly through assignment of pointer values.

The programmer is responsible for retaining the pointer value that references a record; if it is overwritten, there is no way that the record can be accessed. It is also the programmer's responsibility to free and return the space to the system when it is no longer required for a record. No automatic garbage collection is possible in PL/I. The space occupied by a record is returned to the system through a free statement. Any pointers that reference the structure then become invalid. The execution of the free statement does not set them to a null value, and there is no protection against the dangling reference problem.

Pointer values are generally only valid during the execution of a program, and it is not possible to output a data structure for subsequent input. Pointers are usually implemented as actual addresses, and there is no guarantee that the data structure will occupy the same storage when it is input again. As an escape from this problem, PL/I allows the programmer to specify an *area* of storage in which certain data structures are to be allocated. The structures can then be interconnected with a special kind of pointer variable that consists of an offset from the beginning of the storage area. The whole area can thus be relocated, and it is possible to output it for later reinput without destroying the validity of the interconnections.

Pascal

In Pascal, the creation of an instance of a record can be achieved through the use of the dynamic allocation procedure new. The action of this procedure is very similar to the action of the allocate statement in PL/I. Similarly, the dispose procedure corresponds to PL/I's free statement, with the exception that the value of the referencing pointer variable is automatically set to null. Apart from the very real differences between PL/I pointer variables and Pascal reference variables (see Chapter 6), the facilities offered by the two languages for the construction of data structures are essentially similar. Pascal does not provide any means for the output of data structures that contain interconnected records.

Ada

The method for the creation of records in Ada closely matches that of Mini-language Structures. For example, the following program fragment builds a linked list with five elements:

```
declare
    type LIST;   -- incomplete type specification required
                 -- because the definition of LIST is recursive.

    type LINK is access LIST;   -- pointer to a LIST

    type LIST is -- the type specification can now be completed
       record
          VALUE: integer;
          NEXT:    LINK;
       end record;

    P, FIRST, LAST: LINK;   -- automatically given initial value null
    I:              integer;
begin
    for I in 1..5 loop
       P := new LIST(I, null);
       if HEAD = null then
          HEAD := P;
       else
          LAST.NEXT := P;
       LAST := P;
    end loop;
end;
```

Ada has no facility for destroying a record once it has been created; it relies on automatic garbage collection for this service. Neither is there any method by which a data structure containing pointers can be output for later use. Such a structure must be recreated each time it is to be used.

Further Reading

Much of the original work in recursive data statements was done by [Hoare 1972]. A good discussion of the issues presented in this section is given in [Ichbiah et al. 1979]. In the rationale for the Ada programming language, a number of issues and problems associated with dynamic types are discussed.

Exercises

Exercise 13.1 *Programming in Mini-language Structures*

Write a program in Mini-language Structures that will read a sequence of numbers, terminated by zero, and put them into a binary tree. When all the numbers have been read, print the numbers in ascending order.

Exercise 13.2 *Explicit versus Implicit Pointers*

In Chapter 6, we described Mini-language Ref with explicit pointers. Consider a variant of Mini-language Structures with reference variables instead of recursive structure definitions. Thus, the declaration for the type PERSON would be:

```
type PERSON:
    structure
        NAME:        string;
        SS_NUM:      string;
        NEXT_OF_KIN: ref PERSON;
    end structure;
```

A variable that referenced objects of this type would then be declared, e.g.,

```
ADAM: ref PERSON;
```

This mini-language variant requires an explicit dereferencing operator.

Compare the use of explicit versus implicit pointers on the clarity and ease of programming, including comparative examples from the original and variant forms of Mini-language Structures.

Exercise 13.3 *Storage Management*

Mini-language Structures provides no way for the programmer to return storage no longer required to the system. Instead, the implementation must detect and reclaim storage through the use of some *garbage collection* routine. Explain how such a routine could be implemented.

Exercise 13.4 *The Dangers of Explicit Pointers*

It has been suggested that there is an analogy between pointers in a data structure and goto statements in a program. Both are primitive tools capable of increasing the complexity of the program. Provide arguments and examples that support this position and examine how recursive data structures, as used in Mini-language Structures, overcome the problem.

Exercise 13.5 *Notation for Pointers*

Pascal uses an up-arrow (↑) for dereferencing a pointer and producing the object pointed to. For example, if P is a pointer to an integer, P ↑ denotes the integer. At first glance you might prefer a down-arrow to suggest the idea of following down a pointer. Or are there yet better notations?

Propose a notation for declaring and using pointers, and discuss its impact on program readability.

Exercise 13.6 *Queues*

A *queue* is a list of items where items may be inserted at one end, the *rear* of the queue, and deleted at the other, the *front* of the queue. Write a program in Mini-language Structures that will simulate passengers waiting at a bus stop.

The input consists of a sequence of integer pairs. The first integer is a code representing an action. The sequence is terminated by three zeros. The code can be a 1, denoting the arrival of a bus at the stop; a 2, representing the arrival of a group of passengers at the stop; or a 0, marking the termination of the simulation. If the code is a 1, then the second integer represents the number of people for which the bus has room. If the code is a 2, then the second integer represents the number of passengers who join the queue waiting for the bus.

The people are assumed to form a single line, entering the line at the rear and leaving the line at the front to get on the bus. If a bus arrives with room for *n* people, the first *n* people in the queue get on the bus. If there are less than *n* people in the line, they all get on the bus, which does not wait for more people to arrive. The program must model the queue with a dynamic data structure; each time the program reads a pair of integers, it should print out a trace of the action and, after modifying the queue accordingly, a count of the number of people in the queue.

Exercise 13.7 *Do We Need the* new *Option?*

Suppose that assignment automatically causes the construction of a new object as described as pointer semantics in Chapter 6. Discuss how this would affect Mini-language Structures.

14

An Applicative Language: Functions and Recursion

We now turn to a mini-language that is very different from our other mini-languages. This mini-language is devoted to functions and their application to produce values. Perhaps the most striking feature of this mini-language is the absence of commands, such as assignment and repetition, which are common to the other mini-languages.

The material in this chapter has roots in several sources. The most notable is the programming language Lisp. Other roots are the work of [Landin 1965] and the lambda-calculus [Church 1941].

14.1 Mini-language Apply

A program in Mini-language Apply consists of an expression, optionally followed by a sequence of function definitions. The syntax of the language is defined in Table 14.1.

Execution of the program consists of evaluation of an expression and the printing of its value. This may involve invocation of the functions specified by the function definitions.

A function definition associates a name with a function that maps one or more arguments into a single value. Within the function definition, the arguments are denoted by identifiers. The value returned by the function is specified by an expression. The expression can only contain identifiers denoting the parameters of the function and references to other functions, or a combination of these. All functions referenced must either be explicitly defined or be built-in functions of the language.

Table 14.1 **Mini-language Apply**

---

program	::=	`program`
		expression
		[function-definition]. . .
		`end`

function-definition	::=	`where` identifier (identifier [, identifier]. . .) `is` expression
expression	::= |	simple-expression selector-expression
simple-expression	::= | |	[operand +]. . . operand [operand -]. . . operand [operand *]. . . operand

selector-expression	::=	`select`
		condition => expression
		[condition => expression]. . .
		[`else` => expression]
		`end select`

condition	::=	function-application | comparison
comparison	::=	(operand comparison-operator operand)
operand	::= | |	identifier | integer truth-value | integer-list function-application | (expression)
function-application	::=	function-name (expression [, expression]. . .)

function-name	::=
	|
	|
		identifier
		`first` | `last` | `tail`
		`stem` | `append` | `length`

integer-list	::=	`null` | ′ integer [, integer]. . . ′
truth-value	::=	`true` | `false`
comparison-operator	::=	< | = | ≠ | >

For example, consider the function definition:

```
where DOUBLE(X) is
    X + X
```

This definition specifies a function named DOUBLE. The function has one parameter, denoted by the identifier X. The value returned by the function is the sum of X and X. Execution of the simple program

```
program
    DOUBLE(6) + 3
    where DOUBLE(X) is
        X + X
end
```

will cause the application of the function DOUBLE to the argument 6 and then add 3 to the result. Finally, the number 15 is printed.

Expressions

The expressions in Mini-language Apply are of two varieties: simple expressions, whose values can be computed directly, and selector expressions, whose values depend on the truth of one or more conditions. The value of an expression is either an integer, one of the truth values, true or false, or a list of integer values. A special value null denotes a list with no components. For example, we may have the following simple expressions:

```
6          -- an integer
true       -- a truth value
'1,2,3,4'  -- a list with four integers
null       -- the empty list
```

Values can also be computed through the application of a function to arguments. For example, we may have:

```
DOUBLE(1)              -- a simple function application
DOUBLE(1) + DOUBLE(2)  -- an addition of two computed values
```

Assuming that the function named DOUBLE is as specified above, these expressions have the values 2 and 6 respectively.

A number of functions are predefined within the language. These functions are given as follows:

1. first—This function takes a list as an argument and returns the first component of the list. If the list is empty, an execution error results.

2. last—This function takes a list as an argument and returns the last component of the list. If the list is empty, an execution error results.

3. tail—This function takes a list as an argument and returns the list obtained from the argument by removing its first component. If the argument is a list with one component or is empty, the empty list is returned as a result.

4. stem—This function takes a list as an argument and returns a list obtained from the argument by removing the last component of the list. If the argument is a list with one component or is empty, the empty list is returned as a result.

5. append—This function takes two arguments, a list and an integer, and returns a list constructed by appending the given integer to the end of the given list. If the first argument is an empty list, the value of the function is a list consisting of a single element, the second argument.

6. length—This function takes a single argument, a list, and returns an integer, whose value is the number of elements in the given list.

Table 14.2 illustrates the application of each of these functions to various arguments.

As mentioned above, within the body of a function definition, an identifier is used to denote the value of a parameter. For example, we may have the expressions:

```
X + X              -- computes twice X
X + G(X+1)         -- computes X plus the result of G(X + 1)
tail(X)            -- computes the tail of a list
append(L, last(M)) -- appends a copy of the last element of M
                   -- to L
```

The value of each of these expressions depends, of course, on the values of the arguments corresponding to the parameters X, L, and M.

The second form of expression in Mini-language Apply is the selector expression consisting of a sequence of conditions, each associated with a corresponding expression. When a selector expression is evaluated, each of the conditions is evaluated in sequence until one of the conditions evaluates to true. When a true condition is found, the value of its associated expression is the value of the selector expression.

Table 14.2 **Examples of Application of the Predefined Functions**

Expression	Value
first ('1,2,3,4')	1
first ('5')	5
first (null)	error
last ('1,2,3,4,5')	5
last ('5')	5
last (null)	error
tail ('1,2,3,4,5')	'2,3,4,5'
tail ('5')	null
tail (null)	null
stem ('1,2,3,4,5')	'1,2,3,4'
stem ('5')	null
stem (null)	null
append ('1,2,3,4', 5)	'1,2,3,4,5'
append ('5', 1)	'5,1'
append (null, 1)	'1'
length ('1,2,3,4,5')	5
length ('1')	1
length (null)	0

For example, consider the following selector expression:

```
select
    (X < Y) => 1
    (X = Y) => 2
    (X > Y) => 3
end select
```

Depending on whether X is less than, equal to, or greater than Y, the value of this expression will be respectively 1, 2, or 3.

Normally, a selector expression will be terminated by an else part. The expression following the else symbol is returned as the value of the expression if none of the previous conditions evaluates to true. For example, consider the following expression:

```
select
    (X > 5) => X
    else    => X + 1
end select
```

Here if X is greater than 5, the value of X itself is returned. Otherwise, the value of X + 1 is returned. Evaluation of a selector expression for which no condition is true results in an execution error.

The conditions forming a selector expression can be comparisons in which two operands are compared using one of the comparison operators. This is the case in the two examples given above. A condition can also be a function application where the value returned by the function is either true or false.

The body of a function may reference not only the names of other functions but also its own name. Thus, a function may be defined recursively. This recursive invocation causes no problem. When the body of a function is evaluated, evaluation proceeds normally. If it happens that evaluation of the function body requires reapplication of the function itself, the function is simply reapplied to the new arguments before the evaluation of the initial application is completed.

Examples

Consider the program:

```
program
   F(2) + F(6)
   where F(X) is
      select
         (X > 5) => X
         else    => X + 1
      end select
end
```

In the evaluation of the expression F(2) + F(6), the function F is invoked twice, giving the values 3 and 6. Therefore, the number 9 is printed.

In the following example,

```
program
   G(3)
   where G(X) is
      select
         (X > 5) => X
         else    => X + G(X + 1)
      end select
end
```

G is a function defined recursively. If its parameter X is greater than 5, then X is returned as the value of the function; otherwise, G is applied to the

argument X + 1 and the value of this application is added to X. The evaluation process may be viewed as the following steps:

Depth of Call	*Value*
0	G(3)
1	3 + G(4)
2	3 + 4 + G(5)
3	3 + 4 + 5 + G(6)
4	3 + 4 + 5 + 6

Thus, the function G is called four times, and on the fourth call it returns
the simple value 6. The final sum, 18, is printed as the result of evaluating
G(3).

The next example,

```
program
    LENGTH('1,2,3,4')
    where LENGTH(L) is
        select
            (L = null) => 0
            else        => 1 + LENGTH(tail(L))
        end select
end
```

contains a definition of the function LENGTH, which is the same as the predefined function length. This shows that, even though the function length
is predefined, it can also be defined in the language. The result of executing this program is 4.

The name of a function may also be used as an argument to another
function. Consider the following example:

```
program
    G(DOUBLE, 2) + G(TRIPLE, 3)

    where G(P, X) is
        P(X) + P(1)

    where DOUBLE(X) is
        X + X

    where TRIPLE(X) is
        X + X + X
end
```

Here the function G has two parameters, P and X. It returns the value of an
expression in which P is applied twice, once to X and once to the integer

1. For correct execution, the argument corresponding to the parameter P must be the name of a function. In evaluating the expression

```
G(DOUBLE, 2) + G(TRIPLE, 3)
```

the function G is invoked twice. The parameter P takes on two different values, DOUBLE and TRIPLE. When the expression

```
P(X) + P(1)
```

is evaluated during the first invocation of G, it is the equivalent of evaluating

```
DOUBLE(2) + DOUBLE(1)
```

and, in the second invocation, it is equivalent to

```
TRIPLE(3) + TRIPLE(1)
```

The result of executing this program is 18.

14.2 Functions

The dominant feature in Mini-language Apply is that a program is written entirely as the definition and application of functions. Functions have a long history in mathematics, and it is from this concept that functions in programming languages have been developed.

A function f is a mapping or rule of correspondence between one object x, the *argument,* and another unique object y, the *value,* of the function. Thus, we can say that f transforms or maps x into y, or that y is the result of applying f to x. This is generally written:

```
y = f(x)
```

Generally, functions may only be applied to certain kinds of objects and will only produce certain kinds of objects as a result. The set of objects to which a function may be applied is the *domain* of the function. The set of objects that can result from the application is the *range* of the function. In describing a function, it is common to specify the types of the domain and range. For example:

```
DOUBLE:   integer   →   integer
length:   list   →   integer
append:   list, integer   →   list
```

specify the types of the functions DOUBLE, length, and append.

Operations used in expressions are also functions. Thus, an alternative notation for writing the expression A + B would be + (A, B). In Mini-language Apply, the type of the + operator is

```
+:   integer, integer   →   integer
```

The type of a function in Mini-language Apply is not defined explicitly in a declare statement as in other mini-languages. Nevertheless, a mismatch of types will lead to an execution error. For example, if the function G defined by

```
where G(P, X) is
   P(X) + P(1)
```

were invoked by the expression

```
G(1, 2)
```

there would be an execution error when the parameter P was applied to the parameter X, because the constant 1 is an integer, not the name of a function.

One of the fundamental properties of using pure functions is a principle generally known as *referential transparency*. Given an expression of the form

$$F(X_1, X_2, \ldots, X_n)$$

where F is a function and X_1 through X_n denote arguments, referential transparency implies that the expression can always be replaced by its value. The replacement of the expression by its value is entirely independent of the context of the function application. For example, given the definition of DOUBLE shown earlier, the subexpression

```
DOUBLE(2) + DOUBLE(3)
```

may be directly replaced by the value 10, irrespective of the expression in which it is embedded. Even when an expression appears with identifiers denoting arguments, for example, DOUBLE(X), we may still perform the same replacement. That is, DOUBLE(X) always returns a value that is twice its argument. With the property of referential transparency, all we need to know to obtain the value of an expression is knowledge of the values of its components. This property is true of all expressions in Mini-language Apply.

The two major differences between programming in a conventional procedural language like Cobol or Pascal and in an applicative language are:

■ The applicative language has no concept of sequence of operations or flow of control. The whole program execution consists of the evaluation of an expression.

■ The applicative language has no assignment statement. Values are communicated entirely through the use of parameters.

To illustrate the difference between programming in a procedural language and programming in an applicative language, we consider the well-known problem of writing a program to solve the *Eight Queens problem.*

Eight Queens Problem

The Eight Queens problem is stated as follows. We wish to write a program to determine an arrangement of eight queens on a standard chessboard in such a way that no queen can capture any other. A chessboard can be viewed as an 8 by 8 array of squares. One queen can capture another if they are both in the same row, same column, or on the same diagonal.

For example, consider:

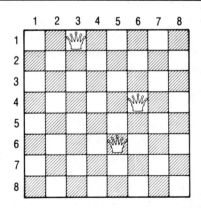

The queen in row 1, column 3 (board[1, 3]) can capture any other queen in row 1 or column 3. She can also capture the queen in board[4, 6] because they are on the same diagonal. The queen in board[6, 5] cannot be captured by either of the other queens. We wish our program to find one of the possible configurations in which the eight queens can be placed.

The straightforward approach would be for the program to form every possible arrangement of eight queens on the board and test each of these as a solution. The difficulty with this approach is the large number of trials that must be made. There are about 4.4×10^9 ways of placing eight queens on the board, and if we assume that we can generate and check a possible solution in 100 microseconds, it will take about 122 hours to check every possibility. We need to find a shortcut. Our solution, based on [Wirth 1971a], is designed to reduce time by eliminating impossible arrangements before they are fully generated.

First of all, we eliminate all configurations with more than one queen in any column. The strategy is to start by placing a queen at board[1, 1]. Since this queen is the only one, she is safe. The next step is to find a safe position in column 2 where the second queen can be placed. Another queen is placed at board[1, 2]. Since this queen can be attacked, the row number is incremented by 1 and the queen is tested on that square. This process continues, successively advancing a queen until a safe position in a column is found. If a configuration arises in which no queen can be placed safely in a given column, the queen already positioned in the previous column is advanced to the next row. The entire process is continued until a complete configuration is found.

So that we can refer to the diagonals, we note that two queens lie on the same downward diagonal if the difference between the row and column coordinates is the same. Similarly, two queens lie on the same upward diagonal if the sum of their row and column positions is identical.

A solution to the Eight Queens problem in the procedural language Pascal is given in Example 14.1. In this solution, the array CONFIGURATION is used to store the row positions of the queens safely placed in each of the columns 1 through 8.

A substantially different solution to the Eight Queens problem is given in Example 14.2 using essentially the same algorithm as in the Pascal solution. This solution to the problem is written using Mini-language Apply. Notice here that there is no use of assignment, no looping control structures, and no global variables. Rather, the solution consists of a single expression

```
QUEENS('1')
```

followed by a sequence of function definitions.

In this program, the board configuration is represented by a list of integers giving the row positions of the queens safely placed in each column that has been processed. The analogs to the Pascal version's quantities ROW and COL in this solution are the last element of the integer list and the length of the integer list. The initial invocation of QUEENS is with an integer

```
program QUEENS (INPUT, OUTPUT);
    type BOARD = array[1..8] of integer;
    var I, ROW, COL: integer;
        CONFIGURATION: BOARD;

    procedure ADVANCECOL(var CONFIGURATION: BOARD;
                         var ROW, COL: integer);
    begin
        CONFIGURATION[COL]  := ROW;
        COL                 := COL + 1;
        ROW                 := 1
    end;


    procedure RETREATCOL(CONFIGURATION: BOARD;
                         var ROW, COL: integer);
    begin
        COL := COL - 1;
        ROW := CONFIGURATION[COL] + 1
    end;


    function ISSAFE(CONFIGURATION: BOARD;
                    ROW, COL: integer): boolean;
        var I    : integer;
            SAFETY: boolean;
```

Example 14.1 **Pascal Solution to the Eight Queens Problem**

---

list that represents the first step toward a solution, placing the queen in the first column in row 1. This list is similar to the array CONFIGURATION in Example 14.1.

The solution of Example 14.2 compares quite favorably with the Pascal solution, when one takes into account the meager facilities of Mini-language Apply. Both programs find the same board configuration as their solution to the problem (Figure 14.1).

```
begin
   SAFETY := true;
   for I := 1 to COL-1 do
      if ((CONFIGURATION[I] + I) = (ROW + COL)) or
         ((CONFIGURATION[I] - I) = (ROW - COL)) or
         (CONFIGURATION[I] = ROW) then
         SAFETY = false;
   ISSAFE := SAFETY
end;

begin
   COL := 1;
   ROW := 1;

   repeat
      while (ROW < 9) and (COL < 9) do
         if ISSAFE(CONFIGURATION, ROW, COL) then
            ADVANCECOL(CONFIGURATION, ROW, COL)
         else
            ROW := ROW + 1;
      if (ROW = 9) then
         RETREATCOL(CONFIGURATION, ROW, COL)
   until (COL = 9);

   for I := 1 to 8 do
      WRITE(CONFIGURATION[I])
end.
```

Example 14.1 **continued**

Figure 14.1 **Configuration of Solution to Eight Queens Problem**

```
program
    QUEENS('1')

where QUEENS(CONFIGURATION) is
    select
       IS_COMPLETE(CONFIGURATION) => CONFIGURATION
       else                       => QUEENS(GET_ANOTHER(CONFIGURATION))
    end select

where IS_COMPLETE(CONFIGURATION) is
    select
       (length(CONFIGURATION) = 8) => IS SAFE(CONFIGURATION)
       else                        => false
    end select

where GET_ANOTHER(CONFIGURATION) is
    select
       (last(CONFIGURATION) = 9)  => ADVANCE(stem(CONFIGURATION))
       IS_SAFE(CONFIGURATION)     => START_NEW_COL(CONFIGURATION)
       else                       => ADVANCE(CONFIGURATION)
    end select

where ADVANCE(CONFIGURATION) is
    append(stem(CONFIGURATION), last(CONFIGURATION) + 1)

where START_NEW_COL(CONFIGURATION) is
    APPEND(CONFIGURATION, 1)
```

Example 14.2 **Mini-language Apply Solution to the Eight Queens Problem**

Functions in a Procedural Language

You may have noticed the use of a function ISSAFE in the Pascal solution to the Eight Queens problem. This is a function in the same sense as those used in Mini-language Apply. Generally, however, the facility for functions in a procedural language is not quite so pure as that in Mini-language Apply. There are often three major differences:

1. In some languages, the value of the argument to the function may be altered during a call to the function.
2. In most languages, execution of the body of the function may result in a change in the value of a variable that is global to the function body.

```
where IS_SAFE(CONFIGURATION) is
   select
      (length(CONFIGURATION) = 0) => true
      else => CHECK_NEW_QUEEN(stem(CONFIGURATION),
                 last(CONFIGURATION),
                      length(CONFIGURATION))
   end select

where CHECK_NEW_QUEEN(CONFIGURATION, ROW, COL) is
   select
      (length(CONFIGURATION) = 0) => true
      POSSIBLE_CAPTURE(last(CONFIGURATION),
                              length(CONFIGURATION),
                              ROW, COL) => false
      else => CHECK_NEW_QUEEN(stem(CONFIGURATION), ROW, COL)
   end select

where POSSIBLE_CAPTURE(ATTACK_ROW, ATTACK_COL, ROW, COL) is
   select
      (ATTACK_ROW = ROW)                          => true
      ((ATTACK_ROW - ATTACK_COL) = (ROW - COL))   => true
      ((ATTACK_ROW + ATTACK_COL) = (ROW + COL))   => true
      else                                        => false
   end select
end
```

Example 14.2 **continued**

3. In every language that we know of, the body of a function may reference variables whose values are global to the function, even if they are not changed.

The first two properties allow functions with side effects to be written in procedural languages. That is, functions can change the values of variables that exist outside the function.

Example 14.3 demonstrates this problem with a very simple Ada program. The expressions in the two computations of the value of C are identical except for the order in which functions F and G are invoked.

Using a left-to-right evaluation, the values printed for C (72 and 75) are not the same. Here, the familiar commutative property of addition is lost

```
procedure MAIN is
   A, B, C: FLOAT;
   use REAL_IO;

   function F(X: FLOAT) return FLOAT is
   begin
      A := A + 1.0;
      return A * X;
   end F;

   function G(X: FLOAT) return FLOAT is
   begin
      A := A + 2.0;
      return A * X;
   end G;

begin
   A := 10.0;
   B :=  3.0;
   C := F(B) + G(B);  -- first computation of value of C
   PUT(C);

   A := 10.0;
   B :=  3.0;
   C := G(B) + F(B);  -- second computation of value of C
   PUT(C);
end MAIN;
```

Example 14.3 **Ada Functions with Side Effects**

because of the assignment to a global variable. Certainly, many programmers would be surprised to learn that

```
F(B) + G(B)
```

is not equivalent to:

```
G(B) + F(B)
```

Since Ada employs conventional mathematical notation, it is dangerous to write functions that violate the properties of established mathematical systems.

The case against references to global variables becomes even stronger when we need to modify a program. Change is a daily occurrence in programming. Someone may find a more efficient algorithm, an error may be detected, or revised specifications may be given. Before a program can be modified, its action must be completely understood. Functions that reference global variables make it more difficult to understand the program because the point at which the function is invoked carries no indication of the variables that will be affected by the invocation. In addition, if a piece of code that is to be changed has external effects, then those effects must be accounted for. This requires delving deeply into the entire program for a clear understanding of what effects a function has on other parts of the program. Adding a few extra lines of code for that desirable change may kill the correctness of another piece of code. As a result, another change may be needed to right matters, and so on.

Even if this process succeeds, it is not likely to add to the clarity or flexibility of the program. Had the original program been written without external references, the function could be changed *without* looking at the rest of the program.

In short, the design of a good facility for functions is an important part of most programming languages. Any deviation from their normal mathematical properties should be handled with great care.

14.3 Recursion

We have already seen in this chapter an example of a recursive definition:

```
where LENGTH(L) is
    select
        (L = null) => 0
        else       => 1 + LENGTH(tail(L))
    end select
```

We have also seen recursive definitions in Chapter 3.

Loosely speaking, a recursive definition is one in which the object being defined is used as part of the definition. For example, the word *descendant* may be defined as:

A descendant of a person is an offspring or a descendant of an off-spring of the person.

In this definition, *all* the descendants of the person are simply and precisely accounted for. A nonrecursive definition of descendant that attempts to take all possibilities into account is the following:

A descendant of a person is a son or daughter, a grandson or grand-daughter of the person, or a great-grandson or great-granddaughter of the person, etc.

In this case, the definition is longer than the recursive definition and avoids infinite length through the use of "etc." Dictionaries try to avoid obvious recursion by defining a descendant as:

One who has a specific person among one's ancestors.

However, an ancestor is defined as:

One from whom a person is descended.

Thus, the recursion is still present, though indirectly.

The concept of recursion presents peculiar difficulties to many programmers. The concept is particularly important in Mini-language Apply where there is no flow of control and all iteration is handled by recursion. Although the two are equivalent, it is important to distinguish between the two.

> *Iteration* is the repeated performance of some action until a particular condition is met. The performance of the action is carried to completion each time before the testing of the condition that decides if the performance is to be repeated.

> *Recursion* involves self-nesting. The performance is not carried to completion before the condition is tested. Instead, the condition is examined as part of the performance of the action and, if the condition is not satisfied, the action is performed again as a subroutine of the as yet uncompleted original action.

Mathematically, recursive definitions are often more succinct than iterative ones, and this applies to programming as well. Iterative definitions seem to require the unsatisfactory device of a string of dots in the middle, for example

$$\text{sum} = a_1 + a_2 + \ldots + a_n$$

The Pascal equivalent of this definition is:

```
function SUM(A: VECTOR; N: INTEGER): INTEGER;
   var PARTIALSUM, I: INTEGER;
begin
   PARTIALSUM := 0;
   for I := 1 to N do
      PARTIALSUM := PARTIALSUM + A[I];

   SUM := PARTIALSUM
end;
```

In Mini-language Apply, the same function is as follows:

```
where SUM(A, N) is
   select
      (N = 0) => 0
      else     => first(A) + SUM(tail(A), N-1)
   end select
```

Here the array is represented by a list. The recursive definition in Apply is simpler because it avoids the use of such extra variables as PARTIALSUM and I.

In general, there is always an iterative equivalent to a recursive definition; however, the iterative version may require a fixed number of extra variables or the use of a stack whose depth depends on the parameters of the recursion.

Fixed Points

We believe that the mathematical concept of fixed points provides the clearest approach to understanding recursion.

A recursive definition has the form:

$$q = \ldots q \ldots q \ldots$$

That is, a definition of some entity q in which the same entity q is used in the definition. In reality, such definitions do not define anything. Rather, they are *equations,* and there must exist some entity that when substituted for q satisfies the equation.

For example, consider the following recursive definitions:

1. $y = y^2 - 12$

2. identifier ::= letter | identifier letter

3. L = (a, L)

4.
```
where F(N) is
      select
      (N = 0) => 1
   else => N * F(N - 1)
   end select
```

What are the "solutions" to these equations? The type of object defined depends on the defining equation:

1. the integers 4 and -3

2. the infinite set of identifiers {A B . . . Z AA AB . . .}

3. the infinite binary list (a, (a, (a, . . .)))

4. the function for computing the factorial of its argument

Notice that in each case, the solution "satisfies" the equation, that is, when the solution is substituted into the defining equation, an identity is produced. The solution to equation 4 is a function object represented by F in just the same way that y in equation 1 represents an object, an integer object. F is a function object of type

    integer → integer

The right side of equation 4 can be considered as a function that is applied to F. That is, we can rewrite the equation as

    F = H(F)

where H is a function that has a single parameter of type

    integer → integer

which we can denote by φ. H is thus the function

```
select
    (N = 0) => 1
    else    => N * φ(N - 1)
end select
```

Since F satisfies the equation

    F = H(F)

we are looking for some function object F that, when operated on by the function H, leaves it unchanged. Such a function is said to be a *fixed point* of the definition.

Let's try the function INCREMENT, which adds one to its argument, as a fixed point of the definition. By replacing F by INCREMENT in our equation we have

```
INCREMENT(N)
    =  select
          (N = 0) => 1
          else    => N * INCREMENT(N - 1)
       end select

    =  select
          (N = 0) => 1
          else => N * N
       end select

    ≠ INCREMENT(N)
```

Thus, INCREMENT is not a solution of the equation.

Now let's try the function FACTORIAL. We have

```
FACTORIAL(N)
   = select
        (N = 0) => 1
        else    => N * FACTORIAL(N - 1)
     end select


   = FACTORIAL(N)
```

Thus, FACTORIAL works and is a fixed point of the equation.

This view leads to an important point. In programming languages there are really no such entities as *recursive functions*. There are recursive definitions or equations whose solution yields a function. A function is a bona fide entity, and it is not *recursive*. Thus, we should not say that F is a recursive function. Instead, we should say that the function F is defined recursively and has a solution that is the factorial function. After all, the factorial function simply maps a number N into N * (N - 1) * . . . * 1.

Understanding Recursion

Consider, for example, the recursive definition:

```
where REVERSE(L) is
   select
      (L = null)     => null
      (length(L) = 1) => L
      else            => append(REVERSE(tail(L)), first(L))
   end select
```

If we read this definition, we know from its name that it has something to do with lists and putting their components in reverse order. Let us assume, for the moment, that the function does compute a list with its elements exactly in reverse order. Thus, our first step in understanding recursion is to develop a clear mental picture of what we assume the definition defines.

Our second step is to test our mentally assumed fixed point against the definition at hand. To do this, we read the recursive definition and constantly test the definition against the assumed fixed point. In the above case, our thinking may go as follows:

a. If the parameter is null, then certainly its reverse is null, and thus the answer given in the recursive definition is correct, at least for this case.

b. If the parameter is a list of length 1, then the list has only one element and the reverse of the list is clearly itself. Thus, the recursive definition gives the assumed fixed point in this case also.

c. Now for the real mental leap. If the list is not null and does not consist of just a single element, then the else clause applies. In this case, our definition calls on us to apply the REVERSE function to the tail of L. Our definition then asks us to form a single list by appending the first element of L to the end of the list formed by reversing the tail of L. With a little thought, we see that this is exactly the reverse of a list with two or more elements.

Of course, our job is not complete. Having verified that our defintion returns the correct answer in all cases stated in the definition, we must finally check that all of the possible input values are covered. In our case above, we see that lists of length zero and one are covered in the first two cases, and that lists of two or more elements are covered by the else clause. Thus, our definition is also complete.

Finally, note that the above discussion presents a model of recursion that can be interpreted statically, that is, without the need for simulating nested recursive calls or employing pushdown stacks.

14.4 Functions as Objects

The definition of the function

```
where F(Y) is
    Y + 3
```

is the equivalent of saying that:

F is the function of Y that is Y + 3

It is a declaration of the identifier F as having a constant meaning or value, just as the Mini-language Ref declaration

```
MAX_COL: integer constant = 72;
```

associates the identifier MAX_COL with a constant value.

We are familiar with the idea of functions having constant meanings, since that is how they generally appear in mathematics. In the expression

```
(x + y) * (x + z)
```

the x and y are regarded as variables that can take on a range of values. The operators + and *, however, always have the same meaning, like the numerals 3, 5, or 7.

In most programming languages, functions are treated as restricted objects that can only be used in certain contexts. For example, in most languages functions cannot be passed as arguments to subroutines. This would be useful, for example, in writing a numerical integration routine where a parameter could be the function that calculates the value of the mathematical function being integrated.

Functions Whose Values Are Functions

We are familiar with functions whose values are integers, lists, or other simple values. We have already seen a function whose parameter is itself a function. We will now see how functions can have values that are functions in their own right.

The plus function is a function of two variables. Thus, we can write (2 + X) as +(2,X). Suppose we introduce a new function +' that takes a single argument, for example, +'(2). The value of the function +' is defined to be a new function of a single argument that adds a constant to it. Thus, the value of +'(2) is a function that adds two to its argument. In other words, its value is the function

    X   →   X + 2

Similarly, the value of +'(5) is the function

    X   →   X + 5

The type of both +'(2) and +'(5) is

    integer   →   integer

Hence the type of the function +' is:

    integer   →   (integer → integer)

That is, +' is a function that takes an integer and yields a new function that takes an integer and yields an integer.

With only a minor change to the syntax of Mini-language Apply, we can write a definition of this function as follows:

```
where PLUS_PRIME(X) is
    G
    where G(Y) is
        X + Y
```

As part of our modification to Mini-language Apply, we now allow the expression in a function definition to refer to an identifier that does not occur in the parameter list. In the function G, the identifier X refers to the parameter of PLUS_PRIME, which contains G. Thus, we have quietly introduced a kind of variable into Apply.

A variable, such as X, whose value is established outside the function definition is known as a *free variable*. A variable that is not a free variable is a parameter, also known as a *bound variable*.

The function PLUS_PRIME consists of a simple expression that names its internal function G. This function is the *value* returned by PLUS_PRIME. This is analogous with a function that consists of the simple expression 5. Evaluation of this function returns the integer object 5. In the case of PLUS_PRIME, it is a function object that is returned, one of the class of integer → integer function objects.

A function object consists of two parts, the body of the function that defines how to calculate the result, and a free variable list that provides the values needed to complete evaluation of the function body. This object is called a *closure*.

In the case of evaluating the expression

```
PLUS_PRIME(K)
```

we would have:

```
body:      K + Y
free variable list:    K
```

Here Y is the parameter of the function object. The free variable list of the function object corresponds to the environment part of a stack frame described in Chapter 11. The environment pointer gives access to the list of nonlocal values of the procedure owning the stack frame. These are the procedure's free variables.

Uses for Function Objects

We have already mentioned the use of parameters that are functions in numerical integration programs. Generalized sort routines can also use such parameters to obtain access to functions that compare and interchange the objects being sorted. In this way, the sort routine does not need to have the definition of the objects and can be used for any set of objects.

In artificial intelligence research, work is being done to devise new ways of representing knowledge. While much can be done through records that contain conventional values, such as integers and character strings, in certain areas it is more convenient to represent knowledge as functions and procedures. For example, the representation of certain classes of patterns can best be done by executable functions that return a truth value that reports if the pattern has been recognized. The inclusion of such functions in a data base is an application of functions as data objects.

While certain languages already allow functions to be treated as objects, much research is still needed in this area.

14.5 Where to Look: Lisp, Val

Lisp

Lisp was first designed and implemented by John McCarthy and a group at MIT around 1960 as an algebraic list-processing language for research in artificial intelligence. The basic ideas of Lisp are:

- computing with symbolic expressions rather than numbers
- representation of symbolic expressions and other information by list structure
- a small set of selector and constructor operations expressed as functions
- composition of functions as a tool for forming more complex functions
- the use of conditional expressions for getting branching into function definitions
- the recursive use of conditional expressions
- the representation of Lisp programs as Lisp data
- the formal definition of the language through a Lisp function that also serves as an interpreter
- the use of garbage collection as a means of recovering unused storage

Like Mini-language Apply, Lisp functions are defined entirely as expressions. Each operator is a function that returns a value, and subprograms are written as single, perhaps complex, expressions.

The language operates on *S-expressions,* for "symbolic expressions," constructed from *atoms.* An atom is a sequence of alphabetic or numeric characters, possibly intermixed, or the special atom NIL, which represents the null list. An atom that consists entirely of numeric characters is a *numeric* atom; all other atoms are *symbolic* atoms. An S-expression is either an atom or a pair, written in the form

(S_1 . S_2)

where S_1 and S_2 are arbitrary S-expressions.

An important subset of S-expressions consists of *lists*. A list is an S-expression that consists either of the atom NIL, or a pair $(S_1.S_2)$ where only S_2 is a list. The following S-expressions are lists:

```
(A . B)
((FRED . 9) . (JOE . (PETER . 27)))
```

It is more convenient to express lists in an abbreviated form known as "list notation":

$(S_1 \ S_2 \ . \ . \ . \ S_n)$

is an abbreviation for

$(S.(S_2.(. \ . \ .(S_n.NIL). \ . \ .)))$

thus

$(X \ Y \ Z)$ is an abbreviation for $(X.(Y.(Z.NIL)))$

Not only are S-expressions manipulated by Lisp programs, but Lisp programs are S-expressions. An expression of the form

$(E_0 \ E_1 \ E_2 \ . \ . \ . \ E_n)$

is an *invocation* where the value of E_0 is the procedure and the values of $E_1 \ . \ . \ . \ E_n$ are its arguments.

Lisp provides a number of primitive functions for manipulating S-expressions. These are:

car	is the equivalent of the Mini-language Apply function first.
cdr	(pronounced "could-er") is the equivalent of the Mini-language Apply function tail.
cons	takes two S-expressions A and B as arguments and returns a new S-expression C such that car(C) = A and cdr(C) = B.
eq	takes two atomic arguments and returns the value true if they are the same atom, otherwise it returns the value false. The function is undefined if either of the arguments is not an atom.
atom	takes an S-expression argument and returns the value true if the argument is an atom (or NIL) and false otherwise.

The strange names car and cdr are historical relics from Lisp's original implementation on an IBM 704 computer. The name car stood for the instruction "contents of the *a*ddress *r*egister" and cdr meant "contents of the *d*ecrement *r*egister".

Boolean functions yield one of the atoms T or NIL. The Lisp function

```
cond((A B) (C D) (T E))
```

may be written in the equivalent more mnemonic forms:

```
if A then B else if C then D else E
```

```
A → B; C → D; T → E
```

in some implementations.

In addition to the functions just described, it is possible for the user to define functions. The form of this definition is based on the lambda-calculus described in [Church 1941]. A function may be defined as

```
(lambda(X Y)(PLUS X Y))
```

which specifies a function of two parameters X and Y that consists of the application of the PLUS function to the two parameters. The function defined in this way does not have a name; it may be bound to a name by

```
(define (ADD (lambda(X Y)(PLUS X Y)))
```

As a result of this definition, the atom ADD has a value that is a function and can be applied to two arguments to produce a result that is their sum.

The features of Lisp described so far have all been applicative. There have been a number of nonapplicative features added to the language for reasons of efficiency. The two principal nonapplicative functions are set, which is a function that acts as an assignment statement, and prog, which takes a list of expressions as its argument and executes them in sequence, thus treating them as statements.

Val

A very different development of applicative languages is that of data flow languages. As the use of computers in scientific applications expands, there is an ever greater demand for faster computers. So far, improvements in hardware technology have been responsible for most of the advances in speed; however, physical constraints such as the speed of light and power-cooling ratios may soon limit the speed that can be achieved by a single processor. A possible solution to this problem is the application of parallel processing on a massive scale, for example, a thousand processors for a single task. To achieve this degree of parallelism, special languages that help identify concurrency in algorithms are required.

Consider the following sequence of statements from Mini-language Core:

```
A := B + C;    -- #1
D := A * C;    -- #2
E := B - A;    -- #3
G := E * D;    -- #4
H := E + A;    -- #5
I := G * H;    -- #6
```

Only some of these statements can be executed concurrently. For example, #1 must be executed before #2 because its result is required in #2's expression. However, once #1 has been executed, #2 and #3 can be executed simultaneously followed by #4 and #5 simultaneously and finally #6 can be executed. To discover these parallelisms requires the same sort of data flow analysis as is used in optimizing compilers. While this can be done for reasonably well structured programs, there are limits to the degree of parallelism that can be achieved. Data flow languages are designed in making this kind of analysis unnecessary and to assist the programmer in writing programs that contain large amounts of concurrency. Typical of this kind of language is the experimental language Val described in [Mc-Graw 1982].

The basic design principles of a data flow language like Val were first described in [Ackerman 1982]:

Freedom from side effects: This is of paramount importance. The language is completely functional and once the values of all inputs to an expression or procedure are known, execution cannot influence the results of any other operations that are ready to execute.

Locality of effect: This means that operations do not have unnecessary far-reaching data dependencies. In conventional languages, temporary data storage is reused in different parts of a program to save space. This prevents concurrent computation because of storage conflicts. In Val, the scope of a data name is very strictly limited.

A "single assignment" convention: A variable may appear on the left side of an assignment only once within its scope.

Unusual iteration forms: These are required by the need for freedom from side effects and the single assignment rule so that each of the iterations can be computed in parallel.

The primitive data types `boolean`, `integer`, `real`, and `character` of Val are similar to those found in most current languages. Each of these types has its own appropriate set of operations and special error values. Some of these special error values are pos over and neg_over to represent numbers that are outside the magnitude capability of the machine, zero_divide for the result of zero division, unknown for a result whose value cannot be accurately determined because of a previous magnitude error condition, and undef for an undefined value. The use of these values avoids the need to stop during a computation because of an error. No operation can abort; if something goes wrong, it returns a value that is within the type of the operation result.

New types can be constructed by aggregating the primitive types into arrays, records, and unions (named oneof). The array bounds are not part of the type definition. Thus, one type describes all finite-length ordered sequences of the elements of the array. Examples of these constructions are:

```
type COORD  = record[X, Y, Z: real];
type LINE   = array[COORD];
type RESULT = oneof[NONE: null; OK: LINE];
```

Here, the program defined type LINE is represented by an array of COORDs. An instance of type RESULT can represent a value of type LINE or of type null. When an object gets a value, one of the forms must be specified together with the appropriate information. For example, this may be done by

```
make RESULT[OK: PERPENDICULAR];
```

where the identifier PERPENDICULAR has been previously bound by a declaration of the form

```
PERPENDICULAR: LINE;
```

to an array of COORDs.

The programming philosophy of Val is value-oriented instead of the more conventional variable orientation. Once a value is computed by some operator, the value is transmitted to all operators that use it as input. The idea of binding values to identifiers is still available; however, once an identifier is bound to a value, the binding remains in force throughout the scope of the identifier and cannot be changed. This is the single assignment convention. This rule applies equally to arrays and records, which are treated as though they were scalars. If a single element in one of them is changed, an entirely new array or record is built; however, this can be done concurrently with other operations. As an example of the single assignment rule, consider the following function:

```
function CALC(X1, X2, Y1, Y2, Z1, Z2: real returns RESULT)
   let
      COORD1:   COORD := record[X: X1; Y: Y1; Z: Z1];
      COORD2:   COORD := record[X: X2; Y: Y2; Z: Z2];
      NEW_LINE: LINE  := [1: COORD1; 2: COORD2];

      in make RESULT*OK: NEW_LINE+
   endlet
```

In this example, there are three temporary bindings before generating the result in the in clause.

One of the most important forms of concurrency available in Val comes from its equivalent of the iterative form. In conventional languages iterations compute sequentially because the language and the target machine operate sequentially. Array construction is often done this way; each pass through the loop computes and stores one value in the array. If the calculations do not depend upon each other, the array could be constructed in one highly parallel, nonlooping expression. This type of concurrency can be represented in Val through the forall statement. For example, in

```
forall I in [L, H]
   ITEM_X: real := LINE[I].X;
   ITEM_Y: real := LINE[I].Y;
   ITEM_Z: real := LINE[I].Z;

   DIST: real := SQRT(ITEM_X * ITEM_X + ITEM_Y * ITEM_Y +
                                        ITEM_Z * ITEM_Z);

   eval plus DIST
endall
```

The range specification [L, H] specifies that a separate ITEM_X, ITEM_Y, ITEM_Z, and DIST are to be created for each of the values of I in the range given by the values of L and H. These separate values of DIST are all computed in parallel. They are then merged into a single result in the eval clause using the binary opertor plus. This merging takes the form of a binary tree of partial sums.

The major advantage of Val is that it does not need any special features to express concurrency or synchronization. The programmer is able to express the algorithm naturally, and the concurrency becomes clear as a consequence. One possible shortcoming of the language is that the designers chose to omit recursion. They did this because of implementation difficulties foreseen with the target hardware, a specially developed "data flow" machine designed to test the concepts of the language. It should be emphasized that Val is a small experimental language for the exploration of highly parallel computation. For further details about the language, the reader should refer to [McGraw 1982].

Further Reading

The basis of Mini-language Apply is taken from Lisp [see McCarthy et al. 1962]. More recent work on the applicative type of languages is contained in [Burge 1975], [Backus 1978], and [Henderson 1980].

A foundation work for treating functions as objects is the lambda-calculus. The original work [Church 1941] and the work in [Curry and Feys 1958] are definitive references on this topic, although certainly hard to read. Numerous applications of the lambda-calculus and derived formal systems can be found. The most famous of these are the works by [Landin 1963] and [Landin 1965]. Other implications are given in [Stoy 1977].

An interesting informal account of recursion and the application of function objects is given in [Hofstadter 1979].

Exercises

Exercise 14.1 *Removing Duplicates from a List*

In Mini-language Apply, a list can have duplicate elements, for example:

```
'1, 2, 3, 1, 2, 3, 4'
'2, 2, 3, 3, 2'
```

Write a function named REDUCE that takes a list as an argument and returns the list without duplicate elements. For example,

```
REDUCE('1, 2, 3, 1, 2, 3, 4')
```

has the value

```
'1, 2, 3, 4'
```

and

```
REDUCE('3, 2, 3, 3, 2')
```

has the value

```
'3, 2'
```

Exercise 14.2 Sorting

Write a program in Mini-language Apply that will rearrange a list of integers into ascending order.

Exercise 14.3 Another List Operation

Write a program in Mini-language Apply that is the converse of the append function already in the mini-language. This function, here called PREPEND, takes two arguments, an integer and a list, and returns a list constructed by inserting the integer at the front of the list. In other words, PREPEND must satisfy the relationship for a list L:

```
L = PREPEND(first(L), stem(L))
```

Exercise 14.4 Finding a Fixed Point

Consider the following definition:

```
where H(X) is
   select
      (X > 0) => 1 + H(X - 1)
      else    => 0
   end select
```

What is the fixed point of H? Once you find it, write a simpler definition of H.

Exercise 14.5 Self-Application

Is X(X) ever meaningful, that is, does it ever make sense to apply an object to itself?

Exercise 14.6 Ackermann's Function

Trace the execution of the following Apply program:

```
program
   ACKERMANN(2, 3)
      where ACKERMANN(M, N) is
         select
            (M = 0) => N + 1
            (N = 0) => ACKERMANN(M-1, 1)
            else    => ACKERMANN(M-1, ACKERMANN(M, N-1))
         end select
   end
```

Exercise 14.7 *Ackermann's Function Again*

Write an iterative equivalent of Ackermann's function defined in the previous exercise. The iterative version may need a stack. If you attempt to execute this program, you should be warned that its value increases very rapidly with increasing argument values. You should only test it for small arguments.

Exercise 14.8 *Applicative versus Conventional Languages*

The nodes in a graph may be labeled with integers, and a connection from one node to another may be given as a pair of integers. In a graph with four nodes, the nodes may thus be denoted as 1, 2, 3, 4. A connection from node 1 to node 3 may be given as (1 3).

A graph is said to be connected if there is a path from each node to every other. Thus, the connections

(1 2) (2 3) (3 4)

and

(1 3) (3 1) (2 4) (3 2)

describe a connected graph, whereas

(1 3) (3 1) (2 4)

does not.

Write one program in Mini-language Apply and another in a conventional language (for example, Fortran, Pascal, or Mini-language Typedef) to determine if a graph is connected. You may give the input data in any suitable form.

Exercise 14.9 *A Strange Function*

Determine the value output by the Mini-Language Apply program:

```
program
    F(14)
    where F(N) is
        select
            (N > 100) => N - 10
            else      => F(F(N + 11))
        end select
end
```

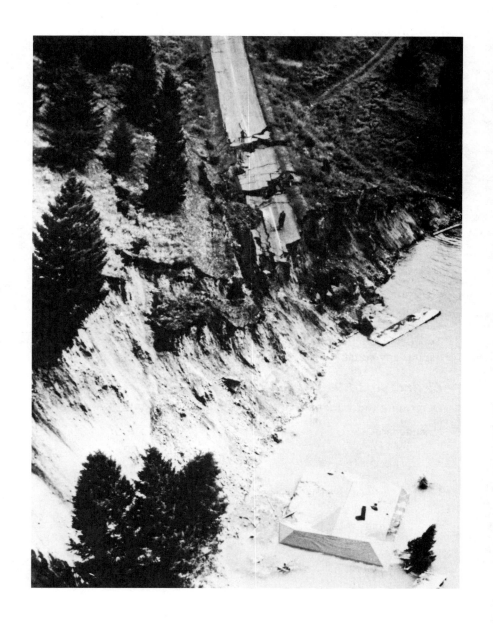

15

Exception Handling

There are "exception" conditions that can arise in every program. Input data may contain values that are out of range, a hardware unit may fail, a table may become full, or the wrong reel of tape may be mounted.

To think of all exception conditions as errors is too limiting. Some exception conditions, though occurring rarely, are required for the proper termination of the program. For example, the end of the input file may mark the end of the input phase of a program and the beginning of its computation phase. Unfortunately, there is no generally accepted distinction between erroneous and normal exception conditions. What is normal in one context may be an error in another.

For our purposes here, we define an *exception condition* as:

A condition that prevents the completion of the operation that detects it, that cannot be resolved within the local context of the operation, and that must be brought to the attention of the operation's invoker.

The action of bringing the condition to the invoker's attention is called *raising* the exception. The corresponding action by the invoker is called *handling* the exception.

Generally, once an exception condition is raised, it must be handled; otherwise, the program is in error. Some languages provide default actions for conditions that are not handled by the program.

Since exception conditions are linked to particular operations, they are *synchronous* in the sense that they can only occur at specific points in the program. For example, a subscript error can only occur during array manipulation. *Asynchronous* events, such as an interrupt caused by a user

445

pressing the break key on a terminal, can occur at any point during a program's execution. The handling of asynchronous events is discussed in Chapter 16. In this chapter, we discuss only synchronous conditions. Mini-language Exceptions is essentially based on Ada.

15.1 Mini-language Exceptions

As illustrated in Table 15.1, our mini-language for this chapter contains many features that have appeared in other mini-languages. As usual, the first part of a program consists of a sequence of one or more variable declarations, and each variable in a program must be declared exactly once. Each identifier may represent either a single integer value or an array of integer values. Integer values may contain at most eight decimal

Table 15.1 **Mini-language Exceptions**

program	::=	`program`
		    variable-declaration. . .
		    procedure. . .
		`begin`
		    statement. . .
		    [exception-handler]
		`end ;`

variable-declaration	::=	identifier [, identifier]. . . : `integer` [`array`] ;

procedure	::=	identifier : `procedure`
		    statement. . .
		    [exception-handler]
		`end ;`

statement	::=	assignment-statement | if-statement | loop-statement | call-statement | raise-statement | input-statement | output-statement
exception-handler	::=	`exception` `when` exception-name `=>` statement. . . [`when` exception-name `=>` statement. . .]. . .
exception-name	::=	identifier | `overflow` | `undefined_value` | `data_error` | `subscript_error` | `end_of_input`
assignment-statement	::=	variable `:=` expression ;

digits. The number of components in arrays is 100, with a subscript range of 1 through 100.

Mini-language Exceptions has a simple procedural mechanism. Each procedure has a name and a body. The body simply consists of a sequence of statements and may also have an exception part, described below.

Most of the statements of this mini-language are familiar; they include:

- Assignment statements

- Loop and if statements

- Call statements

- Input and output statements

In addition, there is a raise statement whose meaning will be explained below.

Table 15.1 **continued**		
if-statement	::=	`if` comparison `then` statement. . . [`else` statement. . .] `end if` ;
loop-statement	::=	`while` comparison `loop` statement. . . `end loop` ;
call-statement	::=	identifier ;
raise-statement	::=	`raise` exception-name ;
input-statement	::=	`input` variable [, variable]. . . ;
output-statement	::=	`output` variable [, variable]. . . ;
comparison	::=	(operand comparison-operator operand)
expression	::=	[expression +] operand
operand	::=	integer | variable | (expression)
variable	::=	identifier | identifier [expression]
comparison-operator	::=	‹ | = | ≠ | ›

Exception Conditions

There are a number of specific situations that can cause exceptions. These exceptions are described in Table 15.2. When one of these situations arises during program execution, the corresponding exception condition is raised. For example, if no value has been assigned to the variable INDEX, then evaluation of the expression

```
INDEX + 1
```

suspends normal execution and raises the undefined_value exception.

Each of the conditions defined in Table 15.2 can also be raised by the execution of a raise statement. For example, execution of the statement

```
raise overflow;
```

causes the overflow condition to be raised, just as it is when overflow occurs during computation. The raise statement can also be used to raise programmer-defined conditions. This allows a subroutine to report the occurrence of an exception condition. For example, the statement

```
raise TABLE_EMPTY;
```

raises the TABLE_EMPTY condition and could be used to indicate that there were no entries in a table. This exception condition is defined by the programmer for the particular program. The appearance of the identifier TABLE_EMPTY in the raise statement defines it to be an exception condition. Whether this would be an error situation would depend on the context in which it was used.

In Mini-language Exceptions, the user may define how a condition is to be handled. The response can range from printing the values of one or more variables, to taking steps to deal with the cause of the exception. If the programmer does not specify how an exception condition is to be handled, the program is in error and is terminated. This applies to both predefined and user-defined conditions.

A response to an exception condition is defined by an exception handler included in a program unit. A program unit is either the main program or a procedure. For example, consider the handler:

```
exception
    when data_error => INVALID_DATA_FLAG := 1;
                       ERROR_COUNT       := ERROR_COUNT + 1;
    when INVALID_ACCOUNT_NUMBER => output ACCOUNT_NUMBER;
```

When an exception condition is raised, normal execution is suspended. If there is an appropriate handler defined in the program unit that was being executed, the corresponding sequence of statements in the given handler is executed. These statements are executed instead of completing execu-

Table 15.2 **Predefined Exception Conditions**

Condition	Cause
overflow	The absolute value of some quantity exceeds 99999.
undefined_value	An attempt to obtain the value of a variable to which no value has been assigned.
data_error	The characters read during the execution of an input statement do not constitute an integer or there is a transmission error due to a hardware malfunction.
subscript_error	The use of an array subscript outside the range 1 through 100.
end_of_input	The execution of an input statement when there are no more data to be read.

tion of the statement that caused the condition to be raised. After execution of the handler, normal execution of the procedure continues at the statement following the one that raised the condition.

If there is no appropriate handler for the exception condition in the program unit, execution of the unit is terminated and the same condition is raised by the call statement that invoked the procedure. This process is continued until either a handler for the condition is executed or the program is terminated. Thus, if the main program does not contain a handler for the condition, the program is terminated.

Consider the simple procedure:

```
INITIALIZE_TABLE: procedure

    END_OF_DATA := 0;
    TABLE_INDEX := 1;
    input X, Y, Z;
    while (END_OF_DATA = 0) loop
        TABLE[TABLE_INDEX] := X + Y + Z;
        TABLE_INDEX        := TABLE_INDEX + 1;
        input X, Y, Z;
    end loop;

    exception
        when end_of_input   => END_OF_DATA := 1;
        when overflow       => TABLE[TABLE_INDEX] := MAX_VALUE;
        when subscript/error => output X, Y, Z;
                                TABLE_INDEX := 1;
    end;
```

This procedure has handlers for three exception conditions. When the condition for end of input is raised, the value of END_OF_DATA is set to 1. Control then returns to the statement following the input statement that raised the condition. The detection of the end of input is thus used to signal the end of the initialization process. The raising of the overflow condition is assumed to be due to the computation of the value to be inserted in the table. When this happens, the table value is set to the constant value MAX_VALUE defined in the containing program, and execution continues normally.

If the input contains more than 100 sets of values, the *subscript-error* condition will be raised. The handler for this condition prints the set of values last read (and ignored), and resets TABLE_INDEX to 1.

15.2 Exceptions

There are two broad classes of exceptions:

- *Domain failure:* The input parameters to the operation do not satisfy the requirements of the operation. In Mini-language Exceptions, the subscripting operation has a domain failure when it is passed a subscript greater than 100.

- *Range failure:* The operation is unable to produce a result that is in its range. For example, an input statement can encounter an end-of-file mark instead of a value. As we have seen, this is not necessarily an error; it depends on the context of the operation. The overflow condition is also a kind of range failure.

The exception handling mechanism of the mini-language treats both classes of exceptions in accordance with our definition of an exception. The raising of an exception condition by a statement brings the exception to the notice of the procedure containing the statement. If the procedure does not have a handler, the condition cannot be handled at that level and must be passed higher in the dynamic invocation chain.

Before we discuss the issues in exception handling, we turn to other common means for handling exceptions.

Unusual Return Value

This is the simplest and most primitive method of handling exception conditions. The operation returns an impossible value, that is, a value that is established by the programmer and that lies outside the normal range of the operation.

In its unadorned form, this method has obvious deficiencies. It requires explicit checking after each return from the operation and can destroy the abstraction of the type of the value returned. This can either lead to incomprehensible code that takes advantage of a particular representation for data or it can lead the programmer into spectacular errors.

For example, suppose an operation is defined to calculate the length of some object. Its range is therefore limited to positive values. If the convention is adopted that a specific value (say -1) is used to indicate the detection of an error, the programmer must always be aware that this impossible value may be returned. To forget this is to accept the risk that the value may be used in subsequent arithmetic operations and lead to erroneous results.

The Error Return

This is a mechanism that involves a nonstandard control structure. A call statement passes one or more label parameters designating error returns. These label values mark the beginnings of handlers for various exception conditions in the calling procedure. For example, consider:

```
GET(I, OVERFLOW, BAD_DATA);
 . . .
OVERFLOW: . . .
BAD_DATA: . . .
```

The idea is that, if the subroutine detects an exception condition, it executes a goto statement to the label value specified by the appropriate parameter. The use of parameters allows the subroutine to be used in a number of contexts since it is not tied to specific handlers. This technique imposes little overhead and requires no checking after each return as is required by an unusual return value. However, it does raise serious program structuring issues since the call to the subroutine does not always return to the following statement. In addition, the programmer may have difficulty in knowing where the program is to be resumed after the error has been handled.

In cases where the operation is a block that is internal to the block that invokes it, the label of the handler does not have to be passed as an argument. This makes the program's control structure even more difficult to understand.

Error Routines

In this case, the operation may be invoked with an entry argument specifying the procedure to be invoked by the operation if an exception is detected. For example,

```
GET(I, E);
```

where E is the name of the error handling procedure that is to be invoked if GET wishes to raise a condition.

The exception handler is a procedure and thus returns to its invoker. The structure of the control flow is therefore preserved; the operation that detected the condition is able to respond to any recovery action taken by the handler.

The use of a procedure as an exception handler does not require that the procedure be passed explicitly to the operation. Instead, the handler to be used can be specified implicitly. The handler can be associated with the object being processed or can be dynamically associated with the condition that is detected.

An example of associating the handler with the object would be to specify, as part of the declaration of a file, the procedure to be executed when the end of that file is detected. Thus, the handler is associated with the file. This is done in Cobol. As another example, the AED language allows a programmer to divide storage into zones and to associate with each zone a subroutine to be invoked if a subsequent space allocation request for that zone cannot be satisfied.

The dynamic association of a handler with a condition is typified by the PL/I on-unit mechanism. This was perhaps the first attempt to provide an explicit exception condition mechanism in a high-level language. It has the disadvantage that, though the handler has many of the attributes of a procedure, there is no parameter passing mechanism. All communication between the operation and the handler must be passed through global variables. This reduces both flexiblilty and clarity.

15.3 Issues in Exception Handling

Is there any real need to worry about exception conditions? Anyone who has ever built a large program that makes any pretense at *robustness* appreciates the problems. As programs grow in size, special cases and unusual circumstances proliferate. Even the performance of a seemingly simple task, like a tape-to-tape copy program, abounds with exception conditions. The end-of-input condition will generally be handled properly since it probably marks the end of the process. However, what can be done about tape label checking and the multitude of possible hardware malfunctions? Exceptions exist in even the simplest task, and the complexity that they induce in the program is large. None of the techniques described in the previous section adequately controls this complexity.

It is clear that, for a program to be robust, any exception condition that can arise must be handled. The difficulty is in designing a simple mechanism of sufficient generality to handle all possibilities.

One common method is to make an explicit test for each exception at all possible points of occurrence. Some argue that this is the best solution since it has the great advantage that no special mechanism is required. In many cases, however, the inclusion of such tests can complicate the structure of the program and hide the algorithm behind a multitude of special cases. Thus, the search continues for some method that is sufficiently general, has manageable complexity, and yet remains clear enough so that the normal is not obscured by the handling of the exceptional.

In the quest for such a method, there are a variety of issues that should be addressed:

- The specification of a handler
- The use of defaults when the programmer has not provided an explicit handler
- The propagation of conditions outside the program unit in which they are detected
- The resumption of execution following handling
- The possibility of suppressing the detection of conditions

Handler Specification

The basic operation of an exception handler is to perform some diagnostic or repair actions. Frequently, a handler will *take over* when some exception condition is raised. To act appropriately, a handler may need access to the environment in which the exception was raised.

One of the critical choices in the design of an exception facility is the method by which the handlers are defined. In Mini-language Exceptions, a very simple mechanism is used. A handler may be specified within a procedure! This handler is supposed to *complete* the work of the operation that raised the condition. Because of the simplicity, the mechanism cannot cope with a situation where different handlers are required at different points in a procedure. While the handler has access to the complete environment of the operation, there is no easy way to determine which one of several operations that have the potential for raising the condition actually raised it. For example, if the procedure has several arithmetic expressions, there is no way of telling which operation caused the overflow condition. However, it is not clear how this information could be used if it were available.

Use of Default Handlers

In Mini-language Exceptions, nearly all of the predefined conditions represent error situations. Generally, these error situations have the potential of being raised at many points in the program. This brings up the need for *default* exception handlers.

A default handler is one that is used in the absence of an explicitly defined handler. The Mini-language Exceptions approach defines a single default action for all conditions—program termination.

Termination may not be adequate for many programs. For example, whenever an overflow occurs, we may wish simply to assign the maximum possible number to the offending expression and then resume normal execution. This brings up a number of issues. Should one be able to define a default handler to be used throughout a program? When should a specifically provided handler override the default handler? The question of the resumption of execution will be taken up later in this section.

The conventional response to an error situation in a programming language is a simple abnormal termination of a program, usually with the printing of some diagnostic message. We may view this action itself as simply the default handler provided for the exception situation raised by the error condition. Accordingly, one test of the adequacy of any exception handling mechanism is that it should be possible to define the normal response to errors provided in a programming language. With Mini-language Exceptions, this test is not satisfied.

Propagation of Exceptions

The underlying reason for devising an exception mechanism is the realization that the context in which a condition is detected may not be the proper context in which to process it. For this reason, notice of its detection must be passed to the context where it can be processed. This is generally another procedure at a different level of abstraction. To preserve the abstraction, the detecting operation should express the exception condition in terms of the abstraction that it defines.

It may not be possible for the recipient of an exception to process the condition completely. The occurrence of the exception may seriously affect its behavior, forcing it to raise an exception as well. To maintain the higher level of abstraction of the recipient, this second exception must be expressed in terms of the abstraction represented by its recipient. In short, it must not simply pass the condition raised by the original operation straight through.

In Chapter 1 we cited the Fortran error message:

```
STATE--ABEND CODE IS: SYSTEM 0200, USER 0000
IO-NONE, SCB=0F10C0, PSW IS 078D2000000A98B7E
```

Here is an example of an exception condition that was originally detected, raised at the level of abstraction of the operating system, and passed to the Fortran run-time support library. This library represents the change of abstraction level from that of operating system to that of programming language. However, in our example, the condition was not modified at that level to maintain the proper abstraction. Thus, the programmer cannot assign any meaning to the message.

This example also illustrates a second problem in design: the unilateral decision by a subroutine to terminate execution rather than to offer the programmer the option of effecting a repair and continuing, or of cleaning up before terminating in an orderly manner. Consider the difficulties that a language module can bring by aborting execution of a data base system instead of propagating the exception upward. Files of the data base may be left in an inconsistent state, potentially causing further erroneous behavior when the data base system is later restored.

A raise statement like that in Mini-language Exceptions provides a simple basis for the propagation of exception conditions while maintaining the proper levels of abstraction. However, because of its extreme simplicity, this mechanism does not provide for passage of information from the detecting operation to the handler. There is no way in which variable information can be passed other than through the clumsy use of global variables.

Resuming Program Execution

With most methods of exception handling, the flow of control passes to some remote program text that defines the action to be taken when the exception is raised. Thus, the handler may be viewed as a sort of *trap*. One basic question about exception handling is, what happens after handling the exception? This amounts to a question of whether resumption of normal program flow is meaningful.

One view of exception handlers is that they are basically subroutines to which control is automatically passed when the exception is raised. As with all subroutine calls, after completion of the subroutine, control resumes at the statement after the subroutine call. With this view, the idea of a trap is still retained, but resumption of normal program flow is implicit.

A second view is that exceptions represent program errors. This means that when an exception occurs in a given environment, this environment is to be terminated. The primary role of an exception handler is to provide some appropriate clean-up operation before termination. With this view, resumption of normal execution is meaningless. The handler may decide to restore the same sequence of actions under better conditions, but it will do so by a different invocation of these actions, not a simple resumption.

The first view of exception handlers is the one adopted in PL/I. However, the question of resumption is not treated in a consistent manner. In some cases, resumption implies repetition of the action that raised the condition with the presumption that some sort of fix-up has been made in the handler. In other cases, resumption takes place at the statement following the one that raised the condition. For a third class of conditions, no sort of resumption is possible without the use of labels and goto statements.

The second view of exceptions is taken by Ada. It treats exceptions errors and provides for their local detection. With this view of exceptions, a handler is part of the program unit in which the exception may be raised. Here, the notion of a trap is perhaps not as appropriate, for the handler takes over in case of a faulty situation within the procedure. In this view, normal program execution resumes at the point in which the procedure is called, just as if there had been no exception raised in the first place.

The view taken by Mini-language Exceptions lies between these two positions. The handler does not really constitute a subroutine, but resumption is possible.

Suppression of Exceptions

It could be said that the detection of exception conditions should never be turned off. There is, however, a counterview to this.

Some exception conditions may be quite inefficient to implement. For example, in a language with arrays whose subscripts are restricted to lie within certain bounds (as is the case with most programming languages), range checks for subscripts may need to be implemented in software. Such checks require an implementation overhead during execution of a program. However, the counterargument that programming reliability is essential should not be forgotten.

In some languages there are exception conditions that certainly require excess overhead. For instance, a language may include the ability for the user to specify assertions that must be true during execution of a program, such as requiring that the value of one variable must always be greater than the value of another. When assertions are themselves present in a programming language, the validity of each assertion must be checked with the underlying software. Such assertion checks can be quite expensive to implement.

Imagine for the moment that you are sure that the program you have written is correct. That is, assume that you tested it, and that in all conceivable cases the output produced by the program is as desired. While we might argue that a program is never fully certified to be correct, in practice we may want to make this assumption. In these cases, the checking of exception conditions is superfluous. For this reason, we may wish a feature in a programming language to indicate that one or more (or all) exception conditions should not be checked. This gives us the notion of *suppression* of exception conditions.

There seem to be two basic views regarding the suppression of exceptions. On the one hand, perhaps the suppression of exceptions is best indicated by a command given in the environment in which the program is run. Such a feature would not have any direct impact on the programming language itself. On the other hand, we may wish to state the explicit suppression of exceptions within the programming language. This question is not addressed in Mini-language Exceptions.

15.4 Where to Look: PL/I, Ada

PL/I

PL/I was one of the first languages to provide any facilities for checking and handling exception conditions. These conditions are divided into six categories; examples from each of the categories are:

1. *Computational conditions*

CONVERSION	Invalid data for attempted conversion
FIXEDOVERFLOW	Invalid fixed point result
OVERFLOW	Invalid floating point result
SIZE	Target variable too small to accommodate number without loss of significance

2. *Input-output conditions*

ENDFILE	Attempted access beyond end of file
TRANSMIT	Transmission error
UNDEFINEDFILE	File access error

3. *Program checkout conditions*

SUBSCRIPTRANGE	Attempt to reference array outside its bounds
STRINGRANGE	Attempt to reference string outside its bounds

4. *Storage management conditions*

STORAGE	Insufficient store for requested allocation

5. *System action condition*

ERROR	General error condition
END	Termination of program

6. *Programmer-defined condition*

CONDITION(identifier)	Condition specified by programmer

It is possible to arrange for these conditions to be monitored so that an occurrence will raise an exception. Such a condition is said to be *enabled.* Conditions can also be disabled to avoid generating the code to detect their occurrence. Enabling and disabling are performed statically and controlled by constructs in the language.

If an enabled condition is detected, it is raised. The programmer can define the handling of a condition that has been raised through a special statement, the on-statement. The form of this statement is

```
ON  condition-name
      on-unit;
```

The on-unit can consist of either a single statement or a block of statements. Executing an on-statement specifies that, if the named condition is raised, then the on-unit is to be executed. The on-unit is treated as a simple parameterless procedure that is invoked when the condition is raised. When the on-unit completes execution, control is returned either to the statement in which the condition was raised or to the next statement. This depends on the particular condition. Exercise 15.3 studies this question.

Once the execution of an on-statement associates an on-unit with a particular condition, this association remains until it is overridden by the execution of another on-statement for the same condition in the same block or until the block containing the on-statement terminates. The association may be pushed down by the execution of another on-statement for the same condition in a descendant block; however, it will be reestablished when the descendant block terminates.

It is possible to simulate the occurrence of a condition by means of the signal statement in the same way that the raise statement was used in Mini-language Exceptions.

Ada

Ada has fewer predefined conditions than PL/I; it recognizes:

CONSTRAINT_ERROR	A range, index, or other constraint has been violated
NUMERIC_ERROR	Raised when a result is out of range
SELECT_ERROR	No guard in a select statement is true and there is no else part
STORAGE_ERROR	The storage allocator cannot obtain needed space
TASKING_ERROR	Intertask communication error

As with PL/I, the programmer is also able to define additional special exception conditions that can be used in a raise statement.

Handlers for exception conditions are defined in essentially the same way as in Mini-language Exceptions. However, their execution differs from those in the mini-language in that they always terminate the block in which they are executed. This reflects the Ada view that all exceptions are errors.

Further Reading

Perhaps the most significant works related to this chapter are the paper [Goodenough 1975] and the thesis [Levin 1977]. These works survey a number of issues regarding exception handling.

An early paper relevant to the discussion here is that by [Hill 1971]. A more recent discussion of exception handling is given in [Ichbiah et al. 1979]. Another view of exception handling is that contained in [Parnas and Wurges 1976]. An interesting discussion of the development of the exception handling mechanism for Clu is in [Liskov and Snyder 1979]. The authors describe various models for exception handling and the compromises that must be made in integrating an exception-handling mechanism into a language.

Exercises

Exercise 15.1 Programming in Mini-language Exceptions

Write a program in Mini-language Exceptions that will calculate and print the largest integer value supported by the implementation.

Exercise 15.2 Using the Raise Statement

Write a program in Mini-language Exceptions that first reads in a sequence of pairs of integers terminated by a pair of zeros. The first integer of each pair represents a part number and the second, the number of parts in stock. The part numbers should be stored in one array and the quantity on hand in another.

Following the table initialization phase, terminated by the two zeros, another sequence of integer pairs is to be read. This is the sequence terminated by end of input. This second sequence represents *additions* to the quantity on hand for certain parts in the original sequence. Thus, for each part number in the second sequence, the table must be searched to find the index so that the corresponding quantity on hand can be updated. Finally, the updated table is to be printed out.

During table initialization, the table must be checked for each new part number to ensure that there are no erroneous duplicate entries. During the updating phase, appropriate error action must be taken if a part number that doesn't exist in the table is supplied. Both phases should use the same table search routine, which should report the fact that the searched-for entry does not exist in the table (using a raise statement).

Exercise 15.3 *Resumption of Execution after an Exception*

There are many points of view on how execution of a program should be resumed after the handling of an exception. In Ada, for example, the action of the handler terminates the execution of the program unit *containing* the statement that raised the exception. Thus, execution is resumed after the statement that invoked the unit. Mini-language Exceptions takes the view that the handler terminates the *operation* that raised the exception. In PL/I, the point of resumption depends on the type of exception, and varies from repeating the operation to aborting the program.

An exception may be raised by an operation that has only partially completed, and it may be inappropriate or undesirable to return control to the precise point at which the exception was raised. Discuss what might be an appropriate set of return points after the following exceptions:

a. Overflow during integer arithmetic.

b. Subscript range error.

c. End of page after output of the second line of a four-line block of printing.

d. Nonnumeric character encountered during conversion of a character string to numeric representation.

e. Insufficient storage during creation of a dynamic data structure.

f. End of file during an input operation.

g. Following the execution of a raise statement.

Exercise 15.4 *Handlers with Parameters*

Mini-language Exceptions has no provision for the passing of parameters to exception handlers. Suggest modifications to the syntax and semantics of the mini-language that will allow this.

Exercise 15.5 *Default Handlers*

Mini-language Exceptions defines a single default action for all conditions—program termination. Propose a more useful set of default handlers for the conditions detected in the mini-language.

16
Parallel Processing

We are all familiar with sets of related actions that take place concurrently. The operation of many moving trains on a rail network and the handling of several lines of customers at a bank are typical examples. In contrast, the traditional stored program digital computer has had as its primary objective the sequential execution of the steps forming a single algorithm. As a consequence, most programming languages address only questions of sequence and ignore parallelism.

However, parallelism has had a place in computers. The desire for increased speed has led to overlapping of input and output with computation, arithmetic units that work in parallel, and multiprogrammed and multiprocessor operating systems. However, this parallelism has generally been hidden from the programmer. In this chapter, we examine the programming language implications of specifying independent, but related, tasks that are to be executed concurrently. These are sometimes known as *concurrent processes* or *cooperating processes.* To achieve concurrency in a controlled and reliable manner, the tasks must be able to communicate and synchronize with each other.

It is not necessary that the component steps of the tasks actually take place concurrently. In a multitasking, single-processor operating system they may be arbitrarily interleaved. The important point is that the execution of the tasks is only required to be synchronized at certain points specified by the programmer. Thus, the requirement for parallel execution poses an extra level of discipline on the programming process.

Our discussion here will make frequent use of a single example. We wish to write a program to decode messages. Let us not worry about what the messages mean. They are generated at some remote field station, decoded, and then printed on a line printer. In particular, we wish to define three program units, named RECEIVE_CODES, DECODE, and PRINT_MESSAGES:

- RECEIVE_CODES: This program unit reads encoded data and passes them on, code by code.

- DECODE: This program unit receives encoded data, decodes them by some method, which does not concern us here, and transmits the decoded characters.

- PRINT_MESSAGES: This program unit receives characters, and when it obtains a full line of text, prints the line on a line printer.

Both the codes and characters are assumed to be represented by integers.

The important point about our example is that the three program units are conceptually independent and can progress at their own rates. Except for specific points of synchronization, the interleaving in time for executing the individual statements of the three program units is of no concern.

Mini-language Parallel is designed to solve such problems. This mini-language is based on the work of [Hoare 1978]; its syntax is inspired by that of Ada.

16.1 Mini-language Parallel

As usual, a program in this mini-language consists of a sequence of declarations followed by a sequence of statements, as shown in Table 16.1. Declarations introduce variables whose values are either simple integers or arrays of integers. The bounds of arrays are unspecified. All variables used in a program must be declared exactly once.

The syntax and semantics of the assignment statement are familiar. Addition and subtraction operators may be used in arithmetic expressions.

Tasks

A task is a program unit that can be executed concurrently with other tasks. Each task has a name and a body. The body of a task simply consists of a sequence of one or more statements.

A start statement specifies the concurrent execution of one or more tasks. All tasks in a start statement may begin execution simultaneously. A start statement terminates successfully when all named tasks have been successfully completed.

Table 16.1 **Mini-language Parallel**

---

program	::=	`program`
		    declaration. . .
		`begin`
		    statement. . .
		`end` ;

declaration	::=	identifier [, identifier]. . . : `integer` [`array`] ;
statement	::=	assignment-statement | start-statement	send-statement | receive-statement	select-statement
assignment-statement	::=	variable := expression ;

start-statement	::=	`start tasks`
		    task-identifier : statement. . .
		    [task-identifier : statement. . .]. . .
		`end tasks` ;

send-statement	::=	`send` variable `to` task-identifier ;
receive-statement	::=	`receive` variable `from` task-identifier ;

select-statement	::=	`select` [`loop`]
		    `when` guard => statement. . .
		    [`when` guard => statement. . .]. . .
		`end select` ;

guard	::=	comparison [`and` comparison]. . . [`and` receive-clause] | receive-clause
receive-clause	::=	`receive` variable `from` task-identifier
comparison	::=	(operand comparison-operator operand)
expression	::=	[operand +] operand | [operand -] operand
operand	::=	integer	variable	(expression)
variable	::=	identifier	identifier [expression]
task-identifier	::=	identifier
comparison-operator	::=	<	=	≠	>

For example, consider the following sketch:

```
start tasks
   RECEIVE_CODES:
      -- statements for obtaining codes

   DECODE:
      -- statements for decoding code values
      -- into character values

   PRINT_MESSAGES:
      -- statements for printing the decoded messages
end tasks;
```

Execution of the start statement results in the parallel execution of the bodies of each named task.

As far as termination is concerned, each task will terminate normally after execution of its last statement. The start statement containing the tasks will terminate when all named tasks have terminated, at which time control continues at the statement following the start statement. In our example above, the start statement will wait at its end for the three tasks RECEIVE_CODES, DECODE, and PRINT_MESSAGES to terminate. If any of the tasks leads to an execution error, the entire program terminates abnormally.

There is one important requirement on the use of tasks within a start statement. Each of the tasks must be *disjoint* in the sense that a task may not use a variable that occurs as a target variable in one of the other tasks. A *target variable* is a variable that occurs on the left side of the assignment statement or a variable that occurs in a receive statement, defined below.

Communications between Tasks

In any system of related tasks, there must be some form of communication. For instance, we clearly do not want the trains on a rail network to collide, we may want to ensure that two bank tellers do not make conflicting transactions on the same account, or we may need to coordinate the actions of the devices in a computing system.

In Mini-language Parallel, the basic form of communication between tasks is through send and receive statements. Communication occurs between two tasks whenever:

- A send statement in one task specifies a value to be transmitted to another task, and
- A receive statement in the other task specifies a target variable whose value is to be obtained from the sending task.

When these two conditions arise, the two tasks are said to meet in a *rendezvous*. A rendezvous in this language is like a rendezvous between people. Generally, the first one to reach the rendezvous waits for the other. If not, there is no guarantee that the meeting will ever take place.

Consider the statement

```
send NEW_CODE to DECODE;
```

which occurs in the task body for RECEIVE_CODES, and the following clause

```
receive CODE from RECEIVE_CODES;
```

taken from the body of DECODE. There are two possibilities for a rendezvous, according to whether the send statement in the task RECEIVE_CODES is executed before or after the corresponding receive statement is reached by the task DECODE. Whichever gets there first waits for the other. When the rendezvous is achieved, the value of NEW_CODE is passed to the variable CODE, and both tasks again proceed independently.

We thus see the two basic functions achieved with a rendezvous:

1. **Synchronization:** The sending task must execute a send statement naming the receiving task and the receiving task must reach a corresponding receive statement, which names the sending task.

2. **Transmission of information:** The sending task transmits a value to the receiving task.

It should be observed that a receiving task can only handle one send statement at a time. Although not illustrated by our example, there could be several tasks with pending send statements to a single receiving task. The send statements are processed on a first-come, first-served basis.

Finally, we note that simple integer values and complete arrays may be transmitted during a rendezvous. The type of the value that is sent must match the type of the corresponding receiving variable; otherwise the program is terminated abnormally. The compiler cannot detect this kind of error since the correspondence between send and receive statements cannot be determined statically.

Guarded Statements

The guarded statements of Mini-language Parallel are based on those introduced by Dijkstra and discussed in Section 7.4. In Mini-language Parallel, a guarded statement (or a guarded sequence of statements) is a statement prefixed by a *guard,* which determines whether or not a statement is to be executed. A guard can contain a sequence of comparisons each separated by and. A guard may also contain a receive clause (defined below).

Such a guard may contain only one receive clause, which must appear as the last element of the guard.

Guarded statements form the alternatives of a select statement, as in:

```
select
   when (LINE_POSITION < LINE_SIZE) =>
      LINE_POSITION := LINE_POSITION + 1;

   when (LINE_POSITION = LINE_SIZE) =>
      send LINE to OUTPUT_DEVICE;
      LINE_POSITION := 1;
end select;
```

This select statement contains two guarded statements: one for the case when the value of LINE_POSITION is less than LINE_SIZE and the other for when LINE_POSITION equals LINE_SIZE.

Execution of a select statement takes place as follows. First, each of the guards in the select statement is evaluated. If none of the guards evaluates to true, the select statement has no effect and is equivalent to an empty statement. If exactly one of the guards evaluates to true, then the statement prefixed by this guard is executed. Otherwise, if more than one guard evaluates to true, then one of the sequences of statements with a true guard is selected arbitrarily and executed. In our example above, where line positions are assumed to be integers in a range of 1 through LINE_SIZE, exactly one of the guards will always be true.

It is important to note that when more than one guard evaluates to true, execution of a select statement is nondeterministic. This is in sharp contrast with our other mini-languages, where a program will always execute statements in a determined order. In Mini-language Parallel, it is possible to write select statements with several true guards, and to give different actions for each true guard. The precise effect of such a select statement cannot be predicted.

As mentioned above, a guard may contain a single receive clause. This has the same form as a receive statement but in this context serves the additional function of a guard. For example, consider the following select statement:

```
select
   when receive MESSAGE_CHAR from DECODE =>
      LINE[LINE_POSITION] := MESSAGE_CHAR;
end select;
```

Here a statement is guarded by a receive clause. A receive clause is said to be:

- **True** if there is a corresponding send statement that is waiting for its information to be received. In this case, the receive clause performs the function of a receive statement and the information is transferred between the tasks. The statement guarded by the receive clause is then executed.

- **Pending** if no corresponding send statement has been issued by the task named in the receive clause and that task is still active.

- **False** if the task named in the receive clause has terminated.

Accordingly, in a select statement, the following cases can arise:

1. One or more guards evaluate to the value true. In this case, one of the sequences of statements with a true guard is executed.

2. One or more of the guards is pending, and the remaining guards evaluate to false. In this case, the select statement is not executed immediately but must await a corresponding send statement from one of the named tasks. When that send statement is issued, the appropriate guarded statement is executed. If all named tasks terminate without issuing a send statement, the select statement is completed with no net effect.

3. All guards evaluate to the value false. In this case, execution of the select statement has no effect.

Thus, we see that a select statement may be immediately executed, or may be delayed until a send statement in another task is executed.

Another form of select statement is used to specify loops. This is the select loop statement. For example, consider the following select loop:

```
select loop
    when (COUNT < N)  =>
        COUNT := COUNT + 1;
end select;
```

As long as the variable COUNT remains less than N, the variable COUNT will continue to be incremented by one. The loop will terminate when the value of COUNT is equal to N.

Execution of a select loop is similar to that of a select statement, except that, as long as guards remain true or contain pending receive clauses, the alternatives in the body of the loop will continue to be executed. In particular, execution of a select loop proceeds as follows:

- If one or more of the guards evaluate to true, one of the corresponding guarded statement sequences is executed, and the select loop is repeated.

- If none of the guards evaluates to true but one or more of the guards contains a pending receive clause, execution of the loop is suspended. When a corresponding send statement is issued, the receive clause is executed and the loop is repeated. If all pending tasks terminate before issuing a send statement, the loop is also terminated.

- If all of the guards evaluate to false, the loop is terminated.

Predefined Tasks

Two tasks are predefined in Mini-language Parallel. The first is a task named INPUT_DEVICE. This task is assumed to be associated with some input device that sends characters to a program containing a corresponding receive clause. The second is the predefined task named OUTPUT_DEVICE. This task corresponds to some output device that receives lines of text containing the number of characters specified by the value of LINE_SIZE, here set to 72. Such lines of text are represented as arrays in Mini-language Parallel.

16.2 A First Solution to the Decoding Problem

We are now in a position to present a solution to the decoding problem described earlier. This solution is given in Example 16.1 and consists of three tasks, named RECEIVE_CODES, DECODE, and PRINT_MESSAGES.

The task RECEIVE_CODES consists of a simple select loop that continues to receive new codes from the input device and transmits these codes to the task named DECODE. Notice that the guard in the select loop for this task consists of a single receive clause. This receive clause continues to wait for values to be transmitted to the target variable NEW_CODE. Notice also that this task may be delayed if no codes are forthcoming for a period of time.

The second task, named DECODE, also consists of a simple select loop. Again, there is a single guarded statement prefixed by a receive clause. When a code is sent from the task RECEIVE_CODES, the value of the code is analyzed and its decoded value is stored in the integer variable named CHAR. Notice here, that in cases where the decoding of codes is time-consuming, this task may operate more slowly than the sending task RECEIVE_CODES. If the data from the input device cannot be delayed, some sort of buffering mechanism will have to be added to RECEIVE_CODES.

```
program

   CODE, NEW_CODE, MESSAGE_CHAR: integer;
   LINE_POSITION, CHAR, LINE_SIZE: integer;
   LINE: integer array;

begin
   start tasks

      RECEIVE_CODES:
         select loop
            when receive NEW_CODE from INPUT_DEVICE  =>
               send NEW_CODE to DECODE;
         end select;

      DECODE:
         select loop
            when receive CODE from RECEIVE_CODES  =>
               -- statements for decoding the value of CODE
               -- and producing the decoded value in CHAR

               send CHAR to PRINT_MESSAGES;
         end select;

      PRINT_MESSAGES:
         LINE_POSITION := 1;
         LINE_SIZE     := 72;
         select loop
            when receive MESSAGE_CHAR from DECODE  =>
               LINE[LINE_POSITION] := MESSAGE_CHAR;
               select
                  when (LINE_POSITION < LINE_SIZE)  =>
                     LINE_POSITION = LINE_POSITION + 1;
                  when (LINE_POSITION = LINE_SIZE)  =>
                     send LINE to OUTPUT_DEVICE;
                     LINE_POSITION := 1;
               end select;
         end select;

   end tasks;
end;
```

Example 16.1 **A Solution to the Decoding Problem**

Finally, the third task, named PRINT_MESSAGES, again consists of a simple select loop. This loop continues to receive message characters from the task named DECODE, fills an array named LINE with these characters and, when a full line is given, sends the value of LINE to the output device.

The three tasks operate quite independently, but are, of course, synchronized through corresponding send statements and receive clauses. As given, the three tasks operate forever, and the program never terminates. In Section 2.2, we said that the meaning of a program is defined only for programs that terminate normally. This simplistic definition excluded programs such as operating systems and real-time programs that, by their very nature, must not terminate. The example that we are considering here is one of this class of nonterminating programs. To cover this class of programs, the definition of the meaning of a program must be extended; the derivation of this extended definition is beyond the scope of this book.

16.3 Putting a Buffer in a Task

The computation performed on a code by DECODE may not be completed by the time the next code is received by RECEIVE_CODES. Since RECEIVE_CODES cannot receive the next code until the transmission of the previous one has been completed, there may be a loss of input data. Of course, on average, the decoding process must be able to keep pace with the reception of codes, but this may not be true over short bursts of input activity. We would like the reception of codes and their decoding to go on much more independently.

In particular, if our decoding process is slow, we would still like RECEIVE_CODES to accept a burst of new data. For this purpose, we can introduce a storage area for characters in the RECEIVE_CODES task as a buffer. The design must be such that as long as the buffer is neither full nor empty, the task is able to accept requests for both input and output.

To do this, the conditions that guard the alternatives must be such that if there is room in the buffer, a new code can be accepted and, if there are characters to be sent, a send request can be performed. Consider the following outline:

```
select loop
    when (COUNT < STORAGE_SIZE)  =>
        -- what to do if more storage space is available

    when (COUNT > 0)  =>
        -- what to do if the storage area is not empty
end select;
```

Only those statements whose guarding conditions evaluate to true can be executed. Importantly, when both guards are true, either guarded statement can be executed. Thus, we have a case of *nondeterminism,* where the choice of actions is not specified by the programmer.

These points are illustrated in Example 16.2. The major change is in the RECEIVE_CODES task where there is an array managed as a circular buffer. That is, whenever the end of the storage area is reached, it is continued again at the beginning. The two indexes, IN_INDEX and OUT_INDEX, are used to denote the elements in the buffer for the next incoming code and the next code for transmission, respectively.

To prevent the RECEIVE_CODES task from being hung up while waiting for the completion of decoding by the DECODE task, the send statement is not executed until a request has been received from DECODE. The request does not have a value that is used, it is merely used as a synchronizing signal.

16.4 Interrupting a Task

On many systems, we have hardware interrupts that are triggered by certain events. For example, we may wish to install a stop button in our decoding system. If no more codes are to be produced, or if for some reason the user wants the program to terminate, the user can press the stop button. All the tasks must then be brought to an orderly completion with all codes printed.

Hardware interrupts can be handled in various ways. Conceptually, we can think of the user as another task that transmits a single piece of information, the pressing of the button. This model fits well with the way that we view a task as executing independently except for a particular rendezvous for the purpose of transmitting data.

Example 16.3 shows the complete solution, incorporating both the buffering described in the previous section and the provision for a stop button. Note that if the user presses the stop button when the input buffer is full, that is, when

```
(COUNT = STORAGE_SIZE)
```

there is the possibility that one of the input codes will be lost. It seems that in such a situation, shutting down the system should take priority.

```
program
    CODE, NEW_CODE, CHAR, MESSAGE_CHAR, COUNT: integer;
    LINE_POSITION, LINE_SIZE, IN_INDEX: integer;
    OUT_INDEX, STORAGE_SIZE, REQUEST_Q, REQUEST_A: integer;
    LINE, STORAGE_AREA: integer array;

begin
    start tasks

        RECEIVE_CODES:
            COUNT        :=    0;
            IN_INDEX     :=    1;
            OUT_INDEX    :=    1;
            STORAGE_SIZE := 500;

            select loop
                when (COUNT < STORAGE_SIZE) and
                     receive NEW_CODE from INPUT_DEVICE  =>
                    STORAGE_AREA[IN_INDEX] := NEW_CODE;
                    COUNT                  := COUNT + 1;
                    select
                        when (IN_INDEX < STORAGE_SIZE)  =>
                            IN_INDEX := IN_INDEX + 1;
                        when (IN_INDEX = STORAGE_SIZE)  =>
                            IN_INDEX := 1;
                    end select;

                when (COUNT > 0)
                     and receive REQUEST_A from DECODE      =>
                    send STORAGE_AREA[OUT_INDEX] to DECODE;
                    COUNT := COUNT - 1;
                    select
                        when (OUT_INDEX < STORAGE_SIZE)  =>
                            OUT_INDEX := OUT_INDEX + 1;
                        when (OUT_INDEX = STORAGE_SIZE)  =>
                            OUT_INDEX := 1;
                    end select;
            end select;
```

Example 16.2 **Putting a Buffer into the Receiving Task**

```
DECODE:
   REQUEST_Q := 1;
   select loop
      when (1 = 1) =>          -- always true
         send REQUEST_Q to RECEIVE_CODES;
         receive CODE from RECEIVE_CODES;
         -- statements for decoding the value of CODE
         -- and producing the decoded value in CHAR
         send CHAR to PRINT_MESSAGES;
      end select;

PRINT_MESSAGES:
   LINE_POSITION := 1;
   LINE_SIZE     := 72;
   select loop
      when receive MESSAGE_CHAR from DECODE  =>
         LINE[LINE_POSITION] := MESSAGE_CHAR;
         select
            when (LINE_POSITION < LINE_SIZE)  =>
               LINE_POSITION := LINE_POSITION + 1;
            when (LINE_POSITION = LINE_SIZE)  =>
               send LINE to OUTPUT_DEVICE;
               LINE_POSITION := 1;
         end select;
      end select;

   end tasks;
end;
```

Example 16.2 **continued**

```
program
    COUNT, CHAR, MESSAGE_CHAR, LINE_POSITION: integer;
    NEW_CODE, IN_INDEX, ON, OFF, OUT_INDEX: integer
    STORAGE_SIZE, LINE_SIZE, REQUEST_Q, REQUEST_A: integer;
    CODE, STOP, STOP_CODE, STOP_FLAG, STOP_DECODING: integer;
    LINE, STORAGE_AREA: integer array;

begin
    OFF        :=    0;
    ON         :=    1;
    STOP_CODE  :=  999;

    start tasks

        RECEIVE_CODES:
            STOP_FLAG    := OFF;
            COUNT        :=    0;
            IN_INDEX     :=    1;
            OUT_INDEX    :=    1;
            STORAGE_SIZE := 500;

            select loop
                when (STOP_FLAG = OFF) and
                      receive STOP from USER  =>
                    STOP_FLAG := ON;
                    STORAGE_AREA[IN_INDEX] := STOP_CODE;
                    COUNT := COUNT + 1;
                when (STOP_FLAG = OFF) and (COUNT < STORAGE_SIZE)
                      and
                      receive NEW_CODE from INPUT_DEVICE =>
                    STORAGE_AREA[IN_INDEX] := NEW_CODE;
                    COUNT := COUNT + 1;
                    select
                        when (IN_INDEX < STORAGE_SIZE) =>
                            IN_INDEX := IN_INDEX + 1;
                        when (IN_INDEX = STORAGE_SIZE) =>
                            IN_INDEX := 1;
                    end select;
```

Example 16.3 **Adding a Stop Button to the Decoding Problem**

```
            when (COUNT > 0) and
                receive REQUEST_A from DECODE =>
            send STORAGE_AREA[OUT_INDEX] to DECODE;
            COUNT := COUNT - 1;
            select
                when (OUT_INDEX < STORAGE_SIZE) =>
                    OUT_INDEX := OUT_INDEX + 1;
                when (OUT_INDEX = STORAGE_SIZE) =>
                    OUT_INDEX := 1;
            end select;
    end select;

DECODE:
    REQUEST_Q      := 1;
    STOP_DECODING := OFF;
    select loop
        when (STOP_DECODING = OFF) =>
            send REQUEST_Q to RECEIVE_CODES;
            receive CODE from RECEIVE_CODES;
            select
                when (CODE ≠ STOP_CODE) =>
                    -- statements for decoding values of CODE
                    -- and producing the decoded value in CHAR
                    send CHAR to PRINT MESSAGES;
                when (CODE = STOP_CODE) =>
                    STOP_DECODING := ON;
                    send STOP_CODE to PRINT_MESSAGES;
            end select;
    end select;
```

program continues on p. 478

Example 16.3 **continued**

```
        PRINT_MESSAGES:
           LINE_POSITION := 1;
           LINE_SIZE     := 72;
           receive MESSAGE_CHAR from DECODE;
           select loop
              when (MESSAGE_CHAR ≠ STOP_CODE) =>
                 LINE[LINE_POSITION] := MESSAGE_CHAR;
                 select
                    when (LINE_POSITION < LINE_SIZE) =>
                       LINE_POSITION := LINE_POSITION + 1;
                    when (LINE_POSITION = LINE_SIZE) =>
                       send LINE to OUTPUT_DEVICE;
                       LINE_POSITION := 1;
                 end select;
                 receive MESSAGE_CHAR from DECODE;
              end select;

           LINE[LINE_POSITION] := STOP_CODE;
           send LINE to OUTPUT_DEVICE;
      end tasks;
   end;
```

Example 16.3 **continued**

16.5 Issues in Parallel Processing

Parallel processing brings up a number of new issues with programming languages. Traditionally, we are quite accustomed to the idea of a program as a purely sequential process. After one statement is executed, the next statement to be executed is specified precisely and in a deterministic manner. However, with the advancement of computer technology, systems with multiple processors and multiple devices are becoming commonplace. Effective use of these resources demands special constructs for parallel processing.

Synchronization

The execution of concurrent tasks is not completely independent. A collection of tasks is executed to solve some problem. Often one task must complete some computation before another task can complete its own computation. This is the general problem of *synchronization.*

In Mini-language Parallel, the synchronization between tasks is handled by corresponding send and receive statements. Before a task can receive a data item, another task must send the data item to the given task.

A synchronization primitive available in some languages is the semaphore, introduced by [Dijkstra 1968b]. The name semaphore evokes the idea of a signal used on railroads to permit or deny entry of a train to a section of track. In its simplest form, a semaphore is a special variable that can take two values, stop and go. We might declare a semaphore variable as

```
S: semaphore;
```

The only valid operations on semaphores are WAIT, originally called P from the Dutch *passeren* meaning "to pass," and SIGNAL, originally called V from the Dutch *vrijgeven* meaning "to release." The two semaphore operations allow a process to cause itself to wait for a certain event and then to be awakened by another process when the event occurs. WAIT and SIGNAL have the following meaning:

WAIT(S): Wait until the value of S is go (it may already be so) and then set its value to stop and continue execution.

SIGNAL(S): Set the value of S to go. This will allow a process that is waiting because it executed WAIT(S) to continue.

Both WAIT and SIGNAL must be performed as a single uninterruptable operation. There can be no partial completion of the operation while something else takes place. On some machines, the equivalent of these operations is implemented as a hardware instruction. The value to which the semaphore is initialized will depend on its application.

Semaphores of this kind are known as *binary semaphores. General semaphores,* which can take positive integer values, are also available in some languages.

An example of how binary semaphores might be used to communicate between tasks is shown in Example 16.4. There, communication between the two tasks is through the variable COUNT, which is shared by the tasks. The semaphore S is used to prevent simultaneous access to COUNT by the two tasks. One difficulty with semaphores is that they are not associated with the shared variable except by a programmer convention. The compiler is thus not able to check that the semaphore is being used to ensure mutual exclusion of the tasks whenever the value of the variable is changed. As a programming language mechanism they are therefore unreliable.

```
program

   COUNT: integer;   -- used to pass information between tasks
   S:     semaphore;

begin
   S     := go;
   COUNT := 0;
   start tasks

      SENDER:
         select loop
            when (1 = 1) =>
               -- code to observe an event
               WAIT(S);           -- prepare to change COUNT
               COUNT := COUNT + 1;
               SIGNAL(S);         -- signal that COUNT is available
         end select;

      RECEIVER:
         select loop
            when (1 = 1) =>
               WAIT(S);        -- prepare to read COUNT and reset it
               print COUNT;
               COUNT := 0;
               SIGNAL(S);      -- signal that COUNT is available
         end select;
   end tasks;
end;
```

Example 16.4 Use of Semaphores

Mutual Exclusion

The fact that different portions of the same program may be executed concurrently can lead to a number of serious problems. These problems arise when two or more tasks have access to the same resource, for example, a location in shared storage. In particular, execution of one of the tasks may update a variable, while another task may not be sure that the value of the variable has been changed. Such a variable is generally called a *shared* variable. To avoid this kind of problem with shared variables, access to a shared resource must involve *mutual exclusion.* That is, access to the shared resource must be restricted so that:

1. Access to the resource is by at most one task at a time.

2. When access to a resource is requested simultaneously by more than one task, it must be granted to one of them in finite time.

3. When a task acquires access to a resource, it must release it in finite time.

4. When a task requests a resource, it must get it within finite time.

5. If a task terminates abnormally while it does not have access to a resource, this must not necessarily affect other concurrent tasks.

6. A task should not consume processing time while waiting for a resource.

Corresponding to the idea in sequential programming of executing to normal termination, as discussed in Chapter 2, concurrent processes have the concept of *liveness.* This means that, if something is supposed to happen, it will happen eventually. Rules 3 and 4 above are examples of liveness.

In Mini-language Parallel, this problem of shared variables is avoided by requiring that each task be disjoint. That is, no task may mention a variable that is updated by another task, and there are thus no shared variables. This restriction clearly simplifies the understanding of concurrently executed tasks. The only means of communication between two tasks is through a rendezvous, as in Ada.

When shared variables are allowed, the construct of a *critical region* is usually introduced, see [Brinch Hansen 1973]. This construct consists of a beginning and ending statement between which there is a sequence of statements. In their simplest form, only one task may be in a critical region at any one time. By enclosing references to shared variables inside a critical region, mutual exclusion may be achieved.

Critical regions solve the problem of preventing undesired access to shared data; however, shared variables are in a sense global variables and entail some of their complexities. Although Mini-language Parallel was not designed to have the scope of variables limited to tasks in which they are declared, this could have been done. This would have ensured disjointness without hindering communication through a rendezvous. However, it would prevent programs such as Example 16.4 from being written.

Another approach to the problem of mutual exclusion is the *monitor.* Essentially, a monitor associates all statements that manipulate shared variables with the variables themselves. These statements are associated with the variables in the form of procedures rather than being distributed through the tasks in critical regions. The shared variables are then manipulated through calls to the procedures in the monitor, which ensures that only one task can be executing any of its procedures at a time.

Communication

In addition to synchronizing their behavior, tasks must also be able to exchange information. In Mini-language Parallel, synchronization of tasks and exchange of information are inseparable. These two requirements are embraced by the concept of a rendezvous. During the rendezvous, the value of an expression is passed to a target variable in another task.

A rendezvous has several strong advantages in the writing of concurrent programs. For one, it allows interactions between tasks to be clearly defined and isolated. Furthermore, there is a pleasant symmetry between send and receive statements. The symmetry helps make the behavior of the tasks quite explicit. Most importantly, aside from a rendezvous, we may view the operation of each task independently from the others.

In Mini-language Parallel, the sending task must name the task to which information is sent, and the receiving task must mention the sending task. In certain circumstances, this symmetry may have drawbacks. In particular, it is difficult to describe the behavior of a task that can accept information from several other tasks, independently of the origin of the information. In the programming language Ada, only the sending task can name the destination to which information is sent. From the receiver's point of view, the information received is anonymous.

Scheduling

In most applications of concurrent processing, there will be senders and receivers of information. In particular, a request to receive information may have been preceded by numerous requests to send the information, presumably from different tasks. In Mini-language Parallel, when this case arises, the requests to send information are presumed to be processed on a first-come, first-served basis. This brings up the question of *scheduling*.

The problem with this method of scheduling is that a first-come, first-served basis may not always be desirable. In particular, there may be certain tasks whose urgency is far greater than that of other tasks. In some languages, tasks can be assigned a *priority,* and tasks with a higher priority are processed first.

It is possible to express urgency entirely within Mini-language Parallel. This can be accomplished by the suitable use of select statements, where outer level guards can be used to handle urgent requests and nested guards can be used to handle less urgent requests. While this kind of solution may appear to be somewhat awkward, it may, in fact, express the desired urgency in an appropriate manner. A final resolution to this matter is not clear.

Deadlock

The most serious breach of liveness is what is known as *deadlock*. This occurs when the computer is no longer able to do any useful work. An example of this in real life is when two polite but obstinate people are trying to go through a door and each insists that the other should go first. In computers, deadlock can occur if two tasks are waiting for a resource that has been acquired by the other and cannot be released until access to the other resource has been acquired.

Imagine for the moment a task named TASK_A and one named TASK_B, which contain the following statements:

```
start tasks
   TASK_A:
      receive VALUE_A from TASK_B;
      send (VALUE_A + 1) to TASK_B;

   TASK_B:
      receive VALUE_B from TASK_A;
      send (VALUE_B - 1) to TASK_A;
end tasks;
```

When these two tasks are initiated, they will immediately deadlock. That is, TASK_A will await a value from TASK_B, and TASK_B will await a value from TASK_A. Since neither value has been sent, both receive statements will be suspended, in this case indefinitely.

The deadlock problem for concurrent tasks is as difficult to avoid as the writing of infinite loops in a sequential language, and the detection of deadlocks is just as difficult. Only the care of the programmer can prevent this circumstance from happening.

Another form of the liveness problem is *lockout*. This occurs when some task is indefinitely delayed although the other tasks are able to continue. Lockout may be even more difficult to discover and correct because it usually only occurs in complex situations where the interaction between tasks serves to prevent one task from obtaining access to a needed resource.

Nondeterminism

In the select statement of Mini-language Parallel, more than one guard may evaluate to true. In this case, one of the corresponding guarded statements is executed. The choice among the guarded statements whose guards evaluate to true is arbitrary. In this sense, the execution of the select statement is *nondeterministic*.

This is consistent with much of concurrent processing. Frequently, a task is used to control a mechanical device, which will typically have a timing variance of more than 100 milliseconds, time enough for more than 10,000 machine cycles. Thus, when an execution of the task is repeated, it will be impossible to obtain synchronization ewithout using special synchronizing constructs. Programmers who are used to repeatability in the execution of simple sequential programs find it difficult to become accustomed to the nondeterminancy of concurrent programming.

Concurrent processing does not necessarily imply a mechanism with nondeterministic behavior, although such is the case in Mini-language Parallel, the proposal by [Hoare 1978], and Ada.

Comments on Parallel Processing

As with most of the topics treated in the mini-languages, a full discussion of all the attendant issues is difficult, and as usual, we make no pretense of treating these areas completely.

Two general remarks are in order. Parallel processing is important, and in many application areas it is essential.

Second, while it may seem superfluous to say, we believe strongly that extreme care is required in the design of any linguistic facility to handle parallel processing. When tasks operate in parallel, the potential chaos to the average programmer is enormous. No expense should be spared to make the facility in a programming language as clear as possible. Any such facility should be designed with a careful eye towards making it one that can be programmed with ease and with clarity.

16.6 Where to Look: Concurrent Pascal, Modula-2, Ada

Concurrent Pascal

Concurrent Pascal was introduced in [Brinch Hansen 1975] as the first language to support monitors. In addition to the normal data types available in Pascal, Concurrent Pascal has three kinds of *system types:*

- **Process type:** this defines a data structure and a sequential statement that can operate on it.

- **Monitor type:** this defines a data structure and the operations that can be performed on it by concurrent processes for synchronization and exchange of data.

- **Class type:** this defines a data structure and the operations that can be performed on it by a single process or monitor, thus providing for mutual exclusion.

Input-output devices are treated as monitors implemented directly in the hardware.

Variables of system type are called *system components* and are initialized by means of a special statement. This statement defines the access rights of the component, allocates space, and gives it an initial value. The access rights define which processes are permitted to operate on the variable.

Modula-2

Modula-2 is a language developed for writing small dedicated computer systems, for example, process control. Communication between processes is either through shared variables or by *signals*. Shared variables are encapsulated in monitors as in Concurrent Pascal. Apart from initialization, only two operations are applicable to signals: a process may send a signal, and it may wait for some other process to send a signal to it. Sending a signal activates at most one waiting task. Signals differ from semaphores in that sending a signal for which no task is waiting is considered as a null operation.

Ada

The primary mechanism for process interaction in Ada is through the use of a rendezvous in a similar manner to Mini-language Parallel. The equivalent to the mini-language send statement is a call to the other process. The equivalent of the receive is the accept statement. Blocking of further execution of the sending task by the call can be avoided by a conditional call, which only performs the call if a rendezvous is immediately possible. Blocking on the accept statement can be avoided by means of a prior enquiry to determine the number of waiting calls.

There is also a mechanism similar to the receive clause on a guard in Mini-language Parallel's select statement. In Ada, a task can also suspend execution for a specific time interval by means of a delay statement. When this statement is used within the guard of a select statement, it ensures that the task will eventually continue even if no other sending task has tried to make a rendezvous.

Further Reading

The basis for this chapter, as mentioned earlier, is the work of [Hoare 1978]. Certainly, this work deserves reading for a further examination of the issues discussed here.

An early survey of parallel processing is presented in [Brinch Hansen 1972]. A further work [Brinch Hansen 1977] describes the actual concepts used to define Concurrent Pascal. A comprehensive general review of the subject is contained in [Andrews and Schneider 1983]. More detailed descriptions with many worked examples can be found in [Holt et al. 1978] and particularly in the excellently written book [Ben-Ari 1982].

Often, concepts are developed that later turn out to be somewhat minor variations of concepts introduced much earlier. Such is the case with the parallel processing facilities introduced in Mini-language Parallel. Here we have in mind the very early work of [Conway 1963], which introduces the idea of a coroutine. *It is here that the notion of a* rendezvous *is introduced.*

An excellent comparison of Pascal, Ada, and Modula-2 is contained in [Coar 1984]. This is one of a series of articles ([Wirth 1984], [Paul 1984], [Ohran 1984], and [Gutknecht 1984]) describing Modula-2, contained in the August 1984 issue of Byte. *The last of these articles discusses the use of coroutines in Modula-2.*

Exercises

Exercise 16.1 Terminology for Parallel Processing

In a difficult area like parallel processing, it is all the more important to define the terminology precisely. Write a one- to four-sentence definition of each of the following terms:

task	critical region
synchronization	deadlock
rendezvous	delay
guard	semaphore

Exercise 16.2 Programming in Mini-language Parallel

Modify the program in Example 16.3 so that there are two separate RECEIVE_CODES tasks, RECEIVE_CODES_A and RECEIVE_CODES_B, which obtain data from different sources and feed their buffered input to DECODE. Each one of them is able to receive a stop signal from its own user. Receipt of a stop signal by either task shuts down the entire program, including the other receiving task, in an orderly manner.

Exercise 16.3 *Mutual Exclusion*

One method of implementing process waiting is through a loop that repeatedly tests the condition for the termination of the wait. The body of the loop is empty. This technique is known as *busy waiting,* since the processor is executing constantly during the waiting period.

Consider the following two implementations of the WAIT and SIGNAL semaphore operations through busy waiting. Supposing that busy waiting is acceptable and that there are two tasks that use the constants THIS and OTHER to distinguish them, that is, THIS = 0, OTHER = 1 in one task and THIS = 1, OTHER = 0 in the second task. Determine whether the following implementations are correct. The first is:

```
WAIT(S):
    S[THIS] := true;
    while (S[OTHER] = true) loop
    end loop;

SIGNAL(S):
    S[THIS] := false;
```

The second is:

```
WAIT(S):
    S[THIS] := true;
    while (S[OTHER] = true) loop
        S[THIS] := false;
        while (S[OTHER] = true) loop
        end loop;
        S[THIS] := true;
    end loop;

SIGNAL(S):
    S[THIS] := false;
```

If either, or both, of these implementations is incorrect, explain.

Exercise 16.4 *Semaphores*

Consider a variant of Mini-language Parallel that does not have the send and receive mechanism defined in Section 16.1, but instead allows the declaration of semaphore variables as described in Section 16.5. Rewrite the program in Example 16.2 using this variant of the mini-language.

Exercise 16.5 *Monitors*

Consider a variant of Mini-language Parallel that does not have the send and receive mechanism defined in Section 16.1, but instead allows the definition of monitors as described in Section 16.5. An outline of a monitor for use in solving the problem treated in Example 16.2 using this variant of the mini-language would be:

```
CHARACTER_BUFFER: monitor
    STORAGE_AREA: integer array;
    IN_INDEX, OUT_INDEX: integer;

    INSERT: procedure(IN_CODE: integer)
        . . .
    end;

    REMOVE: procedure(OUT_CODE: integer)
        . . .
    end;

begin
    IN_INDEX  := 1;
    OUT_INDEX := 1;
end;
```

Complete this outline, write another monitor to handle communication between DECODE and PRINT_MESSAGES, and incorporate these into a revised solution to the decoding problem.

17

Separately Compiled Modules

The work of building a large program can be divided among several people, each of whom must produce part of the whole. The complexity of the program is reduced by dividing it into separate well-defined parts or *modules*. The modules must be separated so that a programmer is able to write one module without needing to know the internal details of another module. All that is important is the interfaces between the modules.

A program is a model of a real-world process, and its success relies on the closeness with which the real-world is modelled. Since the real-world is always changing, programs are always subject to change. The modification of existing programs accounts for well over 50 percent of all software costs. A major aim of the modularization of programs is that of containing the modifications to a program within a few modules. That is, a change in the real-world should be reflected in the modification of the internal details of a very few modules without requiring changes throughout the program. Modularization is rather like the idea of making a ship seaworthy by dividing the hull into watertight compartments. If the hull is damaged and starts to leak, the problem can be contained within a single compartment and the ship prevented from foundering.

A module achieves program simplification by providing an abstraction. That is, its function can be understood through its interface definition without any need to understand its internal details. The term "information hiding" was introduced by [Parnas 1971] to characterize this concept. The idea is that each module "hides" some piece of information about the program so that, if this information should change, only that module needs to be changed.

To be able to gain full advantage from modularization, the modules must be able to be written, compiled, and, if necessary, executed separately. One of the problems of standard Pascal is that a program is a single monolithic entity that must be compiled in its entirety. This makes it very difficult for many people to work on a single Pascal program simultaneously. This is not a criticism of Pascal since it was intended as a pedagogic language and not for the construction of large programs.

In this chapter, we discuss the features that are required by a programming language so that it can support the concept of separately compiled modules and the simplification through abstraction that they afford. Mini-language Modules is designed to illustrate the ideas of separate compilation of modules that provide type abstractions for use in a program. The structure of this mini-language is based on the concept of packages in Ada.

17.1 Mini-language Modules

A program generally consists of a main part (containing the variable declarations and executable statements) and a set of type modules that implement the data types used in the main part. The syntax of Mini-language Modules is defined in Table 17.1. The type modules and the main part are compiled separately and their object modules linked together before execution.

In both the main part and the type modules, the usual assignment, loop, if, input, and output statements can all be used. Declarations in the main part define variables to be either of the primitive `boolean` or `integer` types, or of some types that are defined by type modules of the same name, for example, the following declaration section:

```
TODAY, TOMORROW: DATE;
DAY_NUMBER, MONTH_NUMBER, YEAR_NUMBER: integer;
```

A particular point to note is the major difference between this mini-language and Mini-language Typedef in Chapter 12. In Typedef, the representation and operations for the values of the data type are all described in the part of the program that makes use of the data type. In Mini-language Modules, the main part contains no definition of the data type itself; that is defined separately in the corresponding type module. All that is required is that there must be a type module for each type being used. In this case, there must be a `DATE` type module.

Type Modules

A type module consists of two parts: an interface specification and an implementation part. The interface specification defines the types of the parameters used by the data type's operations. These types can be types defined by other type modules in the program. The operations manipulate values of the type being defined and perform conversions between these values and values of other types. The implementation part contains the actual representation of values of the type and the statements that perform the operations defined in the interface specification.

The interface specification of the DATE type module might, for example, consist of the following operation descriptions:

```
DATE: module
    SET_DATE:     (integer, integer, integer) => DATE;
    DATE_YEAR:    (DATE) => integer;
    DATE_MONTH:   (DATE) => integer;
    DATE_DAY:     (DATE) => integer;
    CHANGE_DATE:  (DATE, integer) => DATE;
```

These definitions show the names of the operations, the types of their parameters, and the type of their returned value. Thus, the type of SET_DATE is defined as

```
integer, integer, integer  →  DATE
```

It is intended to take three integers, representing day, month, and year numbers, and compose them to form a date. The functions DATE_YEAR, DATE_MONTH, and DATE_DAY provide conversions in the opposite direction. CHANGE_DATE takes a DATE value and an integer value, representing an elapsed number of days, and returns a new date.

Armed with this information, it is possible to write the statements that make use of these functions to construct the complete main part of the program, for example:

```
program
    TODAY, TOMORROW: DATE;
    DAY_NUM, MONTH_NUM, YEAR_NUM: integer;
begin
    input DAY_NUM, MONTH_NUM, YEAR_NUM;
    TODAY       := SET_DATE(DAY_NUM, MONTH_NUM, YEAR_NUM);
    TOMORROW    := CHANGE_DATE(TODAY, 1);
    DAY_NUM   := DATE_DAY(TOMORROW);
    MONTH_NUM := DATE_MONTH(TOMORROW);
    YEAR_NUM  := DATE_YEAR(TOMORROW);
    output DAY_NUM, MONTH_NUM, YEAR_NUM;
end;
```

This section of the program is written completely independent of the type module and contains no details of how DATE values are represented.

Table 17.1 **Mini-language Modules**

---

program	::=	main-part [type-module]. . .

main-part	::=	`program`
		    variable-declaration. . .
		`begin`
		    statement. . .
		`end` ;

type-module	::=	identifier: `module`
		    operation-description. . .
		`implementation`
		    type-representation
		    operation-algorithm. . .
		`end module` ;

variable-declaration	::=	identifier [, identifier]. . . : type ;
type	::=	identifier | `integer` | `boolean`
operation-description	::=	identifier: (type [, type]. . .) => type ;

type-representation	::=	identifier : `record`
		        identifier : type ;
		        [identifier : type ;]. . .
		    `end record` ;

operation-algorithm	::=	identifier : `operation` (identifier [, identifier])
		    variable-declaration. . .
		`begin`
		    statement. . .
		    `return` expression;
		`end operation` ;

statement	::= |	assignment-statement | loop-statement if-statement | input-statement | output-statement
assignment-statement	::=	variable := expression ;

Table 17.1 **continued**		

if-statement	::=	if expression then
		    statement. . .
		[else
		    statement. . .]
		end if ;

loop-statement	::=	while expression loop statement. . . end loop ;
input-statement	::=	input identifier [, identifier]. . . ;
output-statement	::=	output identifier [, identifier]. . . ;
expression	::=	[operand operator] operand
operand	::=	integer | boolean | application | variable | (expression)
boolean	::=	true | false
application	::=	identifier (expression [, identifier]. . .)
variable	::=	identifier [. identifier]. . .
operator	::=	< | = | ≠ | > | + | - | * | div

The implementation part of the type module provides the missing details that are required to make the complete program workable. It consists of two parts: a record declaration that describes the representation of values for the type, and the actual algorithms for the operations that were defined in the interface specification. The record declaration for the type DATE might be written as

```
DATE: record
        DAY:   integer;
        MONTH: integer;
        YEAR:  integer;
     end record;
```

The operation algorithms are written very much in the style of the operators in Mini-language Typedef. Each operation has a set of named parameters of a type that is defined in the interface specification. Parameter values are passed by value so that none of the operations can have any side effects. In addition, an operation may make use of local variables that are declared within the operation. The types of these local variables can even be defined by other type modules.

As an example of an operation algorithm, the SET_DATE operation might be written as:

```
SET_DATE: operation(DAY_NUM, MONTH_NUM, YEAR_NUM) => DATE
    CONVERTED_DATE: DATE;
begin
    . . .    -- code to check the validity of parameter values
    CONVERTED_DATE.DAY   := DAY_NUM;
    CONVERTED_DATE.MONTH := MONTH_NUM;
    CONVERTED_DATE.YEAR  := YEAR_NUM;
    return CONVERTED_DATE;
end operation;
```

An alternative way in which dates might be represented is:

```
DATE: record
        JULIAN_DAY: integer;
     end record;
```

where the field JULIAN_DAY contains the number of days that have elapsed since 1 January 4713 B.C. To make this change, only the implementation part of the DATE type module needs to be changed. Since the interface specification can remain the same, the main part of the program does not have to be changed.

The remainder of Mini-language Modules is in the style of the previous mini-languages. The arithmetic operations include div to provide integer division, and the class of operands include the application of an operation to a set of arguments.

Example

Example 17.1 shows a complete Mini-language Modules program. It performs operations on complex numbers represented by the COMPLEX data type. Although in Mini-langue Modules we give identifiers to the operators, a possible variant of the mini-language would allow us to use symbols, such as + and <, and overload the operators as is done in Mini-language Typedef. This type is defined in the COMPLEX type module where complex numbers are represented as records with two elements, REAL and IMAG. These correspond to the real and imaginary parts of the complex numbers.

```
program

    X, Y, Z: COMPLEX;
    R_VAL, I_VAL: integer;

begin
    input R_VAL, I_VAL;
    X := SET_CPLX(R_VAL, I_VAL);

    input R_VAL, I_VAL;
    Y := SET_CPLX(R_VAL, I_VAL);

    if (CPLX_EQ(X, Y)) then
        Z := CPLX_ADD(X, Y);
    else
        Z := CPLX_MULT(X, Y);
    end if;

    R_VAL := REAL_PART(Z);
    I_VAL := IMAG_PART(Z);
    output R_VAL, I_VAL;
end;


COMPLEX: module

    SET_CPLX:   (integer, integer) => COMPLEX;
    CPLX_EQ:    (COMPLEX, COMPLEX) => boolean;
    CPLX_ADD:   (COMPLEX, COMPLEX) => COMPLEX;
    CPLX_MULT:  (COMPLEX, COMPLEX) => COMPLEX;
    REAL_PART:  (COMPLEX) => integer;
    IMAG_PART:  (COMPLEX) => integer;
```

program continues on pages 498 and 499

Example 17.1 **Mini-language Modules Program**

```
implementation

    COMPLEX: record
                 REAL: integer;
                 IMAG: integer;
             end record;


    SET_CPLX: operation(R_PART, I_PART)
       RESULT: COMPLEX;
    begin
       RESULT.REAL := R_PART;
       RESULT.IMAG := I_PART;
       return RESULT;
    end;


    CPLX_EQ: operation(OP_A, OP_B)
       RESULT: boolean;
    begin
       if (OP_A.REAL = OP_B.REAL) then
           if (OP_A.IMAG = OP_B.IMAG) then
               RESULT := true;
           else
               RESULT := false;
           end if;
       else
           RESULT := false;
       end if;
       return RESULT;
    end;
```

Example 17.1 continued

The module provides operations for converting between pairs of integers
and complex numbers, testing complex numbers of equality, addition and
multiplication of complex numbers, and converting the real and imaginary
parts to integers.

An alternative COMPLEX type module might have an internal representation of the values using polar coordinates, that is, the complex number is

```
CPLX_ADD: operation(OP_A, OP_B)
    RESULT: COMPLEX;
begin
    RESULT.REAL := OP_A.REAL + OP_B.REAL;
    RESULT.IMAG := OP_A.IMAG + OP_B.IMAG;
    return RESULT;
end;


CPLX_MULT: operation(OP_A, OP_B)
    RESULT: COMPLEX;
begin
    RESULT.REAL := OP_A.REAL * OP_B.REAL - OP_A.IMAG * OP_B.IMAG;
    RESULT.IMAG := OP_A.REAL * OP_B.IMAG + OP_A.IMAG * OP_B.REAL;
    return RESULT;
end;


REAL_PART: operation(CPLX_VAL)
begin
    return CPLX_VAL.REAL;
end;


IMAG_PART: operation(CPLX_VAL)
begin
    return CPLX_VAL.IMAG;
end;

end;
```

Example 17.1 **continued**

represented by an angle and a distance from the origin of coordinates. To do this would probably require a new type ANGLE and a set of operations including the trigonometic functions. These could be provided in a separate type module. These changes could be made without altering the interface specification for COMPLEX. Thus, the main part of the program would not need to be changed.

17.2 Packaging Subprograms

The division of a program into separate modules has a number of advantages:

- *Reduction in complexity:* Since the program has been reduced into small pieces, the complexity of each piece can be made much smaller than the program as a whole. The COMPLEX type module reduces the complexity of the main part of the program by removing the details of performing complex arithmetic.

- *Ease of team programming:* A large program is almost always the work of a team of programmers. If the program is split into well-defined modules with clear interfaces, the members of the team can work individually on different modules without requiring a great deal of communication among them outside the interface specifications. A very large number of the errors in software can be attributed to failures in communication among the programmers.

- *Improved maintainability:* The principles suggested in [Parnas 1971] suggest that a program be split into modules, each of which "hides" design decisions that are most likely to change. Examples of these decisions are the format of input data or the internal representation of data values. If this is done, it is likely that changes to the program's specifications will result in modifications to the program that are localized to very few modules.

- *Reusability of code:* By splitting programs into modules, it is likely that the solution to one problem can incorporate modules that were part of the solution of another. For example, the COMPLEX type module shown in the previous section could be used for many programs that required complex arithmetic.

- *Project management:* A modular program is easier for a manager to control. The programming of the modules can be assigned to the programmers according to their individual abilities. Since each module represents a modest programming task, no programmer is overwhelmed by complexity. Control of the project is easier because the modules represent milestones in the project's progress.

The idea of packages of subroutines that provide a particular kind of facility have been available in programming since the early days. In fact, packages for performing matrix arithmetic and evaluating mathematical functions were available before the advent of high level programming languages. The ability to construct modules easily as a part of normal program writing is an outgrowth of this idea.

While the construction of a large program is made easier by splitting it into modules, the full advantages of this will not be realized unless the individual programmers are able to compile and test these parts before incorporation into the complete program. Separate compilation of modules has implications for the language design. This is because in the course of compiling one module, information about another module is required in order to ensure consistency.

Three Methods

There are three different ways in which this information can be made available to the compiler:

1. The programmer is responsible for providing this information by repeating it in all contexts where it is required. For example, in Fortran the layout of COMMON storage must be defined in each module, and in PL/I the entry declarations for all called external subprocedures must be defined. In each case, there is no way in which the compiler can check the consistency of the information.

2. The programmer can provide the name of a file that contains the information that is required by the compiler. Examples of this occur in C through #include and in PL/I through %include. While this ensures that the same information will be used for all modules, in the case of interface specifications, there is no assurance that the information contained in the file actually matches the source code of the subroutines.

3. The compiler can obtain the information from the subroutine library. In the case of Mini-language Modules, the compiler is able to access the interface specifications for named data type directly, thus ensuring that the incorporated information actually matches the source code of the subroutine.

The kinds of errors that result from inconsistencies described in methods 1 and 2 above are particularly subtle and difficult to find. Method 3 is not proof against such subtle errors since the interface specification could be changed after the information was incorporated into the invoking program. The prevention of this kind of error requires a strict programming environment with some sort of automatic control of access to source code and recording of modifications. An example of this kind of control is provided by the UNIX™[1] Source Code Control System described in [Rochkind 1975].

Method 3 is the technique supported by Mini-language Modules. The supporting compiler for this language would obtain the interface specifications from the referenced type modules during compiling. The interface specification can be written *before* completing the operation algorithms,

---

[1]UNIX is a trademark of Bell Laboratories.

which can be left as stubs. This technique matches the top-down programming method. As generally understood, this means that programs are coded from the highest level downward. During the coding of one level, only the interfaces with the next lower level are defined. The coding of the lower level is only undertaken when the higher level has been completed.

An important part of the module mechanism of Mini-language Modules is that only the information contained in the interface specification is available to the programmer of the main part. The details of the representation and operation algorithms are kept hidden. In this way, there is no chance that the programmer of the main part can inadvertantly incorporate some knowledge of the type's implementation into the code that uses it. This is important for ensuring the maintainablity of the program.

17.3 Abstract Data Types

A major decision during program design concerns the representation of data. For example, a stack could be represented either by an array or by a linked list of elements. In languages like Fortran or PL/I, the results of the decision are likely to permeate the entire program since the representation is essentially public knowledge. Even though Pascal makes a beginning to a type definition, it is still obvious that the new type is different from a primitive type. Although we might have the type definition

```
type INTEGERSTACK = record
                      TOPOFSTACK: integer;
                      ELEMENTS: array[1..500] of integer;
                    end;
```

the stack will still be accessed directly through subscripts. Thus, we can say that the program uses *concrete operations.*

In contrast to this, a program written in Mini-language Modules, or Ada, which has similar facilities, will operate on the stack through operations provided by the type module. The user is forced to use *abstract operations,* for example, pop and push, because the concrete operations are unavailable because of the hiding of the representation.

The hiding of the representation is consistent with the use of primitive types in a language. The definition of a language gives no clue as to the internal representation of the primitive objects. Integers might be represented as two's complement binary numbers, binary coded decimal digits, or floating point numbers. In most languages, there is no way of finding out the particular representation without going outside the language.

What characterizes the primitive types is the set of operations that manipulate them. A type that is defined entirely by a set of operations is an *abstract data type.* The operations provide a representation-independent specification. A language that supports abstract data types is one that allows the user to define new abstract types beyond the primitive ones. In Mini-language Modules, the specification of a data type is entirely in the operation-description part of the type module.

Advantages and Specification

There are two major advantages to defining a type as a set of operations:

1. The separation of operations from questions of representation results in data independence. The representation can be changed without corresponding changes in the main part of the program, and the correctness of the program will be unaffected.

2. The operations can be defined in a rigorous mathematical manner. In Chapter 4, as part of the axiomatic definition of Mini-language Core in Table 4.5, we gave the set of axioms that defined the operations of integer arithmetic. User-defined abstract data types can be defined similarly to assist in the verification of programs. Axiomatic definitions also ensure that the implementor of the data type knows precisely what is to be implemented and can check that the implementation matches its definition.

A formal specification of an abstract data type consists of two parts:

Syntactic specification: This part gives the name of the type and its operations, together with the types of their parameters and, for functions, the types of the returned values.

Semantic specification: This part defines the axioms that describe in a representation-independent manner the properties of the operations.

The public part of a type module in Mini-language Modules, that is, the part up to the `implementation` symbol, corresponds precisely to the syntactic specification of an abstract data type. There is no equivalent of a semantic specification in the mini-language.

As an example of a semantic specification, we will consider the abstract data type `STACK` for integers. The syntactic definition is:

```
STACK: module
   NEWSTACK: () => STACK;
   PUSH:     (STACK, integer) => STACK;
   POP:      (STACK) => STACK;
   TOP:      (STACK) => integer;
   IS_EMPTY: (STACK) => boolean;
```

The semantic specification consists of equations that link these operations. These equations need some typed variables that are declared first:

```
S:    STACK;
ELEM: integer;

IS_EMPTY(NEWSTACK())      = true;       -- Axiom 1
IS_EMPTY(PUSH(S, ELEM))   = false;      -- Axiom 2
POP(NEWSTACK())           = NEWSTACK(); -- Axiom 3
POP(PUSH(S, ELEM))        = S;          -- Axiom 4
TOP(PUSH(S, ELEM))        = ELEM;       -- Axiom 5
TOP(NEWSTACK())           = undefined;  -- Axiom 6
```

The first axiom states that the IS_EMPTY operation applied to the result obtained from the NEWSTACK operation is true. The second one states that IS_EMPTY applied to a stack that has had an element pushed onto it is false. The third one states that popping an empty stack does nothing. The fourth axiom shows that POP and PUSH are inverse operations. The fifth one shows that TOP returns the last element that has been pushed onto a stack, and the last axiom defines it as an error to apply TOP to an empty stack.

Classes of Operations

There are two distinct classes of operations for an abstract data type: those whose result is a member of the data type (NEWSTACK, PUSH, and POP), and those whose result is a member of some other data type (TOP, and IS_ EMPTY). Neither of the classes should be empty. The first class is needed to generate objects of the data type. The second class is also needed because without it, there would be no way of distinguishing different objects of the data type. In our example of the data type COMPLEX, the members of this class are CPLEX_EQ, REAL_PART, and IMAG_PART.

At first, it may seem that specifications in the form of axioms are difficult to comprehend. However, the alternative of an operational definition has the danger of specifying accidental properties that are part of the definition itself. For example, if we were to define STACK operationally in terms of a linked list, it would be difficult to know whether an array implementation of a stack actually matched the specification. With an axiomatic specification, the test is clear: does the implementation satisfy the axioms? With some practice, one can become quite adept at reading axiomatic specifications.

The major difficulty in constructing these specifications is to decide whether there are a sufficient number of consistent axioms. Generally, completeness is more of a problem than consistency. If one has an intuitive idea of the data type, it is unlikely that one will construct contradictory axioms. However, it is very easy to miss a case, particularly a boundary condition.

17.4 Where to Look: PL/I, Modula-2, Ada, Smalltalk

PL/I

PL/I provides support for separately compiled modules, known as *external procedures*. In the calling routine, there must be an entry declaration for the called procedure. This declaration defines the number and type of the called procedure's parameters and the type of the returned value, if any. For example, consider the following entry declaration:

```
DECLARE SUB EXTERNAL ENTRY(FIXED BINARY(15, 0),
                     CHARACTER(*) VARYING,
                     (1 : 10) FLOAT DECIMAL(6))
                        RETURNS(FLOAT DECIMAL(6));
```

This specifies that the procedure SUB takes three arguments: an integer, a varying length character string of unspecified maximum length, and an array of ten floating point values. SUB is a function procedure that returns a floating point value.

The entry declaration provided in the calling routine must match the parameter declarations in the subroutine for the program to be correct. Thus, the procedure SUB referred to above should have matching declarations, as in:

```
SUB:
PROCEDURE(TYPE_NUMBER, TEXT, COEFFICIENTS) RETURNS(FLOAT DECIMAL(6));
    DECLARE
        TYPE_NUMBER             FIXED BINARY(15, 0),
        TEXT                    CHARACTER(*) VARYING,
        COEFFICIENTS(1 : 10)    FLOAT DECIMAL(6);
```

There is no verification that the entry declaration matches the declarations contained in the source program for the subroutine. This relies on the careful bookkeeping on the part of the programmer. Errors due to such mismatches are common and difficult to find.

Modula-2

Modula-2 is a descendant from Pascal and Modula [Wirth 1977], which grew out of experience in concurrent processing. The major change from Modula to Modula-2 was concerned with the replacement of processes and their synchronization with signals by the lower-level idea of coroutines.

The unit that is processed by the compiler is called a *compilation unit,* or *module.* The main part of the program consists of a main module. The units of data abstraction consist of separately compiled modules called definition and implementation modules. Any identifiers that are to be imported from outside a module must be named in an import list, together with the name of the module from which they are to be imported. Any identifiers that are to be made available for reference outside a module must be named on an export list. The main module may not have an export list. Only the name of an exported type is known outside a module; its representation is not exported. The only way in which a type defined by a module can be manipulated is through exported procedures.

The major purpose of a module is to limit scope and to hide the information about the representation of a type. The definition module specifies the names and properties of types that are relevant to other modules that import from it. The implementation module contains local variables and operations that need not be known by the importing module. The following is an incomplete example based on one in [Wirth 1983] and designed to give the flavor of type definition in Modula-2.

```
definition module BUFFER;
   export PUT, GET, NONEMPTY, NONFULL;

   var NONEMPTY, NONFULL: boolean;
   procedure GET(X: cardinal);
   procedure PUT(var X: cardinal);
end BUFFER;
```

This shows two functions that can used to access a buffer and two variables that can be referenced to test whether it is full or empty. This corresponds closely to the specification part of a type module in Mini-language Modules. One difference is that in Modula-2, the names of the parameters are exported, whereas in the mini-language, they are kept hidden. The corresponding implementation module is:

```
implementation module BUFFER;
   const n = 100;
   var IN, OUT: [0..n-1];
       N: [1..n];
       BUF: array[0..n-1];

   procedure PUT(X: cardinal);
   begin
      if N < n then
         BUF[IN]   := X;
         IN        := (IN + 1) mod n;
         N         := N + 1;
         NONFULL   := N < n;
         NONEMPTY  := true
      end PUT;

   procedure GET(X: cardinal);
      . . .
   end GET;

begin
   N         := 0;
   IN        := 0;
   OUT       := 0;
   NONEMPTY  := false;
   NONFULL   := true;
end BUFFER;
```

The statements at the bottom of the module are initialization code that is invoked when an object of type BUFFER is created.

Ada

The Ada facilities for data abstraction go beyond those of the other languages described in this section. In general, the design of subprograms and type definitions follow the Pascal pattern, and the vehicle of data abstraction is the *package*.

For the flavor of the Ada package, consider Example 17.2 where the type DATE is sketched as an Ada package. The only items that may be known outside of the package are declared in the module header, in the span of the text between the package and private keywords, that is, the type name DATE and the fact that the operator NEXT_DATE takes a DATE value and returns a DATE value. Note that the internal representation of

```
package D is
   type DATE is private;
   function NEXT_DATE(D: DATE) return DATE;
private
   type DATE is
      record
            -- internal structure of a date that is
            -- kept hidden from the user by the module
      end record;
end;

package body D is
   -- local declarations and types

   function NEXT_DATE(D: DATE) return DATE is
     . . .
   end;

   -- definition of other operations

begin
   -- code to initialize data abstractions
end;
```

Example 17.2 **An Ada Package**

type DATE is kept private to the package. A user cannot make use of the fact that a date may be represented by a record structure and cannot access any field of a DATE.

Smalltalk

The language Smalltalk is included in this section because of its data abstraction ideas, which are somewhat different from those of other languages in this chapter.

Computation in Smalltalk consists of sending *messages* to *objects.* An object consists of some memory and a set of operations. Objects may represent numbers, queues, dictionaries, programs, or other kinds of data. The nature of an object's operations depends on the kind of thing it represents. An object that represents a number would have operations that compute arithmetic functions.

A message is a request for an object to perform one of its functions. The message specifies the operation to be performed but not how the operation should be carried out. It is up to the receiver of the message to determine how the operation is to be performed. The set of messages to which an object can respond is its *interface*. In a similar way to the types in Mini-language Modules, the only way in which an object can be manipulated is through its interface. The private memory of an object can only be manipulated by its operations. Thus, we have data abstraction through objects.

Each object is an instance of a *class*. All objects of the same class have identical message interfaces. Each class has a name so that it can be referenced. A class also has a protocol description that lists the messages that can be understood by objects of the class and an implementation description that defines how the operations of the class are implemented.

An example of a class is `FinancialHistory`. Objects of this class have operations available through its interface. These operations are:

1. Create a new object of the class with an initial amount of money.
2. Note that a certain amount of money was spent for a certain reason.
3. Note that a certain amount of money was received from a particular source.
4. Find out how much money is available.
5. Find out how much money has been spent for a particular reason.
6. Find out how much money has been received from a particular source.

The protocol description would list these operations, showing what the parameters are, for example:

```
receive: amount from: source   Remember that amount has been
                               received from source.
```

The implementation description would list the names of variables that belong to each object and the way in which the operations are performed. Thus, part of the implementation description for `FinancialHistory` might be:

class name:	`FinancialHistory`
instance variable names:	`cashOnHand`
	`incomes`
	`expenditures`

instance methods

```
transaction recording
   receive: amount from: source
      incomes at: source
         put (self totalReceivedFrom: source) + amount
      cashOnHand ← cashOnHand + amount
```

The instance variable names are the names of variables individually part of each instance of an object of the class.

The major difference between the class concept of Smalltalk and data abstraction as we have described elsewhere in this chapter is that the variables are typeless; they are thus more flexible than type modules.

Further Reading

The basic idea for abstract data types is based on the concept of a class in Simula 67, which is an instance of a module. Following this pioneering work, there was a sequence of experimental languages—Clu, Mesa, Alphard, Euclid, and Gipsy. This culminated in Modula-2 and the design of the package facility in Ada. The philosophy behind Modula-2 is described in [Wirth 1984] and the rationale for the design of Ada is given in [Ichbiah et al. 1979].

Abstract data types were first introduced in [Liskov and Zilles 1974]. The method of formal specification was first introduced in [Guttag 1977]. The technique is further elaborated in [Guttag et al. 1978a] and [Guttag et al. 1978b]. The question of producing a complete and consistent set of axioms for an abstract data specification is discussed in [Guttag and Horning 1978]. A good general review of the specification and implementation of abstract data types is in [Berztiss and Thatte 1983].

Exercises

Exercise 17.1 Error Handling

In Section 17.1 the example of the data type DATE is sketched. Mention is made that the SET_DATE function checks that the values of the three integers representing day, month, and year number are consistent. However, nothing is said about what should be done if an inconsistency is found. Propose how this should be handled and outline a new type module, perhaps including extra operations.

Exercise 17.2 Floating Point Arithmetic

Design a type module for the data type FLOAT that would allow the language to be extended to include floating point arithmetic.

Exercise 17.3 *Information Hiding*

The actual representation of the values of a data type is in the implementation part of a type module of Mini-language Modules. It is intended that the compiler should not require access to this information while compiling other type modules or the main part of the program. This ensures that the programmer of other parts of the program cannot make use of this private information. Is this possible or must the representation be made available to the compiler? What are the advantages and disadvantages of doing this?

Exercise 17.4 *An Abstract Data Type*

The following is a specification for the abstract data type BAG:

```
BAG: module
   EMPTY_BAG: () => BAG;
   INSERT:    (BAG, integer) => BAG;
   DELETE:    (BAG, integer) => BAG;
   IS_MEMBER: (BAG, integer) => boolean;

BG:  BAG;
INT_A, INT_B: integer;

IS_MEMBER(EMPTY_BAG(), INT_A) = false;

IS_MEMBER(INSERT(BG, INT_A), INT_B) =
               if (INT_A = INT_B) then
                  true
               else
                  IS_MEMBER(BG, INT_B)
               end if

DELETE(EMPTY_BAG(), INT_A) = EMPTY_BAG()

DELETE(INSERT(BG, INT_A), INT_B) =
               if (INT_A = INT_B) then
                  BG
               else
                  INSERT(DELETE(BG, INT_B), INT_A)
               end if
```

Provide an implementation part for the BAG type module in Mini-language Modules extended to include unbounded arrays as an additional data structure as in Mini-language Procedures.

Exercise 17.5 The SET *Abstract Data Type*

Construct a specification for the abstract type SET that corresponds to the mathematical concept of a set. This specification will differ in a small, but important, detail from the specification of the BAG data type in Exercise 17.4. Explain the reason for the difference.

Exercise 17.6 *Facilities for Separate Compilation*

Pick two languages on your system that provide for separate compilation. Write a two- to five-page "user manual" describing only the facilities for separate compilation.

18

The Swamp of Complexity

A programming language is a notation and, as such, serves to record and assist the development of human thought in a particular direction—the formulation of processes to be carried out on a computer. For a notation to be effective, it must carry a mental load for the user and must have, among other properties, economy and the ability to subordinate detail. By *economy* in a programming language we mean that a wide range of programs can be expressed naturally using a relatively small vocabulary and simple grammatical rules.

The ability to subordinate detail, often called abstraction, leads to a reduction in apparent programming complexity. The power of a language to provide abstraction is the source of its usefulness to the programmer. It allows concentration on the problem being solved without worrying about the very detailed stream of instructions that must be given to the machine.

However, there is always a danger of swapping one kind of complexity for another. A language may reduce program complexity by providing simple forms for all circumstances but create a new complexity of its own by the number of different forms and the rules by which they are combined. Although all the mini-languages presented here are small, they nevertheless show complexities, such as the dereferencing rules in Mini-language Ref and the intricacies of scope rules. Real programming languages are many times more complex than any of the mini-languages. It is this complexity that seriously restricts their effectiveness as an adequate notation.

18.1 The Forms of Complexity

There are many forms that complexity takes in a language. All too frequently, a language designer pays only token homage to simplicity, without really making the underlying design simple. Although simplicity may be attempted by building the language from the simplest elements, there is no guarantee that these can be combined clearly to form a coherent whole. In this section, we follow the general organization of the book in examining the forms of complexity.

Complexity Due to Scale

Probably the greatest single symptom of complexity is the scale of the language. Generally, size comes through an attempt to meet the demands of would-be users, who want to see special additions to make their own applications easier. The two largest languages at the moment are, and we hope that this will remain true, PL/I and Ada. In both cases, much of their size has come about through the attempt to meet many isolated special demands.

The design goal for PL/I was a language that would satisfy the needs of scientific, commercial, and special purpose users. Following the release of the initial version of the design, there started a dialogue between the designers and the future users of the language. This dialogue continued up to the production of the ANSI Standard for PL/I. During this period, far more was added than was deleted. As a result, using the language has been likened to "flying a plane with 7,000 buttons, switches, and handles to manipulate in the cockpit" [Dijkstra 1972b].

Ada was designed to meet specifications, produced by the Department of Defense and published as [Whitaker 1978], for a language to be used throughout the Department and the military services. The specifications were drawn up by taking requests for facilities from potential users of the language. These requirements were used by its designers who, in turn, had their own requirements to satisfy as well. Further adding to the cacophony of advice were the many consultants and hundreds of critics. The objective was, of course, to amalgamate all these requirements into a coherent whole. This process has been described as like trying to commission a symphony for an orchestra by constructing it from contributions of a few bars each from a large number of individual composers.

In both PL/I and Ada, the size and complexity of the languages go to the limits of the user's intellectual control. These languages, which were designed by what amounts to very large committees, may be compared to languages that were designed by individuals or small committees, for example, Algol 60, Algol 68, Pascal, and APL. Although they may have other problems, they do not suffer to the same degree from complexity due to absolute size.

A language may be small and yet suffer from complexity due to scale. This can come about through the addition of features that are beyond the scope of the language. Pascal was designed primarily as a language to be used in teaching. Admittedly, Pascal has achieved a popularity beyond that for teaching, but as a pedagogic language, it is extremely large. For example, we question the need for the proposed complicated rules for file types [Addyman et al. 1979], record variants (hardly an introductory topic), the rather elaborate scope rules, the goto statement (of little value in a language with many one-in, one-out structures), set types (of limited use as defined), and so forth. Other complexities in Pascal programs come about through the omission of important abstractions, such as variable length character strings and separate compilation of modules.

Almost every programming language suffers in some way from excessive complexity, either in size, compression of language forms, or special cases. There are several consequences of such complexity:

- Potential and beginning users feel threatened by the magnitude of the language.

- Writing comprehensible tutorial documents becomes almost impossible. As a result, teaching the language becomes unnecessarily difficult.

- Implementation is error prone and inefficient, with diagnostic messages that are difficult to interpret.

- Language forms become overloaded so that subtle and often treacherous distinctions must be made by the user.

- It becomes more difficult for the user to develop a simple set of rules for using the language. Thus, the number of errors made increases.

Syntax

Above all, the high-level syntax should be simple. Consider, for example, the Pascal declaration section. Here everything is static and there is reasonable consistency.

Each statement of the language should have a meaning that matches its intuitive meaning for the user. There should be no "nasty surprises." An example of this is to be found in APL. Throughout our early mathematical education we became familiar with the precedence of multiplication and division over addition and subtraction. In APL, operator precedence runs strictly from right to left. For example, the value of the APL expression (36 / 4 + 5) is 4, not 14, as we would expect from our mathematical experience. It might well be that the APL rule is the best one and traditional mathematics is wrong in its approach. That is beside the point—the APL expression has a different meaning from the intuitive one most of us have. We might argue that a number system based on 16 would be preferable to one based on 10, but until we evolve three more fingers on each hand, it runs counter to everyday experience.

In keeping with the idea of relying on the user's intuitive feeling for the meaning of the forms in the language, the use of English-like constructs helps the English-speaking user. With reservations, we support the direction taken by Cobol. Unfortunately, the form of Cobol is flawed by a lack of clear structure. This makes Cobol programs difficult to understand despite their resemblance to natural language. Following the usage in English, Cobol uses the period to end complete sentences. Unfortunately, the omission of a period is easy to overlook, and this can change the meaning of a program without any warning. For example, in

```
IF TYPE-CODE IS EQUAL TO 'A'
    PERFORM SCALE THROUGH EXIT-SCALE
    ADD 1 TO TITLE-COUNT
ELSE
    PERFORM TITLE-PRINT
    MOVE 1 TO TITLE-COUNT
MOVE BLANK TO TYPE-CODE.
```

the indentation is misleading. The absence of a period at the end of the next-to-last line includes the final line as part of the else clause. BLANK is only moved to TYPE-CODE if TYPE-CODE is not 'A'.

Finally, the syntax should be uniform in its use of constructs. That is, the form of a particular construct should be independent of the context of its use. Consider the punctuation in the two Fortran statements:

```
READ (5) A, B, C, D
GO TO K, (10, 20, 30, 40)
```

In one case there is a comma, in the other none. In one case, the list is in parentheses, in the other, the single item.

Semantics

Probably the greatest contribution to semantic complexity comes from side effects. In various places in this book, we have shown how side effects can lead to loss of clarity. A classic case is a function subprogram that can change the values of its arguments or of global variables in addition to returning a value to the invoker. This can lead to programs that are almost impossible to understand. Indeed, their precise meaning can depend on some quirks of a particular implementation rather than a designed feature of the language.

Functions, although the most commonly mentioned, are not the only sources of side effects in programming languages. In Example 6.1 we saw how the assignment

```
REF_INT_C := INT_B;
```

can affect the outcome of the assignment

```
INT_A := REF_REF_INT_E;
```

even though the two statements do not explicitly reference any common variables. A similar situation arises with lists in Section 13.2. Side effects are the root of the problems with aliasing.

However, it is important to remember that side effects are really endemic to procedural languages since they depend on the side effect of changing the computer store in an assignment. This basic principle of programs descends directly from the original von Neumann design of a computer. Functional languages like Mini-language Apply have no side effects. Indeed, some contend, particularly [Backus 1978], that the continued reliance on the von Neumann model of computation has limited the proper development of functional languages, which are conceptually much simpler.

Control Structures

In Chapter 7, we examine the question of the kinds of control statements that should be available in a programming language. Our conclusion is that the matter reduces to a balance of complexity. On the one hand, a possible reduction of programming effort may be obtained by adding higher-level control structures, such as exit; on the other, the additional statements cause an increased complexity of the language.

We believe that the case for these higher-control structures has yet to be proved. This is not, by any means, a universally held belief. The designers of the language Bliss felt that each specific control environment required its own escape mechanism. Each escape scheme causes control to leave a specific control environment. This seems to us to be an excessive burden of complexity for a single semantic pattern.

Types

One of the problems with the term *type* is that it tends to be overused. PL/I has subsumed the notion of type into the more general one of *attribute,* which includes the ideas of scope and storage management. Our concept of type is limited to the specification of the set of values that may be taken by an object and the class of operations that manipulate the object.

In languages where the choice of type is limited to those fixed in the language initially, the concept remains fairly simple except for the question of conversion from one type to another. Where there are many built-in types, the number of possible conversions is large. Most of these occur between various forms of numeric representation.

A great deal of complexity is added to a language by the many possible conversions, especially if they can occur implicitly, as in PL/I. The addition of the attribute complex doubled the number of potential conversions without adding an adequate return on this investment in complication. By requiring that conversions be mentioned explicitly, some of the complexity is reduced. However, there remains an inescapable residue of complexity due to the variety of numeric representations that are forced on the language designer by the realities of hardware. This is really due to the mapping of the real world's infinite domain of numbers onto the computer's finite one.

Composite data types bring complexities of their own. First, there is the question of operations on composite values. Even such an apparently simple operation as assignment can be anything but simple. For arrays, questions of bounds arise, and for records, of how much alike two records must be to be assignable. If the question of variant records is added, the problem becomes even more difficult. Indeed, the inclusion of variant records of the form described in Section 8.5 adds considerable complexity to the language.

An interesting example of the question of balance between complexity and utility is that of character strings. As discussed in Chapter 8, there are two fundamentally different views of character strings: either as an array of the primitive type character, or as a primitive type in their own right. Making them a part of the already existing array construct would seem at first to be a simplification. However, the need to handle varying length character strings either requires flexible array bounds, an added complication of both the language and the implementation, or puts considerable extra detail into programs, which degrades the utility of the language. On balance, the provision of the character string as a primitive type certainly seems to provide the simpler solution.

Procedures and Parameters

Procedures provide a form of packaging. They simplify programs by allowing details that are not germane at the level of the caller to be replaced by a call statement. The argument-parameter correspondence provides generality so that a single procedure can be used in a variety of contexts.

In order that the full effects of this simplification can be realized, the interface between the caller and the subroutine must be kept as simple as possible. That is to say, the boundary around the procedure should have only one passage for data, the argument-parameter transmission. Any others, such as the use of globals, necessarily weaken the integrity of the structure and reduce its effectiveness as an abstraction.

As discussed in Chapter 10, there are many ways in which the argument-parameter transmission can be defined. Again, simplicity is the criterion. Passing by reference is certainly the simplest; however, care is required to avoid the complexities of aliasing.

While procedures act as statements, functions act as expressions. If clarity is to be preserved, functions must not have side effects since this inevitably brings up questions of evaluation order and a host of rules that hinder more than they help.

Mini-language Apply is a pure function language where there is no possibility of side effects. When this principle is used in procedural languages, then it can cause no change of state, and therefore input-output transmission cannot be permitted. Lisp originally started as a pure applicative language, but later versions included the use of assignments and global variables. It is not obvious that this added complexity was exchanged for a corresponding simplification in programming.

Scope

The original intent of scope rules was to allow localization of names and to permit the reuse of names in other contexts. Thus, the rules of scope define the set of names that may be used at a given point in a program. From the relatively simple concept of block structure, many more complicated schemes have been developed, each ramification being rationalized as rectifying some previous deficiency. Each ramification also added its quota of complexity. Ada provides an example of how scope rules can become greatly complicated, as is attested by the fact that the reference manual devotes an entire chapter to the subject.

The entire issue of scope itself needs to be questioned. Fortran has seldom been criticized on scope grounds, yet the scope rules are simple. Although COMMON variables complicate matters, the underlying idea is simple—nesting is not allowed and everything is local. The Cobol model is also simple, but just the opposite—everything is global.

Input and Output

Generally, the area of input and output has been one of the most complex features of programming languages. While some of the complexity is due to the nature of the problem being solved, much is due to the way in which the approach has evolved. Solutions have tended to be ad hoc without a proper high-level treatment.

Exceptions and Parallelism

At this stage in the development of programming languages, progress in these areas has only occurred recently. Thus, while the earlier attempts at the problem, *fork, join,* and *semaphores* for example, had much complexity and little reliability, there seems to be good progress in the direction of simplification.

18.2   Escaping from the Swamp

A comparison of the languages PL/I, Ada, and Algol 68 is instructive. One of the design goals of Algol 68 was minimization of the number of independent primitive concepts. Power and breadth were obtained by combining these concepts uniformly. A construct that can be used in one context can be used in any other context where there is no semantic ambiguity. Since the primitive concepts are independent, duplication of function is avoided. Both PL/I and Ada lack this uniformity. Although PL/I allows user-defined functions as objects that can be assigned, the built-in functions cannot be used in this way. Ada has task *types,* but no objects or operations that belong to this type.

The mechanism for defining new types and operators allows a language to be extended to suit a particular application. In Algol 68 this mechanism has been used to keep the core of the language very small. All the operators and some types like complex numbers are defined through this mechanism in a *standard prologue.* Conceptually, an implementation of Algol 68 could be realized with a relatively simple compiler for the core language and by processing the text of the standard prologue before each source program. This might not be an efficient method from the point of view of the user.

Much of PL/I's size is due to its attempt to cater, without the benefit of extensibility, to a large community of users. Ada, on the other hand, has been able to take advantage of the technology of extensibility. However, the basis for the extension is a very large language in its own right, many times larger than the core of Algol 68. The core of Ada was designed to economize on concepts and yet meet its many requirements. As a result, many of its elegant features, such as the type model, packages, and one-in, one-out control structures, are obscured.

While the design of Algol 68 is elegant in its basis, its external appearance is not. The definition of the language is forbidding with much new terminology for old concepts. The syntax seems often to have been designed to save keystrokes rather than to promote readability, and the same symbol often serves many purposes, depending on the context.

Nevertheless, the message seems clear. The way to escape the dangers of complexity and yet provide a powerful programming language must be based on:

- a minimum of independent concepts combined in a uniform manner.
- a comprehensive definition mechanism to provide breadth.
- a small core language on which the extensions are based.
- a syntax that is chosen for its readability.

The problems that must be solved with today's languages are not simple. It is important that the programmer's task not be compounded by an additional layer of complexity from the very tool that is being used to solve the problem.

The concept of a programming language as a tool needs to be extended. The task of preparing the program should be integrated more closely with that of translating it into machine instructions. Nowadays, most programs are prepared through an interactive editor, and then the program is analyzed by the compiler for syntactic errors. These errors must then be removed by another cycle through the editing process.

Programs are not text; they are hierarchical arrangements of computational structures and should be edited, executed, and debugged in an environment that supports this view. Recently, much work has been done with *syntax-directed* or *language-sensitive editors*. These editors are sensitive to the syntax of a particular language and ensure that the program retains syntactic integrity. One example of this is the Cornell Program Synthesizer [Teitelbaum and Reps 1981]. This system aims to provide a unified programming environment that promotes programming as a top-down process, ensures that only syntactically correct programs are entered, and provides extensive diagnostic facilities during program execution.

Hitherto, the most popular interactive languages have been APL, Lisp, and Basic. This has not been due to their unsurpassed clarity or ease of expression, but because they have presented the user with an integrated editing, execution, and debugging environment. It is through the use of tools of this kind that we can protect the programmer from many of the frustrating details of programming and improve both reliability and productivity.

Suggested Term Projects

Term Project 18.1 *Implementing a Mini-language*

Language implementations are a popular exercise, and for good reason. By the time you are done, you will have a much deeper knowledge of the language and an appreciation of the difficulty of what first appears to be an easy task. The difficulty of the task is most evident by the many implementations that are never finished.

Your task is to implement *one* of the mini-languages. Obviously, some are more difficult than others. Mini-language Core is probably a good representative language. Mini-language Typedef is quite difficult, and Mini-language Parallel even more so.

There are many characteristics of a good implementation:

1. *Completeness.* The implementation should adhere exactly to the definition.

2. *Correctness.* All difficult cases should be tested. Boundary cases (for example, a program with no variables or with arithmetic over large numbers) should also be tested.

3. *Response to Errors.* This area is always difficult. The implementation should try to give good feedback to a user who makes an error. If a program contains many errors, the implementation should not get completely lost, but should try to recover and go on.

4. *Human Engineering.* The listings provided for the user should be clean and readable. Printing all kinds of diagnostic information may be a poor idea.

5. *Documentation.* The implementation, test cases, summary of its behavior, and performance data should be presented clearly and crisply.

A common complaint in many efforts of this sort is low-quality work resulting from an overly optimistic and ambitious effort. Another complaint is a lack of concern for the user, see [Ledgard et al. 1981]. So don't be afraid to limit the scope of the task. Put your emphasis on the quality of the result.

Term Project 18.2 *Error Assistance*

The possibilities for errors in programs are endless. Often the manual is of little help.

Your task here is to provide a document to be used with one of the mini-languages of your choice. The document is intended to provide as much help as possible to a programmer who has made an error.

The following points are important.

1. *Coverage.* You should attempt to cover all possible errors in both syntax and semantics. The errors will range from simple spelling or punctuation mistakes, to input-output errors, to various ways in which a program will give rise to an infinite loop.

2. *Examples.* You should give examples of each kind of error. The examples should be short and to the point.

3. *Organization.* The organization of the document should allow the programmer with a specific error to get help without wading through each case.

A good place to start this exercise is with a written list of all conceivable cases that could arise. For Mini-language Core, a good document will probably require twenty or more pages.

As samples of such errors, a programmer might write

```
A1 := A1 + 1;
```

instead of

```
A1 := A2 + 1;
```

or might input three values in the wrong order, or might forget to test for a case that leads to division by 0.

Term Project 18.3 *Designing a Mini-language*

The teaching of widely used programming languages is in part difficult because of the larger scale and complexity of the language. One technique to alleviate this problem is to teach only a small (but useful) fragment of the language first. Such a fragment would need its own documentation and its own examples. It would become a "mini-language" in the same sense as those of previous chapters.

Your task is to choose a language you know well, and from it prepare a mini-language subset that would be suitable for teaching. The result of your effort will be a document describing the mini-language. Your mini-language must be small. It should be useful enough that it could be used for several weeks of teaching.

Term Project 18.4 *Literature Review*

Almost any topic in this text is treated, directly or indirectly, by articles in the literature. Subjects like semantics, control structures, or parallelism are heavily treated, while topics like human engineering or scale have been given less attention.

Choose a topic taken from the index of this text and attempt to find at least ten works relevant to the subject. Prepare a report on the topic. The report should discuss the relevance of the topic, debatable concerns, unresolved issues, ramifications in existing languages, and questions of scale and complexity. Your report should clearly state at least one conclusion of your own.

Term Project 18.5 *Language Critique*

When a new book is published, it is common to see book reviews commenting on its significance, its weakness, its bias, and so forth.

Your task here is to do the same for a programming language that is unfamiliar to you. In particular, you are to prepare a twenty- to thirty-page report treating the major issues in its design. You may wish to discuss:

1. The justification for the language
2. The clarity of syntax
3. The documentation
4. Areas in need of more work
5. Constructs that are difficult to use
6. Human engineering of the effort
7. Features that could be deleted

Ada, Modula-2, and Algol 68 are three good general choices. If you wish to try something different, pick a special-purpose language like Snobol, Val, or Prolog. If you are not familiar with some of the older classics, try Basic or Fortran.

Term Project 18.6 *Detailed Paper Review*

Developing a critical perspective of papers in the literature is certainly a strong asset. Each of the following papers is in some way important to the study of programming languages.

[Backus 1978]	[Hoare 1973]
[Beech 1970]	[Knuth 1974]
[McGraw 1982]	[Liskov and Zilles 1974]
[Haberman 1973]	[Tannenbaum 1976]
[Ledgard and Singer 1983]	[Ashcroft and Wadge 1982]
and its response [Wichmann 1984]	[Rowe 1984]
	[Ichbiah 1984]

Your task is to select one of these papers and to provide a *detailed* technical review (10 or 15 pages). Your review should summarize the work, point out its strengths and weaknesses, its clarity, and any other aspect you wish.

References

[Ackerman 1982]
William B. Ackerman, Data flow languages, *IEEE Computer,* vol. 15, no. 2,
February 1982, pp. 15–25.

[Ada]
Department of Defense, *Reference manual for the Ada programming language,*
U.S. Department of Defense, Washington, July 1980 (Also published by Springer-
Verlag, New York, 1983).

[Addyman et al. 1979]
A. M. Addyman, R. Brewer, D. G. Burnett-Hall, R. M. De Morgan, W. Findley, M. I.
Jackson, D. A. Joslin, M. J. Reece, D. A. Watt, J. Welsh, and B. A. Wichamn, A draft
description of Pascal, *Software—Practice and Experience,* vol. 9, May 1979,
pp. 381–424.

[AED]
Softech Inc., *Introduction to AED programming,* 4th. ed., Softech Inc., Waltham,
Mass., 1973.

[Aho and Johnson 1974]
Alfred V. Aho and Stephen C. Johnson, LR parsing, *ACM Computing Surveys,* vol.
6, no. 2, June 1974, pp. 99–124.

[Aho and Ullman 1972]
Alfred V. Aho and Jeffrey D. Ullman, *The theory of parsing, translation, and
compiling,* 2 vols., Prentice-Hall, Englewood Cliffs, N.J., 1972.

[Aho and Ullman 1977]
Alfred V. Aho and Jeffrey D. Ullman, *Principles of compiler design,* Addison-
Wesley, Reading, Mass., 1977.

[Algol 60]
Peter Naur, editor, Revised report on the algorithmic language Algol 60,
Communications of the ACM, vol. 3, no. 1, January 1963, pp. 1–17.

Edsger W. Dijkstra, *A primer of Algol 60 programming,* Academic Press, New
York, 1960.

[Algol 68]
Aard van Wijngaarden, B. J. Mailloux, J. E. L. Peck, C. H. A. Koster, M. Sintzoff, C.
H. Lindsey, L. G. L. T. Meertens, and R. G. Fisker, Revised report on the
algorithmic language Algol 68, *Acta Informatica,* vol. 5, pts. 1–3, 1975,
pp. 1–236 (also reproduced in *Sigplan Notices,* vol. 12, no. 5, May 1977,
pp. 1–79).

Charles Lindsey and S. G. van der Meulen, *Informal introduction to Algol 68,*
North-Holland Publishing Company, Amsterdam 1975.

[Algol W]
Niklaus Wirth and C. A. R. Hoare, A contribution to the development of Algol,
Communications of the ACM, vol. 9, no. 6, June 1966, pp. 413–432.

[Allen 1969]
Frances E. Allen, Program optimization, in *Annual Review of Automatic
Programming,* vol. 5, pp. 239–307, Pergamon, Elmsford, NY, 1969.

[Allen 1970]
Frances E. Allen, Control flow analysis, *Sigplan Notices,* vol. 5, no. 7, July 1970,
pp. 1–19.

[Allen and Cocke 1972]
Frances E. Allen and John Cocke, A catalogue of optimizing transformations, in
Design and Optimization of Compilers, Randall Rustin, Editor, Prentice-Hall,
Englewood Cliffs, N.J., 1972.

[Alphard]
William A. Wulf, Ralph L. London, and Mary Shaw, *Abstraction and verification
in Alphard: introduction to language and methodology,* USC Information
Science Technical Report, University of Southern California, Los Angeles, 1976.

Mary Shaw, William A. Wulf, and Ralph L. London, Abstraction and verification in
Alphard: defining and specifying iteration and generation, *Communications of the
ACM,* vol. 20, no. 8, August 1977, pp. 553–564.

[Ambler et al. 1977]
A. L. Ambler, D. I. Good, J. C. Browne, W. F. Burger, R. M. Cohen, C. G. Hoch,
and R. E. Wells, Gipsy: a language for specification and implementation of
verifiable programs, *Sigplan Notices,* vol. 12, no. 3, March 1977, pp. 1–10.

[Andrews and Schneider 1983]
Gregory R. Andrews and Fred B. Schneider, Concepts and notations for
concurrent programming, *ACM Computing Surveys,* vol. 15, no. 1, March 1983,
pp. 3–43.

[Anklam et al. 1982]
Patricia Anklam, David Cutler, Roger Heinen, Jr., and M. Donald MacLaren, *Engineering a compiler,* Digital Press, Bedford, Mass., 1982.

[ANSI 1966]
American National Standards Institute, *American National Standard Programming Language FORTRAN,* American National Standards Institute, New York, 1966.

[ANSI 1974]
American National Standards Institute, *American National Standard Programming Language Cobol,* ANSI X3.23–1974, American National Standards Institute, New York, 1974.

[ANSI 1976]
American National Standards Institute, *American National Standard Programming Language PL/I,* ANSI X3.53–1976, American National Standards Institute, New York, 1976.

[ANSI 1978]
American National Standards Institute, *American National Standard Programming Language FORTRAN,* ANSI X3.9–1977, American National Standards Institute, New York, 1978.

[ANSI 1983]
American National Standards Institute, *American National Standard Programming Language PASCAL,* ANSI/IEEE 770 X3.97–1983, American National Standards Institute, New York, 1983.

[APL]
Kenneth E. Iverson, *A programming language,* John Wiley and Sons, New York, 1962.

APL language, Form no. GC26–3847–5, IBM Data Processing Division, White Plains, New York, 1983.

[Apt]
Douglas T. Ross, *APT part programmer's manual,* MIT Servo Lab, Cambridge, Mass., 1959.

[Arsac 1979]
Jacques J. Arsac, Syntactic source to source transforms and program manipulation, *Communications of the ACM,* vol. 22, no. 1, January 1979, pp. 43–54.

[Ashcraft and Wadge 1982]
E. A. Ashcraft and W. W. Wadge, Rx for semantics, *ACM Transactions on Programming Languages and Systems,* vol. 4, no. 2, April 1982, pp. 283–294.

[Backus 1978]
John Backus, Can programming be liberated from the von Newmann style? *Communications of the ACM,* vol. 21, no. 8, August 1978, pp. 613–641.

[Backus and Heising 1964]
John Backus and W. P. Heising, FORTRAN, *IEEE Transactions on Electronic Computers,* EC13, no. 4, August 1964, pp. 382–385.

[Barron 1977]
David W. Barron, *An Introduction to the Study of Programming Languages,* Cambridge University Press, Cambridge, England, 1977.

[BCPL]
Martin Richards, BCPL: a tool for compiler writing and system programming, in *Proceedings of Spring Joint Computer Conference,* 1969.

Martin Richards and Colin Whitby-Stevens, *BCPL—the language and its compiler,* Cambridge University Press, Cambridge, 1979.

[Beckermeyer et al. 1974]
Robert Beckermeyer, John Dill, James Elshoff, Michael Marcotty, and John Murray, Handling Asynchronous interrupts in a PL/I-like language, *Software—Practice and Experience,* vol. 4, no. 2, April-June 1974, pp. 117–124.

[Beech 1970]
David Beech, A structural view of PL/I, *ACM Computing Surveys,* vol. 2, no. 1, March 1970, pp. 33–64.

[Bell 1973]
James R. Bell, Threaded code, *Communications of the ACM,* vol. 16, no. 6, June 1973, pp. 370–372.

[Ben-Ari 1982]
M. Ben-Ari, *Principles of concurrent programming,* Prentice-Hall International, Englewood Cliffs, N.J., 1982.

[Berztiss and Thatte 1983]
Alfs T. Berztiss and Satish Thatte, Specification and implementation of abstract data types, in *Advances in Computers,* vol. 22, ed. Marshall C. Yovits, Academic Press, New York, 1983.

[Bliss]
William A. Wulf, D. B. Russel, and A. Nico Habermann, Bliss: a language for systems programming, *Communications of the ACM,* vol. 14, no. 12, December 1971, pp. 780–790.

[Boehm and Jacopini 1966]
Corrado Boehm and Giuseppi Jacopini, Flow diagrams, Turing machines, and languages with only two formation rules, *Communications of the ACM,* vol. 9, no. 5, May 1966, pp. 366–371.

[Bond et al. 1964]
Elaine R. Bond, M. Auslander, S. G. Grisoff, R. Kenney, M. Myszewski, J. Sammet, R. Tobey, and S. Zilles, Formac: An experimental formula manipulation compiler, *Proceedings of ACM National Conference,* Association for Computing Machinery, New York, 1964, pp. K2.1–1–19.

[Brinch Hansen 1973]
Per Brinch Hansen, Concurrent programming concepts, *ACM Computing Surveys,* vol. 5, no. 4, December 1973, pp. 223–245.

[Brinch Hansen 1975]
Per Brinch Hansen, The programming language concurrent Pascal, *IEEE Transactions on Software Engineering,* vol. SE–1, no. 2, June 1975, pp. 199–207.

[Brodie 1981]
Leo Brodie, *Starting Forth,* Prentice-Hall, Englewood Cliffs, N.J., 1981.

[Brosgol 1977]
Benjamin Brosgol, Some issues in data types and type checking in design and implementation of programming languages, *Lecture Notes in Computer Science,* vol. 54, Springer-Verlag, New York, 1977.

[Brown 1974]
Peter J. Brown, *Macro processors, and techniques for portable software,* John Wiley and Sons, London, 1974.

[Brown 1981]
W. Stanley Brown, A simple but realistic model of floating-point computation, *ACM Transactions on Mathematical Software,* vol. 7, no. 4, December 1981, pp. 445–480.

[Bruno and Steiglitz 1972]
J. Bruno and K. Steiglitz, The expression of algorithms by charts, *Journal of the ACM,* vol. 19, no. 3, July 1972, pp. 517–525.

[Burge 1975]
William H. Burge, *Recursive programming techniques,* Addison-Wesley, Reading, Mass., 1975.

[C]
Brian W. Kernighan and Dennis M. Ritchie, *The C programming language,* Prentice-Hall, Englewood Cliffs, N.J., 1978.

[Campbell-Kelly 1980]
Martin Campbell-Kelly, Programming the Mark I: early programming activity at the University of Manchester, *Annals of the History of Computing,* vol. 2, no. 2, April 1980, pp. 130–168.

[Church 1941]
Alonzo Church, *The calculi of lambda-conversion,* Annals of Mathematic Studies, no. 6, Princeton University Press, Princeton, N.J., 1941.

[Clark 1973]
R. Lawrence Clark, A linguistic contribution to goto-less programming, *Datamation,* vol. 19, no. 12, December 1973, pp. 62–63; republished in *Communications of the ACM,* vol. 27, no. 4, April 1984, pp. 349–350.

[Clark et al. 1980]
L. A. Clark, J. C. Wileden, and L. Wolf, Nesting in Ada is for the birds, *Sigplan Notices,* vol. 15, no. 11, November 1980, pp. 139–145.

[Cleaveland and Uzgalis 1976]
James C. Cleaveland and Robert C. Uzgalis, *Grammars for programming languages: what every programmer should know about grammar,* American Elsevier Publishing Company, New York, 1976.

[Clu]
Barbara Liskov, et al., *Clu reference manual,* MIT*LCS*TR–225, Massachusetts Institute of Technology, Cambridge, Mass., 1979.

[Coar 1984]
David Coar, Pascal, Ada, and Modula–2, *Byte,* vol. 9, no. 8, August 1984, pp. 145–152.

[Cobol]
American National Standards Institute, *American National Standard Programming Language Cobol,* ANSI X3.23–1974, American National Standards Institute, New York, 1974.

[Conway 1963]
Melvin E. Conway, Design of a separable transition-diagram compiler, *Communications of the ACM,* vol. 6, no. 7, July 1963, pp. 396–408.

[Cooper 1967]
David C. Cooper, Boehm and Jacopini's reduction of flow charts, *Communications of the ACM,* vol. 10, no. 8, August 1967, pp. 463, 473.

[Curry and Feys 1958]
Haskell B. Curry and Robert Feys, *Combinatory logic,* vol. 1, North-Holland Publishing Company, Amsterdam, 1958.

[Dahl et al. 1968]
Ole-Johan Dahl, B. Myhrhaug, and U. Nygaard, *The Simula 67 common base language,* Norwegian Computing Center, Oslo, 1968.

[Davie and Morrison 1981]
Anthony Davie and Ronald Morrison, *Recursive descent compiling,* Halsted Press, New York, 1981.

[Demers et al 1977]
Alan Demers, James Donahue, Ray Teitelbaum, and John Williams, Encapsulated data types and generic procedures, in *Design and Implementation of Programming Languages,* Lecture Notes in Computer Science, vol. 54, Springer-Verlag, New York, 1977.

[DeMillo et al. 1979]
Richard A. DeMillo, Richard J. Lipton, and Alan J. Perlis, Social processes and proofs of theorems and programs, *Communications of the ACM,* vol. 22, no. 5, May 1979, pp. 271–280. See also *Communications of the ACM,* vol. 22, no. 11, November 1979, pp. 621–630 and vol. 23, no. 5, May 1980, pp. 307–308.

[Department of Defense 1980a]
Department of Defense, *Reference manual for the Ada programming language,*
U.S. Department of Defense, Washington, July 1980 (Also published by Springer-
Verlag, New York, 1983).

[Department of Defense 1980b]
Department of Defense, *Formal definition of the Ada programming language,*
U.S. Department of Defense, Washington, 1980.

[Dijkstra 1960]
Edsger W. Dijkstra, *A primer of Algol 60 programming,* Academic Press, New
York, 1960.

[Dijkstra 1968a]
Edsger W. Dijkstra, Goto statement considered harmful, *Communications of the
ACM,* vol. 11, no. 3, March 1968, pp. 147–148.

[Dijkstra 1968b]
Edsger W. Dijkstra, Cooperating sequential processes, in *Programming
languages,* F. Genuys, editor, Academic Press, New York, 1968.

[Dijkstra 1972a]
Edsger W. Dijkstra, Notes on structured programming, in *Structured
programming* by Dahl, Dijkstra, and Hoare, Academic Press, New York, 1972.

[Dijkstra 1972b]
Edsger W. Dijkstra, The humble programmer, *Communications of the ACM,* vol.
15, no. 10, October 1972, pp. 859–866.

[Dijkstra 1975]
Edsger W. Dijkstra, Guarded commands, nondeterminancy, and formal derivation
of programs, *Communications of the ACM,* vol. 18, no. 8, August 1975,
pp. 453–457.

[Donahue 1976]
James E. Donahue, *Complementary definitions of programming language
semantics,* Lecture Notes in Computer Science, vol. 42, Springer-Verlag, New
York, 1976.

[Dubnow 1981]
Ardyn E. Dubnow, A point-by-point rebuke of revision efforts on Cobol standards,
Data Management, vol. 19, no. 12, December 1981, pp. 32A–32L.

[Elgot and Robinson 1964]
Calvin C. Elgot and Abraham Robinson, Random access stored-program machines:
an approach to programming languages, *Journal of the ACM,* vol. 11, no. 4,
October 1964, pp. 365–399.

[Elson 1973]
Mark Elson, *Concepts of programming languages,* Science Research Associates,
Chicago, 1973.

[Euclid]
Butler W. Lampson, James J. Horning, Ralph L. London, James G. Mitchell, and G. J. Popek, Report on the programming language Euclid, *Sigplan Notices,* vol. 12, no. 2, February 1977, pp. 1–79. Revised Report, Tech. Report, CSL–78–2, Xerox Palo Alto Research Center, Palo Alto, Calif.

[Evans 1968]
Arthur Evans, Jr., Pal: a language designed for teaching programming language linguistics, *Proceedings of the ACM National Conference,* Association for Computing Machinery, New York, 1968, pp. 395–403.

[Feuer and Gehani 1982]
Alan R. Feuer and Narain H. Gehani, A comparison of the programming languages C and Pascal, *ACM Computing Surveys,* vol. 14, no. 1, March 1982, pp.73–92.

[Fisher 1983]
D. L. Fisher, Global variables versus local variables, *Software—Practice and Experience,* vol. 13, 1983, pp. 467–469.

[Floyd 1961]
Robert W. Floyd, A descriptive language for symbol manipulation, *Journal of the ACM,* vol. 10, no. 3, March 1961, pp. 316–333.

[Floyd 1967]
Robert W. Floyd, Assigning meaning to programs, in *Proceedings of symposia in applied mathematics,* vol. 19 (Mathematical aspects of computer science), editor, Jacob T. Schwartz, American Mathematical Society, New York, 1967, pp. 19–32.

[Formac]
Elaine R. Bond, M. Auslander, S. G. Grisoff, R. Kenney, M. Myszewski, J. Sammet, R. Tobey, and S. Zilles, Formac: An experimental formula manipulation compiler, *Proceedings of ACM National Conference,* Association for Computing Machinery, New York, 1964, pp. K2.1–1–19.

[Fortran]
American National Standards Institute, *American National Standard Programming Language FORTRAN,* American National Standards Institute, New York, 1966.

[Fortran 77]
American National Standards Institute, *American National Standard Programming Language FORTRAN,* ANSI X3.9–1977, American National Standards Institute, New York, 1978.

[Gannon and Horning 1975]
John D. Gannon and James J. Horning, Language design for programming reliability, *IEEE Transactions on Software Engineering,* vol. SE–1, no. 2, June 1975, pp. 179–191.

[Garwick 1963]
Jan V. Garwick, The definition of programming languages, in *Formal Language Description Languages,* editor, Thomas B. Steel, North-Holland Publishing Company, Amsterdam, 1963.

[Ghezzi and Jazayeri 1982]
Carlo Ghezzi and Mehdi Jazayeri, *Programming language concepts,* John Wiley and Sons, New York, 1982.

[Glass 1969]
Robert L. Glass, An elementary discussion of compiler interpreter writing, *ACM Computing Surveys,* vol. 1, no. 1, 1969, pp. 55–77.

[Goldberg and Robson 1983]
Adele Goldberg and David Robson, *Smalltalk–80: the language and its implementation,* Addison-Wesley, Reading, Mass., 1983.

[Goodenough 1975]
John B. Goodenough, Exception handling: issues and a proposed notation, *Communications of the ACM,* vol. 18, no. 12, December 1975, pp. 683–696.

[Gordon 1979]
Michael J. C. Gordon, *The denotational description of programming languages: an introduction,* Springer-Verlag, New York, 1979.

[Gries 1971]
David Gries, *Compiler construction for digital computers,* John Wiley and Sons, New York, 1971.

[Gries and Gehani 1977]
David Gries and Nargain Gehani, Some ideas on data types in high-level languages, *Communications of the ACM,* vol. 20, no. 6, June 1977, pp. 414–420.

[Griswold et al. 1971]
R. Griswold, J. Poage, and I. Polansky, *The Snobol 4 programming language,* Prentice-Hall, Englewood Cliffs, N.J., 1971.

[Grune 1977]
Dick Grune, A view of coroutines, *Sigplan Notices,* vol. 12, no. 7, July 1977, pp. 75–81.

[Gutknecht 1984]
Jurg Gutknecht, Tutorial on Modula–2, *Byte,* vol. 9, no. 8, August 1984, pp. 157–176.

[Guttag 1977]
John V. Guttag, Abstract data types and the development of data structures, *Communications of the ACM,* Vol 20, no. 6, June 1977, pp. 396–404.

[Guttag et al. 1978a]
John V. Guttag, Ellis Horowitz, and David R. Musser, The design of data type specifications, in *Current trends in programming methodology,* vol. 4, editor, Raymond T. Yeh, Prentice Hall, Englewood Cliffs, N.J., 1978, pp. 60–79.

[Guttag et al. 1978b]
John V. Guttag, Ellis Horowitz, and David R. Musser, Abstract data types and software validation, *Communications of the ACM,* vol. 21, no. 12, December 1978, pp. 1048–1064.

[Guttag and Horning 1978]
John V. Guttag and James J. Horning, The algebraic specification of abstract data types, *Acta Informatica,* vol. 10, 1978, pp. 27–52.

[Gypsy]
A. L. Ambler, D. I. Good, J. C. Browne, W. F. Burger, R. M. Cohen, C. G. Hoch, and R. E. Wells, Gipsy: a language for specification and implementation of verifiable programs, *Sigplan Notices,* vol. 12, no. 3, March 1977, pp. 1–10.

[Haberman 1973]
A. Nico Haberman, Critical Comments on the programming language Pascal, *Acta Informatica,* vol. 3, 1973, pp. 47–58.

[Harel 1980]
David Harel, On folk theorems, *Communications of the ACM,* vol. 23, no. 7, July 1980, pp. 379–389.

[Henderson 1980]
Peter Henderson, *Functional programming application and implementation,* Prentice-Hall International, Englewood Cliffs, N.J., 1980.

[Higman 1977]
Bryan Higman, *A Comparative study of programming languages,* Elsevier North-Holland, New York, 1977.

[Hilfinger 1983]
Paul N. Hilfinger, *Abstraction mechanisms and language design,* MIT Press, Cambridge, Mass., 1983.

[Hill 1971]
I. D. Hill, Faults in functions in Algol and Fortran, *Computer Journal,* vol. 14, no. 3, August 1971, 315–316.

[Hoare 1969]
C. A. R. Hoare, An axiomatic approach to computer programming, *Communications of the ACM,* vol. 12, no. 10, October 1969, pp. 576–580.

[Hoare 1972]
C. A. R. Hoare, Notes on data structuring, in *Structured programming* by O.-J. Dahl, E. W. Dijkstra, and C. A. R. Hoare, Academic Press, New York, 1972.

[Hoare 1973]
C. A. R. Hoare, *Hints on programming language design,* Technical Report STAN-CS–73–403, Computer Science Department, Stanford University, Palo Alto, Calif., December 1973 (also in Computer Systems Reliability, Infotech State of the Art Report no. 20, Infotech, Maidenhead, England, 1974).

[Hoare 1978]
C. A. R. Hoare, Communicating sequential processes, *Communications of the ACM,* vol. 21, no. 8, August 1978, pp. 666–677.

[Hoare and Wirth 1973]
C. A. R. Hoare and Niklaus Wirth, An axiomatic definition of the programming language Pascal, *Acta Informatica,* vol. 2, 1973, pp. 335–355.

[Hofstadter 1979]
Douglas R. Hofstadter, *Godel, Escher, Bach: an eternal golden braid,* Basic Books, Inc., New York 1979.

[Holt et al. 1978]
R. C. Holt, G. S. Graham, E. D. Lazowska, and M. A. Scott, *Structured concurrent programming with operating systems applications,* Addison-Wesley, Reading, Mass., 1978.

[Horning 1979]
James J. Horning, Programming languages, in *Computing systems reliability,* editors, T. Anderson and B. Randell, Cambridge University Press, Cambridge, England, 1979, pp. 109–152.

[Horowitz 1984]
Ellis Horowitz, *Fundamentals of programming languages,* 2nd. ed., Computer Science Press, Rockville, Maryland, 1984.

[Hunter 1981]
Robin Hunter, *The design and construction of compilers,* John Wiley and Sons, New York, 1981.

[IBM 1976]
OS PL*I checkout and optimizing compilers: language reference manual, Form no. GC33–0009–4, IBM Data Processing Division, White Plains, New York, 1976.

[IBM 1983]
APL language, Form no. GC26–3847–5, IBM Data Processing Division, White Plains, New York, 1983.

[Ichbiah et al. 1979]
Jean Ichbiah et al., Rationale for the design of the Ada programming language, *Sigplan Notices,* vol. 14, no. 6, Part B, June 1979.

[Ichbiah 1984]
Jean Ichbiah, Ada: past, present, future, *Communications of the ACM,* vol. 27, no. 10, October 1984, pp. 990–997.

[IEEE 1981]
A proposed standard for binary floating-point arithmetic, Draft 8.0 of IEEE Task P754 with introductory comments by David Stevenson, *Computer,* vol. 14, no. 3, March 1981, pp.51–62.

[Ingerman 1961]
Peter Z. Ingerman, Thunks: a way of compiling procedure statements with some comments on procedure declarations, *Communications of the ACM,* vol. 4, no. 1, January 1961, pp. 65–69.

[Iverson 1962]
Kenneth E. Iverson, *A programming language,* John Wiley and Sons, New York, 1962.

[Jensen and Wirth 1975]
Kathleen Jensen and Niklaus Wirth, *Pascal user manual and report,* Springer-Verlag, New York, 1975.

[Johnston 1971]
John B. Johnston, The contour model of block structured processes, *Sigplan Notices,* vol. 6, no. 2, February 1971, pp. 55–82.

[Jones and Muchnick 1978]
N. D. Jones and S. S. Muchnick, *Tempo: a unified treatment of binding times and parameter passing concepts in programming languages,* Lecture Notes in Computer Science, vol. 66, Springer-Verlag, New York 1978.

[Kernighan and Plauger 1974]
Brian W. Kernighan and P. J. Plauger, *Software tools,* Addison-Wesley, Reading, Mass., 1974.

[Kernighan and Ritchie 1978]
Brian W. Kernighan and Dennis M. Ritchie, *The C programming language,* Prentice-Hall, Englewood Cliffs, N.J., 1978.

[Knuth 1967]
Donald E. Knuth, Remaining trouble spots in Algol 60, *Communications of the ACM,* vol. 10, no. 10, October 1967, pp. 611–618.

[Knuth 1968a]
Donald E. Knuth, Semantics of context-free languages, *Mathematical Systems Theory,* vol. 2, 1968, pp. 127–145. Correction in *Mathematical Systems Theory,* vol. 5, 1971, p. 95.

[Knuth 1968b]
Donald E. Knuth, *The art of computer programming,* vol. 1, Addison-Wesley, Reading, Mass., 1968.

[Knuth 1969]
Donald E. Knuth, *The art of computer programming,* vol. 2, Addison-Wesley, Reading, Mass., 1969.

[Knuth 1974]
Donald E. Knuth, Structured programming with goto statements, *ACM Computing Surveys,* vol. 6,. no. 4, December 1974, pp. 261–301.

[Knuth and Pardo 1976]
Donald E. Knuth and Luis Trabb Pardo, *The early development of programming languages,* STAN-CS–76–562, Computer Science Department, Stanford University, 1976.

[Kosaraju 1974]
Rao Kosaraju, Analysis of structured programs, *Journal of Computers and System Science,* vol. 9, no. 3, December 1974, pp. 232–255.

[Lampson et al. 1977]
Butler W. Lampson, James J. Horning, Ralph L. London, James G. Mitchell, and G. J. Popek, Report on the programming language Euclid, *Sigplan Notices,* vol. 12, no. 2, February 1977, pp. 1–79. Revised Report, Tech. Report, CSL–78–2, Xerox Palo Alto Research Center, Palo Alto, Calif.

[Landin 1963]
Peter J. Landin, The mechanical evaluation of expressions, *Computer Journal,* vol. 6, no. 4, 1963, pp. 308–320.

[Landin 1965]
Peter J. Landin, A correspondence between Algol 60 and Church's lambda-notation, Part I, *Communications of the ACM,* vol. 8, no. 2, February 1965, pp. 89–101, Part II, *Communications of the ACM,* vol. 8, no. 3, March 1965, pp. 158–165.

[Ledgard 1971]
Henry F. Ledgard, Ten mini-languages: a study of topical issues in programming languages, *ACM Computing Surveys,* vol. 3, no. 3, September 1971, pp. 115–146.

[Ledgard 1977]
Henry F. Ledgard, Production systems: a notation for defining syntax and translation of programming languages, *IEEE Transactions on Software Engineering,* vol. SE–3, no. 2, March 1977, pp. 105–124.

[Ledgard et al. 1981]
Henry F. Ledgard, Andrew Singer, and John Whiteside, *Directions in human factors for interactive systems,* Lecture Notes in Computer Science, vol. 103, Springer-Verlag, New York, 1981.

[Ledgard and Marcotty 1975]
Henry F. Ledgard and Michael Marcotty, A genealogy of control structures, *Communications of the ACM,* vol. 18, no. 11, November 1975, pp. 629–639.

[Ledgard and Singer 1982]
Henry F. Ledgard and Andrew Singer, Scaling down Ada (or towards a standard Ada subset), *Communications of the ACM,* vol. 25. no. 2, February 1982, pp. 121–125. Also in *The Ada programming language: a tutorial,* Sabina H. Sahib and Robert E. Fritz, editors, IEEE Catalog no. EHO 202–2 (1983).

[Lee 1972]
John A. N. Lee, *Computer semantics,* Van Nostrand Reinhold, New York, 1972.

[Lee 1974]
John A. N. Lee, *The anatomy of a compiler,* 2nd. ed., Van Nostrand Reinhold, New York, 1974.

[Levin 1977]
Roy Levin, *Program structures for exceptional condition handling,* Ph.D. thesis, Computer Science Department, Carnegie Mellon University, 1977.

[Lewis et al. 1976]
Philip M. Lewis II, Daniel J. Rosenkrantz, and Richard E. Sterns, *Compiler design theory,* Addison-Wesley, Reading, Mass., 1976.

[Lindsey and van der Meulen 1975]
Charles Lindsey and S. G. van der Meulen, *Informal introduction to Algol 68,* North-Holland Publishing Company, Amsterdam 1975.

[Lisp 1.5]
John McCarthy, Paul W. Abrahams, D. Edwards, T. Hart, and M. Levin, *Lisp 1.5 programmer's manual,* MIT Press, Cambridge, Mass., 1962.

[Liskov and Snyder 1979]
Barbara H. Liskov and Alan Snyder, Exception handling in Clu, *IEEE Transactions on Software Engineering,* vol. SE–5, no. 6, November 1979, pp. 546–558.

[Liskov and Zilles 1974]
Barbara H. Liskov and Stephen N. Zilles, Programming with abstract data types, *Sigplan Notices,* vol. 9, no. 4, April 1974, pp. 50–59.

[Liskov and Zilles 1975]
Barbara H. Liskov and Stephen N. Zilles, Specification techniques for data abstractions, *IEEE Transactions on Software Engineering,* vol. SE–1, no. 1, March 1975, pp. 7–19.

[Liskov et al. 1979]
Barbara Liskov et al., *Clu reference manual,* MIT/LCS/TR–225, Massachusetts Institute of Technology, Cambridge, Mass., 1979.

[Loeliger 1981]
R. G. Loeliger, *Threaded interpretive languages,* Byte Books, Peterborough, N.H., 1981.

[Lucas and Walk 1969]
Peter Lucas and Kurt Walk, On the formal definition of PL/I, *Annual Review in Automatic Programming,* vol. 6, no. 3, Pergamon Press, Elmsford, N.Y., 1969, pp. 108–181.

[MacLaren 1970]
M. Donald MacLaren, Data matching, data alignment, and structure mapping in PL/I, *Sigplan Notices,* vol. 5, no. 12, December 1970, pp. 30–43.

[MacLennan 1983]
Bruce J. MacLennan, *Principles of programming languages: design evaluation and implementation,* Holt, Rinehart, and Winston, New York, 1983.

[Mailloux and Peck 1969]
Barry J. Mailloux and John E. L. Peck, Algol 68 as an extensible language, *Sigplan Notices,* vol. 4, no. 8, August 1969, pp. 9–13.

[Marcotty et al. 1976]
Michael Marcotty, Henry F. Ledgard, and Gregor Bochmann, A sampler of formal definitions, *ACM Computing Surveys,* vol. 8, no. 2, June 1976, pp. 191–276.

[Markov 1954]
Andrei A. Markov, *A Theory of Algorithms,* (in Russian) Academy of Sciences of USSR, Moscow 1954, English translation by U.S. Dept. of Commerce, 1962.

[Markstein et al. 1982]
Victoria Markstein, John Cocke, and Peter Markstein, Optimization of range checking, *Sigplan Notices,* vol. 17, no. 6, June 1982, pp. 114–119.

[Matula 1968]
David W. Matula, In-and-out conversions, *Communications of the ACM,* vol. 11, no. 1, January 1968, pp. 47–50.

[McCabe 1976]
Thomas J. McCabe, A complexity measure, *IEEE Transactions on Software Engineering,* SE–2, no. 6, December 1976, pp. 308–320.

[McCarthy 1960]
John McCarthy, Recursive functions of symbolic expressions and their computation by machine, *Communications of the ACM,* vol. 3, no. 4, April 1960, pp. 184–195.

[McCarthy 1962]
John McCarthy, *Towards a mathematical theory of computation,* Proceedings of IFIP Congress 1962, North-Holland Publishing Company, Amsterdam, 1962, pp. 21–28.

[McCarthy et al. 1962]
John McCarthy, Paul W. Abrahams, D. Edwards, T. Hart, and M. Levin, *Lisp 1.5 programmer's manual,* MIT Press, Cambridge, Mass., 1962.

[McGraw 1982]
James R. McGraw, The VAL Language: Description and Analysis, ACM Transactions on Program Languages and Systems, vol. 4, no. 1, January 1982, pp. 44–82.

[McKeeman et al. 1970]
William M. McKeeman, James J. Horning, and David B. Wortman, *A compiler generator,* Prentice-Hall, Englewood Cliffs, N.J., 1970.

[Mesa]
J. G. Mitchell, W. Maybury, and R. Sweet, *Mesa language manual (version 5.0),* CSL–79–3, Xerox Palo Alto Research Center, Palo Alto, Calif., April 1979.

[Mills 1972]
Harlan D. Mills, *Mathematical foundations for structured programming,* IBM Corporation Report FSC 71–6012, Gaithersburg, Md., February 1972.

[Milne and Strachey 1976]
Robert Milne and Christopher Strachey, *A theory of programming language semantics,* Chapman and Hall, London, 1976.

[Mitchell et al. 1979]
J. G. Mitchell, W. Maybury, and R. Sweet, *Mesa language manual (version 5.0),* CSL–79–3, Xerox Palo Alto Research Center, Palo Alto, Calif., April 1979.

[Modula–2]
Niklaus Wirth, *Programming in Modula–2,* 2nd. ed., Springer-Verlag, New York, 1983.

[Morris 1973]
James H. Morris, Types are not sets, *Proceedings of Sigplan*Sigact Symposium on Programming Languages,* Boston, October 1973, pp. 120–124.

[Muchnick and Jones 1981]
Steven S. Muchnick and Neil D. Jones, *Program flow analysis: theory and applications,* Prentice-Hall, Englewood Cliffs, N.J., 1981.

[Naur 1963]
Peter Naur, editor, Revised report on the algorithmic language Algol 60, *Communications of the ACM,* vol. 3, no. 1, January 1963, pp. 1–17.

[Nicholls 1975]
John E. Nicholls, *The structure and design of programming languages,* Addison-Wesley, Reading, Mass., 1975.

[Ohran 1984]
Richard Ohran, Lilith and Modula–2, *Byte,* vol. 9, no. 8, August 1984, pp. 181–192.

[Organick et al. 1978]
Elliott I. Organick, Alexandra I. Forsythe, and Robert P. Plummer, *Programming language structures,* Academic Press, New York, 1978.

[Overgaard 1980]
Mark Overgaard, UCSD Pascal™: a portable software environment for small computers, *AFIPS Conference Proceedings,* vol. 49, AFIPS Press, Arlington, Va., 1980, pp. 747–754.

[Pagan 1981]
Frank G. Pagan, *Formal specification of programming languages,* Prentice-Hall, Englewood Cliffs, N.J., 1981.

[Pal]
Arthur Evans, Jr., Pal: a language designed for teaching programming language linguistics, *Proceedings of the ACM National Conference,* Association for Computing Machinery, New York, 1968, pp. 395–403.

[Parnas 1971]
David L. Parnas, Information distribution aspects of design methodology, *Proceedings of the 1971 IFIP Congress,* North-Holland Publishing Company, Amsterdam, 1971, pp. 339–344.

[Parnas and Wurges 1976]
David L. Parnas and H. Wurges, Response to undesired events in software systems, in *Proceedings of Second International Conference on Software Engineering,* October 1976, pp. 439–446.

[Pascal]
Niklaus Wirth, The programming language Pascal, *Acta Informatica,* vol. 1, no. 1, 1971, pp. 35–63.

Kathleen Jensen and Niklaus Wirth, *Pascal user manual and report,* Springer-Verlag, New York, 1975.

American National Standards Institute, *American National Standard Programming Language PASCAL,* ANSI*IEEE 770 X3.97–1983, American National Standards Institute, New York, 1983.

[Paul 1984]
Robert J. Paul, An introduction to Modula–2, *Byte,* vol. 9, no. 8, August 1984, pp. 195–210.

[Peterson et al. 1973]
W. Peterson, T. Kasami, and N. Tokura, On the capabilities of while, repeat, and exit statements, *Communications of the ACM,* vol. 16, no. 8, August 1973, pp. 503–512.

[PL/I]
American National Standards Institute, *American National Standard Programming Language PL/I,* ANSI X3.53–1976, American National Standards Institute, New York, 1976.

David Beech, A structural view of PL/I, *ACM Computing Surveys,* vol. 2, no. 1, March 1970, pp. 33–64.

[Pratt 1984]
Terrance Pratt, *Programming languages: design and implementation,* 2nd. ed., Prentice-Hall, Englewood Cliffs, N.J., 1984.

[Richard and Ledgard 1977]
Frederic Richard and Henry F. Ledgard, A reminder for language designers, *Sigplan Notices,* vol. 12, no. 12, December 1977. pp. 73–82.

[Richards 1969]
Martin Richards, BCPL: a tool for compiler writing and system programming, in *Proceedings of Spring Joint Computer Conference,* 1969.

[Richards and Whitby-Stevens 1979]
Martin Richards and Colin Whitby-Stevens, *BCPL—the language and its compiler,* Cambridge University Press, Cambridge, 1979.

[Rochkind 1975]
Marc J. Rochkind, The source code control system, *IEEE Transactions on Software Engineering,* vol. SE–1, no. 4, December 1975, pp.364–370.

[Ross 1959]
Douglas T. Ross, *APT part programmer's manual,* MIT Servo Lab, Cambridge, Mass., 1959.

[Rowe 1984]
Lawrence A. Rowe, Programming language issues for the 1980's, *Sigplan Notices,* Volume 19, no. 8, August 1984, pp. 51–61.

[Rutishauser 1967]
H. Rutishauser, *Description of Algol 60,* Springer-Verlag, New York, 1967.

[Sammet 1969]
Jean E. Sammet, *Programming languages: history and fundamentals,* Prentice-Hall, Englewood Cliffs, N.J., 1969.

[Sammet 1978]
Jean E. Sammet, The early history of Cobol, *Sigplan Notices,* vol. 13, no. 8, August 1978, pp. 121–161, reprinted in [Wexelblat 1981] pp. 199–243.

[Schwartz 1971]
Jacob Schwartz *The SETL language and examples of its use,* Computer Science Department, Courant Institute of Mathematical Sciences, New York 1971.

[Schwenke 1978]
Robert Schwenke, *Survey of scope issues in programming languages,* Technical Report CMU-CS–78–131, Computer Science Department, Carnegie Mellon University, Pittsburgh, 1978.

[Scott 1970]
Dana Scott, Outline of a mathematical theory of computation, *Proceedings 4th Annual Princeton Conference on Information Sciences and Systems,* Department of Electrical Engineering, Princeton University, Princeton, N.J., 1970, pp. 169–176 (also Technical Monograph PRG–2, Oxford University Computing Laboratory, Programming Research Group, Oxford, 1970).

[Scott and Strachey 1971]
Dana Scott and Christopher Strachey, Towards a mathematical semantics for computer languages, in *Proceedings of the Symposium on Computers and Automata,* J. Fox, editor, Polytechnic Institute of Brooklyn Press, New York, 1971 (also Technical Monograph PRG–6, Oxford University Computing Laboratory, Programming Research Group, 1971).

[SETL]
Jacob Schwartz *The SETL language and examples of its use,* Computer Science Department, Courant Institute of Mathematical Sciences, New York 1971.

[Shaw et al. 1977]
Mary Shaw, William A. Wulf, and Ralph L. London, Abstraction and verification in Alphard: defining and specifying iteration and generation, *Communications of the ACM,* vol. 20, no. 8, August 1977, pp. 553–564.

[Shaw et al. 1981]
Mary Shaw, Guy T. Almes, Joseph M. Newcomer, Brian K. Reid, and William A. Wulf, A comparison of programming languages for software engineering, *Software—Practice and Experience,* vol. 11, 1981, pp. 1–52.

[Simula 67]
Ole-Johan Dahl, B. Myhrhaug, and U. Nygaard, *The Simula 67 common base language,* Norwegian Computing Center, Oslo, 1968.

[Smalltalk]
Adele Goldberg and David Robson, *Smalltalk–80: the language and its implementation,* Addison-Wesley, Reading, Mass., 1983.

[Snobol]
R. Griswold, J. Poage, and I. Polansky, *The Snobol 4 programming language,*
Prentice-Hall, Englewood Cliffs, N.J., 1971.

[Softech 1973]
Softech Inc., *Introduction to AED programming,* 4th. ed., Softech Inc., Waltham,
Mass., 1973.

[Stoy 1977]
Joseph Stoy, *Denotational semantics,* MIT Press, Cambridge, Mass., 1977.

[Strachey 1966]
Christopher Strachey, Towards a formal semantics, in *Formal description
languages for computer programming,* Thomas B. Steel, editor, North-Holland
Publishing Company, Amsterdam, 1966, pp.198–220.

[Strachey 1967]
Christopher Strachey, *Fundamental concepts in programming languages,*
International Summer School in Computer Programming, Copenhagen, 1967.

[Strachey 1972]
Christopher Strachey, The varieties of programming language, *Proceedings
of the international computing symposium,* Cini Foundation, Venice, 1972,
pp. 222–233; also Technical monograph PRG–10, Oxford University Computing
Laboratory, Programming Research Group, Oxford, September 1972.

[Tannenbaum 1976]
Andrew S. Tannenbaum, A tutorial on Algol 68, *ACM Computing Surveys,* vol. 8,
no. 2, June 1976, pp. 155–190.

[Teitelbaum and Reps 1981]
Tim Teitelbaum and Thomas Reps, The Cornell program synthesizer: a syntax
directed programming environment, *Communications of the ACM,* vol. 24, no. 9,
September 1981, pp. 563–573.

[Tennent 1976]
Richard D. Tennent, The denotational semantics of programming languages,
Communications of the ACM, vol. 19, no. 8, August 1976, pp. 437–453.

[Tennent 1977]
Richard D. Tennent, Language design methods based on semantic principles, *Acta
Informatica,* vol. 8, 1977, pp. 97–112.

[Tennent 1981]
Richard D. Tennent, *Principles of programming languages,* Prentice-Hall
International, Englewood Cliffs, N.J., 1981.

[van Wijngaarden et al. 1975]
Aard van Wijngaarden, B. J. Mailloux, J. E. L. Peck, C. H. A. Koster, M. Sintzoff, C.
H. Lindsey, L. G. L. T. Meertens, and R. G. Fisker, Revised report on the
algorithmic language Algol 68, *Acta Informatica,* vol. 5, pts. 1–3, 1975,
pp. 1–236 (also reproduced in *Sigplan Notices,* vol. 12, no. 5, May 1977,
pp. 1–79).

[Weil 1965]
Roman L. Weil, Jr., Testing the understanding of the difference between call by name and call by value in Algol 60, *Communications of the ACM,* vol. 8, no. 6, June 1965, p. 378.

[Weiss 1975]
Eric A. Weiss, On the draft proposed PL/I Standard, *Communications of the ACM,* vol. 18, no. 8, August 1975, pp. 431–432.

[Wexelblat 1981]
Richard L. Wexelblat, *History of programming languages,* Academic Press, New York, 1981.

[Whitaker 1978]
William A. Whitaker, The U.S. Department of Defense common high order language effort, *Sigplan Notices,* vol. 13, no. 2, February 1978, pp.19–29.

[Whitehead 1911]
Alfred North Whitehead, *An introduction to mathematics,* Oxford University Press, Oxford, 1911.

[Whorf 1956]
Benjamin Whorf, *Language thought and reality,* MIT Press, Cambridge Mass., 1956.

[Wichmann 1984]
Brian A. Wichmann, Is Ada too big? a designer answers the critics, *Communications of the ACM,* vol. 27, no. 2, February 1984, pp. 98–103.

[Wirth 1971a]
Niklaus Wirth, Program development by stepwise refinement, *Communications of the ACM,* vol. 14, no. 4, April 1971, pp. 221–227.

[Wirth 1971b]
Niklaus Wirth, The programming language Pascal, *Acta Informatica,* vol. 1, no. 1, 1971, pp. 35–63.

[Wirth 1973]
Niklaus Wirth, *Systematic programming: an introduction,* Prentice-Hall, Englewood Cliffs, N.J., 1973.

[Wirth 1974]
Niklaus Wirth, On the design of programming languages, in *Information Processing 74,* Jack L. Rosenfeld, editor, North-Holland Publishing Co., Amsterdam, 1974, pp. 386–393.

[Wirth 1976]
Niklaus Wirth, *Programming languages: what to demand and how to assess them, and Professor Cleverbyte's visit to heaven,* Technical Report 17, E.T.H. Institute für Informatik, Zürich, March 1976.

[Wirth 1977]
Niklaus Wirth, Modula: A language for modular multiprogramming, *Software— Practice and Experience,* vol. 7, no. 1, 1977, pp. 3–35.

[Wirth 1983]
Niklaus Wirth, *Programming in Modula–2,* 2nd. ed., Springer-Verlag, New York, 1983.

[Wirth 1984]
Niklaus Wirth, History and goals of Modula–2, *Byte,* vol. 9, no. 8, August 1984, pp. 145–152.

[Wirth and Hoare 1966]
Niklaus Wirth and C. A. R. Hoare, A contribution to the development of Algol, *Communications of the ACM,* vol. 9, no. 6, June 1966, pp. 413–432.

[Wulf et al. 1971]
William A. Wulf, D. B. Russel, and A. Nico Habermann, Bliss: a language for systems programming, *Communications of the ACM,* vol. 14, no. 12, December 1971, pp. 780–790.

[Wulf et al. 1976]
William A. Wulf, Ralph L. London, and Mary Shaw, *Abstraction and verification in Alphard: introduction to language and methodology,* USC Information Science Technical Report, University of Southern California, Los Angeles, 1976.

[Wulf and Shaw 1973]
William Wulf and Mary Shaw, Global variable considered harmful, *Sigplan Notices,* vol. 8, no. 2, February 1973, pp. 28–34.

INDEX